THE GOSPELS AND ACTS

**This book is to be returned on or before
the last date stamped below.**

AUT

D0587829

TITL

S

Date	Name
. . . .	. . . .
. . . .	. . . .
. . . .	. . . .
. . . .	. . . .
. . . .	. . . .
. . . .	. . . .
. . . .	. . . .
. . . .	. . . .
. . . .	. . . .
. . . .	. . . .

WILLIAM BARCLAY

The Gospels and Acts

VOLUME TWO

The Fourth Gospel
The Acts of the Apostles

SCM PRESS LTD
BLOOMSBURY STREET LONDON

334 00581 7

First published 1976 by
SCM Press Ltd
58 Bloomsbury Street, London WC1
Second Impression 1978

© William Barclay 1976

Filmset by Specialised Offset Services Ltd, Liverpool
Printed in Great Britain by
Fletcher & Son Ltd, Norwich

CONTENTS

Part One: The Fourth Gospel

Part Two: The Acts of the Apostles

Introductory tributes to John

The Gospel of St John – the 'spiritual Gospel', as Clement already calls it – is the charter of Christian Mysticism. Indeed, Christian Mysticism, as I understand it, might almost be called Johannine Christianity; if it were not better to say that a Johannine Christianity is the ideal which the Christian mystic sets before himself. For we cannot but feel that there are deeper truths in this wonderful Gospel than have yet become part of the religious consciousness of mankind. Perhaps, as Origen says, no one can fully understand it who has not, like its author, lain upon the breast of Jesus. We are on holy ground when we are dealing with St John's Gospel, and must step in fear and reverence. But though the breadth and depth and height of these sublime discourses are for those only who can mount up with wings as eagles to the summits of the spiritual life, so simple is the language and so large its scope, that even the wayfaring men, though fools, can hardly altogether err therein.

W.R. Inge

Despite its background of difficult problems, John's theology, presupposing the basic elements of Paulinism, was a mystical fugue on great themes about the 'grace and truth' that were brought into being by the incarnation of the Son of God.

Adolf von Harnack

[Of Dürer's 'Four Saints' at Munich] I could contemplate them with interest for hours; he has contrived to give St John an almost perfect expression of 'divine philosophy'.

T.E. Green

The problem of *alētheia praktikē*, Truth idealized and yet in action, he [Hegel] does not seem to me to have solved; the Gospel of John does.

Benjamin Jowett

PART ONE
THE FOURTH GOSPEL

1

JOHN AND HIS GOSPEL

The most obvious title for the fourth gospel would be 'the gospel which is different'. Even the most untechnical teader, reading in the most cursory way, would be bound to see and to feel the difference between the fourth gospel and the other three. To take an obvious example, there is nothing in the first three gospels even remotely resembling the long speech of Jesus in John 6, after the feeding of the five thousand. Perhaps the most famous description of the fourth gospel is the one of Clement of Alexandria (AD 150–203), quoted by Eusebius in his *History* (6.14.7): 'Last of all, John, aware that the physical facts had been clearly set forth in the other gospels, . . . composed a spiritual gospel.' To talk of a spiritual instead of a physical gospel is far from the whole truth, but it would at least in part be true to say that the first three gospels are based on memory, while the fourth gospel is based on memory plus interpretation.

From the very earliest days the fourth gospel has been regarded by many as the peak and high-water mark of the New Testament. Eusebius (3.24.13) says that John began his gospel with an account of the deity of Jesus, because this task had been reserved for him by the divine Spirit, 'as it were for a superior one'. Jerome says that John was urged by the churches of Asia to write 'more profoundly about the deity of the Saviour, and, so to speak, to break through to the very Word of God', and that what John wrote was 'saturated with revelation'. This passage comes from the preface to his *Commentary on Matthew*, in which Jerome gives a very short account of each of the four evangelists and of the aims and characteristics of their gospels. (He also gives some further information in his short lives of the evangelists in his book *On Famous Men*; the chapter on John is ch. 9. All the quotations from Jerome in the present chapter come from one or other of these two sources. The text and a translation of both of them, and of many other passages quoted in this chapter, are conveniently set out by D.J. Theron in his book, *Evidence of Tradition*.) The Monarchian Prologue (Theron, pp. 58f.) says that John's gospel comes last of the four, not because it is the least of the four, but because 'the last things are perfected by fulness'. Augustine writes in his *Tractates on John* (36.1):

In the four gospels or rather the four books of the one gospel, St John the apostle, not unworthily in respect of spiritual intelligence compared to the eagle, has taken a higher flight, and soared in his preaching more sublimely than the other three, and in the lifting up thereof would have our hearts lifted up likewise.

In that passage Augustine compares John to the eagle. Very early in the history of New Testament interpretation the four beasts of Revelation 4.7 were taken to be symbolic of the four gospels.[1] The emblems are differently allocated by different writers. Irenaeus, for instance, who was probably the first to make the identification, in his book *Against Heresies* (3.11.8) identified Matthew with the man, Mark with the eagle, Luke with the ox and John with the lion (see ch. 2 n. 10 below). The symbols which have won the widest acceptance in Christian art, the man for Matthew, the lion for Mark, the ox for Luke and the eagle for John, make their appearance in the third century in Victorinus of Pettau (in a comment on Rev. 4.7), and again in the preface to Jerome's *Commentary on Matthew* (where, however, they are based on Ezekiel 1.10, not on the verse in Revelation). Augustine, however, writing *On the Agreement of the Evangelists* (1.6), preferred to identify the man with Mark, the lion with Matthew, the ox with Luke and the eagle with John. (It is significant that, even when other allocations differ, the eagle is most frequently assigned to John.) The reasoning behind Augustine's allocation of the symbols is that Mark presents the most human picture of Jesus, and is naturally represented by the man; Matthew presents Jesus as the Messiah, the Lion of Judah, and is naturally represented by the lion; Luke represents Jesus as the Saviour of the world, and is naturally represented by the ox, the animal of the sacrifice; John is represented by the eagle, because of all birds the eagle flies highest, and the eagle is said to be the only living creature which can look straight into the sun and not be dazzled. So John climbs to the heights of truth, and looks most directly into the blaze of the revelation of God.

The fourth gospel was the first New Testament book to be ranked as inspired scripture. Theophilus of Antioch (*c.* AD 174) in his book *To Autolycus* (2.22) quotes the opening words of the fourth gospel – 'In the beginning was the Word and the Word was with God' – as the words of one of the Spirit-bearing men.

For Martin Luther the fourth gospel was 'chiefest of the gospels, unique, tender and true'. He writes in his *Preface to the New Testament*:

In a word, St John's Gospel and his First Epistle, St Paul's Epistles, especially Romans, Galatians and Ephesians, and St Peter's First Epistle are the books that show you Christ, and teach you all that is necessary and good for you to know, even though you never see or hear any other book or doctrine.[2]

Latimer Jackson, in the first chapter of his book *The Problem of the Fourth Gospel*, quotes certain tributes to the fourth gospel. R.W. Dale, he says, tells of a Japanese who became a Christian through the influence of John's gospel.

> The vision of the glory which came to him while reading John's account of our Lord's life and teaching was a vision from another and diviner world; he fell at the feet of Christ exclaiming, 'My Lord and my God!'. . . He saw the divine majesty and the divine grace of Christ; what could he do but worship him?[3]

James Drummond, in his book *The Character and Authorship of the Fourth Gospel*, (p. 2) speaks of 'the tender and unearthly beauty' which pervades the pages of the fourth gospel.

Sybil Thorndike tells how Gilbert Murray, himself a humanist rather than a Christian, told her to read St John's gospel. 'It's bad Greek,' he said, 'but it will open a door for you.' 'And', says Sybil Thorndike, 'what a door it has opened!'

From the second century to the twentieth there is an unbroken chorus of thanksgiving and gratitude to God for this gospel.

Let us then begin by asking what tradition has to tell us about this gospel, about its author, and about its origin.

Tradition has five things to say about the fourth gospel.

(i) According to tradition the author of the fourth gospel is John. Theophilus of Antioch in the passage just quoted introduces the opening words of the gospel with the words, 'John says.' Irenaeus says in his book *Against Heresies* (3.1.1): 'John the disciple of the Lord . . . published a gospel while he was residing in Ephesus.' Jerome says that the fourth gospel is the work of John. The Monarchian Prologue to the fourth gospel (Theron, pp. 58f.) begins, 'This is John the evangelist.' Archbishop Bernard in the introduction to his commentary (p. lviii) refers to two Latin prefaces to John's gospel which he believes to contain very early material. One, found in a ninth-century manuscript in the Vatican, the Codex Regina 14, begins: 'The gospel of John was published and given to the churches by John while still present in the body.' This information is repeated in almost exactly the same words in the preface to the tenth-century Codex Toletanus (see p. 40 below).

Further, this John is said to be the disciple who leaned on Jesus' breast and whom Jesus loved. Irenaeus (*Against Heresies* 3.1.1) says that the gospel was written by John the disciple of the Lord, who also leaned on his breast. Jerome says that the gospel was written by John, whom Jesus loved most. He calls the author John the apostle, whom Jesus loved very much. The Monarchian Prologue says that the gospel was written by John, who was said to have been loved by God (i.e. Jesus) above the others.

So then first of all the gospel is said to be the work of John, and John is identified as the disciple whom Jesus loved.

(ii) This John is frequently, though not always, called an apostle. Tertullian, writing *Against Marcion* (4.2), says that the gospel record had as its authors either apostles or apostolic men, and cites Matthew and John as apostles, and Luke and Mark as apostolic men. Jerome in his preface to the *Commentary on Matthew* begins the account of the fourth gospel: 'Last is John, the apostle and evangelist', and in his life of John says that John the apostle wrote the fourth gospel. The Codex Toletanus says: 'The apostle John . . . last of all wrote this gospel.'

It is true that the John of the fourth gospel is not always called an apostle, but the weight of tradition is that he was.

(iii) According to tradition the fourth gospel was written in Ephesus, to which John had come. Eusebius in his *History* (3.1) reports Origen in his *Commentary on Genesis* (no longer extant) as telling how the different apostles were allocated different parts of the world to evangelize, and says that John was sent to Asia, and lived some time at Ephesus, where he died. Clement of Alexandria introduces a story about John (see pp. 22ff. below) by saying that it happened after John had returned to Ephesus after his imprisonment in Patmos. Irenaeus in his book *Against Heresies* says that John published his gospel in Ephesus (3.3.4), and that John remained with them until the time of Trajan (2.22.5). Polycrates, bishop of Ephesus, in his controversy with Victor, bishop of Rome, about the date of Easter (see p. 43 below), says that John sleeps at Ephesus. Jerome says that John wrote the gospel when he was in Asia. The Vulgate Preface to John describes John's death at Ephesus. The Codex Toletanus repeats the information that the gospel was written in Asia. The Monarchian Prologue (Theron, pp. 58f.) says that John wrote the gospel when he was in Ephesus and describes his death there.

The residence of John in Asia and the writing of the gospel there is deeply fixed in tradition.

(iv) According to tradition the fourth gospel was the last gospel to be written. Irenaeus (*Against Heresies*, 3.1.1f.) describes the writing of the first three gospels, and then says: 'Afterwards John, the disciple of the Lord who also leaned upon his breast, also published a gospel while residing in Ephesus in Asia.' Eusebius in his *History* (6.14.7) quotes Clement of Alexandria as saying: 'Last of all . . . John composed a spiritual gospel.' Eusebius also (6.25.3-10) quotes Origen, who in his review of the books accepted throughout the whole church says: 'Last of all the gospel according to John was written.' And in his own review of the gospels generally accepted by the church Eusebius says (3.24.5-15) that John wrote 'when the three previous gospels had already been delivered to all, including him'. The Monarchian Prologue explains the position of John's gospel among the New Testament books by the fact that it was the last gospel to be written.

Jerome in his chapter on John (*On Famous Men*, 9) says that John wrote last of all, after he had read the books of Matthew, Mark and Luke. A detail preserved by a ninth-century chronicler (see pp. 29f. below) says that, when John wrote, he was the only surviving member of the twelve. Epiphanius (*Against Heresies*, 51.12) says that John was the last to write, and that he wrote unwillingly because of his humility, and was only finally persuaded to write when he was ninety years old.

Tradition is to all intents and purposes unanimous that the fourth gospel was the last of the gospels to be written, and that its author wrote it with knowledge of the other three.

(v) There is one last item in the tradition, which does not occur quite so universally, but which is none the less frequent enough to be worth noting. In the accounts of the tradition it emerges that, while the fourth gospel is undoubtedly the work of one man, it is also the product of the community. The passage from Clement of Alexandria just quoted says: 'Last of all John . . . *urged by his companions*, and inspired by the Spirit, composed a spiritual gospel.' Clearly, the Christian community had a share in the initiation, if not in the actual writing, of the fourth gospel. Jerome, in describing the origin and purpose of the fourth gospel, writes in his preface to Matthew: 'He (John) *was urged by almost all the bishops of Asia at that time and by the delegates of many churches* to write more profoundly about the divinity of the Saviour.' And in his chapter on John he writes:

> John the apostle, whom Jesus loved very much, the son of Zebedee, and the brother of James whom Herod beheaded after the passion of the Lord, last of all, *when asked by the bishops of Asia*, wrote a gospel against Cerinthus and other heretics.

The most highly developed form of this part of the tradition is found in the Muratorian Canon (Theron, pp. 106-113), the first list of New Testament books, which not only lists the books but comments briefly on each one of them:

> The fourth book of the Gospels is that of John, one of the disciples. When his fellow-disciples and bishops urged him, he said: 'Fast together with me today for three days and, what shall be revealed to each, let us tell it to each other.' On the same night it was revealed to Andrew, one of the Apostles, that, with all of them reviewing it, John should describe all things in his own name.

The details of that account, for example, the presence of Andrew at a conference of the bishops of Asia, are incredible, but the general idea that the gospel was communally inspired and initiated, and to some extent communally written, meets us there again, and may well be of very great importance for the interpretation of the form and content of the gospel.

So then, to sum up, the fourth gospel was written by John, who was the beloved disciple and an apostle; it was written in Ephesus; it was the last of the gospels to be written; and there are indications that the Christian community had a vital share in the projecting of it, and perhaps even a share in the writing of it. Such is the account that tradition gives of the fourth gospel.

We have looked at the evidence of tradition in regard to the fourth gospel, and we have seen it points to the apostle John as the author. The classic example of the use of the internal evidence of the gospel to reach the same conclusion is that of B.F. Westcott. Westcott in his commentary (pp. v-xxv) laid out the evidence in a series of five ever-narrowing propositions, and we shall summarize his arguments.

(i)   *The fourth gospel was written by a Jew.* Its author knows the contemporary messianic expectations (1.21; 4.25; 6.14; 40-42; 12.34). He knows the Jewish view of women (4.27); the importance attached to religious education (7.15); the low view of Palestinian Jews concerning the Jews of the Dispersion (7.35); the hatred of the Jews for the Samaritans (4.9); the contempt of the Pharisees for 'the people of the land', the ordinary people who were unable to keep the meticulous details of the ceremonial law (7.49).

He knows the regulations of the Jewish law and the Jewish festivals. He knows, for instance, that the sabbath law is abrogated in the case of circumcision (7.22); that contact with a Gentile would so defile a Jew that he would be unable to share in the Passover (18.28). He knows the ceremonial of the Feast of Tabernacles in detail (7.37f.; 8.12). He knows the relationship of Jewish to Roman law (18.31). His familiarity with Jewish domestic life is seen in his account of the wedding feast at Cana of Galilee and of the mourning at the home in Bethany on the death of Lazarus (2.1-10; 11.17-37).

Westcott would hold that even the style of language in which the fourth gospel is written is 'conclusive as to its Jewish authorship'. The Greek is simple and correct enough, but it is not the Greek that a real Greek would have written. The vocabulary is limited. The style is characteristically paratactic. That is to say, clauses are simply set down side by side, instead of being subordinated to each other, as they would be in Greek – and in idiomatic English too. John writes (1.10):

> He was in the world,
> and the world was made by him,
> and the world knew him not.

A Greek would write: 'When he was in the world, the world did not know him, although the world was made by him.' There is a certain repetition and monotony in the style. It is true that the Greek style of the fourth gospel reads like the style of a man whose native tongue is Aramaic rather than Greek.

Many of the pictures and much of the imagery of the fourth gospel go back to the Old Testament. Such are the pictures of the good shepherd (10.1-18), the living water (4.7-15), the woman in travail (16.21).

'The Old Testament,' as Westcott says, 'is the writer's spiritual home.' The place of the Jewish nation in the economy of God is never doubted (4.22). The scripture cannot be broken (10.35). What is written in the prophets is very certainly that which will be (6.45). Moses wrote of Christ (5.46). Old Testament pictures are used and cited as forecasts and types of Jesus and his work. So the lifting up of the brazen serpent is taken as a type of the lifting up of Jesus Christ (3.14), and the manna as a type of the living bread (6.32).

In many ways it is true to say that John is just as much interested as Matthew in seeing in the events of Jesus' life fulfilments of what the prophets foretold. The treachery of Judas is found predicted in the Old Testament (13.18; Ps. 41.9), as is the hatred felt for Jesus by the Jewish people and their leaders (15.25; Pss. 35.19; 69.4). The cleansing of the temple is connected with the saying of the Psalmist: 'Zeal for thy house will consume me' (2.17; Ps. 69.9). The triumphal entry is seen in terms of the picture in Zechariah (12.14f.; Zech. 9.9). The failure of the Jews to respond is likened to the experience of Isaiah, in whose days the people were fatally dull and blind (12.37-40; Isa. 53.1; 6.10). The division of Jesus' garments by the soldiers (19.23f.) is seen foreshadowed in Psalm 22.18. The cry of thirst (19.28) is illustrated from Psalm 69.21. The fact that Jesus' legs were not broken (19.36) is traced back to Old Testament passages (Ex. 12.46; Num. 9.12; Ps. 34.20). The piercing of his side is taken back to the words of Zechariah (19.37; Zech. 12.10). The thought of John, whatever else it has in it, is saturated in the Old Testament.

One objection has been raised against the assumption that the writer of the fourth gospel is a Jew. Again and again the phrase 'the Jews' occurs – almost 70 times in all. It is argued that the writer of the fourth gospel seems to speak of the Jews from the outside, not as if he were one of them but as if he were detached from them (e.g. 5.10,16; 6.41; 7.15; 8.48, 52, 57; 9.18; 11.8; 18.12; 19.7,12; 20.19). He shows us Jesus speaking to the Jews about 'your law', as if he was quite detached from it (10.34). He shows us Jesus speaking about a word which is written in 'their law' (15.25). It is claimed that such phrases could only be used by one who thought of the Jews as a foreign nation to which he himself did not belong.

It is Westcott's answer that, in looking back on the scenes of the life of Jesus, the writer of the fourth gospel used the phrase 'the Jews' for 'the aggregate of the opinion against Jesus'. The Jews are, as it were, the opposition. He is not really thinking of them in national terms; he is thinking of the Jews as the body of human beings who were at enmity with Christ – and for that very reason he is detached from

them. That is a sound argument, for it is very difficult to see what
other generic name the writer of the fourth gospel could have used for
the opposition to Jesus. This argument does not invalidate the
essential Jewishness of the writer of the fourth gospel. We may take it
that the writer of the fourth gospel was indeed a Jew.

(ii) *The fourth gospel was written by a Jew of Palestine.* The
writer's local knowledge of the geography of Palestine is detailed and
accurate. He appears to be moving in a country with which he is
personally familiar. Cana is in Galilee and he knows its position
relative to Capernaum (2.1, 11; 4.46; 21.1). Bethany which is beyond
Jordan (1.28) is distinguished from the Bethany which is fifteen
furlongs from Jerusalem (11.18). Ephraim is near the wilderness
(11.54). Aenon is near to Salim (3.23). The writer knows the
dimensions of the Lake of Tiberias (6.19).

The writer has local knowledge of the topography of Jerusalem, and
it is to be remembered that, if the fourth gospel was written about AD
100, Jerusalem had for the last thirty years been a heap of ruins, after
its destruction in AD 70. He knows the pool called Bethzatha, with its
five porches, near the Sheep Gate (5.2). He knows the Pool of Siloam
and the Kidron Valley (9.7; 18.1). He knows the headquarters of the
Roman governor, and in his memory he sees the orthodox Jews
refusing to enter it (18.28). He knows the Pavement, in Hebrew
Gabbatha, the raised platform from which the Roman governor
pronounced his judgment (19.13). He knows the place called
Golgotha, and the garden near it (19.17, 20, 41).

He knows the temple. The incident of the cleansing of the temple
(2.13-22) is told more vividly in the fourth gospel than in any other
gospel. The incidents at the Feast of Tabernacles in chs. 7 and 8
shows a knowledge of the ritual of that feast. He knows the Feast of
the Dedication, and its correct date, and how at that time Jesus
walked in Solomon's porch (10.22).

It has been suggested that what John shows is not a native's but an
antiquarian's knowledge of Jerusalem. It is indeed true that in the
twentieth century, with the aid of atlases and maps and Bible
Dictionaries and Historical Geographies, any careful and competent
scholar could reconstruct the situation in Jerusalem and Palestine,
even though he had never been anywhere nearer Palestine than Britain
or America. But, as Westcott says: 'It is monstrous to transfer to the
second century the accuracy of archaeological research, which is one
of the latest requirements of modern art.' We may be reasonably
certain that the writer of the fourth gospel was a Jew of Palestine.

(iii) *The writer of the fourth gospel was an eyewitness of the events
which he describes.* There is in the fourth gospel a wealth of detail,
which can hardly be explained as anything other than the personal
recollection of an eyewitness. For the most part this material is simple

and factual. It is only sometimes possible, and it is never wholly necessary, to read it symbolically. It is either the product of the most consummate literary inventive artistry, or of the personal recollection of an eyewitness. Much of it cannot possibly serve any other purpose than that of additional information and added interest. It is much easier to believe that recollection lies behind it than that invention produced it.

(a) There is regular mention of the great Jewish feasts as dating points in the life of Jesus; the first Passover of his active ministry (2.13, 23), the Feast of the New Year (5.1), the second Passover (6.4), the Feast of Tabernacles (7.2), the Feast of the Dedication (10.22).

(b) Repeatedly there are detailed notices of time. The story begins with the detailed events of a week (1.29, 35, 43). The ending of the story and the resurrection narratives move from day to day (12.1, 12; 13.1; 19.31; 20.1, 26). The Lazarus story is complete with dates (11.16f., 39). The length of the stay in Samaria is dated (4.40, 43).

Not only are days dated. There are in the fourth gospel a number of times when the time of day is noted. The call of Andrew and the other disciple happened at four o'clock in the afternoon (1.39). It was midday when Jesus sat at the well at Sychar (4.6). It was one o'clock in the afternoon when the son of the official at Capernaum was healed (4.52). It was about midday when Jesus was finally led forth to be crucified (19.14). There are references to the early morning (18.28; 20.1; 21.4), to the evening (6.16; 20.19), and to the fact that it was by night that Nicodemus came to Jesus (3.2).

(c) The fourth gospel has a curious fondness for numbers. There were six water-pots at Cana of Galilee (2.6). There were five loaves and two fishes at the feeding of the five thousand (6.9). The disciples had rowed for twenty-five or thirty stades when the storm burst upon them (6.19). There was a party of four soldiers in charge of the crucifixion (19.23). The woman of Samaria had five husbands (4.18). The man at the pool had been ill for thirty-eight years (5.5). The perfume could have been sold for three hundred pence (12.5). The ointment which Nicodemus brought to embalm the body of Jesus weighed one hundred pounds (19.39). The fishing-boat was about a hundred yards from the shore, and the catch of fishes amounted to one hundred and fifty-three (21.8, 11).

Deliberate symbolism has been found in many of these numbers, but it is significant that there never has been any agreement as to what the symbolism is, and in some cases at least there seems to be no motive in supplying the number other than the giving of an additional fact to increase the realism of the story.

(d) There is a gallery of characters who come alive in the fourth gospel, and who, without the material in the fourth gospel, would be to all intents and purposes names and nothing more. It is in the fourth

gospel that Andrew becomes a person (1.40-42; 6.8f.; 12.20-22); that
Thomas acquires a personality (11.1-16; 14.1-6; 20.20-28); that Philip
speaks and acts (6.5-7; 12.20-22; 14.8f.); that Judas not Iscariot
enters the narrative (14.22f.). It is in the fourth gospel that we meet
Nicodemus (3.1-15; 7.50-52; 19.39); that Martha and Mary and
Lazarus become dramatically real (ch. 11); that Simon Iscariot the
father of Judas is mentioned (6.71; 13.2, 26); that Judas Iscariot is
himself more vividly drawn (12.1-8; 13.2, 18-30); that Annas emerges
as a leading actor in the drama of the last days (18.13); that
Nathanael is mentioned (1.43-51; 21.2); that Malchus is named as the
man whom Peter injured in the flash of resistance in the garden
(18.10). It is surprising how much of the vivid detail of the New
Testament story comes from the fourth gospel.

(e)   To all this Westcott adds a more subjective claim. He claims
that the way in which certain stories are told in the fourth gospel
implies an eyewitness. Incidents which seem to him to bear the mark
of an eyewitness are the call of the disciples (1.35-51); the narrative of
the last supper and the footwashing (13.1-20); the admission to the
courtyard of the high priest's house (18.15-17); the appearance by the
lakeside (21.1-14). There are certain vivid details which seem to
Westcott to imply an eyewitness – the fact that in the miracle of the
feeding of the five thousand the loaves are said to be *barley* loaves
(6.9); the statement that at the anointing at Bethany the house was
filled with the odour of the perfume (12.3); the dramatically simple
statement that when Judas went out from the last meal it was night
(13.30); the statement that the robe of Jesus was woven without seam
from the top throughout (19.23); the picture of the grave-clothes in the
tomb lying with the napkin in a place by itself, as if the body had
evaporated out of them (20.7); the detail of Peter making signs to the
beloved disciple to ask him to find out of whom Jesus was speaking
(13.24); Pilate's presentation of Jesus to the crowd with the words:
'Here is the man!' (19.5). This is a subjective argument which will
appear differently to different people, but it is certainly true that the
recollection of an eyewitness would explain at least some of these
passages.

(iv)   *The writer of the fourth gospel was an apostle.* This
conclusion might have been deduced from the facts already stated. If
the author of the fourth gospel was an eyewitness, for example, of the
call of the first disciples, of the events in Samaria, of the events which
led up to the feeding of the five thousand, then he must have been an
apostle, for only an apostle could have been an eyewitness of all these
events. But there are other arguments to support this claim.

The writer of the fourth gospel knows the thoughts of the disciples
at critical moments in the ministry of Jesus, and he could only have
known these thoughts if he belonged to the circle of the disciples. He

knows their reaction after the miracle at Cana in Galilee (2.11). He knows how in time they came to see the real meaning of the cleansing of the temple, and of Jesus' words following it (2.17, 22). He knows the reaction of the disciples when they returned to the well and found Jesus in conversation with the Samaritan woman (4.27). He knows the fear of the disciples when they saw Jesus apparently walking on the water (6.19). He knows how the hard sayings of Jesus daunted them (6.61). He knows how they came to see the meaning of the triumphal entry (12.16). He knows what was going on in the minds of the disciples at the last meal together (13.22, 28).

Even more significant is that he relates sayings of the disciples uttered in private, when there was no outsider there. He knows the conversation at the well of Samaria (4.33). He knows their thoughts when they were alone with Jesus after the last meal (16.17). He knows the conversation which went on with Thomas when the disciples had shut themselves in behind locked doors (20.25). He knows their question about the man who had been born blind (9.2). He knows the private conversation of Jesus with his disciples before the Lazarus miracle (11.8, 12). He knows the questions which they asked Jesus in the upper room (16.29).

He knows the places to which Jesus and the twelve went in times of withdrawal — Ephraim near the wilderness (11.54), the garden across Kidron (18.1f.), the room where they met behind locked doors (20.25).

Perhaps most significant of all, he knows of the mistakes which the disciples made in their thoughts, things which at the time they did not see, things which in time became clear to them. He knows that it was only after the resurrection that the disciples came to see the meaning of the saying about destroying and rebuilding the temple in three days (2.21f.). He knows how at the time they did not understand what Jesus was saying about Lazarus (11.13). He knows that it was only afterwards that they connected the Zechariah prophecy with the triumphal entry (12.16; Zech. 9.9). He knows that it was not until after the resurrection that they understood the scriptures which said that Jesus must rise from the dead (20.9).

It is clear that in the fourth gospel there is either a very great deal of what we might call psychological invention, or else the account of one who was so intimate with the twelve that he knew their thought processes, and must have been one of them. So intimate is the writer of the fourth gospel even with Jesus himself that he can see into the mind and heart of Jesus, and understand even Jesus' inmost thoughts. He knows Jesus' distress of heart at the grief of Mary in her mourning for Lazarus (11.33). And he knows Jesus' own deep grief at the awareness that one of his own men was to betray him (13.21).

(v) *The writer of the fourth gospel was John the apostle, who was also the beloved disciple.* Be it noted that in what follows in this section we are giving the view of Westcott. There is much more than this to be said, and in due time it will be said.

If the fourth gospel was written by an apostle, is there any particular apostle to whom it may be assigned?

(a) The fourth gospel on any grounds makes a claim to be written by someone who was specially intimate with the mind and heart of Jesus. In the synoptic gospels we find three of the apostolic company who constituted a kind of inner circle – Peter, James and John. They were with Jesus at the raising of Jairus' daughter, on the mount of transfiguration, before the apocalyptic discourse, and in the Garden of Gethsemane (Mark 5.37; 9.2; 13.3; 14.33). If someone of special intimacy with Jesus is being sought, it will be natural to seek him among these three. Peter is ruled out, because he appears as one of the characters in the story of the fourth gospel. James is ruled out, because he was martyred very early, long before the fourth gospel was written (Acts 12.1f.). And this leaves John. On perfectly general grounds John would be a strong candidate for the authorship of the fourth gospel.

(b) We now turn to the fourth gospel itself. It identifies its own author (21.24). 'This is the disciple who is bearing witness to these things, and who has written these things.' And this disciple is 'the disciple whom Jesus loved' (21.20). Can we identify this disciple whom Jesus loved? He was next to Jesus at the last meal together (13.23-25). To him Jesus on his cross entrusted the care of his mother (19.26f.). Mary Magdalene went and told Peter and him about the empty tomb, and he and Peter ran to see it for themselves (20.1-10). 'The other disciple' who was known to the high priest and who gained an entry for himself and for Peter to the courtyard (18.15f.) may also be identified with the disciple whom Jesus loved. The disciple whom Jesus loved is at the lakeside at the resurrection appearance of Jesus (21.2, 7, 20).[4]

The passage in John 21 is supremely important for the identification of the beloved disciple. The list of those present on this occasion is given – Peter, Thomas, Nathanael, the sons of Zebedee and two others (21.2). The beloved disciple must have been one of that group. He cannot be Peter, for Peter is shown conversing with him (13.23-25; 20.1-10). He clearly cannot be Thomas. Nathanael is ruled out because he was not one of the twelve. Of the sons of Zebedee James is ruled out, as we have already seen, because of his early martyrdom. This means that the beloved disciple must be either John or one of the two unnamed disciples. Is there anything in the fourth gospel itself to support the identification of the beloved disciple with the apostle John?

i.   There is the odd fact that in the fourth gospel the apostle John is never mentioned from beginning to end. It would be very strange if

John, who was a member of the inner circle in the synoptic narrative, vanished without trace from the fourth gospel. In the fourth gospel the beloved disciple fulfils the role which it would have been perfectly natural for John to play. Unless the beloved disciple is John, John inexplicably vanishes from the narrative altogether.

ii.   In the call of the first disciples, there is a curious form of speech. We are told that two of the disciples of John the Baptist followed Jesus after hearing John call Jesus the Lamb of God who takes away the sin of the world (1.35-42). One of them was Andrew. The Greek then has literally: 'Andrew first found his own brother Simon' (*ton adelphon ton idion*) (v.41). This stressing of '*his own (idion)* brother' is only natural if someone else's brother is involved in this also. This would then mean that the other disciple also had a brother; and if another pair of brothers are involved it must be James and John. So this could be a hidden reference to John.

iii.   The fourth gospel is always meticulous about names. It has a way of not only naming people, but of also identifying them. After his call (1.42) Simon is never simply Simon, as he is in the other gospels, he is always either Simon Peter, or Peter, his new name (6.68; 18.15; 20.2, 6; 21.2; contrast Matt. 17.25; Mark 14.37 = Luke 22.31). Thomas is mentioned four times and in three of them the name Didymus is added (11.16; 20.24; 21.2). Judas Iscariot is the son of a Simon, who does not elsewhere appear (6.71; 12.4; 13.2, 26). Nicodemus is 'he who came to Jesus by night' (19.39). Caiaphas is 'the high priest of that year' (11.49; 18.13). In view of this it is very surprising that the fourth gospel never speaks of John the Baptist, but simply of John. If the gospel was written by John, it is perfectly natural that he does not think to distinguish John the Baptist from himself. To him John the Baptist is not the other John, as he would be to someone who knew them both; he is simply John.

One point remains. If John wrote the fourth gospel, would he be likely to refer to himself as 'the disciple whom Jesus loved'? Would he be likely to single himself out for this specially favoured position, as it were, in contrast with the others? On this point there are two things to be said.

First, the fourth gospel is witness, and it is very concerned to stress the weight and the truth of its witness. The other three gospels are quite impersonal; their authors do not appear at all, except very briefly in the preface to Luke (1.1-4). But the author of the fourth gospel goes out of the way to insist that his witness is guaranteed to be true (19.35; 21.24). The closeness of his connection with Jesus therefore matters, not in the least for his own prestige, but for the guarantee of the truth of his gospel. The author of the fourth gospel stresses his relationship to Jesus in order to make plain the accuracy of his witness.

Second, if he does claim that he was specially dear to Jesus, the claim is not made in pride; it is made in wondering gratitude. As Westcott says (p. xxiv):

> The words express the grateful and devout acknowledgement of something received, and contain no assumption of a distinction above others ... The phrase which is used is no affectation of honour; it is a personal thanksgiving for a blessing which the Evangelist had experienced, which was yet in no way peculiar to himself.

The fact that the writer of the fourth gospel calls himself the beloved disciple is a guarantee of his witness and an expression of his gratitude and love.

So, as Westcott sees it, the fourth gospel is the work of a Jew, a Jew of Palestine, an eyewitness of the events, an apostle; and that apostle is John, who is also the beloved disciple. Such is the case for tradition.

2

THE ATTACK ON TRADITION

We have seen that tradition has five things to say about the fourth gospel. The fourth gospel is the work of John. This John is an apostle. The gospel was written in Ephesus. It was the last of the gospels to be written; and in some sense it was the product of the community as well as the work of a single man. There is none of these propositions which has not come under attack. We must therefore examine the attack, and ask if it has been justified.

To examine the attack is a long and complicated process. Inevitably the question arises: Is it worthwhile? Does it matter what the result of the investigation is? Does it make any difference whether or not the apostle John had anything to do with the writing of the gospel? G.H.C. Macgregor concludes the introduction to his commentary by citing what he calls 'the oft-quoted words of Thiersch':

> If there were a great picture which tradition has affirmed to be painted by Raphael, and it was proved not to have been painted by Raphael, but by some otherwise unknown artist, the world would not have one great painting less, but one great painter the more.

Can this principle be applied to a work like the fourth gospel?

It might be argued that a poem or a picture or a piece of music or a novel is equally great no matter who wrote it, or when or where it was written. But that is not wholly true. Robert Louis Stevenson's adventure stories will read differently if the reader knows that, when he was writing them, Stevenson was coughing his life away, writing in bed when he could not sit, writing with his left hand when he could no longer use his right, saying with a kind of stubborn gallantry: 'I will not let the smell of the medicine bottle get into my books.' W.E. Henley wrote the poem commonly known as *Invictus*, The Undefeated:

> Out of the night that covers me,
>   Black as the Pit from pole to pole,
> I thank whatever gods may be
>   For my unconquerable soul.

> In the fell clutch of circumstance
>   I have not winced nor cried aloud.
> Under the bludgeonings of chance
>   My head is bloody, but unbowed.

It makes a difference to know that Henley had lain in Edinburgh Infirmary, with one foot amputated because of tuberculosis, and the other foot threatened. A listener will hear Beethoven's Choral Symphony differently, if he knows that for twenty-five years deafness had closed further and further in upon Beethoven, so that he never heard the symphony himself, except with what might be called an inner hearing. It is not true to say that the effect of some human product is independent of who produced it. It is obvious that the circumstances in which a thing was produced have a very great deal to do with the impression it makes, and the effect it produces.

But even if we were to grant that it makes no difference who painted a picture, or who wrote a poem, or who composed a symphony, there is one kind of production in the case of which the author is all-important. The author is all-important when the writing is seeking to transmit a personal portrait or the essential teaching of an individual. Quite clearly, if the author has personal contact with his subject, this will be far better than to be dependent on research into written sources or hearsay accounts.

A gospel is not a historical document and nothing else; but a gospel is an attempt to present the portrait and the teaching of Jesus in such a way that those who read it will also take him as Saviour, Master and Lord; and therefore the gospel which goes back to personal contact has a double value. It is therefore not possible to say that we can evade the problems by saying that the value of a gospel is independent of the identity of the writer of it. That is why the investigation of the identity of the author or the source of the fourth gospel is a task which cannot be avoided.

It is argued on two grounds that John is not the kind of man who could have written the gospel.

(i)   It is argued that John was not intellectually capable of writing the fourth gospel, because the fourth gospel is beyond the intellectual range of a Galilean fisherman. J.A.T. Robinson deals effectively with that argument. He writes:

> Incidentally the particular argument that runs, 'This could not have been written by a Galilean fisherman', always seems to me singularly inept. You might have said of Ernest Bevin's speeches as Foreign Secretary, 'These could not have been written by a barrow-boy in east Bristol' – to which, of course, the answer is that they weren't; they were written by a man who *had been* a barrow-boy in east Bristol.[1]

Of course this is true. When John wrote the fourth gospel, if he wrote it or had anything to do with the writing of it, it must have been at least thirty years since he had been a fisherman on the Lake of Galilee – and a lot can happen to a man in thirty years. In any event it is very unsafe to talk about what any man can do and cannot do. In Barrie's *Mary Rose* there is a scene with Mary Rose and Simon her husband, and Cameron the highland gillie. 'What was that book you were reading, Cameron, while I was fishing?' says Simon. 'It iss a small Euripides I carry in the pocket, Mr Blake,' says Cameron. 'Latin, Mary Rose,' exclaimed Simon. 'It may be Latin,' said Cameron, 'but in these parts we know no better than to call it Greek.' For Cameron was a gillie in the summer time, but a student at Aberdeen University during the term. I knew a man who served behind the counter in a city branch of a great multiple-chemist, and that man had with no university education made himself one of the few men in Scotland who were expert in Coptic. In talking to a waiter in an hotel I asked him where he had been for a holiday. He said he had been in Canada. I asked him what took him there. 'I went to visit my son,' he said. 'And what does your son do?' I asked. The waiter answered: 'He is a professor at such-and-such a college,' and he named one of Canada's great teaching institutions. To say that a man could not have written the fourth gospel because he was once a Galilean fisherman is on any grounds a dangerous argument. Kümmel wishes to cite Acts 4.13 as witness to John's lack of education. There Peter and John are said to be 'uneducated, common men'. The Greek uses the words *idiōtēs* and *agrammatos*, which means 'ignorant and unlettered'. Kümmel argues that since the gospel is written in good Greek and since it is an intellectual masterpiece, its writer could not be so described. But what the phrase in Acts means is that Peter and John were technically uneducated; they had never had 'a college education'; they were laymen rather than professional theologians. The phrase in Acts is rather an indication of the intellectual snobbery of the Sanhedrin than it is a criticism of the intellectual ability of Peter and John. As to the Greek of the fourth gospel, it is simple and correct enough, but it is not the Greek that a real Greek would have written. Acts 4.13 does not rule out the possibility that John could have thought and written as the fourth gospel does – unless we are prepared to hold that a university degree is necessary to make a man able to think and write about the deep things of Christianity.

(ii) It is argued that John, to judge from the information that we have about him in the synoptic gospels, is not of a character or personality to be a probable author of the fourth gospel. This argument involves the identification of John with the beloved disciple, a question which we shall discuss more fully in the next chapter. The beloved disciple is the disciple of love; the fourth gospel is the gospel of love; but the John whom we know from the synoptic gospels – so runs the argument – is far from being a figure of love. Let us then set out the picture of John that we do find in the synoptic gospels.

John was the son of Zebedee, who was a fisherman, sufficiently

well-to-do to employ hired servants (Mark 1.19f.). Peter, it seems, was
also a partner in the business (Luke 5.10). Their mother was Salome,
and it is likely that she was the sister of Mary the mother of Jesus.[2]
Since James is usually mentioned before John, it may be that John
was the younger of the two brothers (though occasionally the order is
reversed, e.g. in Luke 8.51; 9.28; Acts 1.13). The brothers James and
John were among the very first disciples to be called by Jesus (Matt.
4.21f.; Mark 1.19f.). It is possible that the brothers had a still earlier
contact with Jesus. The fourth gospel (1.36f.) tells of the two disciples
of John the Baptist who very early attached themselves to Jesus, when
they heard John call Jesus the Lamb of God. Andrew was one of these
two, and the story says of him: 'He first found his brother Simon'
(1.40f.). There is something slightly odd about that expression. Why
'first'? In the Greek, if taken literally, it is 'his own brother'.[3] When
these two things are put together, it is suggested that the other person
must in turn have also gone to find his brother. And since there
are only two pairs of brothers among the twelve,[4] the other of John the
Baptist's disciples must have been one of the sons of Zebedee, who
went off to find his brother, when Andrew went off to find Peter. This
however is a speculation rather than a certainty.

    John was clearly one of the leaders of the apostolic company. His
name always appears in the first section of the lists of the twelve
(Mark 3.17; Matt. 10.2; Luke 6.14; Acts 1.13). He was one of the
inner circle, the three whom Jesus took with him on special occasions,
the raising of the daughter of Jairus (Mark 5.37), the mountain of
transfiguration (Mark 9.2; Matt. 17.1; Luke 9.28), the agony in
Gethsemane (Mark 14.33; Matt. 26.37). If their mother Salome was
the sister of Mary the mother of Jesus, they would have been Jesus'
cousins, and this may well have given James and John a special place;
the fact that they laid claim to the seats on the right and the left of
Jesus in his kingdom makes it not improbable that they were already
accustomed to occupying these places (Mark 10.37). That John held a
leading place among the twelve is clear. The synoptic gospels make it
evident that he was one of those who were close to Jesus.

    It is none the less true that from the narrative of the synoptic
gospels John does not emerge as a very attractive character. Right
from the beginning Jesus called James and John 'sons of thunder',
Boanerges, a name which could only be given to an explosive
character liable to violent eruptions (Mark 3.17). John appears as a
rigidly exclusive character. To him anyone who was not one of the
apostolic company had no right to act in the name of Jesus (Mark
9.38; Luke 9.49). When a Samaritan village refused to give hospitality
to Jesus and his company, the first instinct of James and John was to
blast it out of existence (Luke 9.51-56). The two brothers were
vengeful and intolerant. The brothers were ambitious; they wanted to

assure themselves of the premier places in Jesus' kingdom (Mark 10.37) (or, as Matthew 20.21 tells the story, their mother did). In the gospel (22.8) he and Peter are sent forward to make preparations for the Passover, and in Acts John always appears in the company of Peter, but never himself speaks (3.1, 11; 4.13; 8.14). John is mentioned only once in the letters of Paul, and then he appears as a pillar of the church (Gal. 2.9). As we have already noted, it is said in Acts (4.13) that Peter and John had no technical education, which made their defiance of the Sanhedrin even more amazing. It is a remarkable fact that John does not appear in the fourth gospel by name at all, and the sons of Zebedee are only mentioned once (21.2).

If tradition is right, John left Palestine and came to Ephesus. We do not know when. Nicephorus Callistus, a fourteenth-century ecclesiastical historian, records in his *History* (2.3) that Mary lived with John in Jerusalem for eleven years after Jesus had entrusted her to him (John 19.26f.). The likeliest time for John to leave Jerusalem would be in AD 68, when the Christians left Jerusalem in view of its impending destruction and moved to Pella. Eusebius in his *History* (3.5.3) tells the story:

The people of the church in Jerusalem were commanded by an oracle given by revelation before the war to those in the city who were worthy of it to depart and dwell in one of the cities of Peraea which they called Pella. To it those who believed in Christ migrated from Jerusalem, that when holy men had altogether deserted the royal capital of the Jews and the whole land of Judaea, the judgment of God might at last overtake them for all their crimes against the Christ and his apostles, and all that generation of the wicked be utterly blotted out from among men.

(Epiphanius in his book *On Weights and Measures*, 15, also speaks of the departure to Pella.) It would be at this moment that all the apostles who were there would leave Jerusalem, and John must have made his way to Ephesus because at that time it was the centre of the Christian faith.

Tradition identifies the writer of Revelation with the John of the fourth gospel, and there is a consistent line of tradition that John, after being banished to Patmos, was later released to return to Ephesus. 'I John', says the writer of Revelation, '... was on the island called Patmos on account of the word of God and the testimony of Jesus.' We may set out the main patristic evidence.[5] Clement of Alexandria introduces a long story about John (see pp. 22f. below) by saying that it happened when after the death of Domitian John had returned from the island of Patmos to Ephesus. Origen writes in his *Commentary on Matthew* 16.6 (on Matt. 20.23): 'The Roman emperor, so tradition tells us, condemned John to the island of Patmos because of his witness for the word of truth.' Tertullian, listing the apostolic churches in his book

On the Prescription of Heretics (36), says: 'You have Rome . . . where the apostle John was first plunged into boiling oil, and thence remitted to his island exile.' Victorinus, in a comment on Rev. 10.11, says that John saw his visions when he was in the island of Patmos, condemned to the mines by the Emperor Domitian. On the death of Domitian the sentence was repealed; John was released from the mines and passed on the Apocalypse which he had seen. Epiphanius in his *Heresies* (51.33) speaks of John delivering his prophetic message when he was on the island of Patmos during the reign of Claudius (i.e. between AD 41 and 54, which seems impossibly early). Jerome (*On Famous Men*, 9), writes:

> Fourteen years after Nero, when Domitian began to persecute [the Christians], John was banished to the island of Patmos and there wrote the Apocalypse. On the death of Domitian, when his acts had been repealed by the senate because of their excessive cruelty, John returned to Ephesus during the reign of Nerva.

Eusebius writes in his *History* (3.18.1):

> It is said that in this persecution [the persecution initiated by Domitian] the apostle and evangelist John, who was still alive, was condemned to dwell on the island of Patmos in consequence of his testimony to the divine word.

There is a consistent line of tradition connecting John with Patmos, but it is true to say that the whole thing might well stem from nothing more than the simple statement in Revelation 1.9.

(iii)   We have now exhausted the New Testament evidence for the life and character of John. We must go on to take account of legend and speculation. No one is going to claim that the legends are history, and that they in every case represent actual fact, but the stories which are told about a man do show what kind of a man a man was taken to be; they are indications of his character and personality as the world knew them. The legends which gather round the name of John are of two kinds. There are the legends which are obviously not to be accepted as factually true, and there are the legends which may very well have a historical basis.

First then, let us glance at the legends which are clearly apocryphal. Eusebius in his *History* (5.18.13) records a story told by a certain Apollonius, who is said to have been a bishop of Ephesus about AD 200, 'that by divine power a dead man had been raised by John himself in Ephesus'. Tertullian relates a story (already mentioned) that John in Rome was seized by the authorities and plunged into a cauldron of boiling oil, only to emerge completely unharmed. Jerome further embroiders the story by saying that John came out of the boilding cauldron purer and fresher than before he had been thrown into it.[6] The Latin *Acts of John* (20) tell how, at the challenge of Aristodemus the heathen priest John drank a cup of poison, after seeing two condemned criminals drink the same cup and immediately die, and the poison did him no harm.[7] In a late Greek version the poison drinking is said to have taken place in the presence of Domitian. Further marvels there include the story that, also in the presence of Domitian, John raised to life a girl killed by an evil spirit, and that when John was recalled from Patmos by Nerva, he was shipwrecked and escaped by swimming on a cork until he reached Miletus.[8] It is in the *Acts of John* (60f.) that there is the story of John and the beg bugs. In a deserted inn John lay down on the only bed and was promptly bitten by hordes of bed bugs. So he said, 'I tell you, you bugs, to behave yourselves, one and all; you must leave your home for tonight and be quiet in one place and keep your distance from the servants of God.' Thereupon the bugs left the bed and John spent the night peacefully sleeping undisturbed. When the morning came the bugs were discovered waiting at the door of the inn, whereat John for their obedience invited them to return to the bed which they did. Thereupon John drew the lesson that it would be well if men were as obedient to the voice of God as the bugs had been to him. Last of these incredible tales there is the story connected with the death of John, which Augustine passed down in his *Tractates on John* (124.2, on John 21.22f.) – and apparently believed. When John was buried, even in the grave, there was proof that he lived, for, it was said, 'he showed that he was still alive by the movement of the dust above, which was stirred by the breath of the saint'. And Augustine adds:

> I think it needless to contest the opinion. Those who know the place must see whether the soil is so affected as it is said, since I have heard the story from men not unworthy of credence.

On the other hand, there are legends of John which have every appearance of being true. There is the story of John's encounter with the heretic Cerinthus. Eusebius passes down the story of Irenaeus, who got it from Polycarp:

> The apostle John once entered a bath to bathe. But when he learned that Cerinthus was within, he sprang from the place and rushed out of the door, for he could not bear to remain under the same roof with him. And he advised those who were with him to do the same. 'Let us flee,' he said, 'lest the bath fall, for Cerinthus the enemy of truth is inside.'[9]

The 'son of thunder' was not yet dead!

There is the story which Cassian tells in his *Collations* (24.21):

> It is told that the most blessed evangelist John, when he was gently stroking a partridge with his hands, suddenly saw one in the dress of a hunter coming to him. The man wondered that one of such repute and fame as John should demean himself to such small and humble

amusements. 'Are you that John,' he said, 'whose eminent and widespread fame has enticed me also with a great desire to know you? Why then are you taken up with such mean amusements?' The blessed John said to him: 'What is that that you are carrying in your hands?' 'A bow,' he said. 'And why,' said John, 'do you not always carry it about with you at full stretch?' 'I must not do that,' the man answered, 'lest by constant bending the strength of its vigour be wrung and grow soft and perish, and when there is need that the arrows be shot with much strength at some beast, the strength might be lost by excess of continual tension, and a forcible blow cannot be dealt.' 'Just so,' said the blessed John, 'let not this little and brief relaxation of my mind offend you, young man, for unless it eases and relaxes sometimes by remission of the force of its tension, it will grow slack through unbroken rigour, and will not be able to obey the power of the spirit.'

As the proverb has it: 'The bow that is always taut will soon cease to shoot straight.'

There is perhaps the most famous of all the fragments of tradition about John, handed down by Jerome in his *Commentary on Galatians* (6.10):

> When John lingered in Ephesus to extreme old age, and could only with difficulty be carried to the church in the arms of his disciples, and was unable to give utterance to many words, he used to say no more at their meetings than this: 'Little children, love one another.' At length the disciples and fathers who were there, wearied with always hearing the same words, said: 'Master, why do you always say this?' 'It is the Lord's command,' was his reply, 'and, if this alone be done, it is enough.'

Here indeed speaks the disciple of love.

Finally, there is the story told by Clement of Alexandria in *The Rich Man's Salvation* (42), which may well have in it more of the essential John that any other. Once on a visit to a congregation John saw a young man, exceptionally handsome, and obviously of a spirited personality. John pointed at the young man, and said to the bishop of the church: 'This man I entrust to your care with all earnestness in the presence of the church and Christ as witnesses.' The bishop accepted the trust and pledged himself to it. He took the young man into his own home, cherished him, taught him, and finally baptized him. Then he relaxed his care and vigilance too soon. The youth fell into evil company who seduced him into dissolute luxury and taught him to be a robber.

The young man became accustomed to this new kind of life. 'Like a restive and powerful horse which starts aside from the right path and takes the bit between its teeth, he rushed all the more violently because of his great nature towards the pit.' The youth himself decided that he had drifted beyond the mercy of God, and he organized a robber band, of which he became chief, 'the most violent, the most blood-thirsty, the most cruel'.

So the day came when John revisited the church in which he had first seen the youth. He said to the bishop: 'Now, bishop, return to us the deposit which Christ and I entrusted to your care in the presence and with the witness of the church over which you preside.' The bishop was amazed. He thought at first that it was some entrusted money about which John was speaking. 'It is the youth,' said John, 'and the soul of your brother than I demand back.' With sorrow in his voice the bishop answered: 'The man is dead.' 'By what death did he die?' asked John. 'He is dead to God,' said the bishop, and went on to tell how the youth had slipped from grace, and had become a robber chieftain. John rent his clothes. 'A fine guardian of our brother's soul it was that I left!' he said.

John called for a horse and a guide, and rode straight from the church to find the youth. When he came near the headquarters of the robber band he was captured by their sentries. He made no attempt to escape. 'It was for this very purpose I came,' he said. 'Take me to your leader.' So he was brought to the leader who was waiting fully armed, but, when he recognized John, he was smitten with shame and turned and fled from his presence. Forgetting his old age John pursued him. 'Why do you flee from me, my child,' he said, 'from your own father, from me, a poor, old, unarmed man? Have pity on me, and do not fear. You have still hope of life. I myself will give account to Christ for you. If need be, I will willingly undergo penalty of death, as the Lord did for us. I will give my own life in payment for yours. Stand! Believe! Christ has sent me!'

When he heard this, the youth threw away his weapons and fell to trembling and to tears. With bitter contrition he repented, and John assured him that he had found pardon with his Saviour for him. He brought him back to the church. He never ceased to keep his grip upon him. In the end the young man was so changed by Christ that he became the bishop of the congregation. There is no story about John which so expresses the strength and the gentleness which were combined in John's character as this one does.

(iv) We have looked at the legends which have gathered around John. We end this study of him by looking not at a legend but at a speculation. F.C. Burkitt in *The Gospel History and its Transmission* (pp. 248ff.) advances the theory that John, before he became a Christian, was a Sadduccee. If John was a Sadducee, he may well have had priestly connections, for the priests were almost all Sadducees. If John had priestly connections, two things might well be explained. Polycrates – to whom we shall later return – was bishop of Ephesus about AD 190. He was involved in a controversy with Victor, bishop of Rome, about the date of Easter, which the churches of Asia Minor observed on a different date from the church of Rome and the churches of the rest of Christendom. In his letter to Victor (p. 43

below) Polycrates, in justification of the Asian date, cites the great apostolic figures who had been connected with Ephesus, among them John 'who was both a witness and a teacher, who reclined upon the bosom of the Lord, and being a priest wore the *petalon*'. In the Septuagint (Ex. 28.36; 29.6) the *petalon* was the plate or diadem worn by the high priest on his mitre (RSV: turban). Where Polycrates got his information and just what he meant is quite uncertain, but, if John was a Sadducee, he might well have priestly connections, although it is surely impossible to think of John as ever being high priest. The whole matter is very obscure, but if John was a Sadducee, then the one-time priestly connection becomes a possibility. Another crux of Johannine interpretation occurs in John 18.15f. There we find Peter in the company of 'another disciple'. This 'other disciple' has frequently been identified with the beloved disciple, and therefore, on the traditional view, with John. This other disciple was instrumental in bringing Peter into the courtyard of the high priest's house. This he was able to do because he was 'known to the high priest'. This once again provides John with a priestly connection. We shall return later to this passage.

What evidence then does Burkitt offer for his suggestion? In the first place, it is an odd fact that the writer of the fourth gospel, familiar as he seems to be with Jerusalem, never once mentions the Sadducees. Matthew mentions the Sadducees six times (3.7; 16.1, 6, 12; 22.23f.), Mark once (12.18) and Luke once (20.27). Burkitt suggests that John regarded the name Sadducee as a nickname and therefore preferred not to use it. The Sadducees did not believe in a resurrection, nor in angels, nor in spirits (Acts 23.8). The attitude of the fourth gospel to these things could be significant. John certainly believes in them, but he does seem to imply that they all entered the world with the Christian revelation. John says of the Spirit that during Jesus' earthly life 'the Spirit had not yet been given' – literally 'was not yet' (7.39). It is after the resurrection that Jesus breathes the Spirit into his disciples (20.22). In Luke, however, both Zachariah and Elizabeth, for example, are 'filled with the Holy Spirit' (1.67, 41). Mary Magdalene saw two angels in the tomb where Jesus had lain (John 20.12). True, Jesus had promised Nathanael that he would see the angels of God ascending and descending upon the Son of man (1.51), but it was not until after the resurrection that the angels became visible to any mortal eye. This is particularly so in regard to the resurrection of the dead. The Pharisees, and to some extent the people, believed in a resurrection. Martha, in the midst of her grief, says of Lazarus: 'I know that he will rise again in the resurrection at the last day.' Thereupon Jesus says to her: '*I* am the resurrection and the life' (11.24f.), and in the Greek the *I* is very emphatic. It is as if to say that apart from him there is no resurrection. With that phrase John, as it were, expresses at one and the same time his disbelief in the old

Pharisaic resurrection and his belief in the new Christian resurrection.
Burkitt sets side by side two sentences. First, 'You will be repaid at the
resurrection of the just' (Luke 14.14). There the resurrection is an
accepted and established fact. Second, 'I will raise him up at the last
day' (John 6.40) – and once again the *I* is intensely emphatic. In Luke
the resurrection is part of the established order. In John it is part of the
new dispensation. It is certainly true that a case can be put up for
finding the mind of a converted Sadducee behind the fourth gospel.

What then shall our conclusion be? Can we say that John the son of
Zebedee sat for the portrait of the beloved disciple? Or must we
eliminate him entirely on intellectual and personal grounds? We have
seen that it would be dangerous to say that from the intellectual point
of view John could not have written the fourth gospel. But what of the
personal point of view?

Of one thing we must beware. We cannot say that the synoptic
material portrays John as explosive, intolerant, ambitious, and then go
on to say that in the course of the long years the grace of God so
worked upon him that in the later days he did become the apostle of
love. As G.H.C. Macgregor writes in the introduction to his
commentary (p. xlv), the memories which the synoptics leave us of
John are those of a 'son of thunder' rather than the apostle of love.

And if it be argued that the grace of God may have transformed the fiery
zealot into the tender intimate of Christ, the reply is that the title 'Beloved
Disciple' has reference not to the Apostle's old age, but to the days of his
'thundering'.

The man who was the beloved disciple was the beloved disciple in the
days in Palestine long before the days of Ephesus.

There are nevertheless two things that we may well say. First, if the
synoptic narrative is to be accepted at all, John was one of the inner
circle, one of those whom Jesus in his moments of crisis did choose to
be with him. Second, it is possible to interpret at least some of the
actions of John in two different ways. We may, if we choose, say that
the demand of James and John for the chief places in the kingdom was
sheer vaulting ambition. But it is to be noted *when that demand was
made*. The three verses which immediately precede the request (Matt.
20.17-21; cf. Mark 10.32-37) are:

And as Jesus was going up to Jerusalem, he took the twelve disciples
aside, and on the way he said to them: 'Behold, we are going up to
Jerusalem; and the Son of man will be delivered to the chief priests and
scribes, and they will condemn him to death, and deliver him to the
Gentiles to be mocked and scourged and crucified, and he will be raised
on the third day.'

The request for the first places follows that immediately. Three things can be said of this juxtaposition. First, it may be said that the juxtaposition means nothing, and that the two incidents need have no connection at all, if the gospels are composed of nothing but disconnected units. Second, it may be said that James and John totally and completely misunderstood Jesus, and refused to be moved from their belief in a worldly Messiah. But, third, it can well be held that the request of James and John is a magnificent example of fact-defying faith. It is difficult to see how anyone could see a journey to Jerusalem as likely to end in anything but disaster; but in spite of that the brothers never doubted the ultimate triumph. If that is so, there is faith here on a heroic scale. This is exactly the kind of action which is again illustrated in Clement's story of how John reclaimed the youth turned robber.

We do not need at this stage to commit ourselves to the conviction that John is the beloved disciple, but we can go the length of saying that it is not impossible that he was.

Zahn has said that there was an ancient faction in the church which had declared war on all the Johannine writings. In the last quarter of the second century we find certain attacks on both the fourth gospel and the Revelation. It is argued that, if there was no doubt that the author was the apostle John, the beloved disciple, it is extremely unlikely, if not impossible, that any such attack should have developed, for no one would have attacked writings of such high apostolic authority. Let us set out the evidence for this doubt about the fourth gospel.

(i) It is argued that the last verse but one of the gospel (21.24) indicates the existence of a doubt: 'This is the disciple who is bearing witness to these things, and who has written these things; and we know that his testimony is true.' This is what we might call an authenticating guarantee, and – it is claimed – no one offers that sort of guarantee unless it is needed. The very fact of the insertion of the guarantee implies the existence of a doubt.

(ii) In the last quarter of the second century there was a direct attack on the fourth gospel. Hippolytus (AD 170–236) wrote a book entitled: *A Defence of the Gospel according to John and of the Apocalypse.* And, as G.H.C. Macgregor says (p. liv): 'No one defends that which nobody attacks.' At about the same time a Roman presbyter called Gaius certainly attacked Revelation and may well have attacked the gospel as well. Hippolytus answered his attacks in his *Heads against Gaius.* There is no doubt at all that the Johannine writings did come under fire.

In particular the attack came from a group of people whom Epiphanius describes in Book 51 of his *Heresies.* He calls them the Alogi because 'they do not receive the Logos preached by John'. The name Alogi was no doubt regarded as doubly appropriate, because it also means irrational or unreasonable people. Their main attack was based on the discrepancies between the fourth gospel and the synoptic gospels, and on the results of taking Revelation absolutely literally. One of their best known charges was that Revelation must be rejected because no church existed at Thyatira, and there was in it a letter to the church at Thyatira (2.18-29).

The Alogi were never very numerous. But the most significant thing about them is that their orthodoxy was not really questioned. Epiphanius says of them (51.4): 'They seem to believe just as we do.' And further, they were never excommunicated from the church. It is significant that it was possible to reject the fourth gospel and yet to be regarded as orthodox. V.H. Stanton in *The Gospels as Historical Documents* (I, pp. 210f.) quoted Harnack's opinion that they were 'good Christians', 'Christians who agreed with the great Church in the Rule of Faith'.

At the end of the second century there is good evidence that the fourth gospel was under attack. The attack was quickly repelled and the position of the gospel established, but the attack is difficult to understand, if there never was any doubt that the apostle John was the undisputed author.

(iii)   There is the attitude of the Muratorian Canon (AD 170, an important item in Theron's *Evidence of Tradition*). It is the first list of church books, and probably represents the situation in the church at Rome towards the close of the second century. It could be significant that, as Macgregor points out (p. liv), the Muratorian Canon takes seven lines to deal with Luke and twenty-five lines to deal with John. It could be held that the Muratorian Canon seems to feel a special necessity and obligation to justify the place of the fourth gospel in the canon of the New Testament, a necessity and obligation of which it would not have been conscious if the Johannine authorship was beyond question.

(iv)   There is the insistence of Irenaeus on the essential necessity of a fourfold gospel, and his attack on those who do not abide by this necessity (*Against Heresies* 3.11.8f.). He writes:

> It is not possible that the gospels can be either more or fewer in number than they are. For, since there are four zones of the world in which we live, and four principal winds, while the church is scattered abroad throughout all the world, and the pillar and ground of the church is the gospel and the spirit of life, it is fitting that she should have four pillars, breathing out immortality on every side, and vivifying men afresh.

He supports this argument from the fact that the cherubim are four-faced — the lion, the ox, the man and the eagle — and the creatures symbolize the gospels.[10] Irenaeus then goes on to condemn anyone who for his own purposes makes the gospels either more or fewer in number.

> These things being so, all who destroy the form of the gospel are vain, unlearned and audacious too; those, I mean, who represent the aspects of the gospel as being either more in number than we have stated, or, on the other hand, fewer. The former do so that they may seem to have discovered more than is of the truth; the latter that they may set the dispensations of God aside.

And he goes on to cite those who refuse to accept the teaching of John's gospel about the Spirit. It is clear from the words of Irenaeus that there were those who added gospels to the universally accepted four to suit themselves, and there were those who refused to accept some gospel because its teaching did not suit them, and Irenaeus makes it clear that there were those who rejected the fourth gospel – and once again it has to be said that the rejection of a gospel coming undisputedly from John the apostle would be difficult to understand.

(v) Finally in this matter, it has been suggested that there is something odd in the way in which Justin Martyr (martyred in Rome in AD 165) and Ignatius, who flourished in the first quarter of the second century, quote the fourth gospel. Justin refers to the Memoirs of the Apostles. He quotes the synoptic gospels over one hundred times, and the fourth gospel only three times. Frequently he quotes texts from the synoptic gospels which are not really appropriate and omits texts from the fourth gospel which would have been conclusive. Macgregor quotes Streeter in *The Four Gospels* (p. 441):

> In fact Justin acts like a modern apologetic writer, trying to establish the pre-existence of Christ, but, in deference to critical objections, attempting to do so without reference to the Fourth Gospel.

It is the same with Ignatius. Ignatius was deeply influenced by the fourth gospel, but he does not quote it as he does Matthew. Streeter says of him (p. 455):

> His whole outlook and his theology have been profoundly influenced by the study of this Gospel; but his use of it suggests that it is not yet recognized in his own Church as on the same level of authority as Matthew.

The scarcity of quotations from the fourth gospel shows that the gospel tended to be slow in acquiring its authority, slower perhaps than one would expect in a gospel which went back to the apostle John.

The result of our whole investigation is to show that the fourth gospel did have opposition and hesitation to meet before it finally established itself – and there are those who would wish to use this circumstance to argue that it cannot have come from the apostle John.

There is a line of tradition which says that John died an early death as a martyr, probably in Jerusalem before AD 70, and if that is so he certainly had nothing to do with Ephesus, and it is very unlikely that he had anything to do with the writing of the fourth gospel.[11]

The debate as to whether or not John died an early death is one of the unsolved questions of the New Testament. The main tradition makes him live until an extreme old age, until he was so frail that he had to be carried to church (see the story told by Jerome, quoted on p. 22 above). In two places in his book *Against Heresies* (2.22.5 and 3.3.4) Irenaeus tells us that the Christians in Asia said that John continued among them until the time of Trajan. According to Eusebius (*History*, 3.20.11), it was when Nerva came to the throne and repealed Domitian's savage legislation that John was released from Patmos and crossed over to Ephesus. Nerva's dates are AD 96–98 and Trajan's are 98–117. If John survived until then, he was a very old man, and indeed the *Chronicon Paschale* (quoted by J.B. Lightfoot, *Biblical Essays*, p. 53), says that he died at the age of one hundred and four. In popular tradition John is always thought of as surviving to a great age.

We shall first of all set out without comment the evidence which is used to suggest the early martyrdom of John; then, when we have presented the case, we shall go back and test each link in the chain, from the latest to the earliest.

(i)   The first evidence to be called is a statement said to be from Papias, and transmitted through two sources. The first source is Philip of Sidē. Philip moved from Sidē in Pamphylia to Constantinople early in the fifth century. There he became the friend of Chrysostom, by whom he was ordained as deacon. He produced an enormous historical work in thirty-six books called *A Christian History*. Our information comes from an eighth-century epitome of this work, and in particular from a fragment of it known as the de Boor fragment. Theron (pp. 30f.) translates:

> Papias, who was bishop of Hierapolis, a hearer of John the Theologian [the Divine], and a companion of Polycarp, wrote five books of *Oracles of the Lord*, in which, when making an enumeration of the Apostles, he enrolled among the disciples of the Lord, together with Peter and John, Philip and Thomas and Matthew, Aristion and another John whom he also called a presbyter ... Papias in the second book says: 'John the Theologian and James his brother were put to death by the Jews.'

The second source is George Hamartōlos, George the Sinner, a Byzantine chronicler who lived in the ninth century. He wrote a Chronicle in four books, which entended from creation down to AD 842. The relevant passage appears in Codex Coislinianus 305 and must be quoted in full (Theron, pp. 30f.):

After Domitian Nerva reigned one year – who recalled John from the island and permitted him to settle in Ephesus. He was the only one of the twelve disciples still living at that time, and when he had written his Gospel, he was counted worthy of martyrdom. For Papias the Bishop of Hierapolis, since he was an eye-witness of this one, says in the second book of the *Oracles of the Lord* that he was put to death by the Jews; having fulfilled evidently with his brother the prediction of Christ concerning them and their own confession and approval concerning this. For when the Lord said to them: 'Are you able to drink the cup which I drink?' and when they had readily agreed and assented, he said: 'My cup you shall drink, and with the baptism with which I am baptized you shall be baptized.' And rightly, for it is impossible that God should lie. So also the very learned Origen in his commentary on the Gospel according to Matthew confirms that John suffered martyrdom, indicating that he had learned this from the successors of the apostles. And also the very learned Eusebius says in his *Ecclesiastical History*: 'Thomas received Parthia by lot, but John Asia, where he settled and died in Ephesus.'

(ii)   Next there is the evidence of the ecclesiastical calendars and martyrologies (set out by J.H. Bernard in *Studia Sacra*, pp. 275-9). To this day the dates are as follows:

December 26 : The Feast of St Stephen
December 27 : The Feast of St John
December 28 : The Feast of the Innocents.

It is argued that in a context like this, coming between the proto-martyr and the slaughtered children, this can only mean that John was martyred. All existing calendars go back to what is called the Hieronymian Martyrology, or the Martyrology of Jerome. This was a kind of amalgamation of all the calendars put together about the beginning of the sixth century. Its entry for December 27 reads:

Assumptio S. Joannis evangelistae : et ordinatio episcopatus S. Jacobi fratris domini qui ab apostolis primus est Judaeis Hierosolymis est episcopus ordinatus et tempore paschali martyrio coronatus.

That simply commemorates the death of John, not necessarily a martyr, and the elevation of James the brother of Jesus to the Jerusalem episcopate, and adds the information that James won the martyr's crown at the Passover time. It has nothing to say about James the brother of John, whose day comes on July 25, as it does now.

There are two calendars to be taken into consideration. In the West the calendar of Carthage dates to about AD 505. Its datings are:

December 26 :   *S. Stephani, primi martyris.* St Stephen, the first martyr.
December 27 :   *Johannis Baptistae et Jacobi Apostoli quem Herodes occidit.* John the Baptist and James the Apostle, whom Herod killed.
December 28 :   *Sanctorum infantum quos Herodes occidit.* The holy infants whom Herod killed.

The name of John the Baptist must be a mistaken intrusion, for this calendar itself commemorates John the Baptist on June 24. In the East there is the Syriac calendar, originally made in Nicomedia about AD 360, and copied in Edessa in AD 411:

> December 26 : Stephen chief martyr.
> December 27 : John and James the Apostles at Rome.
> December 28 : In the city of Rome Paul the Apostle and Simon Cephas, the chief of the Apostles of our Lord.

The Armenian Calendar has the same listing.

Once again, at least at first sight, John seems to be counted with the martyrs.

(iii)   The Syrian Aphraates, writing *On Persecution* in AD 344, says (ch. 23):

> Great and excellent is the martyrdom of Jesus. After him was the faithful martyr Stephen, whom the Jews stoned; Simon also and Paul were perfect martyrs. And James and John walked in the footsteps of their master Christ... Others also of the apostles afterwards in different places confessed and proved themselves true martyrs.

(iv)   The anonymous African work *On Rebaptism*, written about AD 250, says (ch. 14):

> He said to the sons of Zebedee, 'Are you able to drink of the cup...?' (Mark 10.38). For he knew that men had to be baptized not only in water but in their own blood.

(v)   There is a passage in Heracleon, a gnostic teacher and scholar who flourished about AD 145, and who wrote a commentary on John's gospel. In connection with the saying about being brought before rulers and authorities (Luke 12.11f.), Clement of Alexandria (*Miscellanies* 4.9) quotes Heracleon as saying: 'Matthew, Philip, Thomas, Levi and many others have escaped public testimony to Christ.' (The understanding of Matthew and Levi as different persons occurs elsewhere also.) This is taken to mean that the persons listed escaped 'red martyrdom', and it is argued that John is so important that, if he had escaped martyrdom, his name was bound to have been included in the list.

(vi)   Clement of Alexandria seems to be on both sides. In the *Miscellanies* (7.17) he says that all the apostles were dead by the reign of Nero. This would mean that they were all dead shortly before AD 70; and yet the same Clement regularly speaks of John in Ephesus in his old age, as he does in *The Rich Man's Salvation* with the story of John's rescue of the young man turned robber chief (pp. 22f. above).

(vii)   Chrysostom is like Clement. In *Homily* 65.2. *on Matthew* (on Matt. 20.23), he interprets Jesus' words as meaning: 'You shall be counted worthy of martyrdom and shall suffer those things I suffer.

You shall close your lives by a violent death.' Yet in *Homily* 76.2 he says: 'John lived a long time after the taking of Jerusalem', that is, after AD 70.

Both Clement and Chrysostom seem to know traditions both of an early martyrdom and a long Ephesian residence of John.

(viii)   There is the situation which the Muratorian Canon seems to reflect. It says of the fourth gospel (Theron, pp. 106-9):

> The fourth book of the Gospels is that of John, one of the disciples. When his fellow-disciples and bishops urged him, he said: 'Fast together with me today for three days and, what shall be revealed to each, let us tell it to each other.' On the same night it was revealed to Andrew, one of the Apostles, that, with all of them reviewing it, John should describe all things in his own name.

That passage seems to describe a situation which could only happen in Jerusalem before the destruction of that city in AD 70. It is highly unlikely, if not impossible, that there could have been a meeting of the apostles in Ephesus; this could happen only in Jerusalem. But later (Theron, pp. 110f.), in introduction to Paul's letters there comes an even more astonishing statement: 'The blessed Apostle Paul himself, *imitating the example of his predecessor, John*, wrote to seven churches.' Paul began writing about the year AD 48 and finished about AD 64, and if the Muratorian Canon is to be taken seriously the Revelation was written before Paul began to write at all, for its seven letters served as a pattern for Paul. That is a situation which it is surely impossible to contemplate, but it is interesting that as early as AD 170 someone could think of John's writing preceding that of Paul.

(ix)   Sometimes a phrase in the letter of Polycrates bishop of Ephesus to Victor bishop of Rome is quoted in this connection. The letter was written to support the Asian date of Easter, and we shall say more about it later (pp. 42f. below). Polycrates cites the great figures of the Asian church, whose names give weight to the Asian custom, and among them he cites John *martus kai didaskalos*. The word *didaskalos* without doubt means 'teacher'; but there often is a question as to the meaning of *martus*. *Martus* can mean either 'witness' or 'martyr', a very natural double meaning in an age when any witness to Christianity had to be prepared to become a martyr. Witness and martyrdom were close kin to each other. But what is the meaning here? Is Polycrates calling John a *witness* and a teacher, or a *martyr* and a teacher? In the same letter Polycrates uses the word *martus* of Polycarp, Thomas of Eumenia and Sagaris, undoubtedly in the sense of 'martyr'. But in the Ephesian tradition the martyrdom of these other great figures was never in doubt, while the martyrdom of John has no place there. Therefore it must be held that in the case of John *martus* is used in the sense of witness, and that this passage from Polycrates is not relevant to the discussion of the alleged martyrdom of John.

(x) We come finally to what would be regarded by many as the main piece of evidence. Both Mark (10.35-45) and Matthew (20.20-28) tell of the request of James and John for the chief places in the kingdom. In Mark's version Jesus replies:

> 'You do not know what you are asking. Are you able to drink the cup that I drink, or to be baptized with the baptism with which I am baptized?' And they said to him: 'We are able.' And Jesus said to them: 'The cup that I drink you will drink; and with the baptism with which I am baptized, you will be baptized; but to sit at my right hand or at my left is not mine to grant, but it is for those for whom it has been prepared.'

It is argued that this is a prophecy of Jesus that James and John would suffer martyrdom, and that a prophecy of Jesus must be fulfilled. There are those who would go further, and who would say that this is a *post eventum* prophecy, that is to say, that there is here put into the mouth of Jesus a prophecy of that which had already happened by the time the gospel was written. In any event, it is claimed that the New Testament itself in the very words of Jesus provides the witness to the martyrdom of John.

Let us now examine the most significant of these pieces of evidence. We begin by looking at the evidence of Philip of Sidē (p. 29 above). Philip was a notoriously incompetent historian. Socrates the ecclesiastical historian says of him that he was a laborious student who had amassed many books, but that his history was useless, because it is loose and inexact, especially in matters of chronology.[12] (Lightfoot in his *Biblical Essays*, p. 95, gives several examples of Philip's factual errors.) On the face of it, Philip of Sidē is not a historian whose information can be confidently accepted. Let us test his information.

(a) Philip says, first, that Papias was 'a hearer of John'. It is true that Irenaeus does say this. 'These things,' writes Irenaeus in his *Heresies* (5.33.4) 'are attested by Papias, an ancient man who was a hearer of John and a companion of Polycarp.' But Eusebius in his *History* (3.39.2) correctly contradicts this:

> These are the words of Irenaeus. But Papias himself in the preface to his discourses by no means declares that he was himself a hearer and eyewitness of the holy apostles, but he shows by the words which he uses that he received the doctrine of the faith from those who had known them.

Philip then begins with an incorrect statement.

(b) Philip then says that Papias spoke about John the Theologian, or John the Divine, as the AV calls him in the title of the Revelation. Whatever else Papias said, he did not call John *theologos*, the theologian, the divine, because that title was not applied to John until the fourth century and Papias was writing in the second century.

(c) Lastly, Philip says that James the brother of John was put to death by the Jews. But this is incorrect; he was executed by Herod

(Acts 12.2). It is entirely likely that Philip was confusing James the brother of John with James the brother of Jesus, who was executed by the Jews, as reported both by Josephus in his *Antiquities* (20.200) and by Hegesippus (in a passage preserved by Eusebius, *History*, 2.23.4-18). Errors such as these do not promote confidence in the accuracy of any historian.

Let us now look at the material which George the Sinner supplies (pp. 29f. above).

(a)   Whatever else we may say of it, George's material is highly confused. He says that after the death of Domitian Nerva allowed John to return to Ephesus. Nerva's dates are AD 96-98. On the other hand, he says that John was put to death by the Jews. If John was executed by the Jews, it must have been before AD 70, the year of the destruction of Jerusalem. Moreover, the Jews could not have executed anyone in a Roman province. True, the Jews were often, as Tertullian says in his book entitled *An Antidote to the Scorpion's Bite* (10), the source of persecution. And, further, they did often take part in martyrdoms, as in the case of Polycarp. Workman, in his *Persecution in the Early Church* (pp. 305-10), retells the story from *The Martyrdom of Polycarp*. When Polycarp confessed himself a Christian,

> A howl of vengeance rose from the heathen, in which the Jews, who were present in large numbers, joined – it was 'a great sabbath', probably the Feast of Purim, and their fanaticism was specially excited. 'This', they cried, 'is the teacher of Asia, who has perverted so many from sacrifice and adoration.' . . . The wood for the stake, torn in an instant from shops and baths, was carried to the spot by eager hands, the Jews as usual freely offering their services.

The Jews could inflame and even initiate persecution, but in a Roman province they could not have executed anyone.

(b)   Further, George completely misunderstood Origen. What Origen wrote in his *Commentary on Matthew* 16.6 (on Matt. 20.23) was:

> The sons of Zebedee drank the cup and were baptized with the baptism, since Herod indeed killed James the brother of John with the sword; but the Roman emperor, so tradition tells us, condemned John to the island of Patmos because of his witness for the word of truth.

Origen's whole point is that a Christian can be a martyr either by losing his life for Christ or by witnessing in his life for Christ – that John was a martyr not by dying but by living.

(c)   George's concluding quotation from Eusebius' *History* (3.1.1) has nothing at all to do with any kind of martyrdom, but simply says that John's allotted sphere of service was Asia, where in Ephesus he died a natural death.

When we examine the credentials of Philip and of George it is difficult to avoid the conclusion that he would be a reckless man who would regard either of them as trustworthy sources of information. It is very difficult to believe that Papias ever did say that John was martyred by the Jews, because quite certainly both Irenaeus and Eusebius had actually read the works of Papias, and we would have to believe that for some reason they both suppressed the information about the death of John. But, if Papias did not ever speak of the martyrdom of John, what has happened?

In the case of Philip, J.H. Bernard in *Studia Sacra* (pp. 270-5) suggests that there may have been a corruption of the text. Omitting the word *theologos*, the theologian, the divine, which, we have seen, Papias could not have used of John, since it was not applied to John until the fourth century, we get the sentence: 'John and James his brother were put to death by the Jews.' Two things may be said about that sentence. First, the order John and James is unusual; the regular order is James and John. Second, the phrase translated 'put to death by the Jews' is the phrase which is commonly used to describe the death of James the brother of our Lord. Suppose that the original had been: 'The brother of the Lord, James, was killed by the Jews'. 'The brother of the Lord, James' is in Greek *adelphos kuriou Iakōbos*. (We must remember that in the ancient manuscripts there was no space between the words, and the writing was in Greek capital letters, which were much more easily confused than the small letters later used). Now suppose that *adelphos kuriou Iakōbos* got corrupted into *adelphos autou kai Iakōbos*. It would mean 'his brother and James'. That is an odd phrase, and it would soon be further corrupted to the much easier 'John and James'. This would explain why John unusually comes before James, and why the words used of the martyrdom are the words normally used of the martyrdom of James the brother of the Lord. It is at least possible that what was originally a perfectly correct reference to James the brother of the Lord was corrupted into a wrong reference to John and James.

Now let us turn to the George Hamartōlos passage. In the first place it is worth noting that the Codex Coislinianus, which is unquestionably the oldest and the best manuscript, says: 'When John had written his gospel he was counted worthy of martyrdom.' But there are no fewer than twenty-six other manuscripts which read: 'When he had written his gospel, he died in peace', and which then go on to the last sentence, 'Concerning whom the very learned Eusebius says in his *Ecclesiastical History*; Thomas received by lot Parthia and John Asia, where he remained and died in Ephesus.' This is not to say that the Codex Coislinianus is wrong; it is the best manuscript. But it is to say that copyists found the statement of the death of John at the hands of the Jews so totally incredible that they altered the text to tell of John's long life and natural death in Ephesus.

In the case of George, J.B. Lightfoot in his essay on Papias (p. 212) has a suggestion to make. He suggests that George was working with a manuscript of Papias which had a gap in the text where a whole line had been omitted in the copying. So he suggests that the full reading (with conjecturally omitted part in brackets) was:

> Papias says that John [was condemned by the Roman Emperor and sent to Patmos for his witness, while James] was put to death by the Jews.

It is thus not impossible that Philip's statement comes from a corrupted text, and George's from the fact that he was using a defective text of Papias from which a line had dropped out.

Let us now examine the evidence from the calendars (pp. 30f. above). Before we do so directly it will be well to note two general facts. First, we must bear in mind the enormous prestige of martyrdom. Workman writes in *Persecution in the Early Church* (p. 343):

> At times there swept over all sections an extravagant thirst for self-immolation, and Christians, in plain disregard of the teaching of Jesus, courted death with culpable recklessness, and exalted martyrdom into the one royal road to perfection.

By martyrdom, says the Shepherd of Hermas (*Parables*, 9.28.3), 'all sins were healed'. Persecution, said Tertullian in his treatise *On Baptism* (16), was 'the second baptism in blood which stands in lieu of fontal baptism when that has not been received, and restores it when lost'. Workman (p. 344) continues:

> A certificate from a martyr, transferring, so to speak, his merit to another, not always specifically named, was looked upon by the lapsed as sufficient pardon for their denial of their Lord ... a cause of much trouble to the early Church, especially in North Africa, and which led in later times to further erroneous developments of the doctrine of Indulgences.

To be a martyr was to belong to the royalty of Christianity. Second, there always remained a certain ambiguity about the word *martus*; in both Greek and Latin it can mean 'witness' and it can mean 'martyr'. So there came to be two kinds of martyrdom: 'red martyrdom' in which the martyr died for Christ, and 'white martyrdom' in which he witnessed for Christ, no matter what the cost. Thus Tertullian writes in his treatise *On Flight in Persecution* (12): 'Can Christ claim that you, as a *martyrem* for him, have steadfastly shown him forth?' Eusebius records in his *History* (5.18.5f.) how angry Apollonius was at two Montanists, Themiso and Alexander, who arrogantly claimed to be martyrs. So we bear it in mind that 'martyr' was the highest title which could be given to any Christian, but to call a man a martyr did not necessarily mean to say that he had died for the faith; it could mean that he had lived for it. Bearing these things in mind, let us now go to the calendars.

The calendars make it clear that after Christmas it was the custom to commemorate a group of men – Stephen, James, John, Peter, Paul. There are two passages in the works of Gregory of Nyssa which are very illuminating.[13] The first occurs in his *Panegyric on St Basil*, and there he says that it was customary after Christmas to celebrate the memory of Stephen, Peter, James, John and Paul. In an earlier work, *In Praise of St Stephen*, he tells how this group is selected. The praise of Stephen the proto-martyr is fitly followed by the praise of the apostles, 'for neither are martyrs without apostles, nor apostles separated from [martyrs]'. He then goes on (I quote from J.H. Bernard's translation, *Studia Sacra*, p. 281):

> To this Stephen all the precious stones [of the spiritual temple] were immediately joined together – the most divine heralds of the gospels; after them the martyrs; and after them again those who have shone with saving virtue – principally those commemorated at this present season, who flash forth the beauty of piety far and brightly, I mean Peter and James and John, the leaders of the apostolic chorus, and the crowns of the church's glory.

He is thus saying that these great figures of the Church are commemorated not primarily because they were martyrs, but because they are 'the leaders of the apostolic chorus'. Then he goes on to say that those who are so honoured for their witness to Christ 'endured the combat with different kinds of martyrdom'. Peter was crucified, James was beheaded, and John's witness was fulfilled, first in his trial when he was flung into the cauldron of boiling oil, and secondly in his continual willingness to die for the name of Christ. And we find Gregory of Nazianzus saying exactly the same in his *Panegyric on St Basil* (76). He ranks Basil with this very same group, not that he did end his life in 'red martyrdom', but because he was always willing to do so. This evidence is earlier than that of the calendars, for Gregory of Nazianzus died in AD 395. It is therefore clear that the name of John appears on the calendars not because he was a 'red martyr', but because he was a leader of the apostolic chorus, and because by his witness he had demonstrated his willingness to die for Christ. The calendars are not a witness to the martyrdom of John.

We may here look at the Heracleon passage (p. 31 above). It is a comment on Luke 12.8-12, the passage which insists on the necessity of confessing Jesus before men, and which promises the help of the Holy Spirit to the Christian when he is brought before the synagogue, the rulers and the authorities. The point which Heracleon is making concerns the extravagant claims made for 'confessors', for, as we have already seen, martyrdom did have a fascination and did beget spiritual pride. Heracleon says that there are two kinds of confession, that which is made with the voice before the magistrate, and that which is the effect of a quiet and consistent Christian life. The distinction is between those who have had to make confession before the magistrate and those who have never been so called. He cites as examples of those who have never had to appear before the magistrate Matthew, Philip and Thomas. It has been argued that, since John's name is not mentioned, he must have been a martyr. But Heracleon could not possibly have included John in this list, for John had been condemned to Patmos for his witness to the faith (Rev. 1.9). Heracleon is not really a relevant witness at all.

So we come finally to the passage in Matthew and Mark (p. 33 above) in which Jesus deals with the claim of James and John to the chief places in the kingdom. Jesus says that they will be baptized with the same baptism as he is baptized, and that they will drink the same cup as he drinks (Matt. 20.22f.; Mark 10.38f.).

Matthew and Mark give slightly different versions of the words of Jesus. Matthew has: 'Are you able to drink the cup that I am to drink?' Mark has: 'Are you able to drink the cup that I drink, or to be baptized with the baptism with which I am baptized?' Matthew refers only to the cup; Mark also has the idea contained in the word 'baptism'. What exactly do the two phrases mean and imply?

(a) In the first place, the tenses of the verbs are to be noted. The tense in both cases is *present*, not future. Jesus did not say that James and John would drink the cup which he was going to drink, and be baptized with the baptism with which he was going to be baptized. The reference is not in the first place to the cross. Jesus said that they must drink the cup which at that moment he was drinking and be baptized with the baptism with which he was at that moment being baptized. It is Jesus' present experience they must share – the experience of rejection, humiliation, treachery, misrepresentation, misunderstanding, unpopularity, hatred, not necessarily the experience of actual martyrdom.

(b) In the second place, the meaning of the words must be carefully examined. First, the words 'baptism' and 'to be baptized'. The Greek words are *baptisma* and *baptizein*. To us these words have only one meaning; they describe the sacrament of reception into the church. But in ordinary secular Greek they have many meanings. *Baptizein* means 'to dip', and therefore 'to bathe', 'to wash', 'to submerge'. In the Septuagint it is used in II Kings 5.14 of Naaman *dipping* himself seven times in the Jordan and so being cleansed; it is used of Judith, when she was staying in the camp of Holofernes, going out at night to the valley of Bethulia to *bathe* in the spring; and it is used in Sirach (Ecclesiasticus) 34.25 of the futility of *washing oneself* after touching a dead body and then going and touching it again. Polybius uses it of a ship *sinking* (1.51.6; 16.6.2). But the word is also very commonly used not of literal submersion, but of being *submerged* in some experience. Josephus in the *Jewish War* (4.137) speaks of

Jerusalem being submerged by the crowds flooding through the streets. There is an epigram in the *Greek Anthology* (11.49) on wine, recommending that it be well diluted with water: 'Then it is most suited for the bridal chamber too, but if it breathes too fiercely, it puts the Loves to flight, and plunges us in a sleep that is neighbour to death.' In Plato's *Symposium* (176B) Pausanias suggests that they drink sparingly and Aristophanes agrees, saying that yesterday he was *bebaptismenos oino*, 'sunk, soaked in wine', dead drunk. Plutarch (*Galba*, 21) says of Otho that he was *bebaptismenos* with debts, immersed in debt, head over ears in debt. Plato in the *Euthydemus* (277D) uses it of a lad who is beginning to be submerged in a flood of arguments which he cannot understand and questions while he cannot answer, much as English colloquially uses the word 'sunk' of a student who is defeated by the questions in an examination. Achilles Tatius (6.19) says that both love and anger are flames. But 'love is overwhelmed by anger and *sinks in its flood*'. Bebaptismenos is a medical term for being *overcome* by sleep.[14]

All this is to say that, in a book written before the Christian church had established its sacraments, *baptizein* would make the reader think of being submerged by an experience of bitterness rather than of the idea of baptism. So the Psalmist says (Ps. 42.7): 'All thy waves and thy billows have gone over me.' What Jesus is saying to James and John is: 'Can you survive the bitter experience in which I am at the moment submerged, the experience of the hatred and the rejection of men?'

The other phrase, *to drink the cup*, does not necessarily imply death. It is common in the Old Testament. Psalm 11.6 says: 'A scorching wind shall be the portion of their cup.' In God's hand there is a foaming cup which the wicked must drink to the dregs (Ps. 75.8). Isaiah speaks of 'the cup of God's wrath' (51.17). And in Gethsemane Jesus prays for release from 'this cup' (Matt. 26.39; Mark 14.36; Luke 22.42). To drink the cup is to pass through some bitter experience, which may, but need not necessarily, involve death.

It is unnecessary to take Jesus' words to James and John as a prophecy of martyrdom. In view of the present tenses of the verbs it may indeed be unjustified. Jesus was saying to the brothers: 'Can you face the same bitter experience as I am facing? Can you be submerged in the same sea of troubles as is rolling over me?' It is certainly a warning that the way of the Christian will not be an easy way, but it is not necessarily a prophecy of martyrdom, and taken in this sense there is not the slightest necessity to assume that it is a *post eventum* prophecy, for there was no need of prophetic genius to foresee that the way of the Christian would be hard.

(c) In the third place, it is not without significance that Luke omits the incident, and moves the saying on humility (Mark 10.42-44; Matt.

20.25-28) to the last supper (Luke 22.24-27). There are three possible reasons why Luke should omit it. First, he may have hesitated to transmit a story which seemed to limit the power of Jesus, with its statement (Matt. 20.23; Mark 10.40) that the chief places were not his to give. Second, he may not have wanted to hand down a story which showed the apostles in an unsatisfactory light. Third, he may have omitted it because by the time he came to write the martyrdom motif had been read into the story – and yet no martyrdom had happened in the case of John. The silence of Luke may well be an argument against the early martyrdom of John.

There are many reputable scholars who accept the early martyrdom of John, but we believe that from start to finish the evidence is unsatisfactory and that each link in the chain is weak. J.H. Bernard, more than fifty years ago, concluded his essay on the subject: 'It may be said, I believe, that for reasonable suspicion that John the son of Zebedee came to a violent end there is no ground whatever.' And much more recently, J.N. Sanders, in the introduction to his commentary, writing of Philip of Sidē and George Hamartōlos, said: 'It is safer to leave the death of John the son of Zebedee unexplained than to rely on such dubious information.'

Finally, in our examination of the attack on tradition, we must investigate the view that John never had any connection with Asia and Ephesus, and that the supposition that he lived and worked and wrote in Ephesus is all based on a mistake. To do this we must put the evidence for John's residence in Asia under examination. We shall set out this evidence in reverse order. That is to say, we shall begin with the late witnesses and work back to the earliest witnesses for John's connection with Asia.

(i) We begin with the Latin preface to John in the Codex Toletanus, a tenth-century Bible at Madrid.[15] Here we read:

> The Apostle John whom the Lord Jesus loved most, last of all wrote this Gospel, at the request of the bishops of Asia, against Cerinthus and other heretics, and specially against the new dogma of the Ebionites, who say that Christ did not exist before He was born of Mary.

This preface has no doubt that the writer of the fourth gospel is John, that he is the apostle, and that he wrote in Asia.

(ii) The next witness to be called is a ninth-century manuscript from the Vatican, Cod. Reg. 14 (Theron, pp. 32f.). We quote it in J.B. Lightfoot's translation (from his essay on Papias, p. 210).

> The Gospel of John was made known (*manifestatum*), and given to the Churches by John while he yet remained in the body, as one Papias by name, of Hierapolis, a beloved disciple of John, has related in his *Exoterics*, that is, in his last five books; but he wrote down the Gospel at

the dictation of John, correctly. But Marcion the heretic, when he had been censured by him, because he held heretical opinions was cast off by John. Now he (Marcion) had brought writings or letters to him from the brethren in Pontus.

There are things there which are improbable and impossible. That Papias was John's amanuensis is highly improbable, and that John ever met Marcion is impossible. But this passage attributes the gospel to John, and if Papias is stated to be John's amanuensis, then the writer must believe that the gospel was written in Asia.

(iii) There is the Latin preface to the Vulgate text of John (quoted by J.H. Bernard in his commentary, p. lvii), which is probably sixth-century. It says that John, the Evangelist, one of the disciples of God, wrote the gospel in Asia, having already written the Apocalypse in Patmos, and it tells how, when John knew that the day of his death had come, he called his disciples together in Ephesus for his last message. Once again John is firmly connected with Ephesus.

(iv) Next there is the witness of Jerome (AD 340–420). In the preface to his commentary on Matthew (Theron, pp. 52ff.) he writes:

Last is John, the Apostle and Evangelist, whom Jesus loved most, who, reclining on the breast of the Lord, drank the purest streams of teachings and who alone merited to hear from the cross: 'Behold thy mother.' He – when he was in Asia, and at that time the seeds of the heretics, Cerinthus, Ebion, and others, who deny that Christ came in the flesh, whom he himself also calls Antichrists in his epistle, and at whom the Apostle Paul frequently lashes out, were already shooting up – was urged by almost all the bishops of Asia at that time and by delegates of many churches to write more profoundly about the divinity of the Saviour and, so to speak, to break through to the very Word of God – not so much with boldness as with fortunate haste [in view of the fact that he died soon afterwards]. When he was urged by the brethren to write, he is said to have replied that he would do so, if, when a general fast had been proclaimed, all would pray to God. When this was carried out, saturated with revelation, he burst into that heaven-sent Prologue: 'In the beginning was the Word, and the Word was with God, and this Word was God. The same was in the beginning with God.'

Once again, John is unequivocally connected with Asia.

(v) The next witness is Eusebius. Speaking of the reign of Trajan he writes in his *History* (3.23.1):

At that time the apostle and evangelist John, the one whom Jesus loved, was still living in Asia, and governing the churches in that region, having returned after the death of Domitian from his exile on the island.

Eusebius without question connects John with Asia.

(vi) Next there is the Monarchian Prologue, which probably dates to about AD 320. The Prologue to John is a fairly lengthy document. The relevant sentence is: 'He (John) wrote this Gospel in Asia after he had written the Apocalypse in the island of Patmos' (Theron, pp. 58f.).

(vii) Our next witness is Origen (AD 182–251). He was one of the greatest scholars of his day, as even the pagans would admit. Eusebius in his *History* (6.25.9) tells us that he made an investigation into the books which were universally accepted throughout the church. 'Why need we speak of him,' he writes, 'who reclined on the bosom of Jesus, John who has left us one Gospel, though he confessed that he could write so many that the world would not be able to contain them?' There he definitely assigns the fourth gospel to John, but does not speak of Asia and Ephesus, but Eusebius also tells us (3.1.1) that Origen in his *Commentary on Genesis* says that, when the apostles and disciples of the Lord were dispersed throughout the world, Parthia was allotted to Thomas, Scythia to Andrew, Asia to John. So Origen too is a witness to the common tradition.

(viii) Next comes Clement of Alexandria (AD 150–203). We have already told (pp. 22f. above) the famous story from *The Rich Man's Salvation* of the lad who became the robber chieftain after being entrusted to the care of the bishop. There Clement tells how John, whom he calls the apostle, dealt with the situation in the days 'when after the death of the tyrant (Domitian) he removed from the island of Patmos to Ephesus'. Clement of Alexandria is still another who locates John in Ephesus.

(ix) Next comes Apollonius. About Apollonius we know next to nothing. A fifth-century tradition makes him bishop of Ephesus, but it is a tradition without credibility. He wrote against Montanism, and Jerome (*On Famous Men*, 40) reports him as saying that he wrote forty years after Montanism had emerged, which would date him about AD 200. Eusebius has in his *History* a chapter about him which includes the statement: 'He tells how by divine power a dead man was raised by John himself at Ephesus' (5.18.13). With the accuracy of the report we are not concerned; the point is that Apollonius connects John with Ephesus.

(x) Our next witness is Polycrates. Polycrates was bishop of Ephesus about AD 190. He was very much a churchman, with long-standing family connections within the church. Eusebius (5.24.6) reports him as saying: 'Seven of my relatives were bishops, and I am the eighth.' Polycrates comes under our consideration because of his connection with the Quartodeciman controversy which concerned the date of Easter. The churches of Asia celebrated the Easter events on 14 Nisan, the day of the Jewish Passover, no matter what day of the week that was, since they regarded the whole festival as the Christian Passover. The Roman church celebrated Easter Sunday on the first Sunday after the first full moon after the spring equinox, which we do to this day. The controversy stretched over a long period. Polycarp had been involved in argument with Anicetus, the then bishop of

Rome; but Polycarp and Anicetus had had their argument in Christian love, and had in the end agreed to differ and yet to remain in Christian fellowship (see Eusebius' *History*, 5.24.16f.). In the days of Polycrates, Victor was bishop of Rome. He was a very overbearing and arrogant character, and proceeded to excommunicate Polycrates, a step of which the rest of the church did not approve. The matter dragged on until it was settled at Nicaea in AD 325, although as late as the fifth century a Quartodeciman sect still existed. Polycrates defended the Asian custom in a letter to Victor, in which he lists the great figures of the Asian church who had observed the Asian date. The relevant part of the letter (Eusebius, *History*, 5.24.2f.) runs:

> We observe the exact day, neither adding nor taking away. For in Asia also great lights have fallen asleep, which shall rise again on the day of the Lord's coming, when he shall come with glory from heaven, and shall seek out all the saints. Among these are Philip, one of the twelve apostles, who fell asleep in Hierapolis, and his two aged virgin daughters, and another daughter, who lived in the Holy Spirit, and now rests at Ephesus; and, moreover, John, who was both a witness and a teacher, who reclined upon the bosom of the Lord and, being a priest, wore the sacerdotal plate. He fell asleep at Ephesus.

It is true that Polycrates here seems to confuse the Philip who was one of the twelve with the Philip who was one of the seven (see p. 00 below). But the statement about John concerns his own see, and it is clearly difficult to disregard the evidence of a bishop about his own see, and of a man with such an intimate family connection with the church; and it is clear that Polycrates is asserting that John the apostle lived and worked and died in Ephesus.

(xi) The next witness is Papias, who presents us with a series of problems. His dates are probably about AD 70–145. He was bishop of Hierapolis and an indefatigable collector of the traditions of the early church. Eusebius (3.39.13) dismisses Papias as a man of very limited intelligence, but it may well be that Eusebius was heavily prejudiced against Papias because of Papias' pronounced millenarianism. The trouble begins with the fact that Irenaeus in his *Heresies* (5.33.4) calls Papias 'the hearer of John, and a companion of Polycarp'. That Papias was a hearer of John, Eusebius flatly denies. In his *History* (3.39.2) he writes:

> These are the words of Irenaeus, but Papias himself in the preface to his treatises makes plain that he in no way been a hearer and eyewitness of the holy apostles, but he shows by the words which he uses that he had received the doctrines of the faith from those who had known them [i.e. had known the apostles].

What in fact did Papias say? The famous or notorious quotation preserved by Eusebius in his *History* (3.39.4f.) runs as follows (We quote Barrett's translation from the introduction to his commentary, p. 89, and it is his explanation of the grammar of the passage that we are using.)

> But I shall not hesitate also to put down for you along with my interpretations whatsoever things I have at any time learned carefully from the elders and carefully remembered, guaranteeing their truth. For I did not, like the multitude, take pleasure in those that speak much, but in those that teach the truth; not in those that related strange commandments, but in those that deliver the commandments given by the Lord to faith, and springing from the truth itself. If, then, anyone came who had been a follower of the elders, I inquired into the sayings of the elders – what Andrew, or what Peter said, or what Philip, or Thomas, or James, or John, or Matthew, or any other disciples of the Lord said – and the things which Aristion and the Elder John, the disciples of the Lord, were saying. For I did not think that what was to be had from the books would profit me as much as what came from the living and abiding voice.

To evaluate this quotation correctly we may note the following points. The elders are not the ecclesiastical order of church officials; the elders are the generation immediately following the apostles, the generation who had been in direct living touch with the twelve. The word is used much as we would use the expression 'the fathers of the church'. 'I inquired' is *anekrinon*. What the disciples of the lord 'said' is *eipen*, the aorist tense, and must mean that Papias inquired what these men *had said* in the past. In the case of the second group, Aristion and the elder John, the verb is *legousin*, which is the present tense, and which must refer to the same time as the main verb *anekrinon*; the meaning will therefore be that Papias inquired what these men were actually saying at the time. So in the Papias quotation there are three groups. The first group, about which Papias investigated what they had said, is the apostles. Papias' connection with them was at two removes. After the apostles came the elders, the fathers of the church; then, thirdly, after the elders, came the followers of the elders; and it was from the followers of the elders that Papias drew his information. It is apparent that the second group, Aristion and the elder John, were alive when Papias was making his investigation which, as we have seen, must have been about AD 100. John the elder and Aristion are described as disciples of the Lord. Is it possible that round about AD 100 there were still alive people who had actually been disciples of the Lord?

Barrett (p. 91) offers four possibilities. First, quite simply Papias may have been mistaken, and Aristion and John the elder may not have been actual disciples of Jesus. Second, the text may be wrong. As the text starts, Aristion and John the elder are said to have been disciples *tou kuriou*, of the Lord; perhaps it ought to say that they were not disciples *tou kuriou*, but disciples *touton*, 'of these', that is, of the disciples. This would make Aristion and John the elder, not disciples of Jesus, but disciples of the disciples of Jesus, not first-generation, but second-generation Christians. Third, it is possible, but surely in the context unlikely, that 'disciples of the Lord' means no more than 'Christians' as you might call a loyal follower of Jesus in any age a disciple of Jesus. Fourth, it may well be that Papias was right. As Barrett says: 'Each of these suggestions is possible; but none seems decisively preferable to the view that two personal disciples of Jesus lived till *c.* AD 100.'

Before we leave this problem, we may note certain other suggestions, even if it would be too much to call them possibilities.[16] Robson has suggested that in the first group, instead of 'James and John' we should read 'the mother of James and Joanna'. In Greek *Iōannes*, John, and *Iōanna*, Joanna, are indeed very similar. The two are mentioned together in Luke 24.10; and Robson comments: 'a natural and proper pair to whom enquirers after authentic records would always resort.' M. Krenkel identifies John the elder with John the apostle, and the John of Papias' first group with John Mark. Larfeld suggests that in the second group the reading should be not 'the disciples of the Lord', but 'the disciples of John', and argues that Aristion and John the elder were disciples of the apostle John. It is just remotely possible to argue that both Johns are the same, that the John of the first group and John the elder of the second group are the same person, and that the name John occurs in both groups because he is the one apostle whose life spans both groups, and thus it was possible to enquire both what he had said and what he was saying. When all is said and done, the best solution is to agree with Barrett that Papias was right, that these two men did survive, for none of the alternatives makes any better sense.

It is of interest to note how, as the generations passed, the name of Papias became ever more closely associated with the name of John. All that Papias himself claimed was that he had sought out those who had been followers of the fathers of the church who had known John and the first apostles. Irenaeus (*Against Heresies*, 5.33.4) turned him into a hearer of John, as did Jerome (*On Famous Men*, 18). In Philip of Sidē (p. 50 above) he is a hearer of John and a companion of Polycarp. In George the Sinner (pp. 29f.), Papias is an eyewitness of John. In the Vatican codex mentioned above (pp. 40f.) he is a beloved disciple of John, who wrote the gospel 'at the dictation of John.'[17]

Papias in fact does not in so many words himself link John the apostle to Ephesus. If Irenaeus had not mistakenly called Papias a hearer of John, he would most likely not have appeared in the list of witnesses at all.

(xii) We come finally to Irenaeus, and he is the most important witness of all, for his evidence is the foundation on which all the other evidence is built, and this means that, if Irenaeus can be proved to be mistaken, the whole edifice will collapse. Irenaeus lived from about AD 130 to 201. He was educated at Ephesus, and heard at least some of the teaching of Polycarp, and upon Irenaeus' recollection of Polycarp's teaching the evidence for the residence of John in Ephesus very largely depends. Irenaeus left Ephesus for Rome not later than AD 155. He became bishop of Lyons in Gaul in AD 177. Irenaeus may have had another contact with the early days of the faith in Ephesus. His predecessor as bishop of Lyons was Pothinus, and tradition makes Pothinus a native of Asia Minor. Pothinus was martyred in the persecution of the churches of Lyons and Vienne in AD 177, and at the time of his martyrdom he was more than ninety years old. This would mean that he was born about AD 80. And it may be that Pothinus too contributed something to Irenaeus' knowledge of the church in Ephesus.

Polycarp was martyred in AD 155 or 156. When he was invited to save his life by publicly blaspheming Jesus Christ, he made his famous reply: 'Eighty and six years have I served Christ, and he has never done me wrong. How can I blaspheme my King who saved me?'[18] It is not certain whether the eighty-six years represent his whole life-time or the time that he was a Christian, but in any event he too goes back to about AD 70 in his connection with Ephesus.

On the face of it, it would seem that Irenaeus' sources are good. Irenaeus has no doubt about John's authorship of the fourth gospel, of his connection with Ephesus, and that he was the apostle. Irenaeus ends his account of the process by which the gospels were written with the words: 'Afterwards, John, the disciple of the Lord, who also had leaned upon his breast, himself published a Gospel during his residence at Ephesus in Asia' (*Against Heresies*, 3.1.1). He guarantees a tradition about Jesus by saying: 'Those who were conversant in Asia with John the disciple of the Lord, affirm that John conveyed to them this information. And he remained among them up to the time of Trajan' (2.22.5). He speaks about 'the church in Ephesus, founded by Paul, and having John remaining among them until the time of Trajan', and says that it is 'a true witness of the tradition of the apostles' (3.3.4). In the same passage, also reproduced by Eusebius (4.14.3-7), he speaks of the connection of both Polycarp and John with the church at Ephesus, and of his own connection with Polycarp:

> Polycarp was not only instructed by apostles, and conversed with many who had seen Christ, but was also by apostles in Asia appointed bishop of the church in Smyrna, whom I also saw in my early youth, for he tarried on earth a very long time, and, when a very old man, gloriously and most nobly suffering martyrdom, departed this life, after always teaching the things which he had learned from the apostles, and which the church has handed down, and which alone are true. To these things all the Asiatic churches testify, as do also those men who have succeeded Polycarp

down to the present time, – a man who was of much greater weight, and a more steadfast witness of truth, than Valentinus and Marcion and the rest of the heretics ... There are also those who heard from him that John, the disciple of the Lord, going to bathe in Ephesus, and perceiving Cerinthus within, rushed out of the bath-house without bathing. 'Let us flee,' he exclaimed, 'lest even the bath-house fall down, because Cerinthus the enemy of truth is within.' And Polycarp himself replied to Marcion who met him on one occasion and said: 'Do you know me?' 'I do know you the firstborn of Satan.'

The document in which Irenaeus most directly talks of himself and Polycarp and John is the letter to Florinus. Florinus was an old friend of his, who had strayed into gnostic Valentinianism, and Irenaeus is seeking to recall him to the right way by reminding him of the old days when they were both young students. Eusebius (5.20.4-8) gives the letter (the translation is that of C.K. Barrett, p. 84):

> For when I was a boy, I saw thee in lower Asia with Polycarp, moving in splendour in the royal court, and endeavouring to gain his approbation. I remember the events of that time more clearly than those of recent years. For what boys learn, growing with their mind, becomes joined with it; so that I am able to describe the very place in which the blessed Polycarp sat as he discoursed, and his goings out and his comings in, and the manner of his life, and his physical appearance, and his discourses to the people, and the accounts which he gave of his intercourse with John, and with the others who had seen the Lord. And as he remembered their words, and what he heard from them concerning the Lord, and concerning his miracles and his teaching, having received them from eyewitnesses of the 'Word of Life', Polycarp related all things in harmony with the Scriptures. These things being told me by the mercy of God, I listened to them attentively, noting them down, not on paper, but in my heart. And continually, through God's grace, I recall them faithfully.

Clearly, Irenaeus had no doubt that he had heard Polycarp tell how he had listened to the teaching of the apostle John in Asia.

On the face of it the evidence looks good, even indisputable. But one curious fact emerges: Irenaeus hardly ever calls this John an *apostle*; he nearly always describes him by the title *disciple* (sometimes even '*the* disciple', a title which he gives to no one else). Already in this section we have quoted four examples of this, and there are many more. 'As John the Lord's disciple says' is Irenaeus' normal way of introducing a quotation from the fourth gospel (e.g. *Against Heresies*, 2.2.5; 3.16.5). In 3.11.3, when quoting John 1.14, he omits the name 'John' and simply calls him 'the disciple of the Lord'. Irenaeus also ascribes the Revelation to 'John the disciple of the Lord' (4.3.4), and we find the same phrase introducing a quotation from II John 11 (1.16.3).

We must then ask if it is possible that Irenaeus was mistaken, that he gained the impression that Polycarp was talking about John the apostle, when he was in fact talking about another John, John the disciple. It is clear that whenever Irenaeus talks about his John, the title 'John the disciple of the Lord' comes automatically to his tongue or pen. There are very few who would question that Irenaeus *thought* that he was talking about John the apostle. One of those who would was C.F. Burney. Burney held that Irenaeus made no mistake, that when he talked of John the disciple of the Lord, he knew what he was doing, and he was referring, not to John the apostle, but to John the elder about whom Papias speaks. According to Burney, the person who made the mistake is Eusebius, who jumped to the conclusion that the writer of the gospel must be the apostle, and who was thus responsible for making it seem that Irenaeus had made a mistake.[19] But that is a view which few would take. As we shall see, questions can be asked regarding the evidence of Polycrates, but it does seem that Polycrates too must have believed that he was talking about John the apostle, because it would be an apostle's evidence which was to him essential to support his position in regard to the Quartodeciman controversy. And Polycrates' date is about AD 190, long before Eusebius.

Is there any further possible evidence for this John the disciple of the Lord as a separate person? The Monarchian Prologue to John begins: 'This is John the Evangelist, one of the *disciples* of God.' When we look at the letter of Polycrates (quoted on p. 43 above), we notice that there is something rather odd about it. Polycrates cites his witnesses for his side of the Quartodeciman controversy:

> Philip, one of the twelve apostles, who fell asleep in Hierapolis, and his two aged virgin daughters, and another daughter, who lived in the Holy Spirit, and now rests at Ephesus; and John who was both a witness and a teacher, who reclined upon the bosom of the Lord, and, being a priest, wore the sacerdotal plate.

It could be argued that there are two curious things there. First, Philip is cited before John, and normally John would come far ahead of Philip. Second, John is called a witness and a teacher but he is not called an apostle, although Philip is.

There is something strange about the way in which the Muratorian Canon (Theron, pp. 106-9) mentions John.

> The fourth book of the Gospels is that of John,*one of the disciples*. When his fellow-disciples and bishops urged him, he said: 'Fast together with me today for three days and, what shall be revealed to each, let us tell it to each other.' On the same night it was revealed to Andrew, *one of the Apostles*, that, with all of them reviewing it, John should describe all things in his own name.

It is odd that John should be so definitely called one of the disciples and Andrew equally definitely one of the apostles.

Before we begin to ask our questions and to evaluate our evidence, we must qualify one piece of evidence and add two more.

First, as we indicated above, there are examples of Irenaeus calling John an apostle, although they are very rare. In *Against Heresies*, 1.9.2, he introduces the sentence, 'And the Word was made flesh, and dwelt among us', with the statement that it was the apostle who said it. In 2.22.5 he says that some of the elders saw not only John, 'but the other apostles also', which calls John an apostle at least by implication. Of the church at Ephesus Irenaeus says (3.3.4) that since it was founded by Paul, and since John resided there down to the time of Trajan, it was 'a true witness of the tradition of the apostles', and there once again John is called an apostle by implication. But beyond this Irenaeus does not go, and the title by which he habitually describes his John is 'the disciple of the Lord'.

The two further pieces of evidence consist of two very surprising omissions. John, according to Irenaeus, was the teacher of Polycarp, and yet when Polycarp wrote his letter *To the Philippians*, he never mentions John's name. He three times mentions the name of Paul. In 3.2 he writes:

> Neither am I nor is any other like me able to follow the wisdom of the blessed and glorious Paul, who when he was among you in the presence of the men of that time taught accurately and stedfastly the word of truth, and also in his absence wrote letters to you, from the study of which you will be able to build yourselves up in the faith given to you.

In 9.1. he urges them to show the same endurance as they have seen 'not only in the blessed Ignatius and Zosimus and Rufus, but also in others among yourselves, and in Paul himself and the other apostles'. In 11.3 he describes the Philippians as those among whom the blessed Paul laboured and who are praised in the beginning of his letter. But there are no references to John at all. Is that so very surprising? Paul had the closest possible contact with the church at Philippi. It might well be that the Philippians hardly knew who John was, for John was not one of the wide-travelling apostles, and Polycarp's letter may well have been written in the first quarter of the second century, before John's gospel had become widely known and accepted. On the whole there was no reason for Polycarp to mention John to the Philippians.

A much more surprising omission is that Ignatius makes no mention of John in his letter *To the Ephesians*. Ignatius was martyred in Rome sometime near AD 110; and it was on his way to Rome that he wrote his letters. He himself was bishop of Antioch. When he writes *To the Romans* (4.3), he mentions Peter and Paul. 'I do not order you as did Peter and Paul; they were apostles, I am a convict; they were free, I am until now a slave.' That is to say, in writing to Rome he mentions the apostles who were most closely connected with the

Christian church there. It is strange, therefore, that in writing to Ephesus Ignatius makes no reference to John, who, if tradition is correct, was the greatest glory of the Ephesian church, whereas he does mention Paul. In 12.4 he tells the Ephesians:

> You are fellow-initiates with Paul, who was sanctified, who gained a good report, who was right blessed, in whose footsteps may I be found when I shall attain to God, who in every letter makes mention of you in Christ Jesus.

It may be that Ignatius mentions Paul and not John because Paul like himself had been a martyr for Jesus Christ, and is therefore far more in his mind than John.

One small point should also be mentioned here. Those who hold that Acts is a late work, and that the speeches in Acts are not authentic but later compositions, argue that if John had been the leader of the Ephesian church, whoever wrote Acts could not have written the sentence in Paul's farewell speech to the Ephesian elders (Acts 20.29f.):

> I know that after my departure fierce wolves will come in among you, not sparing the flock; and from among your own selves will arise men speaking perverse things to draw away the disciples after them.

Of course if the speech is not a fiction but represents the words of Paul, there is no problem, for when Paul made the speech no one had any idea that John would arrive in Ephesus. But in any case, even when John was there, the church at Ephesus still had its heretics, to deal with whom both the fourth gospel and the first letter of John were written.

Are we then from the evidence in front of us and from the general probabilities of the case to assume that Irenaeus had got the whole matter wrong, that Polycarp did not speak of John the apostle but of John the disciple of the Lord, an entirely different person, and that Irenaeus' mistake set up a kind of chain reaction in which his error was perpetuated, and in which John the apostle was assigned a connection with Asia and Ephesus which he never had?

(a) It is suggested, for example by G.H.C. Macgregor in the introduction to his commentary, (p. lviii), that Irenaeus in his letter to Florinus is making much more of his connection with Polycarp than the facts warranted, that his stay in Asia Minor and in Smyrna was very brief, that he had no more than a brief, casual and distant contact with Polycarp, and that in any event he was at the time too young to have any real understanding or recollection of what was said.

The question of Irenaeus' age when he had contact with Polycarp is important. In the letter to Florinus (see p. 47 above) he says that it was 'when I was still a boy'. In *Against Heresies* (3.3.4) he says it was 'in my early youth'.[20] Just what does the phrase mean? When Irenaeus is discussing the age of Jesus (in *Against Heresies*, 2.22.25), he says that Jesus was baptized when he was about thirty, *adhuc iuvenis* (the passage exists only in the Latin version), while still a young man. Irenaeus is talking about how Jesus sanctified the various ages of life, and he says that thus Jesus sanctified the first stage of life; he goes on 'that the first stage of life embraces thirty years (*quia autem triginta annorum aetas prima indolis est iuvenis*), and that this extends onward to the fortieth year, everyone will admit.' It is extremely probable that this is the same as 'early youth'. But since it was at the beginning of his first age of life that Irenaeus claims to have been in contact with Polycarp, it may well be that at the time he was seventeen or eighteen. At least it is certain that when he listened to Polycarp he was not a child; and there is no reason why his memory of what Polycarp said should not have been quite accurate, and there is still less reason for assuming that he did not understand what Polycarp was saying.

(b) It is pointed out that Irenaeus did misunderstand Papias, and in his book *Against Heresies* (5.33.4) called him 'a hearer of John' when he was not. True, but Irenaeus was *reading* Papias – and it would not have been difficult to misread him – while he was *listening* to Polycarp, and listening to something which Polycarp clearly often repeated. It is further pointed out that Irenaeus' information about Polycarp appears to be wrong. He says of Polycarp (*Against Heresies*, 3.3.4):

> Polycarp was not only instructed by apostles, and conversed with many who had seen Christ, but was also by apostles in Asia appointed bishop of the church in Smyrna.

This is information which Eusebius also transmits in his *History* (3.36.1):

> At that time Polycarp, a disciple of the apostles, was a man of eminence in Asia, having been entrusted with the episcopate of the church of Smyrna by those who had seen and heard the Lord.

Macgregor (p. lviii) reminds us that this differs from the account in the life of Polycarp ascribed to Pionius, who says that Polycarp was ordained deacon and nominated as his successor by Bucolus, bishop of Smyrna, and even Bucolus was not the first bishop. But the fact that Irenaeus was wrongly informed about the biography of Polycarp would make no difference to his ability to understand what Polycarp was saying. It is not necessary to have read someone's entry in *Who's Who* in order to understand his lectures.

There is no compelling reason to believe that Irenaeus must have misunderstood or in fact did misunderstand Polycarp.

(c) Suppose there were two persons both called John, both prominent in the church, and both connected with Asia and Ephesus, is it possible that the two could become confused, and that one might be mistaken for the other? The Papias quotation presents us with two Johns. Papias sets himself to enquire what Andrew, or Peter, or Philip, or Thomas, or James or John or Matthew had said; and he also makes enquiry as to what Aristion and the Elder John, the disciples of the Lord, used to say. This means that, presumably, there was in the church a John who had been a member of the twelve, and a John who was not a member of the twelve, but who was a well-known figure in the church and an original disciple of Jesus. Is there any possibility that the two Johns could have become confused with each other?

The answer is that such a confusion was indeed possible. There is apparently widespread confusion between Philip the apostle, who was a member of the twelve, and Philip the evangelist, who is named in Acts 6.6 as one of the seven. This confusion emerges in Polycrates' letter to Victor of Rome, in which he cites the great figures who may be taken to support the Asian side of the Quartodeciman controversy; he includes among them, 'Philip, *one of the twelve apostles*, who sleeps in Hierapolis, with his two aged virgin daughters, and another daughter, who lived in the Holy Spirit and now rests at Ephesus.' In his *History* (3.31.3-5) Eusebius cites this part of Polycrates' letters, and then goes on to cite the evidence of Proclus the Montanist in his *Dialogue* with Caius. Proclus there says: 'After him there were four prophetesses, the daughters of Philip in Hierapolis in Asia. Their tomb is there and the tomb of their father.' Eusebius finally cites the words of Luke in Acts 21.8f.: 'We came into Caesarea; and entering the house of Philip the evangelist, who was one of the seven, we stayed with him. Now this man had four daughters, virgins, who prophesied.' It is extremely unlikely that both Philips had such similar families of virgin daughters who were prophetesses. Quite clearly it was Philip the evangelist who was buried in Hierapolis, but Polycrates cites him as Philip the apostle.

Irenaeus himself confuses James the son of Zebedee and James the brother of the Lord. In his book *Against Heresies* (3.12.15) he is commenting on Galatians 2.12, which describes the conduct of Peter: 'Before certain men came from James, he ate with the Gentiles; but when they came, he drew back and separated himself, fearing the circumcision party.' Irenaeus points out how Peter and James and presumably John (cf. Gal. 2.9) still insisted on observing the Mosaic law, and he says: 'Thus did the apostles, whom the Lord made witnesses of every action and of every doctrine – for upon all occasions do we find Peter and James and John present with him – scrupulously act according to the dispensation of the Mosaic law.'

Irenaeus is, of course, referring to the fact that Jesus took Peter and James and John with him on very special occasions, the raising of Jairus' daughter, the mount of transfiguration, the Garden of Gethsemane (Mark 5.37; 9.2; 14.33). But the James who was one of the chosen three in the gospels was the brother of John and the son of Zebedee, while the James of Galatians is the brother of our Lord, and in any event the James of the gospels had been martyred by Herod, as recorded in Acts 12.2, before the Galatians events happened. The common confusion of the two Philips and Irenaeus' own confusion of the two Jameses makes it clear that people of the same name could and did get confused with each other. It is therefore theoretically possible that Irenaeus could have confused the two Johns, John the apostle and John the elder, although that he could have done so is no proof that he actually did so.

(d) We must finally enquire whether or not the fact that Irenaeus consistently calls John the disciple of the Lord, and only very rarely an apostle, will bear the weight of the argument which has been erected on it. The argument is that Irenaeus thought that he was speaking about John the apostle, but the very fact that he regularly speaks of John the disciple of the Lord is the proof that, although Irenaeus was unaware that it was so, the person involved is not the apostle, but some one else.

We must begin by establishing the meaning of the words which are used, always remembering that, while we can establish the technical and exact meaning of the words, we cannot always be sure that a writer is going to use them with absolute accuracy.

When the apostolic company met to replace the traitor Judas, the qualifications of an apostle were laid down (Acts 1.21f.). He must be 'one of the men who have accompanied us during all the time that the Lord Jesus went in and out among us, beginning from the baptism of John until the day when he was taken up from us'. The function of such a man is to 'become with us a witness to his (Jesus') resurrection'. When Paul's apostleship is questioned, his demand (I Cor. 9.1) is: 'Have I not seen Jesus our Lord?' In other words, an apostle must have been a companion of Jesus throughout the days of Jesus' earthly life in the body, and in the end a witness of the resurrection. Clearly, the apostolic company is going to be very limited, and equally clearly, in the process of time the apostles are a vanishing order. The word disciple had both a wider and a narrower significance. In its wider meaning it is to all intents and purposes the same as the word Christian; it means simply a follower of Jesus Christ. In its narrower meaning it means one of the original followers of Jesus. It therefore can be seen that all apostles were disciples, but not all disciples were apostles. Both words originally describe those who were followers of Jesus during his earthly ministry. In a writer like Irenaeus, the word 'elders' means the immediate successors of the apostles, not the ecclesiastical order which the word was later to describe. The elders are those, who, as Irenaeus says (*Against Heresies*, 4.26.2), 'possess the succession from the apostles'. He speaks about 'the elders who were the disciples of the apostles' (5.5.1). Irenaeus can also speak of one of his sources for the correct teaching of scripture as 'a certain elder who had heard it from those who had seen the apostles, and from those who had been their disciples' (4.27.1). The elders in this sense were very much what we would call the fathers of the church.

Let us then see how these words are actually used. It is the surprising fact that in the fourth gospel the word 'disciple' occurs seventy-eight times, and the word 'apostle' only once. And on the one occasion on which it is used, it is used in a quite non-technical sense. The word apostle, *apostolos*, means 'one who is sent'. And in John 13.16 we read: 'Truly, truly I say to you, a servant is not greater than his master; nor is he who is sent (*apostolos*) than he who sent him.' In John 2.2 Jesus' company both collectively and individually are called disciples. Jesus was invited to the marriage feast at Cana in Galilee, with his disciples. In the Lazarus story the dialogue is continually between Jesus and his disciples (John 11.7, 12, 16). In the account of the last supper in the fourth gospel, Jesus is said to wash his disciples' feet (13.5), and we read (13.22) that when Jesus spoke of the traitor 'the disciples looked at one another, uncertain of whom he spoke'. The group to whom the resurrection appearance at the lakeside was made (21.1f.) is collectively described as 'the disciples'. Simon, Thomas and the sons of Zebedee, who were members of the twelve, are named; Nathanael, who did not belong to the twelve, is also named; and there were two other disciples. We also find the term 'disciple' applied to individuals, Andrew (6.8), Judas Iscariot (12.4), and the 'other disciple' who accompanied Peter (18.15f.). The word is equally common in the synoptic gospels; for instance we read in Matthew 20.17: 'As Jesus was going up to Jerusalem he took the twelve disciples aside.'

When we move outside the New Testament, we find that the Monarchian Prologue describes John as 'one of the disciples of God', that is, of Jesus (Theron, pp. 58f.). Eusebius writes in his *History* (3.24.5): 'Of all the disciples of the Lord, only Matthew and John have left us written memorials.' Philip of Sidē (Theron, pp. 30f.) says of Papias,

> When making an enumeration of the apostles, he enrolled among the disciples of the Lord, together with Peter and John, Philip and Thomas and Matthew, also Aristion and another John whom he also called an Elder.

George the Sinner (also quoted by Theron, pp. 30f.) says of John in the reign of Nerva: 'He was the only one of the twelve disciples still living at that time.' Papias (see p. 44 above) wrote: 'I made enquiry . . . what Andrew or what Peter had said, or what Philip, or what Thomas or James, or what John or Matthew, or any other of the disciples of the Lord.' We may well conclude that the words 'disciples' and 'apostles' continued to be used interchangeably, so that it was still possible for a late writer like George to speak, as the gospel writers did, of the 'twelve disciples'. It seems clear that to argue that Irenaeus' John could not be an apostle because Irenaeus calls him 'the disciple of the Lord' is extremely precarious. Our conclusion must be that the fact that Irenaeus called John the disciple of the Lord will not bear the weight of the argument erected upon it.

Our examination of the evidence shows that it is not such as to preclude the possibility that John the apostle lived and worked and wrote in Ephesus. It does not prove that he did, but it does bar us from saying that he could not have done so.

3

THE BELOVED DISCIPLE

He who would write about the fourth gospel is constantly confronted by an ever-recurring difficulty. The problems of the fourth gospel tend to interlock. It is not possible to take one problem, to write about it in one section, to come to some solution of it, and then to pass on to the next problem, and so to work in a series of self-contained sections, each complete in itself. In the case of the fourth gospel this is impossible, because the problems are interwoven and interconnected. This present chapter proposes to deal with the beloved disciple. We have to discuss who he was. In order to do that we have to discuss whether or not ch. 21 is an authentic and integral part of the fourth gospel. And then we have to discuss what part the beloved disciple played in the writing of the fourth gospel. All these problems are interlocked.

'The disciple whom Jesus loved' does not appear until the closing scenes of the fourth gospel. He appears first in John's account of the last meal together (13.21-25). Jesus had indicated that one of the twelve would betray him. The beloved disciple was next to Jesus, leaning on Jesus' shoulder, and Peter signed to him to ask who the traitor was. So the beloved disciple did ask the question and was given the answer which indicated the identity of the traitor. The intimacy of the beloved disciple with Jesus is shown by his place next to Jesus at the table, and by the fact that Peter turns to him to ask Jesus this specially intimate question.

The beloved disciple next appears at the foot of the cross, when Jesus gives him to Mary as a son, and Mary to him as a mother; and where it is said that from that time he took Mary to his own home (19.25-27).

He next appears on Easter morning, when Mary Magdalene came and told him and Peter that the stone was rolled away from the entrance to the tomb. He outstripped Peter as they ran to the tomb. At first he did not enter the tomb, but, when Peter went into the tomb, he followed him. And when he saw the empty grave clothes, 'he saw and believed' (20.2-10).

We next meet the beloved disciple in Galilee after the resurrection, when Jesus has appeared to the disciples beside the lake, and where care is taken to correct a misapprehension, apparently common, that Jesus had said that the beloved disciple would not die (21.20-23). On this occasion the beloved disciple is said to be the witness to the things contained in the fourth gospel, and to be its author (21.24). This last passage is to be taken in close connection with 19.35, which seems to claim the beloved disciple as a witness to the water and blood which flowed from Jesus' side when the soldiers pierced it as Jesus hung on the cross. So in these passages the beloved disciple is being cited at least as the witness whose authority lies behind the story of the gospel, and most probably as its author.

One other passage is usually taken as a reference to the beloved disciple, although in it his name is not actually mentioned. It is told that after the arrest of Jesus, Peter followed Jesus with 'another disciple'. This other disciple was known to the high priest and arranged that Peter should be admitted to the courtyard of the high priest's residence while the interrogation of Jesus was in progress, thus introducing Peter to the situation in which he so tragically three times denied his Lord (18.15-18, 25-27).

The beloved disciple is identified as having leaned upon the breast of Jesus at the last supper. The description comes from the way in which at that period guests sat at table. In fact they did not sit; they reclined on low couches, leaning on the left elbow, leaving the right hand free to deal with the food, and with the legs stretched out behind. Sitting or reclining thus, a guest had his head resting on the shoulder of the person on his left. So the phrase, which in the early church becomes a kind of standard description of the beloved disciple,[1] means that he was sitting on Jesus' right.

Who then was this beloved disciple? Tradition is unanimous that he was John the son of Zebedee. Irenaeus (*Against Heresies*, 3.1.1) speaks about 'John the disciple of the Lord who leant upon his breast'. Polycrates (see p. 43 above) speaks of John 'who reclined upon the breast of the Lord'. Origen (quoted by Eusebius in his *History*, 6.25.9) says: 'What must be said of John who reclined upon Jesus' breast?' Eusebius introduces his two long chapters on John (3.23f.) with the phrase 'the very disciple whom Jesus loved'. The tenth-century Codex Toletanus (see p. 40 above) speaks of John as 'the apostle whom Jesus loved most of all'. J.H. Bernard writes in the introduction to his commentary (I, p. xxxvii): 'This is a point on which tradition could not have gone astray, and there is no other tradition.' J.B. Lightfoot (*Biblical Essays*, p. 40), asks the question, 'How do we know that the fourth gospel was written by John the son of Zebedee?' He answers: 'I answer, first of all, that it is traditionally ascribed to him, as the *Phaedo* is ascribed to Plato, or the *Antigone* to Sophocles.' To anyone who is prepared to give a dominant weight to tradition, the identity of John the son of Zebedee and the beloved disciple is beyond argument.

First, let us set down the arguments in favour of identifying the beloved disciple with John the son of Zebedee, as presented by Lightfoot in the passage just quoted, and in their commentaries by Barrett (pp. 97-101) and Bernard (pp. xxxiv-xxxvii).

(i) The beloved disciple was present at the last supper (13.23), and in the account of the last supper in the synoptics it is clear that only the twelve were present on that occasion. 'When it was evening, he sat down at table with the twelve disciples' (Matt. 26.20; cf. Mark 14.17; Luke 22.14). Therefore it is a strong probability that we must look for the beloved disciple among the twelve.

(ii) The beloved disciple is to be looked for in the group enumerated in John 21.2 as having been present at the appearance of Jesus by the lakeside – Simon Peter, Thomas called the Twin, Nathanael of Cana in Galilee, the sons of Zebedee, and two others of his disciples. J.N. Sanders in his essay 'Who was the Disciple whom Jesus Loved?' (p. 75n.) says that it is 'conceivable' that in that passage *the sons of Zebedee* is an explanatory gloss on the two other disciples and is therefore not part of the original text, but would then be the earliest evidence for the view – not the fact – that the beloved disciple was John the son of Zebedee. That is so precarious an assumption that we do not need to consider it. If the beloved disciple is in that group, he cannot be Peter, for Peter and the beloved disciple are earlier reported as talking to each other (John 13.23-25). He clearly cannot be Thomas, who does not fit the part at all (cf. John 20.19-29). He cannot be Nathanael, for Nathanael was not one of the twelve. He cannot be James, for the implication in ch. 21 is that the beloved disciple was long-lived, while James was the first of the twelve to be martyred (Acts. 12.2). By elimination we therefore arrive at the conclusion that the beloved disciple was either John, the other son of Zebedee, or one of the two anonymous disciples.

(iii) If the beloved disciple was a member of the twelve, we should expect to find him a member of the inner circle, and the inner circle was composed of Peter, James and John, who were with Jesus at the raising of Jairus' daughter (Mark 5.37; Luke 8.51), on the mount of transfiguration (Mark 9.2; Matt. 17.1; Luke 9.28), on the occasion of the apocalyptic discourse (Mark 13.3) and in Gethsemane (Mark 14.33; Matt. 26.37). C.F. Nolloth in his book *The Fourth Evangelist* (p. 27) stresses this point:

> It is not reasonable to suppose that the close intimacy of our Lord with the three, recorded in the Synoptics, should have been encroached upon by the addition of another disciple, who is not once named in those Gospels. As a mere question of fitness and congruity in narration, it is wholly improbable. Psychologically and as a matter concerned with the character of our Lord's human affections, it is unlikely. The sacred ties that bound him to the three favoured apostles, leading him to desire their presence in the times of his sorest need, are hardly likely to have been

stretched beyond the limits assigned by the first three Evangelists. The addition of a fourth favourite if we may use the term, is a disturbing feature in the Gospel story and brings into it a jarring note.

If the beloved disciple was one of the twelve, then, it is argued, surely his place must be within the chosen three – in which case he must be John.

(iv)   Jülicher in his *Introduction to the NT* (p. 413) holds that there is only one thing in favour of identifying John and the beloved disciple. The beloved disciple is the disciple who leaned on Jesus' breast. This is to say he was occupying a position on Jesus' right hand. Jülicher says that this immediately sends our memories to the request of James and John to sit on the right and on the left of Jesus in his kingdom (Mark 10.37; Matt. 20.21). He then argues that this request would be unlikely to have been made, unless John and James were in fact already accustomed to occupy these places. This is the one fact which might justify our looking for John at Jesus' right hand, where the beloved disciple must have been.

(v)   It would appear that Salome was the mother of James and John, and that she was the sister of Mary the mother of Jesus (see ch. 2 n.2). This would mean that James and John were first cousins of Jesus, and it might be held that this closeness of kinship and of blood gave them a special place in the affection of Jesus.

(vi)   The beloved disciple is consistently found in the company of Peter or in special contact with him – at the last supper (John 13.23-25), on the resurrection morning (20.2-10), and by the lakeside (21.20-30). But in the synoptic gospels (e.g. Luke 22.8) we regularly find John in association with Peter, and this is especially true in Acts (where they form an inseparable pair, as in 3.1; 4.13; 8.14), and it occurs again in Galatians (2.9). Peter's connection both with John and with the beloved disciple suggests that John and the beloved disciple may be the same person.

(vii)   Unless the beloved disciple is John the son of Zebedee, there is no mention of John at all in the fourth gospel (except as one of 'the sons of Zebedee' in the list in 21.2). It would be odd if John, the member of the inner circle, were to vanish without trace from the story – but this is what happens if the beloved disciple is not John.

(viii)   The last point is a rather subtle one. The first three gospels regularly speak of John the Baptist, especially at the beginning of a narrative in which he appears, or in cases where his actual work of baptism is not mentioned (e.g. Matt. 3.1; 11.11; Mark 6.14,24; Luke 7.20, 33; 9.19). In Luke 3.2 he is 'John the son of Zechariah'. In the fourth gospel, however, John the Baptist is always just 'John' (1.6, 19, 26, 28, 32, 35, 40; 3.23f., 27; 4.1). This is to say that the synoptic gospels feel the need to distinguish John the Baptist from some other John; the fourth gospel feels no such need, because if John the son of

Zebedee was concerned in the writing of it, there was of course only
one John, other than himself.

To all this J.B. Lightfoot adds something which is not so much an
argument as a subjective impression. In his *Biblical Essays* (p.
41) he says that the scenes in which the beloved disciple took part are related
'with peculiar minuteness and vividness of detail' – the conversation at
the last supper, the scene in the firelight in the courtyard of Caiaphas'
house, the crucifixion incidents, and the lakeside resurrection
appearance.

A good case can certainly be made for identifying the beloved disciple
with John the son of Zebedee; but there is another side to the matter,
and we must now look at the objections to that identification which
have been made by several commentators, particularly C.K. Barrett
(pp. 97-101), G.H.C. Macgregor (p. xlv) and J.N. Sanders (pp. 73f.)

(i)   That the beloved disciple is found at the cross at all contradicts
the synoptic narrative that all the disciples forsook him and fled (Matt.
26.56; Mark 14.50), a fact to which reference is made also in the
fourth gospel itself (16.32). It would seem that if the beloved disciple
was at the cross, he cannot be one of the twelve, and therefore cannot
be John the son of Zebedee.

(ii)   In the fourth gospel Mary is left to the care of the beloved
disciple. How could she, it is asked, be left to the care of a man who
had been bidden to abandon his home and to become a wandering
preacher? He would not have a home to which to take her.

(iii)   At the beginning of Acts (1.14) Mary is found, not with John,
but with the brothers of Jesus.

(iv)   In the narrative of the fourth gospel the beloved disciple
appears only in Jerusalem and has connections with Jerusalem. When
he received charge of Mary, we are told, 'from that hour the disciple
took her to his own home' (19.27), which certainly sounds as if his
home was in Jerusalem. The connections of John the son of Zebedee
are with Galilee; those of the beloved disciple are with Jerusalem, and
this is against their identification.

(v)   If we do accept that the 'other disciple' of John 18.15 refers to
the beloved disciple, as is generally assumed, is it likely that a Galilean
fisherman would be so well known to the high priest as to have access
to his house? It is said that he was 'known to the high priest'. The
word is *gnōstos*, which means more than 'known to'. It can also mean
an intimate friend. It is used only twice elsewhere in the gospels. When
the boy Jesus went missing on his first visit to Jerusalem, his parents
searched for him amongst their kinsfolk and *gnōstoi* (the plural of the
word, Luke 2.44). And Luke also tells us (23.49) that at a distance
from the cross of Jesus there stood 'his *gnōstoi* and the women who
had followed him from Galilee'. In Psalm 55.13, when the Psalmist

speaks of being wounded by the cruelty of his companion, his 'familiar friend', this is the word used in the Greek version (54.14). In all these cases the word *gnōstos* appears to mean more than a mere acquaintance; it means an intimate friend. It is not very likely that a Galilean fisherman would be the intimate friend of the high priest.[2]

H.V. Morton, writing in the thirties, cited an interesting, if speculative possibility:

> There is in one of the back streets of Jerusalem a dark little hovel, now, I believe, an Arab coffee-house, which contains stones and arches which were once part of an early Christian church. The Franciscan tradition is that this church was erected on the site of a house which had belonged to Zebedee, the father of St John. The family, said the Franciscan, were fish merchants of Galilee, with a branch office in Jerusalem, from which they used to supply, among others, the family of Caiaphas, the High Priest.[2]

If there is any truth in this story, then John would be well-known to the high priest as a tradesman who came regularly to deliver his goods. Even at that it still remains difficult to see how the Galilean fish merchant or fisherman could be an intimate friend of the high priest.

(vi) It has always seemed difficult to some people to understand how, if John is the beloved disciple and John did write the fourth gospel, he could call himself the disciple whom Jesus loved, as if to say: 'I was the one whom Jesus loved more than any of the others.' It has always seemed to indicate an attitude of pride and self-conceit. It would have been easy for someone else, knowing the intimate relationship between Jesus and this disciple, to refer to him as the disciple whom Jesus loved, but for him to refer to himself in those terms is, so they say, quite another matter. So it is argued that John cannot have both written the gospel and been the beloved disciple.

But it is possible that for John to call himself the beloved disciple was an act of grateful and wondering love, as if to say: 'I am what I am – and yet he loved me.' Somewhere Plato tells of a man who was asked near the end of his life for what he was most thankful, and his answer was: 'That being such as I am, I have had the friends I had.' So for a man to call himself the beloved disciple could be an act, not of pride, but of deep humility. Plummer has suggested in his commentary (p. xxxiv) that it is possible that the title 'the beloved disciple' was given to John by others before he used it himself, so that, when he did use it, he was simply using the name by which he was ordinarily called.

(vii) One further objection is raised. There is in all the records a close connection between John and Peter. So in view of this connection Macgregor (p. xlv) has asked:

> Is it probable that John, whom the Synoptists represent as the close companion of Peter, can be the source of a stream of tradition so

divergent from the Synoptic stream, which Mark is said to have derived from Peter?

This question would only be valid, if we are certain that Mark and John were trying to do the same thing. It could be argued – it has been argued, as we shall later see – that John begins where Mark leaves off, that the difference is due to the fact that they may be covering in essence the same ground, but John is not simply re-telling the story, he is interpreting it – hence the difference.

Before we come to any decision as to whether or not the beloved disciple is to be identified with John the son of Zebedee, we must ask if there is any better and more probable candidate for that title.

There are some New Testament scholars who would regard the whole investigation as useless, because we do not know and cannot know who the beloved disciple was. Jülicher writes in his *Introduction to the NT* (p. 413): 'This chosen one, who in his turn stands opposed to the other chosen ones, is a figure which can find no place in the Synoptic tradition; he is in fact not a figure of flesh and blood at all.' Kümmel in his *Introduction* (p. 168) is equally definite: 'There is no possibility of establishing the identity of the disciple whom the Gospel of John cites as its authority for its report about the passion of Jesus.' Nevertheless, the difficulty – or the impossibility – of the task has not deterred many people from putting forward their suggestions.

(i) · We may begin by taking up the statement of Jülicher that the beloved disciple is not, and was never meant to be, a figure of flesh and blood, but that he is an idealized figure. Schmiedel could speak of Nathanael as 'that exquisite creation of a devout imagination, the disciple whom Jesus loved'.[3] He is the picture of the perfect Gnostic, the discple who really *knows* Jesus. Scholten, with an allusion to Hebrews 7.3, says that the beloved disciple is another Melchizedek, without father, without mother, without genealogy.[4] Bultmann in his commentary (p. 481) quotes the suggestion of Joseph Martin that in Jesus and John we have the Greek commonplace 'of the "love pair", developed in the Symposia literature under Plato's influence: "Jesus and John are firmly anchored in the last supper by the well established *topos* [commonplace situation] of the two who love each other".'

According to Bacon (*The Fourth Gospel in Research and Debate*, pp. 317f.), the scene at the cross, when Jesus commits his mother to the beloved disciple and him to her, is to be read in either of two ways. First, it may be read in the light of the saying in Luke 11.27f.:

As he said this, a woman in the crowd raised her voice and said to him, 'Blessed is the womb that bore you, and the breast that you sucked!' But he said, 'Blessed rather are those who hear the word of God and keep it!'

The mother stands, not for any human relation, but for her who hears the word of God and keeps it. Second,

Perhaps in a narrower sense Mary is the representative of the adherents of an older faith which had not known the day of its visitation, finding a home with that younger *ecclesia* which took its start from the cross as the essence and substance of the gospel.

In the scene with Peter on resurrection morning, where in face of the empty tomb the beloved disciple 'saw and believed', Bacon says (p. 319) that he is 'the type of that faith which does not wait for ocular demonstration but is quickened to full life by "knowing the scripture that he must rise from the dead"'. Bacon finally comes to the conclusion that, if the beloved disciple is to be individualized, he is the prototype of Paul. Referring to the episode in Galatians 2.11-21, he says (pp. 325f.):

> The term 'disciple whom Jesus loved' cannot well have been coined ... without a primary reference to that great Apostle who, when even Peter was recreant and blind to the real significance of the doctrine he professed to follow, cut into the rock foundation of the Church the true gospel of the redemption. No language ever framed can so express the whole heart secret of the Fourth Gospel as that great utterance of Paul, wherein, as against the inadequate apprehension Peter had shown of the true meaning of the cross, he pours out his soul's experience of Christ. If the Fourth Gospel be 'the heart of Christ', the heart of the Fourth Gospel is Paul's confession of his faith in Galatians 2.20: 'I have been crucified with Christ; yet I live; and yet no longer I, but Christ liveth in me: and the life which I now live in the flesh, I live in faith, the faith which is in the Son of God, WHO LOVED ME, and gave himself up for me.' In this sense Paul, and whosoever has had Paul's experience, whether in the body or out of the body, whosoever has come to 'know him and the power of his resurrection' – is the 'disciple whom Jesus loved'.

For Bultmann, the beloved disciple stands for Gentile Christendom, 'which has achieved its own true self-understanding ... emancipated from the ties of Judaism' (p. 484). So Bultmann sees the meaning of the scene at the cross (p. 673):

> The beloved disciple represents Gentile Christianity, which is charged to honour [Jewish Christianity] as its mother from whom it has come, even as Jewish Christianity is charged to recognize itself as 'at home' within Gentile Christianity, i.e. included in the membership of the one great fellowship of the church.

A little later (p. 685) Bultmann sees the significance of the race to the tomb by Peter and the beloved disciple in the relationship between the two disciples, Peter standing for Jewish and the beloved disciple for Gentile Christianity:

> Each in his way achieves precedence of the other ... The first community of believers arises out of Jewish Christianity, and the Gentile Christians attain to faith only after them. But that does not signify any precedence of the former over the latter; in fact both stand equally near the Risen Jesus,

and indeed readiness for faith is even greater with the Gentiles than with the Jews: the beloved disciple ran faster than Peter to the grave!

– even if Peter entered it first.

The trouble about this kind of approach is twofold. First, if the beloved disciple is so much the one who understands the mind of Jesus, why does he appears so seldom, and why only in the closing scenes of the gospel? And second, if this is so, quite certainly no ordinary reader of the gospel would know that it is so. If these inner meanings are going to be read into the gospel, then the gospel is going to be a closed book to the ordinary man – and, if a gospel is not for the ordinary man, for whom is it?

(ii) If then the beloved disciple is not an idealized figure, with whom has he been identified?[5]

We begin with what on the face of it is the most unlikely suggestion. The beloved disciple has been identified with Judas Iscariot. This identification has been made in two connections.

(a) First, it has been made in connection with the 'other disciple' who obtained access for Peter to the courtyard of the high priest's house, when the trial of Jesus was in progress (John 18.15f.). There is no definite statement that the 'other disciple' was the beloved disciple, although it is often, even generally, assumed that he was. Bultmann (p. 645) holds that there is 'no basis' for the identification, and that his appearance with Peter on this occasion proves nothing. The view that this 'other disciple' was Judas has been worked out by E.A. Abbott.[6] This other disciple was 'known' to the high priest. How? In the question addressed to Peter by the maidservant, there is in all the gospels one rather odd word. John (18.17) has: 'Are not you *also* one of this man's disciples?' Matthew (26.29) has: 'You *also* were with Jesus the Galilean.' Mark (14.67) has: 'You *also* were with the Nazarene, Jesus.' Luke (22.56) has: 'This man *also* was with him.' Why *also*? As well as whom? Abbott's argument is that the maidservant, who kept the door, had seen Judas constantly come and go on his traitorous business; she knew him well by sight. She had seen Peter come in with him, and she actually thought that Peter too was engaged with Judas on the business of selling Jesus to the authorities. There is unquestionably a case here; this is a reconstruction which does make sense. But this does not identify Judas with the beloved disciple; it simply assumes that the 'other' disciple has no connection with the beloved disciple.

(b) But, second, Judas has been definitely identified with the beloved disciple, and has been taken to the author of the fourth gospel. Noack[7] saw in Judas the one person who really understood the mind of Jesus, and argued that his 'betrayal' of Jesus was not an act of treachery, but a deliberate playing into Jesus' hands, in order to allow Jesus to fulfil his purposes. But, quite apart from what Jackson calls the offensiveness of this theory, the narrative of John 13.21-30 clearly shows that the beloved disciple and Judas Iscariot cannot have been the same person.

(c) Two further alleged pieces of evidence have been adduced in favour of Judas. There is a very odd phrase in Mark 14.10. The English translations have it: 'Then Judas Iscariot, who was *one of the* twelve, went to the chief priests in order to betray him to them.' But, if the Greek is translated literally, it is not 'one of the twelve'; it is *'the one of the twelve'*. It can be argued that the initial 'the' is not to be stressed, and that this is simply a Hellenistic Greek form, meaning no more than 'one of the twelve'. But it has been argued by some[8] that to call Judas *the* one of the twelve is to call him the chief, the leader, the first, the top man of the twelve. It would almost certainly be unsafe, however, to place any great weight on a phrase of such uncertain meaning.

(d) The other argument comes from the story of the last meal together in John 13. We have already seen how the seating arrangements were made. The guests did not sit; they reclined, leaning on the left elbow, with the feet stretched out behind. This meant that the guest on the right of the host reclined with his head on the host's shoulder. But the place of the highest honour was the place on the left of the host, for the host reclined with his head on the shoulder of the guest on the left. We have already seen that John must have been on Jesus' right, thus reclining with his head on Jesus' shoulder. Now when we read that narrative, the conversation between Jesus and Judas seems quite clearly to have been private and not overheard. If the eleven had been aware that Judas was going out to complete the arrangements for betrayal, surely he would never have got out of that room at all. If the conversation with Judas was private and not overheard, then clearly Judas can only have been sitting on Jesus' left, with Jesus' head on his shoulder, the place of highest honour. This does not do away with the difficulty that Judas and the beloved disciple are clearly distinguished in the narrative, but it does make it possible that Judas did occupy a very high place in the apostolic company.

(iii) Any investigation of the identity of the beloved disciple must at least take account of the list in John 21.2: 'Simon Peter, Thomas called the Twin, Nathanael of Cana in Galilee, the sons of Zebedee and two others of his disciples'. We may glance briefly at the anonymous two. Bernard (II, pp. 693f.) mentions that Nonnus, who about the year 400 produced a paraphrase in hexameters of the fourth gospel, names Andrew as one of them. The end of the apocryphal *Gospel of Peter* (quoted on p. 78 below) names Andrew and Levi. Bernard himself suggests Philip, who like Peter and Andrew was from Bethsaida (John 1.44), is associated with Peter, Andrew, John and

Nathanael (John 1.37-46), and is always listed among the first five apostles (Mark 3.18; Matt. 10.2; Luke 6.14; Acts 1.13). Jackson (p. 165) suggests Nathanael, the Israelite in whom there is no guile (John 1.47). Undoubtedly Nathanael is the kind of person we would expect the beloved disciple to be. But he was not a member of the twelve, and it is highly probable that the beloved disciple was. Moreover, Nathanael was a Galilean from Cana, and the likelihood is that the beloved disciple was from Jerusalem. Of the other apostolic names Matthias has been suggested.[9]

(iv) The beloved disciple has been identified with a person who in the synoptic gospel narrative Jesus is said to have loved. In Mark's version of the story of the rich young ruler we read: 'And Jesus looking upon him loved him.'[10] The story has been vividly reconstructed.[11] It is suggested that he was a follower of John the Baptist and that through him he met Jesus. Always he felt the fascination of Jesus, and Jesus' treatment of the children (Mark 10.13-16) greatly impressed him. The incident of the children comes immediately before his own approach to Jesus. At that moment he made the great refusal, but he did not part completely from Jesus; he was always potentially a disciple. It is suggested that he was the 'goodman of the house' where the last supper was held (Mark 14.14 AV), and that from then on he became the beloved disciple. H.B. Swete writes: 'Who shall say that Christ's love did not avail to bring him back? or that on his return he may not have attached himself to Jesus with a fervour and whole-heartedness which justified the Lord's immediate recognition of his worth?'[12]

This is one of these reconstructions of which we can only say that we wish they were true, but unfortunately imagination, however devout and beautiful and skilful, is not evidence.

(v) We come now to a theory about the beloved disciple which has won wide acceptance, in the words of G.H.C. Macgregor (p. xlvi):

a theory which finds the Beloved Disciple in a young Jerusalemite of good family, possibly with priestly connections, not one of the Twelve, but a 'supernumerary', whom Jesus admitted to a peculiar intimacy during the closing period of his ministry.[13]

This theory is based on two deductions. Bousset wrote: 'Only a one-sided criticism, which overshoots its mark, can ignore the fact that the gospel of John supplies, as compared with the synoptics, an independent and in many respects superior account as soon as Jerusalem becomes the stage of the gospel drama.'[14] It would seem that some special source is needed to explain the special vividness of the Jerusalem narrative. The first deduction is then that when the beloved disciple enters the narrative, it takes on a special quality. Therefore he comes from Jerusalem. The other deduction comes from

John 18.15f., which is taken to refer to the beloved disciple, and which shows him as having a special connection with the household of the high priest.

So this young Jerusalemite is held to be an aristocrat of priestly family, perhaps one of those referred to in John 12.42. This explains a number of things – how he knows that the name of the servant of the high priest who had his ear cut off was Malchus (18.10); how he knew that one of Peter's questioners was a relative of Malchus (18.26); how he had special knowledge of Nicodemus, a member of the Sanhedrin (3.1; 7.50; 19.39); how he had special knowledge of what went on at meetings of the Sanhedrin (7.45-52; 11.47-53). So closely does Delff connect the beloved disciple with Jerusalem that he removes from the gospel all Galilean incidents as later insertions.

Just possibly this theory might be used to find a solution to the very surprising statement of Polycrates (quoted above, p. 43) that John wore the *petalon*, the plate on the high priest's turban (Ex. 28. 36-8; 29.30f.). The high priest wore his full regalia only on the Day of Atonement. In an emergency his place could be taken by a substitute, and Delff thinks that this young Jerusalemite, who was in time to become John of Ephesus, acted as substitute. The theory is that this young Jerusalemite, after the destruction of Jerusalem, found his way to Ephesus, that he was also called John, and that he was, if not the actual writer, at least the authority behind the fourth gospel. To the question of authorship we shall later return. So Sanday describes this person as 'one who although, perhaps on account of his youth, not actually admitted to the number of the twelve, yet had all – and even more than all – of their privileges'.

At the moment we will be content to have stated the theory. We shall not examine it until we come to deal with the question of the authorship of the gospel, with which it is obviously most intimately connected.

(vi) The beloved disciple has been found by some in Lazarus.[15] The reason for this identification is the statement in 11.5; 'Now Jesus loved Martha and her sister and Lazarus.' It is also suggested that the report that had spread abroad 'that this disciple was not to die' (21.23) was particularly applicable to Lazarus, who had been raised by Jesus from the dead. But, as Latimer Jackson says (p. 166):

> It is still not easy to conceive of any chain of circumstances which would have converted Lazarus of Bethany into the *theologos* [the divine, the theologian], the leader of Greek Christianity who survived under the name of John to the end of the first century.

A very much elaborated version of the Lazarus theory has been offered by J.N. Sanders in his commentary (pp. 29-31), and more fully in his essay on the beloved disciple. Sanders noted that two Greek words are used in the Fourth Gospel for the word 'loved'. In 13.23; 19.26; 21.20 the verb is *ēgapa*, the imperfect tense of the verb *agapan*. In 20.2 the verb is *ephilei* from the verb *philein*. Further in John 20.2 the disciple is called 'the other disciple', and 'another disciple' is again found in 18.15, the disciple who gained entry for Peter into the courtyard of the high priest's house. It is Sanders' theory that there were therefore two disciples, one of whom Jesus *ēgapa* and one of whom Jesus *ephilei*.

On that differentiation Sanders proceeded to build a complicated and highly speculative reconstruction. Lazarus is the disciple whom Jesus *ēgapa*. The disciple whom Jesus *ephilei* is John, but not John the apostle. He is John Mark, the son of Mary, whose house was the headquarters of the early church in Jerusalem (Acts 12.12), the John Mark who went on the first missionary journey to Cyprus (Acts 13.5). In due time this John settled in Ephesus and he is the Elder, John the Presbyter, cited by Papias (see p. 44 above) as one of his sources for information about the life and teaching of Jesus. In Ephesus this John Mark who was also John the Presbyter wrote the three letters of John, the Revelation and the fourth gospel. For the fourth gospel he used the reminiscences, either oral or written, of Lazarus, the disciple whom Jesus *ēgapa*.

One of the immense difficulties of this piece of ingenuity is that John Mark is firmly fixed in tradition (as recorded by Eusebius in his *History*, 3.39.15) as the author of the *second* gospel and the transmitter of the memories of Peter. And, if he wrote the fourth gospel he certainly did not write the second gospel. Sanders' reply in his essay (pp. 73f.) is:

> But it is not surely a very great strain on our credulity to suppose that there were two men with the surname Mark connected at different periods of his career with Peter . . . Anyone who boggles at two Marks in the first century may be reminded that in Cambridge after the Second World War there were two Ravens, two Burnabys, and two Chadwicks in Anglican orders holding College and University posts. Imagine the confusion that will cause to research students in 4000 AD.

Not even the Cambridge parallel will convince many people that John Mark wrote the fourth gospel and that we must find another Mark for the second gospel. And it can well be held that the theory has collapsed long before that stage, for its basis, the difference between *agapan* and *philein* is an extremely shaky foundation. With few exceptions the commentators hold that it is impossible to distinguish between the two words.[16] The usage of the two words in the fourth gospel is fully discussed by J.H. Bernard in his commentary (II, pp. 702-4), and we summarize his conclusions.

(a) In classical Greek it is true that *philein* is used of all kinds of love, and that *agapan* is 'more dignified and restrained', but the words

are used interchangeably. Aelian speaks of a man who loved (*agapan*) his brothers very much, and who in turn was loved (*philein*) by them.[17]

(b)   In the Septuagint *agapan* is used of sexual love. It is used of Ammon's illegitimate love for his sister Tamar (II Sam. 13.4). It is used in the Song of Solomon (2.5) of being sick with love. But in Ecclesiasticus 9.8 *philia* is used of the passion kindled by the sight of a beautiful woman, and Proverbs 7.18 uses it of the seductive invitation to delight ourselves with love. Normally the Septuagint uses *agapan* for loving God. The faithful abide with God in love (*agape*), says the writer of Wisdom (3.9), but in Proverbs 8.17 the divine voice says: 'I love those who love me', and the word is *philein*.

(c)   In the fourth gospel God's love for man is expressed by *agapan* in 3.16; 14.23; 17.23; and by *philein* in 16.27. The Father's love for the Son is expressed by *agapan* in 3.35; 10.17; 15.9; and by *philein* in 5.20. Jesus' love for men is expressed by *agapan* in 11.5; 13.1; 14.21; 15.9; and by *philein* in 11.3. The love of man for man is expressed by *agapan* in 13.34; 15.12,17 and by *philein* in 15.19. The love of men for Jesus is expressed by *agapan* in 8.42; 14.15, 21, 23 and by *philein* in 15.19.

In the fourth gospel there is clearly no distinction in meaning between *agapan* and *philein*. In the Arabic version of Tatian's Diatessaron there is no difference in the translation of the two words and this is also true of the Old Syriac and the Peshitta. In the Old Latin versions both words are translated by *amare*, though the Vulgate uses *amare* for *philein* and *diligere* for *agapan*.

The precariousness of any differentiation is shown by the fact that those who do make a differentiation do not agree as to what the difference is. The most famous juxtaposition of the two words is in the conversation between Jesus and Peter in John 21.15-17. Twice Jesus asks Peter if he loves him (*agapan*); and twice Peter replies that he does (*philein*). The third time Jesus asks the question he uses *philein* and Peter continues to use *philein* to reply. Westcott (p. 303) holds that Jesus in using *agapan* is asking for 'the higher love which is to be the spring of the Christian life', while Peter in using *philein* is professing no more than natural affection. This is to say that *agapan* is the higher word of the two. G.H.C. Macgregor (p. 373) quotes the differentiation which R.H. Strachan makes. *Agapan* implies the esteem existing between benefactor and recipient; *philein* denotes the personal affection existing between members of the same family. So Peter, it is claimed, deliberately changes the colder word into the warmer. 'To love Jesus as a benefactor and to love him for himself are lower and higher stages of love.' Here *philein* is taken as the higher word and *agapan* as the lower.

There is no discernible difference in the fourth gospel between *agapan* and *philein*. In any event it would be difficult to believe that there were two beloved disciples, each of whom Jesus loved with a different kind of love. It is unlikely enough that Lazarus is the beloved disciple on general grounds; but Sanders' edifice of speculation has so insecure a foundation that it is not unlikely, it is impossible.

Now that we have surveyed the material concerning the beloved disciple, we can move on to examine the bearing of all this on the question of the authorship of the gospel. There are three passages in the fourth gospel which may be taken to be claims that the gospel is the work of an eyewitness of the life of Jesus, or at least of certain parts of that life.

(i)   The first of these passages is John 1.14:

> And the Word became flesh and dwelt among us, full of grace and truth; we have beheld his glory, glory as of the only Son from the Father.[18]

Along with this passage are to be taken the first three verses of the first letter of John:

> That which was from the beginning, which we have heard, which we have seen with our eyes, which we have looked upon and touched with our hands, concerning the word of life . . . that which we have seen and heard we proclaim also to you, that you may have fellowship with us.

The first question we have to ask is, what is the meaning of the word 'beheld'? Does it imply actual physical, sensible seeing, or does it mean seeing with the inward eye, the eye of faith?

It has to be admitted that the obvious meaning of John 1.14 at first sight, especially when the passage from the first letter is taken into account, is physical eyewitness. And that is the way in which many New Testament scholars take it. The verb 'to see, to behold' is *theasthai*. It occurs twenty-two times in the Greek New Testament, and apart from this passage, it is always of actual physical seeing.[19] In the passage from the first letter it does seem that a distinction is being drawn between the *we* who have actually seen and the *you* to whom the story is being passed on by the eyewitnesses. Further, the tense of the verb is the aorist tense, and the aorist tense looks back to a completed action in past time. Westcott says: 'The whole point of the passage is that the Incarnation was historical, and that the sight of the Incarnate Word was historical.' Hoskyns and Davey say: 'If a contrast is implied, it is between the original disciples, who believed in consequence of the actual vision of the Christ incarnate, and those who have not seen and yet have believed (20.29), but who nevertheless believe because of the witness of the original apostles.' And they quote Lagrange who says: 'A sensible vision forms the point of departure for faith.' C.K. Barrett says: 'The faith of the Church rests on a real beholding of one who, however glorious, was a historical person.'

Stanton says: 'The theme of the whole passage plainly is, that the Divine glory was manifested in a human life, and that it had been perceived through contact with that life while it was being lived on earth.'

But there are those who wish to take the seeing as the seeing of faith. Bauer, quoted by Hoskyns and Davey, speaks of seeing with 'immortal eyes'. G.H.C. Macgregor quotes Loisy as saying that the seeing refers 'not to physical sight but to the penetrating vision of enlightened faith'. If that be so, J. Drummond says, 'we' would denote 'Christians in their corporate unity, and ascribe to the general body what was the actual experience of only the first disciples, the emphasis not being on the persons, but on the act of seeing'. Bultmann states this view most fully and most penetratingly. The seeing is the seeing neither of the natural eye nor of the natural man. After all, the Jews saw Jesus Christ with the natural eye and did not see his glory. The Johannine seeing is not concerned with eyewitnessing in an historical or a legal sense; nor has it anything to do with 'spiritual' sight, found in the Greek contemplation of ideas or mysticism. 'The seeing is neither sensory nor spiritual, but it is the sight of *faith*.' It is not limited to the contemporaries of the Revealer; but it is passed on by them to all succeeding generations. In fact it cannot be passed on without them, because it is not the contemplation of some timeless truth but of the Word become flesh. The 'eyewitnesses' are not the guarantors of some past bit of history; they are those who confront every age with the offence of the glory become flesh.

No one would deny the beauty and the truth of this conception, but it seems to us that we cannot evade the fact that the Greek text as it stands is an eyewitness claim in the sensible physical sense of the words.

(ii) The second reference which implies the account of an eyewitness is at one and the same time much more definite and just as obscure. It is the authenticating parenthesis in 19.35. The previous verse tells how one of the soldiers pierced Jesus' side with a spear, and at once there came out blood and water.

> He who saw it has borne witness – his testimony is true and he knows that he tells the truth – that you also may believe.

Who is the 'he' who saw it and bore witness? The last person to be mentioned is the beloved disciple (19.26f.), when Mary is committed to him and he to Mary. It therefore seems entirely likely that it is the beloved disciple who saw it, and who is the witness-bearer. 'His testimony is true, and he knows that he tells the truth' – who is the 'he' in the 'he knows'? Who is, so to speak, the guarantor of the witness? This is a passage and a problem which have produced endless discussion.[20] The 'he' in 'he knows' is in Greek *ekeinos*, which means

'that one'. *Ekeinos* is a favourite Johannine word; it comes 54 times in
Matthew; 19 times in Mark (3 times in Mark 16.9-20); 32 times in
Luke; 71 times in John; 8 times in I John.

> He who saw it has borne witness – his testimony is true and that one
> knows that he tells the truth – that you also may believe.

Who is 'that one'? Four answers have been given.

(a) It is held that 'that one' refers to the witness himself, and that
the meaning is really 'I saw it; I witness to it; and I know that I am
telling the truth.' Undoubtedly *ekeinos* can be used like that. Jesus so
uses it in John 9.37 which is literally: 'Jesus said to him: "You have
seen him, and it is that one (*ekeinos*) who speaks to you."' In the
Jewish War (3.202) Josephus tells how he thought of escaping from
the city, and how the people besought him to stay:

> All this they did, I cannot but think, not because they grudged that one
> (*ekeinos*) his chance of safety, but because they thought of their own; for,
> with Josephus on the spot, they were convinced that no disaster could
> befall them.

He tells the story about himself in the third instead of in the first
person. Drummond points out (p. 392) that this can occur even in
English. Thackeray's *Esmond* masquerades as an autobiography, but
the hero consistently uses the third person throughout. On one
occasion he writes: 'In this report the Major-General was good
enough to mention Captain Esmond's name with particular favour;
and *that gentleman* carried the despatch to head-quarters the next
day.' There is no doubt that it is possible that 'that one' could refer to
the witness himself. Westcott says that this crucial incident of the
water and the blood makes the evangelist 'separate himself as a
witness from his immediate position as a writer'. C.C. Torrey believed
that the fourth gospel was originally in Aramaic, and that here we
have simply an over-literal translation of an Aramaic original which
means no more than, 'I know that he is telling the truth'.[21] He himself
translated the verse: 'And he who saw this testified to it, and his
testimony is reliable – and I myself know that his word is true – that
you also may believe.' And he subjoins a footnote: 'Literally, *that one*
(Aramaic *hahu gabra*), a common Jewish substitute for the pronoun
of the first person singular.'[22] There is no doubt that 'that one' could
refer to the witness himself, but we cannot help agreeing with Bacon,
when he says (p. 192): 'Whoever heard of a writer employing such
ambiguities to make the simple statement: "I myself saw this"?'

(b) *Ekeinos* is used by John for God. John 1.33 reads literally:
'That one (*ekeinos*) who sent me to baptize with water said to me.'
John 5.19 is literally: 'For whatsoever that one (*ekeinos*) does the Son
does likewise.' John 6.29 is literally: 'I came not of my own accord,

but that one (*ekeinos*) sent me.' So Moffatt translates 19.35: 'He who saw it has borne witness (his witness is true; God knows he is telling the truth), that you may believe.' This makes good sense. The beloved disciple as witness, so to speak, swears to God that his witness is true.

(c) *Ekeinos* is used by John of the Holy Spirit. John 14.26 is literally: 'But the Counsellor, the Holy Spirit, whom the Father will send in my name, that one (*ekeinos*) will teach you all things.' John 15.26 is literally 'But when the Counsellor comes ... even the Spirit of truth ... that one (*ekeinos*) will bear witness to me.' John 16.13 is literally: 'When that one (*ekeinos*) comes, the Spirit of truth, he will guide you into all the truth.' This could be an appeal to the Spirit as the guarantor of truth, which would be specially appropriate in the fourth gospel.

(d) *Ekeinos* is used of Jesus in the fourth gospel. John 1.18 is literally: 'No one has ever seen God; the only Son who is in the bosom of the Father, that one (*ekeinos*) has made him known.' John 3.30 is literally: 'That one (*ekeinos*) must increase, but I must decrease.' John 7.11 is literally: 'The Jews were looking for him at the feast, and saying, "Where is that one (*ekeinos*)?"' Bultmann (p. 678) says that *ekeinos* 'cannot be the eye-witness himself, but must be another who is in a position to guarantee the truth of the testimony. In that case however only Jesus can be meant.' He reminds us that the Pythagoreans referred to Pythagoras as *ekeinos*. Bultmann makes the suggestion that the text is wrong. John 21.24 which is closely parallel reads: 'This is the disciple who is witnessing about these things ... and we know that his witness is true.' So he suggests that here instead of reading *ekeinos oiden hoti alēthē legei*, 'he knows that he is telling the truth', we should read *ekeinon oidamen hoti alēthē legei*, 'we know that he is telling the truth' – which would be much simpler, and which Nonnus evidently translated in his metrical paraphrase of the fourth gospel. But for this there is no manuscript evidence whatsoever, however attractive it may sound.

On the whole, it seems likeliest that the *ekeinos* is Jesus.

We come now to the most important passage of all, John 21.24:

> This is the disciple who is bearing witness to these things, and who has written these things; and we know that his testimony is true.[23]

But before we consider this verse, we must consider ch. 21 as a whole.

It is widely held that, whoever the author of ch. 21 was, and whenever and wherever it was written, it is an addition to the body of the gospel. Bernard calls it an appendix and an afterthought; Jackson and Kümmel also refer to it as the Appendix; Sanders, Westcott call it the Epilogue; Barrett calls it an addendum; Kümmel uses the word supplement; Bultmann calls it a postscript. But though it is often regarded as an addition, it is not regarded as secondary in quality. Streeter says that there are many hypotheses but 'all those which do not begin by recognizing that the chapter is a work of genius may be dismissed'. 'The style,' he says, 'of the added conclusion to Mark (Mark 16.9-20) is pedestrian; the Appendix to John is great literature.' Stanton (III, p. 17) records that as long ago as 1641 Hugo Grotius suggested that the chapter was added by the Ephesian church after the apostle's death. What then are the reasons for regarding ch. 21 as an addition and an afterthought and an appendix?

(i)   It is clear that 20.31 is the true ending of the gospel:

> Now Jesus did many other signs in the presence of the disciples, which are not written in this book; but these are written that you may believe that Jesus is the Christ, the Son of God, and that believing you may have life in his name.

As Stanton says, anything that comes after that can only come as an anticlimax. As Barrett says of ch. 20, it is a unit which needs no supplement. The gospel builds up to its impressive ending at 20.31, and, so it is argued, for the author himself to have wrecked his own conclusion by an addition would have been an incredibly clumsy proceeding. This is no modern feeling. Tertullian knew ch. 21, for in *The Antidote to the Scorpion's Bite* (15) he speaks of how the day came when Peter was indeed girt by another (v. 18). But in his book *Against Praxeas* (25) he speaks of 20.31, 'that you might believe that Jesus Christ is the Son of God' as being *ipsa quoque clausula*, at the very termination of the gospel. The great commission of 20.21-23 and the great definition of aim in 20.31 are things to which nothing can be added.

(ii)   The events of this chapter are out of place in their context. This is said to be the third appearance of Jesus to his disciples, but it looks far more like the first. It is incredible that the events of ch. 21 should follow the events of ch. 20. How could the disciples fail to recognize their risen Lord when, as the sequence of events stands, they had met him twice already (20.19-23, 26-29)? As Bernard says, we would expect the disciples after the events of ch. 20, especially after having the Holy Spirit breathed into them by Jesus, to be 'sensitive . . . to every slightest indication of the presence of Jesus'. Again, they had received the great commission: 'As the Father has sent me, even so I send you . . . If you forgive the sins of any, they are forgiven; if you retain the sins of any, they are retained.' Would an author, asks Barrett, spoil the effect of that tremendous commision by adding on a narrative in which the disciples had gone back to their old jobs, and in which they failed to recognize their risen Lord when they saw him? As Stanton has it, the whole attitude is one of listlessness, which is incomprehensible after the events of ch. 20, followed by astonishment, as if the events of ch. 20 had never happened. As Hoskyns and Davey say, the return to the fishing after the great commision is an act of apostasy, and a fulfilling of the prophecy (16.32) that the disciples would abandon everything and scatter to their own homes. There is not even any word of their going back to Galilee. Chapter 20 happens in Jerusalem, ch. 21 in Galilee, and there is no transition. The events of ch. 21 would be perfectly intelligible, if they were telling the story of the *first* resurrection appearance to a band of desolate and despairing men, but they are difficult, if not impossible, to understand, following the two appearances and the great commission of the previous chapter.

(iii) Bultmann adds some small but possibly significant points. The sons of Zebedee appear for the first time in ch. 21. Strangely enough, nowhere else in the fourth gospel is there any mention of the disciples being fishermen. It is strange that Nathanael is defined as coming from Cana here and not on his first appearance in 1.45. The first two points belong to the synoptic rather than to the Johannine tradition.

(iv) Chapter 21 differs at least in some respects in theological outlook from the rest of the fourth gospel. It is generally agreed that one of the aims of the fourth gospel was to spiritualize the whole idea of eschatology, and in particular of the second coming. In the earliest days of the church the expectation was that Jesus would physically and visibly and at a definite date return upon the clouds of heaven, that that event would happen soon. In point of fact it did not happen. John took the whole idea and spiritualized it. Instead of a visible physical second coming at some given time in the future he saw the second coming in the coming of the Spirit. To this we shall later return. 'I will not leave you desolate; I will come to you' (14.18). 'If a man loves me, he will keep my word, and my Father will love him, and we will come to him, and make our home with him' (14.23). These things, as that chapter shows, were to be fulfilled in the coming of the Spirit, the Paraclete. There was now a sense in which death was irrelevant, or even non-existent. 'Truly, truly, I say to you, if anyone keeps my word, he will never see death' (8.51f.) – a saying which infuriated and exasperated the Jews. But John 21.22f., with its talk of an actual return and of a tarrying until Jesus came, is back at the old beliefs from which the fourth gospel had turned away. It is very difficult – although it is not impossible – to set the eschatology of ch. 21 beside the eschatology of the rest of the Gospel.

(v) There is the matter of the linguistic evidence. Does the vocabulary of ch. 21 suggest that it was written by the same author as the first twenty chapters, or by a different author? There are three things to be said about this. First, ch. 21 is far too short a passage to make any test of vocabulary. Second, vocabulary depends on what a writer is talking about. It is true that there are 28 words in ch. 21 which do not occur in the rest of the gospel, but, to mention only one relevant fact, ch. 21 is the only chapter in the fourth gospel which is concerned with fish and fishermen. Thirdly, in this matter of vocabulary there is total disagreement between experts. J.B. Lightfoot in his *Biblical Essays* (pp. 194-7), J.H. Bernard (pp. 687-9) and Hoskyns and Davey (p. 534) are all satisfied that the author of ch. 21 is also the author of chs. 1-20. Macgregor (p. 367) and Bultmann (pp. 700f.) insist on different authors. B.H. Streeter in *The Four Gospels* (p. 472) talks of 'certain minutiae of diction' which indicate difference of authorship, differences which are listed by Moffatt in his *Introduction to the Literature of the New Testament* (p. 572). C.K. Barrett (p. 479) is uncertain.

Clearly, matters of vocabulary and style can only properly be treated in relation to the Greek text; but there are certain things which can be appreciated without a detailed examination of the Greek. Lightfoot, when presenting the case for the common authorship of ch. 21 and chs. 1-20, notes the following points. *(a)* The Greeks had a way of tying each sentence to the sentence which goes before by little connecting words. Often these words represent rather a tone of voice, and a writer's use of them can be very individual and very characteristic. Two of these words have special characteristics in John. The first is the word *oun* meaning 'therefore' or 'so', and denotes some kind of logical connection with what goes before. John has what can only be called an addiction to this word *oun*. He uses it as some speakers in English have a habit of beginning almost every sentence with 'now', used with no particular meaning at all. Mark has *oun* 6 times, Matthew 51 times, Luke 30 times, all the Pauline letters put together 104 times; John has it over 200 times. In ch. 21 it occurs in vv. 5, 6, 7 (twice), 9, 11, 15, 21, 23. It is used with typical Johannine frequency. The second of these tying words is *de* (the *e* short as in 'begin'). It can mean 'but', although not very strongly; it is the commonest Greek connecting word, and often means no more than 'and' and is sometimes not translatable at all. Oddly enough, John uses *de* sparingly. To take an example: in Luke 8. 1-25 *de* occurs 20 times; in the 25 verses of John 21 it occurs only 9 times. Once again, in regard to *de* ch. 21 is characteristically Johannine. *(b)* John has a tendency to begin the sentence with the verb; the English does not always show this. In ch. 21 the verb begins the sentence in vv. 2, 3, 5, 7, 10, 11, 12, 13, 23, 25. *(c)* Often John does not have connecting links at all. Unlike a native writer of Greek he simply sets down sentences with no connection. This is called *asyndeton*, which means absence of links. This asyndetic abruptness occurs in verses 3, 12, 13, 16, 17. *(d)* John has a habit of introducing a parenthetic explanation. For example: 'When Simon Peter heard that it was the Lord, he put on his clothes – for he was stripped for work – and sprang into the sea' (v. 7; there is another example in v. 8). *(e)* John is much given to using the double name Simon Peter – 5 times in ch. 21, 12 times elsewhere in the fourth gospel; otherwise only in Matthew 16.16; Luke 5.8; II Peter 1.1. 'Simon Peter' is characteristically Johannine. *(f)* John alone uses 'Verily, verily', and it occurs in v. 18. *(g)* John has a liking for definiteness. So in v. 6 we have the *right* side of the boat; in v. 8 they are said to be a hundred yards from the shore; in v. 14 this is the third resurrection appearance. *(h)* 'To show by what death he was to glorify God' (v. 19) is a Johannine phrase (cf. 12.33; 18.32). *(i)* John has a habit of designating places and people – so Thomas 'called the Twin' and Nathanael 'of Cana in Galilee' (v. 2); the disciple 'whom Jesus loved' (vv. 7 and 20); Simon 'son of John' (v. 15). *(j)* The relationship of Peter and John is typically Johannine – 'the spiritual insight of John', 'the impetuosity and curiosity of Peter'. It is an impressive case; and Lightfoot would hold that ch. 21 is by the author of chs. 1-20, and that it was published with the gospel, or at least very shortly after it, a suggestion which is rendered very probable by the fact that no manuscript exists without it.

On the other hand there are certain 'minutiae of diction' which may be cited against common authorship. Bultmann (pp. 700f.) has collected a number which do not occur elsewhere in the gospel. Some of these, e.g. 'beach' (v. 4), the verb 'to fish' (v. 3), to have breakfast (v. 12), to grow old (v. 18), he relegates to a footnote, as merely emerging from the situation and not really significant. But others are more striking: 'brethren (v. 23) is not otherwise a Johannine word for Christians; 'children' (*paidia*, v. 5) is not usual as an address to the disciples; the word for 'ask' in v. 12 is *exetazein* instead of the usual *erotan*; the word for 'be able' in v. 6 is *ischuein* instead of the common *dunasthai*. There are other small points which make some believe that ch. 21 came from a different hand, and even long after. Bacon, for instance, would hold that the chapter was written and added about AD 150 in Rome for ecclesiastical purposes.

The weight of the evidence would seem to prove that, if chapter 21 was not written by the author of chapters 1-20 – and it may well have been – it was written by a member of the Johannine school who was saturated in his master's style, and it was written very soon after the main body of the gospel. Afterthought it certainly is, but afterthought very closely connected with what goes before.

(vi) We may next ask, What are the sources from which the information in chapter 21 is drawn? If we are to claim that the whole gospel is an eyewitness account set down by the apostle John – and to this we will return – then of course the question does not arise. But for those who cannot take that way one interesting suggestion has been made. It has been suggested that the resurrection appearance of John

21 was part of the lost ending of Mark. And it is further suggested that the story in the lost ending of Mark is to be found in part in the apocryphal Gospel of Peter. That gospel breaks off before its end, but the last bit of it extant reads like this:

> Now it was the last day of unleavened bread, and many were coming forth of the city and returning to their own homes because the feast was at an end. But we, the twelve disciples of the Lord, were weeping and were in sorrow, and each one, grieved at what had happened, departed to his own house. But I Simon Peter and Andrew my brother took our nets and went to the sea; and there was with us Levi the son of Alphaeus, whom the Lord . . .

—and there the fragment breaks off.[24] It is suggested that this is the beginning of the story told in John 21, and that it comes from the lost ending of Mark – but this must remain a speculation.

Another point arises. What is the connection – if any – between the story of the miraculous draught of fishes in Luke 5.1-11, with its commission of Peter, and the story in John 21? Undoubtedly there are resemblances. Loisy suggests that they are indeed the same story, but that Luke omitted it from his resurrection narrative, because he deliberately omits the Galilean appearances, and concentrates the appearances in Jerusalem. But, Loisy goes on, Luke did not wish to lose the story altogether, because of its symbolic value, so he retained it by using it, not as the story of the rehabilitation of Peter, but of his original call.[25]

Now we come to a much larger question – What were the motives and purposes which prompted the inclusion or the addition of ch. 21?

(i) It is clear that the chapter has something to do with Peter – but what?[26]

(a) There are those who have seen in the fourth gospel a consistent and deliberate playing down of Peter. The synoptic tradition is Petrine, and here Bacon sees 'a subtle correction of the Petrine story'. John, says Kümmel, stands with Peter in some kind of 'competitive' relationship, which Jülicher traces. The beloved disciple regularly appears side by side with Peter, and as regularly eclipses him. At the last supper Peter wishes to know the name of the betrayer, but does not dare to ask Jesus himself and signs to the beloved disciple to ask the question (13.23-26). At the arrest he and Peter follow Jesus and he gains an entry for Peter into the courtyard of the high priest's house (18.15-17). There Peter cowardly denies his master, while the beloved disciple accompanies him the whole road to death. And there beneath the cross he is given to Mary as her son, becoming thereby in the fullest sense the heir of Jesus (19.25-27). The beloved disciple and Peter run to the tomb on Easter morning. The beloved disciple arrives

first, but Peter is the first to enter the tomb; but it is of the beloved disciple that it is said: 'He saw and believed' (20.8). And in the incident of 21.15-23 Peter receives what is little less than a rebuke for his impulsive curiosity. But surely, if there is any comparison at all, the aim of it is not to denigrate Peter but rather to highlight the beloved disciple. Even C.K. Barrett says: 'It is conceivable, though this is pure speculation, that there is a polemical allusion to Mark, the Gospel guaranteed according to tradition by Peter, from which John differs in certain notable points.' It is very unlikely that in the fourth gospel Peter is deliberately denigrated; his eclipse is due to no fault of his own but to the effulgence of the beloved disciple.

(b) The chapter does stress the partnership of Peter and John, each great in his own way. C.K. Barrett writes of Peter and the beloved disciple: 'They are represented as partners, of whom neither can take precedence of the other. Peter is the head of the evangelistic and pastoral work of the Church, but the beloved disciple is the guaranttee of its tradition regarding Jesus.'

(c) The chapter quite certainly relates the rehabilitation of Peter. The three questions and the three answers of Peter surely take our minds back to the three denials (18.17, 25-27). Bernard says that ch. 21 contains a necessary postscript to place on record the rehabilitation of Peter. Although the denial is reported in great detail both in the synoptic gospels and in the fourth gospel, his rehabilitation, his forgiveness, and his restoration to apostolic leadership are not told. Yet in Acts Peter is depicted as leader. 'How were the other apostles reassures as to his stability?' 21.15-19 is the only explanation preserved. Chapter 21 preserves a scene without which the drama of Peter would be incomplete.

(d) Some have held that the chapter lays down the primacy of Peter. Roman Catholic exegetes have often taken the 'lambs' whom Peter must feed as the faithful in general, while the 'sheep' are other pastors, thus making Peter not simply *primus inter pares* but also *episcopus episcoporum*, an interpretation for which there can be no justification.

(e) Bultmann (pp. 712f.) refuses to accept the idea of rehabilitation. There is, he says, no word of the denial, no word of repentance, no word of absolution from Jesus. He sees in the story a variant of Peter's commission as leader as told in Matthew 16.17-19. And we might well take the matter further and say that the prophecy of Peter's death is a reminiscence of the saying (Matt. 16.24-26) that for a Christian there must be a cross.

(ii) Chapter 21 has another object; it is added to remove a misunderstanding, which, if it has been allowed to continue, might well have been destructive of faith. In the early church there were many for whom belief in the second coming *was* the gospel. It seemed on the face of it that Jesus had promised his return within the lifetime of some who had actually seen him in the days of his flesh. Had he not said: 'Truly, I say to you, there are some standing here who will not taste death before they see the Son of man coming in his kingdom' (Matt. 16.28; cf. Mark 9.1; Luke 9.27). The Thessalonians were so sure of the second coming in their own lifetime that they were worried as to whether those who had died before the second coming arrived would miss the glory – which Paul assured them would not be the case (I Thess. 4.13-18). Paul in his early days believed that the second coming would happen *before* some of the Corinthians fell asleep in death, that is, he was confident that the second coming would arrive within the lifetime of at least some of that generation (I Cor. 15. 51f.). Bit by bit those who had actually seen Jesus slipped away in death. But there still remained the venerable figure of the beloved disciple. So the report had arisen that Jesus had said that he, as the last survivor, would survive until the second coming. Now either he had died or, perhaps more likely, he knew that his days were numbered, and, if he too went before the prophecy of Jesus was fulfilled there were Christians who were going to be sadly disconcerted. So ch. 21 is added to say that Jesus did not in fact say that the beloved disciple was to survive until he came again. What he did say was: 'If it is my will that he remain until I come, what is that to you?' So this is an effort to clear up a misunderstanding of what Jesus said.[27]

We will end our consideration of ch. 21 with Streeter's dramatic reconstruction (*The Four Gospels*, pp. 468-78) of how the text reached its present form. For Streeter the author of the fourth gospel is John the elder, and he added the postscript himself. If the appendix is added by the original author, his work stops at 21.23. He cannot have given himself the certificate in John 21.24f.; these concluding verses are the words of the person or persons who are guaranteeing the gospel. This presents us with the spectacle of an astonishing ending to the gospel. The original gospel ended at 20.31, a magnificent ending, a true climax dramatically and artistically worked up to. But add the appendix and take out the certificate and how does the gospel end?

> The saying spread abroad among the brethren that this disciple was not to die; yet Jesus did not say to him that he was not to die, but, 'If it is my will that he should remain until I come, what is that to you?'

That is a very strange ending indeed, with nothing like the artistry and the force of 20.31. Why then was 20.31 sacrificed? The only reason possible is that John the elder thought it was so important to say what v. 23 says that he was quite prepared to stop the gospel there. In other words, if this theory is true, it is for v. 23 that ch. 21 mainly exists.

How does Streeter arrive at that conclusion? John the Elder, as

Streeter sees it, was one of the great thinkers of the church – whoever wrote the fourth gospel was a great thinker. He did two things. First, he introduced the Logos doctrine, 'the boldest "restatement" of Christianity in terms of contemporary thought ever attempted in the history of the Church'. Second, and more important for our present investigation, he did not absolutely deny an apocalyptic judgment, 'nevertheless for all practical purposes he substitutes the Coming of the Comforter for the visible Return of Christ'. The first letter is intended to follow up and commend this startling gospel. With the 'progressives' this was effective apologetic and propaganda. But the 'conservatives' would recoil from this 'philosophising mysticism'. The gospel was published about AD 90, not long before Domitian's persecution broke out. The spiritualizing teaching of the Gospel was largely accepted. Then Domitian's persecution broke. Persecution always rekindles apocalyptic; it always begets a return to the belief in – or at least the longing for – the visible breaking in of God and the visible return of Christ to save his people from their distresses. This one was no exception; it resulted in the violently apocalyptic book of Revelation. So the Christians waited for the 1290 days of Daniel 12.11 to be accomplished and for Jesus to come again (Rev. 11.2; 13.5). Then in AD 96 Domitian was assassinated. The 1290 days came to an end – *and there was still no second coming*. This was a blow to a faith based on apocalyptic. What had happened to Mark 9.1? There was still hope; all would be well if Jesus came back while there was still *some one* of the original disciples alive. John the Elder was still alive – but he knew that death was close. He *knows* his spiritual view is correct. He *must* confute 'the fanatic hope of an immediate return', kindled by the Revelation.

> All that he could do was to add something to his Gospel which would provide, as it were, a reserve trench against the hour of disillusionment, which he saw to be inevitable – to append to it a word of the Master, which would be there when he was gone, as an evidence that it was, not the Lord, but their own misunderstanding that had misled them: 'Yet Jesus said not . . .'.

Streeter thinks that John the Elder knew John the apostle, and it was the apostle's death – perhaps early by martyrdom – which confronted himself with the whole problem and led him to his own solution. For many the return of Jesus was 'the great good news for a despairing world'. If that hope was disappointed, faith would be shattered, unless it was rediscovered in the Paraclete and the doctrine of the spiritual return to every faithful and obedient soul. The Appendix was added to forestall despair. John's new theology had been accepted by those who were willing to set out on the adventure of thought; but by way of reaction it also produced in those who recoiled

from it a more determined obscurantism, which in the end was
doomed to be shattered. Hence John ended his gospel with a word
from Jesus which he hoped would rescue faith and save the situation.

It is a dramatic reconstruction, and undoubtedly some of the truth,
if not the whole truth, is in it.

So we come back to the key verse, 21.24: 'This is the disciple who is
bearing witness to these things, and who has written these things; and
we know that his testimony is true.' It may sound a simple enough
statement, but every phrase in it has produced endless discussion.[28]

(i) *the disciple*   There is surely no doubt that this is the beloved
disciple, since the immediately preceding passage has been speaking of
him. It does not settle who the beloved disciple was, but it does settle
that the witness of the beloved disciple lies behind the fourth gospel.

(ii) *who is bearing witness*   What does this phrase say about the
witness whose evidence is being cited? This is the present participle.
Does this then mean that the witness is still alive and still bearing
witness? Not necessarily. In quoting we can and do quite naturally
say: 'As Plato says in the *Apology*', or, 'As Shakespeare writes in
Hamlet'. The fact that 'is bearing witness' is in the present tense is not
an argument either way, although the fact that it is a present participle
that is used rather than the present indicative, the fact that it is 'is
bearing witness' rather than simply 'witnesses', makes it rather more
likely that the witness is still alive.

(iii) *and who has written these things*   Does this mean that it is
being certified that the beloved disciple actually did the writing, the
composing, or does it rather mean 'caused these things to be written'?
We read in John 19.19 that 'Pilate wrote a title and put it on the
cross', and the meaning is, not that Pilate did the writing himself, but
that he caused, or ordered, that such a title should be written. Paul
says to the Romans (15.15): 'On some points I have written to you
very boldly by way of reminder,' but we know from 16.22 that the
actual writer of the letter was in fact Tertius. I may well say to
someone: 'I wrote you a letter last week', when in fact it was my
secretary who wrote; I may not even have dictated the letter; if I have
a good secretary, I may well say: 'Send so and so a note about such
and such a thing', and then leave it to her to write, and myself do no
more than sign it. If 'who has written these things' is to be taken
literally, then the beloved disciple is the author of the fourth gospel; if
it means 'caused or arranged to be written', he remains the source
behind the gospel, the person who provided the information, but he is
not the actual author.

Both V.H. Stanton and G.H.C. Macgregor think that 'and who has
written these things' is in any event an afterthought, and that the real
stress is on the *witnessing* and not on the *writing*; they even think that

the way it is put implies a certain kind of doubt or uncertainty.

No one can say that these questions cannot be raised; but no one can say that they raise themselves. The plain intended meaning is that the beloved disciple is both the witness to, and the author of, these things.

(iv)   *these things*   There are four possible meanings here:

(a)   The incident concerning Peter and the beloved disciple in 21.20-23; *(b)* the whole of ch. 21, *(c)* the whole gospel, *(d)* that part of the gospel from ch. 13 onwards in which the beloved disciple appears. It would be on the whole seem most likely that the reference is to the whole; it seems most natural that a closing certificate of authentication should refer to everything that goes before.

(v)   *we know that his testimony is true*   Who are 'we'? At least four suggestions have been offered. It has been suggested that this is an authenticating certificate appended by the Ephesian elders, if indeed it was in Ephesus that the gospel first appeared. Hoskyns and Davey suggest that 'we' denotes the fellow-disciples of the author. They say that 'we' is regularly so used in the Johannine literature. 'The Word became flesh and dwelt among us . . . *we* have beheld his glory' (John 1.14). 'That which *we* have seen and heard *we* proclaim also to you' (I John 1.3). J.N. Sanders says:

> 'We know that his witness is true' is not the comment of a kind of editorial committee . . . but an instance of an author taking his readers into his confidence, and assuming that they share his opinions.

This is the testimony of the beloved disciple and you and I know that it is true. We have already noted that for Sanders this would mean that it is a statement by John Mark referring to Lazarus.

G.H.C. Macgregor introduces us to another view of the fourth gospel. He holds that this verse is a saying of the redactor, as is 19.35. Macgregor's opinion is that the witness is the beloved disciple, a young unnamed Jerusalemite disciple, the author is John the Elder, and that after it was written the gospel underwent a process of redaction and of further editing.[29] He argues (p. xlvii) that the tradition that the witness is the evangelist rests on 21.24, which 'cannot be from the hand of the original author, and represents a late, and probably erroneous, tradition'.

We would rather ourselves conclude that, though the verse is not from the hand of the original author, it and ch. 21 were additions to the gospel made at a very early date, probably even before the gospel began to be circulated, and indeed that ch. 21, apart from this verse, may well be from the hand of the author of the gospel. Further, we would hold that this certificate of authentication is to be taken in its obvious meaning, which is that the beloved disciple is the witness to the facts of the gospel and also its author.

We can now no longer evade facing the supreme question – what does this mean in regard to the authorship of the gospel? The obvious meaning of 21.24 is that the beloved disciple is the authority for, and the author of, the gospel. And the consistent tradition of the early church is that the beloved disciple is John the apostle. But to many who have studied the gospel, both these statements seem incredible.

(i)   It is held that it is very improbable that the beloved disciple is the author of the gospel. Jülicher writes in his *Introduction to the NT* (p. 415):

> It is, in fact, the one unassailable proposition which criticism, dealing solely with the internal evidence, can set up concering the Fourth Gospel, that the author was not 'the disciple whom Jesus loved'.

This argument is based on two assertions. We set forth the first in the words of Streeter (*The Four Gospels*, p. 432):

> If the Fourth Gospel had come down to us, as originally published, without the last two verses, everyone everywhere would have taken it for granted that the author intended to distinguish himself from the Beloved Disciple, and we should have inferred that its author stood in much the same kind of relationship to the Beloved Disciple as Mark, the author of another of our Gospels, stood to Peter.

It is quite true that up to 21.24 the beloved disciple seems to be rather a character in the story than the author of the story.

The second argument, which is very widely put forward, is that it is very difficult to think of the beloved disciple calling himself by that title, whereas it is easy to think of one of his own disciples calling his master by it. It is difficult to think of anyone saying: 'I was the disciple whom Jesus loved most of all', whereas it is easy to think of someone else saying: 'This was the disciple who was closest and dearest to Jesus.' The beloved disciple does not appear on the scene until ch. 13, and it is difficult to think of him as the authority behind and the author of the whole gospel.

For this reason there are some (for instance, Macgregor, p. xlvii, and Kümmel in his *Introduction to the NT*, p. 166) who think that it is possible that the beloved disciple is the authority behind the gospel, the source of its information, that he is the witness, but not the author.

(ii)   It is held that it is equally improbable that John could be the author of the gospel. It is a fact of New Testament study that the Johannine authorship of the fourth gospel was not questioned until late in the eighteenth century. According to Drummond (pp. 67f.), the earliest attack was made by Edward Evanson in 1792 in a book entitled *The Dissonance of the Four Generally Received Evangelists and the Evidence of their Respective Authenticity Examined*. In Germany the most able attack was made by K.T. Bretschneider in 1820 in *Probabilia de Evangelii et Epistolarum Joannis Apostoli*

Indole et Origine (Probabilities concerning the Nature and Origin of the Gospel and Epistles of the Apostle John). Kümmel (p. 140) tells us that Bretschneider argued against the Johannine authorship of the gospel on the grounds of its alleged divergence from the teaching of Jesus in the synoptic gospels, its non-Jewish character, and the late testimony to it. At the time of the writing of his book he held it to have been written by a Gentile, probably in Egypt about AD 150, and to have been brought to Rome by the Gnostics. He wrote in Latin so as not to give offence to the unlearned, and so that learned men in any country could read it. Four years later he withdrew his critical views and accepted the traditional position.

We have already discussed in ch. 2 the attack on the traditional view of the Johannine authorship of the gospel, but we wish very briefly to repeat the evidence and to add some additional points. Kümmel (p. 151) cannot agree that the writer of the fourth gospel is an eyewitness who was drawing, not on sources, but on his own memory for his facts. Gardner in his book *The Ephesian Gospel* (p. 54) was very definite: 'Who he [the author of the Fourth Gospel] was will never be determined with certainty. But that he was John the son of Zebedee is so improbable that we may regard this view as set aside.' What then are the arguments?

(a) It is argued that from the point of view of personality, character and temperament John the son of Zebedee could never have sat for the portrait of the beloved disciple, that it is impossible to identify the quick-tempered, ambitious, thunderer of the synoptic gospels with the author of the fourth gospel.

(b) It is argued that from the point of view of mentality John could never have written the fourth gospel. As Gardner put it: 'As a literary composition it is quite beyond the powers of the fisherman of Galilee.'

(c) It is argued (e.g. by Macgregor, p. xlv) that from the point of view of theology John could not have written the fourth gospel. The stream of tradition is so different from that of Mark that it is impossible to hold that John wrote it. Kirsopp and Sylvia Lake in their *Introduction to the NT* (p. 51) point out that the real Johannine problem is the difference between Mark and John. If we take the view that Mark gives a correct account of the ministry of Jesus and Matthew a correct account of his teaching, 'the fourth gospel is so different that it must be largely, if not altogether, fictitious and written by an Hellenistic Christian to support the sacramental theology which finds a centre in the divine Jesus.'

(d) If the early martyrdom be accepted as history (see pp. 29ff. above) then clearly John could not have written the fourth gospel.

(e) It is known that the fourth gospel came under attack, and it is argued that, if the fourth gospel had been certainly known to be the

work of John the apostle, no one would have dared to attack it. B.H.
Streeter writes in *The Four Gospels* (pp. 436f.):

> The most notable theologian of the Church of Rome during the period AD
> 190 to 235 was Hippolytus. On his death a statue of him seated was set
> up, and this was discovered in an old cemetery in Rome in 1551, and is
> still preserved in the Lateran Museum. On the chair of the statue is
> inscribed a list of his numerous works. Near the beginning of the list is
> mentioned a 'Defence of the Gospel and Apocalypse of John'. No one
> defends what nobody attacks.

That the fourth gospel did come under attack is held to be an
indication that its apostolic authorship was by no means certain. It
can even be argued that the very fact that the certificate of
authenticity is given in 21.24 is the proof that such a certificate was
regarded as necessary, and, it is argued, no such certificate would
have been necessary in the case of a gospel about which there was no
doubt.

(*f*) It is pointed out that John the apostle was connected with the
Jewish side of the church in the records of the early church (e.g. Gal.
2.1-9), whereas, it is claimed, the fourth gospel is thoroughly
Hellenistic. This is a matter which is in fact under debate. In 1933
B.W. Bacon wrote a book about the fourth gospel which he entitled
The Gospel of the Hellenists. E.J. Goodspeed in his *Introduction to
the NT* (p. 308) writes: 'The [Fourth] Gospel may be said to be
intensely Greek from Prologue to Epilogue in every fibre of both
thought and language.' And he concludes his introduction to the
fourth gospel (pp. 314f.) with these words:

> The thoroughly Greek character of the thought and interest of the Gospel,
> its literary (dialogue) cast, its thoroughly Greek style, its comparatively
> limited use of the Greek scriptures (roughly about one-fifth of Matthew's),
> its definite purpose to strip Christianity of its Jewish swaddling clothes, its
> intense anti-Jewish feeling, and its great debt to the mystery religions –
> combine to show that its author was a Greek, not a Jew. In the Gospel of
> John the Greek genius returns to religion.

B.H. Streeter is just as emphatic. He writes of the fourth gospel (p.
467): 'It gave the church an expression of its belief intellectually
acceptable to the Greek mind, yet true to the Jewish thought of God
as personal and as one', and speaks of the doctrine of the Logos (p.
468) as 'the boldest "restatement" of Christianity in terms of
contemporary thought ever attempted in the history of the church'.
Earlier (p. 367) he can say: 'The author of the Fourth Gospel stands
between two worlds, at the confluence of the two greatest spiritual and
intellectual traditions of our race. In him Plato and Isaiah meet.'

On the other hand, William Temple, introducing his *Readings in St
John's Gospel* (p. xix), could write: 'The Gospel is through and

through Palestinian. The notion that it is in any sense Hellenistic is contrary to its whole tenour.' And J.B. Lightfoot in his *Biblical Essays* (p. 135) said that the fourth gospel was 'the most Hebraic book in the New Testament, except perhaps the Apocalypse'. Clearly this is not a safe argument.

(g) There is the fact that, when Ignatius wrote to Ephesus, he mentions Paul in his letter, but makes no mention of John (see pp. 49f. above).

(h) There is the problem of the evidence of Irenaeus (pp. 45ff. above). Irenaeus tells how he heard Polycarp tell about his connection with John. It is beyond doubt that Irenaeus thought that Polycarp was speaking about John the apostle, and, when Irenaeus speaks about John and Asia, he believes himself to be speaking about the apostle, but the odd fact is that Irenaeus mentions this John eighteen times, and sixteen times he refers to him as the disciple of the Lord, and only twice – and that indirectly – as an apostle. Streeter (p. 444) argued from this that Irenaeus was speaking, not about John the apostle, but about another John, although he was unaware that he was doing so.

Here then is the case for divorcing the fourth gospel from the apostle John, the son of Zebedee. What are we to say to it? It will not be possible to assess the strength of the case against John's authorship until we see what alternative is offered.

There are those who would hold that the whole matter is veiled in a mystery which it is impossible to penetrate. Kümmel writes (p. 168):

> There is no possibility of establishing the identity of the disciple whom the Gospel of John cites as its authority for its report about the passion of Jesus. The supposition which continues to be the most probable is that the author of John was associated with a disciple who lived very long, and upon whom had been bestowed the title of honour 'he whom Jesus loved'. But so far as the clarification of the problem of authorship is conceived, this statement helps us no further.

But supposing we are not content to leave the matter in mystery, where can we turn?

We may start from the deduction that there quite certainly was a John of some kind in Asia Minor. Quite certainly Irenaeus heard Polycarp speaking about a John. As B.H. Streeter puts it (p. 445): 'The less you accept Irenaeus' evidence for the Apostle the weightier it is for another John.' To the evidence of Irenaeus must be added the evidence of Justin Martyr who had lived in Asia Minor. In his *Dialogue with Trypho* (p. 81) Justin writes:

> And, further, a certain man among us whose name was John, one of the apostles of Christ, in a revelation made by him, prophesied that those who believed our Christ would spend a thousand years in Jerusalem.

Whether or not Justin Martyr was right in calling this John an apostle, there was a John. Is there any direct evidence for such a John?

There is. We turn again to the famous Papias quotation. It comes from the Preface to his *Expositions of the Oracles of the Lord*, recorded by Eusebius in his *History* (3.39.3):

> I shall not hesitate also to put down for you along with my interpretations whatsoever things I have at any time learned carefully from the elders and carefully remembered, guaranteeing their truth. For I did not, like the multitude, take pleasure in those who speak much, but in those that teach the truth . . . If then anyone came who had been a follower of the elders, I questioned him in regard to the words of the elders, – what Andrew or what Peter said, or what was said by Philip, or by Thomas, or by James, or by John, or by Matthew, or by any other of the disciples of the Lord, and what things Aristion and the presbyter John, the disciples of the Lord, say.

Here we find a John the presbyter, or John the elder, in additon to John the apostle, and since Papias speaks of investigating what he said he must in all probability have still been alive when Papias wrote.

In addition to this there is an odd story of there being two tombs or monuments of John in Ephesus. These are mentioned twice in Eusebius. The first mention is in the chapter just quoted, where Eusebius goes on to say:

> This shows the truth of the statement that there were two persons in Asia that bore the same name, and that there were two tombs in Ephesus, each of which, even to this present day, is called John's.

The second reference (in 7.25.16) is in an extract from the letters of Dionysius of Alexandria, in connection with his views on the Revelation. He could not believe that the Revelation was by the author who produced the fourth gospel and the first epistle. The spirit, the style the character, the mode of expression, above all the Greek is so very different that identity of authorship is not possible. Dionysius did not doubt the inspiration of the Revelation, nor did he doubt that it was written by John; but it was a different John. And he finds some support for his contention in the fact that 'they say that there are two monuments in Ephesus, each bearing the name of John'. (Jerome also mentions two monuments, *On Famous Men*, 9.) No one is very likely to place much stress on this argument. Jülicher writes in his *Introduction* (p. 408): 'The story of the two graves at Ephesus will scarcely impose upon any historian acquainted with the legends of the saints.'

It is to be added that the *Apostolic Constitutions*, a fourth-century work purporting to give the institutions that the apostles laid down for the church, gives a list of the bishops of the great churches (7.46), and for Ephesus lists Timothy ordained by Paul, and John ordained by

John the apostle. Again, this is not evidence, but there are indications that there was more than one John in Ephesus.

Whatever we say about the two tombs and the *Apostolic Constitutions*, Papias does mention two Johns. It is barely conceivable and highly improbable that Papias is talking about only one John, that John is the one figure who bridges the two groups, that Papias includes him among the disciples of the Lord who spoke, and the disciples of the Lord who still speak – but this is very unlikely. A more valid point is that there is no indication within the quotation itself that either John the apostle or John the elder is to be definitely associated with and located in Ephesus. The assumption that they have to do with Ephesus is the result of bringing together the tradition and the words of Papias – a proceeding which may well be justified.

If we assemble all the information we have set down, we have to come to the conclusion that there are three Johns in question – John the apostle, John the elder, and, if, as is almost certain, we must assign the Revelation to still another author, John the seer. But on the view which we are discussing just now, we have to leave John the apostle out of it, for the argument is that he was never in Ephesus at all. Is there then any evidence at all which would lead us to believe that the author of the fourth gospel was in fact John the elder and not John the apostle?

The fourth gospel and the first letter do not directly state any claim to authorship, but the second and third letters of John do. The second letter begins: 'The elder to the beloved Gaius.' So these two letters are the work of the elder. All the probability is that the first letter is by the same author as the second and third, and it is highly probable that the fourth gospel is by the same author as the author of the first letter. If then, on this argument, the elder wrote second and third John he also wrote the fourth gospel, and here, it is claimed, is the proof that the author of the fourth gospel is John the elder and not John the apostle.

If we bring John the elder into the centre of the picture there still remain some uncertainties. If John the elder is to be regarded as the author of the fourth gospel, four different possibilities emerge.

(i) John the elder is both the author and the witness. That is to say, John the elder is both the author of the fourth gospel and the beloved disciple. The main objection to this view comes from the matter of age. If we put it in very round figures, Jesus was crucified about AD 30 and the fourth gospel was written about AD 100. If the beloved disciple was a youth fifteen to twenty years old in the closing days of Jesus' ministry on earth, then when he wrote the gospel he must have been between eighty-five and ninety. This is not impossible, and tradition does in fact make John an aged figure when he wrote. Indeed it is often said or implied that he was asked to write because his death was near, and his disciples wanted his written story to compensate for the loss of his spoken word. B.H. Streeter points out (p.456) that Gladstone at the age of eighty introduced the second Home Rule bill into the House of Commons in a four-hour speech in no way inferior to the oratorical triumphs of his middle age. The first Temple did not become archbishop of Canterbury until he was seventy-five, and he still had the energy to leave a permanent mark on the Church of England. Titian died at ninety-nine, producing masterpieces to the very end. The age of John the elder would not necessarily rule him out as both the witness and the author, as both the beloved disciple and the evangelist.

(ii) If, however, the age is felt to be a valid objection, then it is possible that John the elder is the author of the gospel and the beloved disciple is the witness, that John the elder is a younger contemporary of the beloved disciple. This is the view of G.H.C. Macgregor (p. xlviii):

> The evangelist was not himself the Beloved Disciple-witness, but rather a younger contemporary and admiring follower of the latter, standing in much the same kind of relation to him as did Mark, the author of another of our Gospels, to Peter.

B.H. Streeter, who also holds this view, thinking of the age of John the elder, believes (p. 433) that his contact with the beloved disciple may well have been fairly tenuous:

> A brief, and as it seemed in the halo of later recollection, a wonderful connection – perhaps also a few never-to-be-forgotten words of Christ derived from his lips – would make the attitude towards the Beloved Disciple expressed in the Gospel psychologically explicable.

(iii) But there still remains a question – who was the beloved disciple? If the beloved disciple was the apostle John, and if John the elder had him as his ultimate source, then it still remains true that the fourth gospel is still the gospel according to John; John may not have written it, but John remains the source behind it.

(iv) But if the beloved disciple is the aristocratic young Jerusalemite, who, as has been suggested, became very close to Jesus in the last days in Jerusalem, then John the apostle has nothing whatever to do with the fourth gospel.

If John the elder is introduced as the author of the fourth gospel, then at the most John the apostle may retain a distant and possibly rather tenuous connection with the gospel as one of its sources; at the least John the apostle completely vanishes from the scene.

At this stage certain questions have to be asked. It must certainly be asked who this John the elder was. It must be said that the only evidence we have – if it is evidence – that he ever existed is the Papias information, transmitted by Eusebius (3.39.3). Let us once again set down the salient lines:

If then anyone came who had been a follower of the elders, I questioned him in regard to the words of the elders, – what Andrew or what Peter said, or what was said by Philip, or by Thomas or by James or by John or by Matthew, or by any other of the disciples of the Lord, and what things Aristion and the Elder John, the disciples of the Lord, say.

That quotation contains the sum total of our information about John the elder, and on this slender foundation an elaborate superstructure has been erected. C.F. Nolloth in his book *The Fourth Evangelist* (p. 35) calls him a 'nebulous' figure. J. Armitage Robinson, writing on *The Historical Character of St John's Gospel* (p. 101), will have nothing to do with him: 'That mole never made such a mountain.' Jülicher in his *Introduction* (p. 409) calls the whole tradition of John of Asia 'worthless'. We shall have to examine the evidence more carefully before we allow ourselves to speak as sweepingly as that. There are three views of this John.

(i) It is held that this John never existed. (See for instance C.F. Nolloth, pp. 33-6, 61-4; T. Zahn, *Introduction to the NT* II, pp. 435-8, 452f.) This is argued partly from the Eusebius quotation itself, and partly from the tradition of the church. The tradition of the church does not know of two Johns in Ephesus. About the year 250 Dionysius of Alexandria came to the conclusion on the grounds both of matter and of style that it was impossible that the same author could have written both the fourth gospel and the Revelation. He did not doubt that the fourth gospel was the work of the apostle John, and he did not doubt that the Revelation was written by a man called John. He knew about the alleged two monuments to John in Ephesus; he knew about the existence of John Mark, but could in no way connect him with Ephesus. He therefore left the identity of the second John in suspense, because he could suggest no one, although, as he said, John was so common a name that he had no difficulty in supposing that there was another John (Eusebius, *History*, 7.25.14). About seventy-five years later Eusebius came across the Papias preface, and there he seemed to himself to find just the other John who was wanted. In point of fact, Eusebius grabbed the second John with both hands, for Eusebius was one of the many who had the gravest doubts about the Revelation, and was eager to find some other John in order to disconnect the apostle from it. So Eusebius (3.39.6) comments on Papias' statement:

This shows the truth of the statement that there were two persons in Asia who bore the same name, and that there were two tombs in Ephesus, each of which, even to this present day, is called John's. It is important to notice this. For it is probable that it was the second, if one is not willing to admit that it was the first, who saw the Revelation which is ascribed by the name of John.

Eusebius was not entirely unbiased in his quickness to believe that Papias was speaking about two Johns, for the second John provided him with the opportunity to get rid of the apostolic authorship of the Revelation.

Now, however, we turn to the passage itself, which has been interpreted differently.

> If then anyone came who had been a follower of the elders, I questioned him in regard to the words of the elders, what Andrew or what Peter said, or what was said by Philip, or by Thomas or by James, or by John or by Matthew, or by any other of the disciples of the Lord, and what things Aristion and the elder John, the disciples of the Lord, say.

The question is, Who are the elders? The word could be used as we speak of the fathers of the church, and it was also the description of an ecclesiastical office. Here it is clearly used in the first sense. But does the phrase 'the words of the elders' mean 'what Andrew and Peter and the rest of them said'? Or does it mean 'what the elders related that Andrew and Peter and the rest of them said'? Are there, so to speak, three layers – first, followers of the elders; second, elders; third, the apostles? Or are there only two layers – first, followers of the elders; second, apostles, who are called elders in the sense that they are the fathers of the church? Did Papias question followers of elders who had been followers of the apostles? Or did he question followers of the elders, elders who *are* the apostles? If Papias is distinguishing between elders and apostles then almost certainly there are two Johns; if he is speaking of the apostles as elders, then there may well be only one John. And this John is the one figure who bridges the two groups; he belongs both to the group whose followers transmit their teaching, and to the group who still teach. And if there is only one John, he must be John the apostle, and John the elder, as Zahn puts it in his *Introduction to the NT* (III, p. 230) owes his existence 'to the critical notes and arts of Eusebius'.

(ii)   It is held that Papias does intend to indicate that there were two Johns. Kümmel in his *Introduction* (p. 171) regards it as 'hardly understandable' that anyone should argue for anything else. But there are those who hold that there is no indication that the elder John ever had any connection with Ephesus. C.K. Barrett writes in the introduction to his commentary (p. 92):

> That there was an Elder John need not be doubted ... But equally there seems to be no convincing ground that the Elder ever lived in Ephesus; nor is there any positive evidence that he wrote the Fourth Gospel, or was in any way connected with it.

Bacon (p. 78) said of the Papias quotation:

> The passage quoted clearly implies that neither one of the two Johns was

accessible to Papias. The apostle had long since been dead; the Presbyter, though living, was accessible to Papias only through report of travellers 'who came this way'.

Bacon (p. 452) would not have it that John the elder had anything to do with any of the Johannine literature, gospel or letters. He believes him to be a real person, but even for Papias a dim and distant figure. He believes him to be a resident of Jerusalem, where the authoritative tradition of the church was preserved, and where the 'elders', the fathers of the church, were to be found. C.K. Barrett in the passage to which we have already referred makes a further point. The journey from Hierapolis, where Papias had his episcopal seat, to Ephesus was not great, and there was a main road connecting the two towns. One would therefore have expected Papias to make an actual visit to see the famous John, rather than to be dependent for his sayings on chance travellers, if John was really a resident in Ephesus.

Can we then simply say that the elder John had no connection with Ephesus, and therefore no connection with the Johannine literature?

This brings us to another of the problems. In the passage we are considering Papias speaks of inquiring what Peter, Philip, Thomas and all the other members of the first group *said*; but of enquiring what Aristion and the elder John *say*. Why is the one verb in the past tense and the other in the present? Three reasons have been given.

(a) Lightfoot in his essay on Papias (p. 150) suggested that 'say' is an historic present and really refers to the past, and is used simply for stylistic variation. This view he takes, because he does not think that any of the original disciples could still be alive in the time of Papias.

(b) Drummond in his book *The Character and Authorship of the Fourth Gospel* (p. 200) suggests that the reference is to books, and that what Papias means is what Aristion and John say in books, either by themselves or by others about them. Although it is getting on for two thousand five hundred years since Plato died, we can still regularly write: 'As Plato says in the *Phaedo* . . .'

(c) Undoubtedly, the obvious meaning is the best meaning. The difference between the two groups is that the first group are dead and no longer speak; the second group are alive and still speaking.

Even if we take it that Aristion and John are still alive, that does not mean that they are alive in Ephesus. But when we read what Eusebius says of Papias' relationship to these two, it does look as if John was much nearer than in Jerusalem. He quotes Papias (3.39.15) as beginning his account of Mark's gospel by saying: 'This also the elder said . . .' Eusebius himself writes (3.39.7): 'Papias, of whom we are now speaking, confesses that he received the words of the apostles from those who followed them, but says that he was himself a hearer of Aristion and the elder John.' Then Eusebius corrects himself, for

Papias did not say that in so many words – 'At least he mentions them frequently by name, and gives their traditions in his writings.' And Eusebius goes on (3.39.14) to say: 'Papias gives also in his own work other accounts of the words of the Lord on the authority of Aristion who was mentioned above, and traditions as handed down by the elder John.' We get the impression that the contact of Papias with Aristion and John was not at a distance, but fairly close. It is true that it is never said that the elder John was in Ephesus, but the impression given is that he was, and Eusebius has no doubt that Papias' contact with him was direct.

(iii) But in contrast to those who obliterated the elder John altogether, or those who accepted that there was such a person, but who denied that he had any connection with Ephesus or with the Johannine literature, we come to the third group, those who, like Eusebius many centuries ago, grasped at the elder John as the solution of their problems. Among those who have argued that the elder John had a very large share in the production of the fourth gospel, we may particularly refer to Streeter (*The Four Gospels*, pp. 430-61), J.H. Bernard (I, pp. lxviii-lxxi) and Macgregor (pp. xliv-lxviii).

Students of the fourth gospel found themselves in a dilemma. If they accepted the early martyrdom of John, if they accepted the theory that, though Irenaeus thought he was talking of the apostle, his continuous talk of 'John the disciple' showed that he was not, then John the apostle could not have been in Ephesus towards the end of the first Christian century and so could not have written the gospel. But it was indisputable that there was some one called John in Ephesus who was a leader and teacher of the church. The elder John supplied just the figure who was needed, the more so that the second and third letters of John state that they were written by the elder. So it has become a commonly accepted viewpoint that the elder John had a very great share in the production of the fourth gospel, whether he, as the author, knew the apostle, and drew on the apostle's memories, so that the gospel is the gospel *according* to John, or whether the apostle does not enter into it at all and the elder John is the man responsible for the Johannine literature.

There are three questions to ask. First, is it possible that the apostle and the elder could have got confused and even identified with each other? Second, if it is possible, how could it have happened? Third, can we believe that it did take place, and are we to accept the elder John as the author, or at least the compiler, of the fourth gospel?

First, then, could the confusion have taken place? Theoretically it could. Two parallel confusions can be cited. There is the case of the tomb of Philip in Hierapolis (see p. 52 above). Polycrates refers to this as the tomb of Philip the apostle, but it is clear from the details given that the Philip in question was the member of the seven, the evangelist of Acts (8.4-8, 26-40; 21.8f.). Such a confusion was natural enough, for Hierapolis would much rather be able to boast of its connection with one of the twelve than with one of the seven. As Streeter says (p. 454), 'tradition always errs on the patriotic side'.

Even Irenaeus himself can nod. When talking about the episode recorded in Galatians 2, when Paul clashed with Peter, James and John for refusing to eat with the Gentiles, he comments (3.12.15):

> Thus did the apostles whom the Lord made witnesses of every action and of every doctrine – for upon all occasions do we find Peter and James and John present with him – scrupulously act according to the dispensation of the Mosaic law.

But the James who was one of the inner circle in the gospels is James the brother of John, the son of Zebedee, whose death is recorded in Acts 12.2; the James of Galatians 2 and Acts 15, who with the others Judaized to the anger of Paul, was James the brother of the Lord. The two Jameses were confused.

The two Philips were confused; the two Jameses were confused; and therefore it cannot be held to be impossible that the two Johns were confused.

Second, how could the confusion have arisen, if indeed it did? Two things could have combined to bring it about.

(a)   In Ephesus there was more than one John. There was the John who wrote the Revelation. There was the elder John. And perhaps there was the apostle John. At that time the church was building up the New Testament, and the primary condition for a book to become a book of the church was that it should have apostolic authorship. This, for instance, is how the letter to the Hebrews finally came to rest under the protection of the name of Paul, although everyone was well aware that Paul was not the author of it. If the Ephesian church wished to preserve books written under the name of John, and if it wished to consider them as books of the church, they had to be regarded as apostolic, and therefore all the Johns in question would tend to be identified with John the apostle. Thus Justin in his *Dialogue* (81) can speak of Revelation as written by 'a man named John, one of the apostles of Christ'. Books tended to gravitate towards the names of apostles.

(b)   In the early days the fourth gospel was the happy hunting-ground of the Gnostics, and the Alexandrian Valentinus by midway through the second century was busy turning Christianity into what Sanders in his commentary (p. 38) calls 'a hellenistic theosophical system'. The first commentary on the fourth gospel was written by the Gnostic Heracleon, in the latter half of the first century; a work on the fourth gospel by Ptolemaeus – who was the first to assign that gospel to John in so many words – is preserved by Irenaeus, and one by Theodotus is preserved by Clement of Alexandria. The Gnostics had annexed the fourth gospel, and, since it was gnostic practice to attribute apostolic status to their documents, they would readily assign the fourth gospel to John. The church had to authenticate and authorize the fourth gospel or abandon it to the Gnostics. Further study of the fourth gospel would readily show that instead of being pro-gnostic it could in fact provide the best defence against, and attack on, Gnosticism. And it could well be that the church, so to speak, took over the fourth gospel, with its ascription to John as well.

It is possible to conceive of a situation in which apostolic authorship was assigned to the fourth gospel to preserve it for the church and to rescue it from the Gnostics, with the result that the John who wrote it became identified with the apostle, whether he was the apostle or not.

Third, we have now to ask our most important question. We have seen that confusion of two persons with the same name is a possibility, that indeed it did on occasion happen; we have seen how it could have happened; and now we have to ask, Did it happen? Can we believe in face of the evidence available that John the apostle and the elder John were so confused that the works of the elder were attributed to the apostle, that the confusion is so complete that it is probable that John the apostle was never resident in Asia Minor at all? We believe that two things have to be asserted.

First, if John the apostle was martyred early, then he cannot have been in Asia Minor. But we have argued (pp. 33-40 above) that the evidence for the early martyrdom of John is quite unacceptable and ought to be disregarded. W.F. Howard transmits the verdict of Lord Charnwood, whom he calls 'a historian of renown coming to the problem with a fresh mind trained in other fields of research'. Lord Charnwood wrote of the case for the early martyrdom of John:

> There could be no better example of a vice which microscopic research seems often to induce, that of abnormal suspiciousness towards the evidence which suffices ordinary people, coupled with abnormal credulity towards evidence which is trifling or null.[30]

The story of the alleged early martyrdom of John cannot be used as evidence to suggest that John had no connection with Asia Minor.

Second, I do not believe that there is any sufficient ground for doubting the evidence of Irenaeus. That Irenaeus could have made a mistake is no doubt possible; that he could have remained uncorrected in that mistake is far less probable. Drummond writes (p. 348):

> Critics speak of Irenaeus as if he had fallen out of the moon, paid two or three visits to Polycarp's lecture room, and never known anyone else. In fact he must have known all sorts of men, of all ages, both in the east and in the west, and among others his venerable predecessor Pothinus, who

was upwards of ninety by the time of his death. He must have had numerous links with the early part of the century, and he must have known perfectly well, whether the Gospel was older than himself or not.

Are we to assume that Irenaeus made his mistake and that he was so isolated that no one ever corrected him? And are we further to assume that Irenaeus' mistake brought about a situation in which the whole church was mistaken?

What has not been sufficiently realized is that the situation in which the fourth gospel is ascribed to John are polemical situations, in which, if it had been possible to deny the apostolic authorship of the gospel, it would quite certainly have been denied.

There is first the letter of Irenaeus to Florinus (quoted above, p. 47). In that letter Irenaeus reminds Florinus of how they had both heard Polycarp tell of his friendship with 'John and with others who had seen the Lord'. It is clear that to Irenaeus the John in question is the apostle. Eusebius tells us in his *History* (5.15) that Florinus was a presbyter of the Roman church who had fallen into heresy. He had become a Valentinian Gnostic, and he was arguing that, if it was insisted that there was only one God, then that God must be taken to be the creator of evil, and no doubt he was preaching the gnostic doctrine of two gods, one the God of spirit, the true and real God, the God and Father of Jesus Christ, the other the distant, ignorant, hostile, evil God of creation. Now it is to face and contradict this that Irenaeus wrote his letter *On Monarchy* and his book *On the Ogdoad*. Since there is no mention of Florinus in *Against Heresies* it is entirely probable that Florinus emerged after Irenaeus had written his great work. This is to say, first, that, if Irenaeus had made a mistake in thinking that Polycarp had been speaking of John the apostle, he had had ample time to discover that he was mistaken, and, second, if Irenaeus had made a mistake by bringing John the apostle into it at all, then one would have expected Florinus at once to have said so, and so to take the sting out of Irenaeus' implied rebuke.

We have already quoted (p. 43 above) the letter of Polycrates, supporting the Asian date for the observance of Easter in opposition to Victor, bishop of Rome, in which he enumerated the great teachers of Asia who had observed the Asian date, including 'John, who was both a witness and a teacher, who reclined upon the bosom of the Lord'. (Jerome in his brief biography of Polycrates [*On Famous Men*, 45] also says that Polycrates wrote a letter 'in which he says he follows the authority of the apostle John and of the ancients'.) Irenaeus also became involved in this controversy, and Eusebius in his *History* (5.24.16) quotes a letter in which Irenaeus tells how Polycarp had discussed the very same question with Anicetus, a previous bishop of Rome, and how Anicetus could not persuade Polycarp 'not to observe what he had always observed with John the disciple of the Lord, and the other apostles with whom he had associated'. It is obvious that if in the circumstances Anicetus or Victor could have pointed out that there was any doubt about the connection of John the apostle with Asia, he would have been quick to do so.

There is no adequate reason to doubt the evidence of either Irenaeus or of Polycrates. It is not at all probable that there was any confusion of the two Johns, and there is no good reason to doubt the connection of John the apostle with Asia.

Before we make our final decision in regard to the authorship of the fourth gospel there are two things that we must do. First, we must make a quick survey of the external evidence for the existence of the gospel and for its authorship.[31]

(i)   We begin with two witnesses from among the papyri. The first is P[52], the famous Rylands Papyrus. The Rylands Papyrus is the oldest known New Testament papyrus fragment. It measures $2\frac{1}{2}$ by $3\frac{1}{2}$ inches. It contains John 18.31-33 and 37f. It was acquired by B.P. Grenfell in Egypt in 1920. It lay unnoticed in the John Rylands Library in Manchester until 1934, when it was identified by C.H. Roberts, who dated it before AD 150. F.G. Kenyon says: 'It is in a hand which can be confidently assigned to the first half of the second century.' A. Deissmann would put it possibly as early as the time of Trajan (AD 98-117), and certainly as early as Hadrian (AD 117-138).[32] The fourth gospel must therefore have been copied, and must have reached Egypt well before AD 150, which means that it must in all probability have been first written in Ephesus about fifty years before.

The second papyrus witness is Papyrus Egerton 2,[33] which comes from about the same date. Fragment 1 begins and ends with an unknown saying of Jesus and the main body of it seems to depend on the fourth gospel. In it Jesus is in controversy with the Jewish authorities:

> Jesus said to the lawyers: 'Punish every wrong-doer and transgressor, but not me . . .' And turning to the rulers he spake thus: 'Search the scriptures in which you think you have life; these are they which bear witness of me. Do not think that I came to accuse you to my Father. There is one who accuses you, even Moses, on whom you have set your hope.' But when they said: 'We know well that God spoke to Moses; but as for you we do not know where you are from.' Jesus answered: 'Now already is your unbelief accused.'

On the other side of this fragment, the authorities are trying to arrest Jesus:

> . . . drag him away and to carry stones and to stone him. And the rulers tried to lay hands on him, that they might take him away and hand him

over to the crowd; and they could not take him because the hour of his betrayal had not yet come.

The importance of these fragments is that they prove once and for all that any theory which wishes to date the fourth gospel as late as AD 150 must be wrong. For the fourth gospel to be current in Egypt by then means that it must date to about fifty years earlier.

(ii)   Next we come to Clement of Rome, the first of the group of Christian writers known as the apostolic fathers. In his letter to the Corinthians, known as *I Clement*, we find four possible echoes of fourth gospel language:

> 43.6: that the name of the true and only Lord may be glorified. Cf. John 12.28; 17.3.

> 49.1: Let him that has love in Christ keep the commandments of Christ. Cf. John 14.15.

> 49.6: Jesus gave his flesh for our flesh. Cf. John 6.51.

> 60.2: Cleanse us with the cleansing of thy truth. Cf. John 17.17.

The date of I Clement is AD 96, which makes it in all probability contemporary with the fourth gospel. It may therefore well be held that these passages are resemblances rather than quotations, or even echoes.

(iii)   Next comes the letter of Barnabas. J.B. Lightfoot dated it tentatively from AD 70-79, in which case there will obviously be no connection with the fourth gospel; but it is probably later than that, about AD 100-130. Barnabas 12.7 sees the serpent in the wilderness as the type of Jesus (cf. John 3.14):

> Moses said to them: 'Whenever one of you be bitten, let him come to the serpent that is placed upon the tree, and let him hope in faith that it, though dead, is able to give life, and he shall immediately be saved.' And they did so. In this also you have again the glory of Jesus, for all things are in him and for him.

(iv)   Next comes Ignatius, the dates of whose activity are about AD 110-118, who wrote his seven letters to certain churches in Asia Minor, when he was being taken from Antioch, where he was bishop, to Rome to be flung to the lions in the arena. Ignatius lived before there was an accepted Canon of the New Testament. As Bernard says (p. lxxi), 'He never quotes directly or avowedly from the Gospels or Apostolic Epistles.' But his thought and his writing come from the same cradle as the fourth gospel.

> *To the Magnesians* 7.1: As then the Lord was united with the Father *and did nothing without him*, neither by himself nor through the Apostles, so do you do nothing without the bishop and the presbyters. Cf. John 5.19,30; 8.28.

To the Romans 7.2f.: My lust has been crucified, and there is in me no fire of love for material things; but only *water living* and speaking (possibly, *springing up*) in me, and saying to me from within: 'Come to the Father.' I have no pleasure in the food of corruption or in the delights of this life. I desire *the bread of God which is the flesh of Jesus Christ*, who was of the seed of David, and *for the drink I desire his blood*, which is incorruptible love. Cf. John 4.10; 7.38; 6.33.

To the Magnesians 8.1: ... God who *manifested himself* through Jesus Christ his Son, *who is his Word*, proceeding from silence, *who in all respects was well-pleasing to him who sent him.* Cf. John 1.14; 8.29.

To the Philadelphians 9.1: He is the *door* of the Father. Cf. John 10.7,9.

To the Ephesians 17.1 and 19.1: *The Prince of this world.* Cf. John 12.31.

To the Ephesians 6.1: For everyone whom the master of the house sends to do his business ought we to receive as him who sent him. Cf. John 13.20.

To the Romans 3.3: Christianity is not the work of persuasiveness but of greatness, *when it is hated by the world.* Cf. John 15.19.

It is not possible to claim that Ignatius is actually quoting the fourth gospel, but he certainly spoke the same language.

(v) There are no actual quotations of the fourth gospel in The Shepherd of Hermas. The dates of Hermas are AD 100-145. There may be a very few remote echoes.

Similitudes 9.12.5: 'If you wish to enter into a city, and that city has been walled round, and has one gate, can you enter into that city except through the gate which it has?' 'No, sir,' said I, 'for how is it possible otherwise?' 'If then you are not able to enter into the city except through the gate which it has, so,' said he, 'a man cannot otherwise enter into the kingdom of God except through the name of his Son, who was beloved by him... The gate is the Son of God, this is the only entrance to the Lord. No man can enter in to him otherwise than through his Son.' Cf. John 3.5; 14.6.

Similitudes 5.6.3: When, therefore, he had cleansed the sins of the people, he showed them the way of life, and gave them the law *which he had received from his Father.* Cf. John 10.18.

Apart from these echoes C. Taylor deduced that Hermas knew the four gospels. *Vision* 3.13.3 gives a picture of the church in the form of a woman 'sitting on a couch; the position is secure, for a couch has four feet and stands securely, for even the world is controlled by four elements'.[34] Taylor, with Drummond's approval, takes the four feet of the couch to symbolize the four gospels, and in support of this he cites the famous passage (*Against Heresies*, 3.11.8) in which Irenaeus lays it down that it is just as inevitable that there should be four gospels as it is that there are four winds and four quarters of the earth.

The connection of Hermas with the fourth gospel can only be regarded as possible but very doubtful.

(vi) The *Didachē*, The Teaching of the Twelve Apostles, is the church's first service order book, the first book of church discipline and administration, and the first book of instruction for those entering the church for the first time. It is possible that it is as early as AD 100. In the eucharistic prayers there may be echoes of the fourth gospel:

> 9.4: As this broken bread was scattered upon the mountains, but was brought together and became one, so let thy Church be gathered from the ends of the earth into thy kingdom. Cf. John 11.52.
>
> 10.2: We give thee thanks, Holy Father, for thy holy name which thou didst cause to dwell in our hearts. Cf. John 17.11.
>
> 10.5: Remember, O Lord, thy Church to deliver her from all evil and to perfect her in thy love. Cf. John 17.15, 23, 26.

After the worshippers are *satisfied* with the food of the eucharist, the *Didachē* gives the prayers that are to be prayed, and the word used for 'satisfied' is the same word as is used in John 6.12 for those who had shared in the miracle of the loaves and the fishes, when they had 'eaten their fill'.

Once again the connection between the *Didachē* and the fourth gospel is doubtful; they may well both be using standard eucharistic language.

(vii) Next we come to Justin Martyr whose dates are about AD 110 to 165. He was born in Flavia Neapolis in Samaria; he began by being a philosopher, a searcher in many schools. When he was converted, he became a Christian preacher and teacher. We know that he spent some time in Ephesus, and that he lived for a considerable time in Rome. With Justin things are different. He does not quote the fourth gospel or John by name, but it is clear that he knew that gospel.[35]

Justin knew John's theology; in particular a number of statements in his two *Apologies* make it clear that he knew and held the Logos doctrine of Jesus: 'The Word of God is his Son. . . . Jesus Christ is the Son of God and his Apostle, being of old the Word' (1.63). 'The first power after God the Father and Lord of all is the Word, who is also his Son' (1.32). 'The Word who is the first-born of God' (1.21; 1.33). 'Jesus Christ is the only Son who has really been begotten by God, being his Word and first-begotten.' 'His Son, who alone is properly called Son, the Word who also was with him and was begotten before the works, when at first he created and arranged all things by him, is called Christ' (2.6).

We have said that Justin does not name John, but there are times when he does seem definitely to refer to the fourth gospel. In *Apology* 1.13 he speaks of Jesus and his crucifixion and says that he *was born for this purpose.* And this probably refers back to Jesus' saying to Pilate: 'For this was I born, and for this I have come into the world, to bear witness to the truth' (John 18.37). There are Justin's words about John the Baptist in the *Dialogue with Trypho* (88): 'Men supposed him to be the Christ; but he cried to them, I am not the Christ but the voice of one crying; for he that is stronger than I shall come, whose shoes I am not worthy to bear.' The first part of that saying is only in the fourth gospel (1.20, 23). Thirdly, there is the passage concerning baptism in *Apology* 1.61. After those who wish to enter the Christian church have been instructed, have fasted and prayed and have made their vows, they are baptized:

> Then they are brought by us where there is water, and are regenerated in the same manner in which we were ourselves regenerated. For in the name of God, the Father and Lord of the universe, and of our Saviour Jesus Christ, and of the Holy Spirit, they then receive the washing with water. For Christ also said: 'Except you be born again, you shall not enter into the kingdom of heaven.' Now, that it is impossible for those who have once been born to enter into their mothers' womb is manifest to all.

Even if there are slight variations, probably due to quotation from memory, there can be little doubt that this is a quotation from John 3.3f.

(viii)   Next we come to Tatian, who was born about AD 110, and who did his main work about AD 150. In two ways Tatian is a landmark. First, he is the first person to quote the fourth gospel verbatim. He still does not quote it as John's, but twice in his *Oration to the Greeks* (13.1 and 19.4) he quotes the prologue to the gospel exactly: 'The darkness does not comprehend the light.' 'All things were made by him, and without him not one thing was made.' Second, Tatian was the first man to make a harmony of the gospels, that is, to weave the four of them into one connected narrative. And it is our four, and no more, that he uses, including John. This is to say that by the time of Tatian the fourth gospel is firmly established beside the other three.

(ix)   Theophilus of Antioch, who was active between about AD 170 and 180, is the first Christian writer to name the gospel as John's and to rank it as inspired scripture. In his book *To Autolycus* (2.22) he quotes the saying, 'In the beginning was the Word, and the Word was with God' as a saying of John, who was one of the Spirit-bearing men.

(x)   We next find a group of Gnostic thinkers and writers, all clearly with knowledge of the fourth gospel. Valentinus was one of the great Gnostics. He was born in Egypt probably about AD 100-110, and he lived and worked in Rome from AD 136 to about 155. Tertullian tells us that he was of such standing in the church that he had the expectation of becoming a bishop, and that it was when he was disappointed in his hopes that he left the orthodox church.

Tertullian hated him but in his book *On the Prescription of Heretics* (30) admits that 'both as to talent and eloquence he was an able man'. It is highly probable that Valentinus was the author of *The Gospel of Truth*.[36] *The Gospel of Truth* knows the fourth gospel. It says that the gospel 'gave them a Way, and the Way is the Truth' (18.19-21; cf. John 14.6). The true Gnostic is 'wont to do the will of him who called him and is wont to wish to please him' (22.9-11; cf. John 7.17). The Word was not a mere sound, but 'became a *soma*, a body' (26.5-8; cf. John 1.14). The Father 'breathed into' his own (30.34; cf. John 20.22). He is the shepherd of the sheep who have strayed (31.36-32.3; cf. Matt. 18.12-14 and John 10.11, 14). It was the Gnostic Heracleon who wrote the first commentary on the fourth gospel. Ptolemaeus, a pupil of Valentinus wrote a commentary on the prologue of the fourth gospel which is preserved by Irenaeus (*Against Heresies*, 1.8.5), and he may have been the first of all to ascribe it to John. Clement of Alexandria preserves parts of a commentary on the fourth gospel by another Gnostic, Theodotus. The Gnostics found the fourth gospel saying many of the things they wanted to say.

(xi) The matter is clinched by Irenaeus. After listing the other three canonical gospels, he concludes (3.1.2): 'Then John the disciple of the Lord, who also had leaned against his breast, himself published the gospel when he was living at Ephesus in Asia.' From then on, Christian writers accept the authorship of John the apostle as unquestioningly as the student of English literature accepts it as a fact which does not need proving that John Milton wrote *Paradise Lost*. Clement of Alexandria (see p. 1 above) says that last of all John wrote a spiritual gospel. Tertullian, writing *Against Marcion* (4.2), speaks of John and Matthew as instilling faith into us. Eusebius in his *History* (3.24.5-15) explains how John wrote to supplement the first three gospels. Jerome in the preface to his *Commentary on Matthew* ascribes the fourth gospel to 'John, the apostle and evangelist'.

Raymond E. Brown writes in the introduction to his commentary (I, p. xcii):

> It is fair to say that the only ancient tradition about the authorship of the Fourth Gospel for which any considerable body of evidence can be adduced is that it is the work of John the son of Zebedee. There are some valid points in the objections raised to this tradition, but Irenaeus' statement is far from being disproved.

Even when all legitimate objections have been taken into account the tradition that John the apostle wrote the fourth gospel at Ephesus is very strong.

We must now bring matters to a head by asking, Who is the author of the fourth gospel, if he is not the apostle John? C.K. Barrett on the opening page of his commentary called the question of the authorship of the fourth gospel a 'tantalizing' question – and so indeed it is. B.W. Bacon in *The Fourth Gospel* (p. 3) said that its Johannine authorship is 'the question of questions in all the domain of biblical science'. J.B. Lightfoot went very far. He wrote in his *Biblical Essays* (p. 47):

> The genuineness of St John's Gospel is the centre of the position of those who uphold the historical truth of the record of our Lord Jesus Christ given us in the New Testament. It enunciates in the most express terms the Divinity, the Deity of our Lord, and at the same time professes to have been written by the one man of all others, who had the greatest opportunities of knowing the truth.

It is probably true that in our day we would not care to make such an issue of the matter as that, but it is an important question. We must then briefly review, even if it involves some repetition, the candidates suggested for authorship other than the apostle John.

(i)   We begin with John the presbyter or the elder John, whether it be assumed that he is the independent author of the fourth gospel, or the author who had as his authority the apostle himself. The difficulty about the elder John is just this – we *know* nothing whatever about him. We may speculate, we may deduce, we may infer, but we do not *know*. Nor has tradition ever connected him with the gospel. Raymond E. Brown writes (p. xci): 'There is not the slightest positive evidence in antiquity for making John the Presbyter the author of the Fourth Gospel.' It does seem an extremely rash assumption to attribute the high-water mark of New Testament thinking to a man about whom nothing is known but his name, and about whose connection with the fourth gospel tradition is completely silent.

(ii)   The claims of John Mark have been advanced. This is the theory of J.N. Sanders (pp. 44-52). Briefly to recapitulate: Sanders held that there are two beloved disciples, Lazarus of whom the verb *agapan* is used, and Mark of whom the verb *philein* is used. Mark, Sanders believed, was exiled from Jerusalem (*relegatio in insulam*) to Patmos. On release from Patmos he went to Ephesus because it was so near, settled there, attained to a position of leadership, and wrote the Johannine literature, basing the gospel, or at least the latter part of it, on the memoirs of Lazarus. This theory breaks down on the alleged difference between *agapan* and *philein*, on the fact that Mark is no way connected with Ephesus, and on the necessary conclusion, if this is true, that Mark cannot have had anything to do with the second gospel, which bears his name. There are some late traditions about John Mark noted by R.E. Brown (p. xc), which are evidence of confusion in antiquity between John the apostle and John Mark. Acts 12.12 speaks of 'the house of Mary, the mother of John whose other name was Mark', and Chrysostom takes this to refer to John the apostle. A fifth-century Egyptian writer identifies Mark with the unnamed disciple in the incident recorded in John 1.35-42. A sixth-century tradition from Cyprus says that Jesus met John Mark when healing the paralysed man at the Pool of Bethzatha, a story which is told only in the fourth gospel (John 5.1-18). Spanish ecclesiastical writers of the sixth to the eighth centuries identify John the apostle as the relative of Barnabas mentioned in Colossians 4.10. A tenth-century Arabic work, drawing on earlier sources, says that John Mark was one of the servants who handled the water-made-wine at Cana of Galilee (John 2.1-11). No one would claim that this material has any claim to be history, and the tenuous line of tradition which does connect John Mark and John the apostle does not amount to support for Sanders' theory.

(iii) B.W. Bacon assigns the fourth gospel to a complete unknown. He does not believe that either the apostle John or the elder John had anything to do with Ephesus (pp. 78, 106). If the elder was an authority on church tradition Jerusalem would be the natural place for him (p. 452). But, Bacon goes on to suggest, there was an elder in Ephesus as the opening verses of II and III John show. Who was this elder, for it is he who is behind the Johannine literature? Bacon suggests (pp. 207f.) that he may be found in the elder to whom Justin Martyr the one-time philosopher owed his conversion. At the time Justin was studying with a distinguished Platonist, but his doubts were far from being stilled. In his *Dialogue with Trypho* (3) he says:

> I used to go into a certain field not far from the sea. And when I was near that spot one day, and when, once I reached it, I proposed to be by myself, a certain old man, by no means contemptible in appearance, but exhibiting meek and venerable manners followed me at a distance.

The old man resolved Justin's doubts by pointing him to a revelation that Plato never knew, a revelation that made the immortality of the soul not intrinsic but the gift of God – 'To live is not its attribute for it is God's' – and they talked about the prophets who spoke by the divine Spirit far more wisely than the philosophers. Then (ch. 7) the elder continued in language which, Bacon holds, has Johannine echoes:

> For they did not use demonstration in their treatises, seeing that they were witnesses to the truth which is above all demonstration, and worthy of faith: and those events which have happened, and these which are now happening, compel you to assent to the utterances made by them, although indeed they were entitled to credit because of the miracles which they performed, since they both glorified the Creator, the God and Father of all things, and proclaimed his Son the Christ sent by him, which indeed the false prophets who are filled with the lying unclean spirit neither have done or do ... But pray that above all things the gates of light may be opened to you, for these things cannot be perceived or understood by all,

but only by the man to whom God and his Christ have imparted wisdom.

Bacon says that we cannot hold that there was no one in Ephesus to write the fourth gospel when the ancient man could speak like that. So he takes him as the original author of the fourth gospel, which gained a wider circulation and was then edited and redacted into the form in which now we have it. Bacon even 'for convenience' calls the old elder *Theologos* (p. 453). This is not so much a theory as a speculation, which is both completely unprovable and highly improbable.

(iv) We may close the list of candidates by grouping together a number of entirely unlikely candidates mentioned by H.L. Jackson in his book *The Problem of the Fourth Gospel* (pp. 107-110). W. Lock in his article on Ephesians in Hastings' *Dictionary of the Bible* (I, p. 717) remarked that it would be, as he saw it, a tenable view that Ephesians was written by the writer of the fourth gospel writing in the name of Paul. Tobler suggested that the writer of the letter to the Hebrews was the same person as the writer of the fourth gospel, a convert from Judaism, versed in Alexandrian learning, in touch with John the Baptist's disciples and subsequently with John the Apostle. Apollos, Tobler thought, would fit both works.

Lutzelberger suggested that Andrew was the beloved disciple. The gospel, he thinks, was written on the borders of Parthia, where according to legend Andrew and Thomas laboured, probably in Edessa. The evangelist was neither a Jew nor a Greek; he was a Syrian, born in Samaria who had fled with his parents to Edessa as a boy at the outbreak of the Jewish War. He became a Christian and perhaps a bishop and knew Andrew the beloved disciple. He wrote the main fabric of the gospel; another hand finished it and added chapter 21 in Ephesus.

Kreyenbuhl was certain that the author was the beloved disciple, who, he held, is not the apostle, nor a disciple of the apostle, nor the presbyter, nor John the high priest, nor the author of the epistles. The beloved disciple = Lazarus = the sick boy (4.46) = the impotent man (5.5) = the man born blind (9.11) = the author = the Gnostic Menander! An exclamation mark is comment enough on that theory.

E. Iliff Robson suggested that the beloved disciple is Aristion, which is the same as Ariston, which, he says, comes from *aristos*, which means *the best*, and which was a nickname of honour he enjoyed in Ephesus and Smyrna. The author is John Mark; he, not the apostle, spent his old age in Ephesus. As the years passed by Mark grew more and more discontented with his first attempt at a gospel – Mark. He therefore embarked on a spiritual gospel based on deeper reflection and maturer education. He had no eyewitness knowledge of his own, so he turned to Ariston the beloved disciple. Ariston is the witness of 19.35. In Rome Mark was Marcus, but in Ephesus he was known by his Jewish name Johannan – hence the Gospel is called John's. This is surely imagination rather than deduction.

So, after travelling the long way round, it seems to me that in the end there is no better candidate for the authorship of the fourth gospel than John the apostle. That he could not have written it on the grounds of intellectual ability or personal quality is a statement which no one can make as a certainty. That he called himself the disciple whom Jesus loved could be the outcome of astonished humility rather than of pride. That Irenaeus was mistaken is not, and cannot be, proved, and that he led everyone else away on the same mistaken track as himself is next door to incredible. Above all there is the unbroken and almost unwavering tradition, which cannot be lightly disregarded, unless a better candidate for authorship is produced. R.H. Lightfoot wrote in the introduction to his commentary (p. 2): 'This traditional ascription (to the apostle John) still receives support, and has never been shown to be impossible' – and with that verdict I agree.

4

THE DISCOURSES OF THE FOURTH GOSPEL

Even the most casual reader must see the difference between the synoptic gospels and the fourth gospel in regard to the words of Jesus and the form of his teaching. Justin Martyr in his *First Apology* (14) said of Jesus: 'Short (*bracheis*) and pithy (*suntomoi*) are his discourses; no sophist was he.' Writing of the words of Jesus in the fourth gospel Hoskyns and Davey ask (p. 60):

> Where are the sharp, crisp, isolated, aphoristic utterances . . .? Where are those terrifying imperatives?. . . Where are the parables and parabolic sayings? . . . In the synoptic gospels the whole visible panorama of nature and the whole visible business of human behaviour burgeon with a mighty secret yearning to be made known: and in his parables Jesus does manifest this secret or *mystery* (Mark 4.11), thereby conferring upon the smallest and most insignificant occurrences the supreme dignity of the revelation of God.

It is very different in the fourth gospel.

Jülicher thinks the difference so wide that it is inconceivable that the same person could have taught in the style of both the synoptic gospels and the fourth gospel. Everything, he says, prayers and discourses alike, are in the evangelist's language. There are scarcely two or three sentences in common with the sayings of Jesus as given by the synoptists. Instead of the synoptic gospel parables there are colourless allegories and ambiguous metaphors. Instead of pithy, practical wisdom there is theological speculation. Instead of a constant relationship to actual circumstances there is a prevailing character of timelessness. The sole theme of the speaker is himself. Just as unhistorical is the long high-priestly prayer in ch. 17, which could scarcely have been uttered in the presence of the disciples and recorded by them immediately after. There is only one verse in the synoptic gospels which recalls the discourses of the fourth gospel — Matthew 11.27 = Luke 10.22:

> All things have been delivered to me by my Father; and no one knows the Son except the Father, and no one knows the Father except the Son, and anyone to whom the Son chooses to reveal him.

It has to be a choice between the fourth gospel and the synoptic gospels.

For a Jesus who preached alternately in the manner of the Sermon on the Mount and of John 14-16 is a psychological impossibility; the distinction between his so-called exoteric and esoteric teaching is a palpable absurdity ... There may be authentic fragments (e.g. John 16.21f.) ... But the specifically Johannine material, of which chapter 17 is the type, was produced and created by a single brain, and that the brain of the Evangelist (p. 421).

It is quite true that in the fourth gospel there is such a sameness of style that it is sometimes impossible to be certain when Jesus has stopped speaking and when John is speaking in his own person. As Kümmel says in his *Introduction to the NT* (p. 138), in the Nicodemus story, Nicodemus is lost sight of after 3.11; and so uniform is the style that the RSV concludes Jesus' words at 3.15, while the NEB carries them on to 3.21. Further, John's long discourses, as for instance, in chs. 3, 4, 5, 6, 9, 11, grow out of a previous narrative, and they are quite definitely all of a piece, whereas in the synoptic gospels, when a long discourse does occur, as in the case of the sermon on the mount in Matthew 5-7, the discourse is not a unified whole delivered at the one time, but is formed out of a collection of different fragments. In his famous article on John's Gospel in the *Encyclopaedia Britannica*, von Hügel noted how in the synoptic gospels words and actions are only loosely connected, while in John, as we have just noted, deeds and words are inextricably connected, so that 'history tends to become one long allegory'.

Further, not only is there a difference in the form of Jesus' teaching between the synoptic gospels and the fourth gospel, but there is also a difference in atmosphere. The Jesus of the fourth gospel is highly argumentative and by no means conciliatory. F.C. Burkitt in *The Gospel History and its Transmission* (p. 227) puts this very strongly: he says that in the synoptic gospels our sympathies are naturally with Jesus against the Pharisees and Sadducees.

But in the Fourth Gospel it is altogether different. Here I cannot but think that the natural sympathy of the non-Christian reader must go time after time with the Jews. There is an argumentativeness, a tendency to mystification, about the utterances of the Johannine Christ, which, taken as the report of actual words spoken, is positively repellent.

Burkitt takes as an example the difference in the way in which Jesus deals with the sabbath question. In the synoptic gospels in Mark (2.27) he defends his actions by saying that the sabbath was made for man and not man for the sabbath; in Matthew (12.7) he insists that God will have mercy and not sacrifice; in Luke (13.15f.) he says that to loose on the sabbath day a bond by which Satan had bound a daughter of Abraham was as good, and most surely as lawful, as loosing a beast from its stall to take it to drink. But in John 5 it is

Jesus' discourse after healing the impotent man which infuriates the Jews as much as the action, for in that discourse Jesus talks about himself as the special object of his Father's love, of his full and immediate knowledge of the Father, of how his Father has given him the supreme attributes of life and judgment, of how already he is able to give life to whom he will, of how already he judges with righteous judgment, for his judgment is one with the will of God who sent him. He does not bear witness to himself; the Father has already done that. The Jews have never heard the Father's voice, nor seen his form. Like speaks to like and they are not like. 'It is quite inconceivable,' says Burkitt (p. 228), 'that the historical Jesus of the Synoptic Gospels could have argued and quibbled with opponents as he is represented to have done in the Fourth Gospel.'

In the article we have already quoted von Hügel also comments on this change of atmosphere. He talks about the intolerance of Jesus in the fourth gospel (e.g. 8.21, 44; 10.7f.; 15.22), which contrasts strangely with his brooding over Jerusalem (Matt. 23.37-9; Luke 13.34f.), or his 'Father, forgive them' (Luke 23.34). Unquestionably there are these differences, both in form and in atmosphere.

Some people have thought that the writer of the fourth gospel drew his discourse material from a separate sayings source. So it has been suggested[1] that the fourth gospel was originally a 'gospel of signs', containing only narrative, and only one journey from Galilee to Jerusalem, and that this basic material was later expanded with discourses, written earlier, which were then inserted into the original material, and that finally the whole was transformed into a Passion Gospel, although it was never finally completed and revised. Bultmann (p. 7) held that the fourth gospel used a sayings source, which did not originate from Jesus at all, but which was composed of gnostic revelation discourses, emanating from some gnostic group, who may have been disciples of John the Baptist. Bultmann identifies this alleged gnostic-originated source[2] as follows:

1. Logos sayings: 1.1-5, 9-12, 14, 16
2. Flesh and Spirit: 3.6, 8, 11-13, 18, 20, 21, 32-36
3. The water of life: 7.37f.; 4.13f.
4. The bread of life: 6.27, 35, 48, 47, 44f., 37
5. Father, Son and eternal life: 5.17, 19-21, 24f.; 11.25
6. The glory: 5.31f., 39-44; 7.16-18; 8.14, 16, 19; 7.7, 28f.; 8.50, 54f.; 7.33f.; 8.43, 42, 44, 47, 45, 46, 51
7. The light of the world: 8.12; 12.44f.; 9.39; 12. 47-50; 8.23, 28f.; 9.5, 4; 11.9f.; 12.35f.
8. The shepherd-door: 10.11f., 1, 4, 8, 10, 14f., 27-30, 9
9. The coming of the hour: 12.27f., 23, 31f.
10. Freedom through truth: 8.31f., 34f., 38

11. The revelation of glory: 17.1-4-6, 9-17; 13.31f.
12. The vine and the branches: 15.1f., 4-6, 9f., 16
13. The departure of the revealer and the arrival of the Paraclete: 15.18-20, 22, 24, 26; 16.8, 12-14, 16, 20, 22-24, 28; 14.1-7, 9, 14, 16-19, 26f.; (18.37?)

Kümmel doubts this source theory, because (p. 153) he finds the discourses to be thoroughly Johannine in style and thought and to have no sign of coming from an external source.

The discourses follow a standard pattern. Dibelius (*A Fresh Approach to the NT*, p. 97) says: 'By foolish questions and very erroneous misunderstandings the hearers repeatedly give Jesus occasion to state again what he has said, in what might be called a monologue.' So in the Nicodemus story in ch. 3 Jesus makes a statement of the necessity of the new birth from above (v. 3); Nicodemus misunderstands it, taking it in physical terms (v. 4); Jesus tries to clear up the misconception (vv. 5-8); there follows another question (v. 9); Jesus expands his answer (vv. 10-15). In the incidents and discourses in chs. 4 and 6 exactly the same pattern recurs – statement, misunderstanding, fuller restatement, question, expansion.

We are bound to ask how far we may take the discourses to be authentic utterances of Jesus. Streeter (*The Four Gospels*, pp. 369-73) has a full and illuminating treatment of this question, which we now outline. There was a difference between the Jewish and Greek transmission of the teaching of the wise men. The Jewish wise men gave their teaching in vivid, concise, epigrammatic form and the original form was carefully preserved. Originally the teaching tended to be anonymous, as it is in the collections in Proverbs, Ecclesiastes and Wisdom; later the author of Ecclesiasticus, Jesus the son of Sirach, is named by his grandson who edited and transmitted his work, and from then on more and more sayings were preserved under their authors' names. It is in this form that the sayings of Jesus are transmitted in the synoptic gospels, and naturally so, for the teaching was first given to, and preserved by, Jewish communities.

The Greek method was different. We have already quoted (in Vol. I, p. 226) Thucydides' account (1.22) of how he composed his history. Of the speeches which form so significant a part of it he said:

> As to the speeches that were made by different men, either when they were about to begin the war or when they were already engaged therein, it has been difficult to recall with strict accuracy the words actually spoken, both for me as regards that which I myself heard, and for those who from various other sources have brought me reports. Therefore the speeches are given in the language in which, as it seemed to me, the several speakers would express, on the subjects under consideration, the sentiments most befitting the occasion, though at the same time I have

adhered as closely as possible to the general sense of what was actually said.

In other words Thucydides says that he is as accurate as memory and research make it possible for him to be, but he makes no claim to verbal accuracy. And this was for Greek writers a restrained view of the subject, for many Greek historians, when it came to transmitting speeches, made no secret of the fact that the speeches were their own composition.

Plato will give us an even better illustration. Plato owed everything to Socrates, and he spent a long life writing a series of dialogues in which Socrates discusses with people seeking knowledge or with opposing philosophers, but he made no attempt whatever to hand down the *ipsissima verba* of Socrates.

> In most of the series the views which Socrates is represented as expounding are those which Plato himself, at the date of writing a particular dialogue, had come to entertain. Plato attributed his whole philosophical system to the original inspiration of Socrates; and it is probable that in the earlier dialogues the speeches of Socrates, though written in the style and language of Plato, do not inadequately represent opinions entertained by Socrates. But in the later dialogues Plato had developed his system far beyond anything which is at all likely to have been in the mind of the historic Socrates.

John was writing in Ephesus to a Greek audience, trained in Greek literature, familiar with Greek methods.

> The original readers of the Fourth Gospel would never have supposed that the author intended the speeches put into the mouth of Christ to be taken as a verbatim report, or even as a précis, of the actual words spoken by Him on the particular occasions on which they are represented as having been delivered. They would not have supposed that the author meant that the doctrine propounded in these discussions was verbally identical with what was actually taught by Christ in Palestine, but rather that it was organically related to what Christ taught, in such a way as to be the doctrine which Christ would have taught had he been explicitly dealing with the problems confronting the Church at the time the Gospel was written.

John had his own tradition, and on it he had long meditated. 'But what he does give us is not the saying as it came to him, but the saying along with an attempt to bring out all the fulness of meaning which years of meditation had found in it.' Streeter points out that a thing may be given, and yet the means of expression consciously chosen. 'The poet Blake in one passage speaks of a poem as given him by an angel, and then proceeds to give the reason for the choice of a particular metre.'

Streeter sums up the matter. The speeches in John are not like the speeches of the Greek historians, for the speeches in John are the product of the Spirit.

> John knows that they are interpretations of the essentials of Christianity rather than the *ipsissima verba* of the historic Jesus; but they have come to him through the direct inspiration from the risen Christ himself. That is why he insists, 'The Spirit shall lead you into all truth.' John knows quite well that his theology is a development of the original apostolic teaching, but it is a development directly inspired by the Spirit. It is Christ himself, speaking in the Spirit, who says, 'I have many things to tell you but you cannot bear them now.' It is thus he fulfils the promise, 'The Paraclete, when he comes, he shall take of mine, he shall glorify me.' 'Glorify me' can only mean 'lead you to perceive the truth that I am the incarnation of the Word'. John had reached this conclusion; but he believed that he had reached it, not by his own intellectual efforts, but by direct revelation of the Spirit of Jesus.

In other words, John claims that his interpretation is the work of the Spirit, and therefore – a point to which we will return – the discourses must be classified with prophecy rather than with history or biography.

At various times the attempt has been made to explain the differences between the synoptic gospels and the fourth gospel by holding that they are both the teaching of Jesus, but that they represent different kinds of his teaching, given in different contexts and in different circumstances. Westcott writes in his commentary (pp. lxxxf.):

> There is no scene in St John which answers to those under which the Sermon on the Mount, or the chief groups of parables were delivered; and conversely there are no scenes in the Synoptists like those with Nicodemus and the woman of Samaria. . . . On the one hand is the Gospel of the common people who heard him gladly; on the other is the Gospel of such as felt the deeper necessities and difficulties of faith.

In contrast to the gospel of the crowd we have the gospel of the individual, or of the dedicated group (e.g. chs. 3, 4, 9, 14-17). It has even at times been suggested that Jesus was a trained rabbi. That he was a carpenter would not render this at all unlikely, for every rabbi had to have a trade by which he made his living, since he was not allowed to take money for teaching. And then it is suggested that in the synoptics we see Jesus teaching 'popularly', and in the fourth gospel we see him teaching 'rabbinically'. It may not unfairly be said that this kind of approach to the fourth gospel is as convincing or unconvincing as most efforts at harmonization are.

Let us now look at certain things the discourses have been said to be and to do.

(i) B.H. Streeter (pp. 365f.) said of the whole gospel that it is 'an

inspired meditation on the life of Christ'. There is no doubt that it
would be right to call the discourses inspired meditations. Streeter
further said that in his opinion the fourth gospel belongs neither to
history nor to biography, but to 'the Library of Devotion'. He went on
to say (p. 371) that John, like Paul, was a 'Christocentric mystic', but
that he lived longer and meditated more than Paul. It is also not
unimportant to remember that the fourth gospel did not have 'the
hectic background' of the Pauline letters, the day-to-day struggle with
active hostility which Paul had to carry on, and so John was able to
give 'a simpler, clearer, and, in a sense, calmer expression to his creed'.
From the point of view of devotion, E.J. Goodspeed in his
Introduction to the NT (pp. 301f.) ranks the fourth gospel with the
Psalms. There is nothing equal to it in Paul; Paul is too argumentative.
There is nothing like it in the synoptic gospels; the sermon on the
mount is too didactic. But he says of John 14-17 in particular: 'Of all
New Testament literature [these chapters] alone possess that great
devotional quality.' The fourth gospel in a unique way unites the
intellectual and the mystical. So then in the first place the discourses
are meditations on Christ.

(ii) The discourses are explanation and interpretation. R.H.
Lightfoot speaks (p. 28) of 'the large interpretative element in the
fourth gospel', and calls John 'the interpreter of the synoptists' (p. 34).
He thinks that the fourth gospel presupposes the synoptic gospels. He
asks whether, if John had thought his gospel the only gospel, he would
have written as he did. Would he really have left out any account of
the institution of the Lord's Supper, for example, if he was not well
aware than the account was there already? He continues (p. 32):

> It seems that St John's gospel, if considered by itself, in isolation, is a
> riddle; but that if it is regarded as the crown and completion of our gospel
> records, it falls forthwith into place.

Its position, the very fact that it comes fourth, means that the others
have to be read first, before the reader comes to it. Holtzmann writes:

> Originally Jesus spoke in a way that the disciples did not understand. The
> discourses are the result of thought and meditation on things not
> originally understood ... It was the Christian consciousness, stirred by
> reflection, and enlightened by the Spirit, which evolved the speeches.[3]

J.N. Sanders' way of putting it (pp. 13f.) is that what is implicit in the
synoptic gospels becomes explicit in the fourth gospel, in particular
Jesus' claim to be Messiah. To this we shall return. On this view the
fourth gospel develops and interprets the other three.

(iii) There is another way in which to put this – the fourth gospel,
and especially the discourses, are based under the guidance of the
Spirit on the developing experience of the church. Percy Gardner
writes in *The Ephesian Gospel* (p. 335):

Though the Fourth Gospel contains valuable historic material, yet, what is its main treasure, the speeches of the Lord contained in it, belongs not to the life-time of the Founder, but to the early experiences of the Church.

G.H.C. Macgregor (p. xxvii) looks upon the fourth gospel as 'interpretation in the light of personal religious experience', and that is specially true of the discourses. E.J. Goodspeed says (p. 307): 'The writer has ... read back the Jesus of experience into the Jesus of history.' And again (p. 309), 'The Gospel of John is a charter of Christian experience. For the evangelist, to know Christ through inner experience matters more than to have seen him face to face in Galilee.' 'Blessed are those who have not seen yet believe' (John 20.9). There is therefore in the fourth gospel what Burkitt calls 'a sovereign freedom in remodelling'. And he goes on to quote J.A. Robinson:

The old disciple needs no documents ... The whole is present in his memory, shaped by years of reflection, illuminated by the experience of a life-time. He knows the Christ far better now than he knew him in Galilee or Jerusalem half a century before.[4]

Memory, experience, thought, meditation, all under the control of the Spirit combined to write these discourses.

(iv) We now return to a matter on which we previously touched. If the discourses of the fourth gospel are all this, then they are to be regarded as the work of a prophet. They are material which it would be quite correct to introduce with the words: 'Thus saith the Lord.' E.J. Goodspeed writes (p. 368):

To ignore the phenomenon of prophecy is to study the Fourth Gospel apart from its environment. And, for myself, I must say that the more I read the discourses of the Fourth Gospel, the more it is borne in upon me that its author was regarded by himself, and by the Church for which he wrote, as an inspired prophet.

J.N. Sanders writes more fully (p. 16):

The clue to the understanding of the form of the Johannine teaching attributed to Jesus may be that the material in the fourth gospel consisted originally of sermons, preached by a man who was a Christian prophet, whose words were as truly 'words of the Lord' as those spoken by Jesus beside the Sea of Galilee or in the upper room. In his sermons the prophet not only quoted what we mean by 'the words of the Lord', but also paraphrased and adapted them. In John 16.14, which refers to the Spirit taking what is Christ's and telling it to the disciples, we have the explanation and justification of the way in which the prophet handles the teaching of Jesus. He would no doubt have regarded the scruples of the modern critic as miserable pedantry.

Thus in John 6 the feeding of the five thousand becomes a 'text' for a Passover sermon, and John 13 becomes a sermon on the other sacrament, the washing of the disciples' feet being the text. The narrative units become sermon *texts* rather than sermon *illustrations*.

There is something of real value in this view, something which no one who believes in the Holy Spirit can totally discard.

(v)   But it may well be that the thing that most strikes anyone who reads the speeches is the unsurpassable height of the claims which Jesus makes in them. Von Hügel in the *Encyclopaedia Britannica* article says that the speeches of the fourth gospel talk of Jesus' person and work with 'a didactic directness, philosophical terminology, and denunciatory exclusiveness' unmatched in the synoptic gospels. R.H. Lightfoot rightly says (p. 40) that in the fourth gospel it was not what Jesus did that led to his crucifixion, but what he claimed to be; and, of course, the claims are most prominent in the discourses. Lightfoot goes on to point out how, as his ministry went on, and when it drew near its close, Jesus' claims became higher and higher. 'Before Abraham was I am' (8.58). When the man who was blind asks who the Son of man is, Jesus answers: 'It is he who speaks to you' (9.35-37). 'I and the Father are one' (10.30). And in the incident which in the fourth gospel is the spark which kindles the final explosion, Jesus claims to be Lord even over death (11.25f.). 'I am the resurrection and the life; he who believes in me, though he may die, yet shall he live, and whoever lives and believes in me shall never die.' E.J. Goodspeed (p. 307) says of Jesus in the fourth gospel: 'He does not teach in parables, and his teaching deals, not as in the other Gospels with the Kingdom of God, but with his own nature and his inward relation with God.' In his debates with the Jews he defends his union with the father, his pre-existence, his sinlessness.

In these speeches Jesus talks of his right to judgment (3.16-21); of how he alone can satisfy the thirst of the soul (4.7-15); of how his Father has delegated all things to him (5.19-47); of how he alone can satisfy the hunger of the soul with the living bread which is himself (6.25-59); of how he is the light of the world, and how men are judged by their reaction to him, and of his special and unique relationship with the Father (8.12-58); of the fact that he and the Father are one (10.22-39); of his possession of the life which death is powerless to touch (11.25f.); of how to hate him is to hate God (15.18-27); of how he came from glory and goes to glory which he can share with his own (ch. 17).

But there is one supreme claim in these discourses, a claim not made in so many words, but made by the use of an expression which for the world of Jesus' time made it unmistakable. R.M. Grant in his *Historical Introduction to the NT* (p. 149) points out that in the fourth gospel Jesus uses the word 'I' 120 times; that the Father is identified as 'he who sent me' 26 times; that there are 120 references to God as Father, not so much of men as of Jesus. The particular point which we wish to stress here is the way in which Jesus uses the expression 'I am', *egō eimi* in Greek.

Of course 'I am' can be quite colourless, as in 'I am Joseph' (Gen. 45.3); 'I am Jesus whom you are persecuting' (Acts 9.5). But in the Old Testament there is a special and widespread use of 'I am', *egō eimi*, on the lips of God. It is what has been called 'the style of deity'.[5] It is used on occasions when the language is intended to be deeply impressive. So in the Greek Old Testament we have: 'I am your God' (Gen. 17.1); 'I am the Lord your healer' (Ex. 15.26); 'I am your deliverance' (Ps. 35.3); 'I am the Lord who loves justice' (Isa. 61.8). In cases of special stress the phrase is doubled, *egō eimi, egō eimi*, which in English is usually translated 'I, I am he'. 'I, I am he (*egō eimi, egō eimi*) that comforts you' (Isa. 51.12). 'I, I am he (*egō eimi, egō eimi*) who blots out your transgressions' (Isa. 43.25).

This language of deity comes into the New Testament, and again on the lips of God. 'I am the Alpha and the Omega' (Rev. 1.8). 'I am ... the first and the last, the beginning and the end' (Rev. 22.13). So then 'I am', *egō eimi*, is the standard language of deity in the Old Testament, and in the fourth gospel it is constantly on the lips of Jesus:

I am the bread of life (6.35).
I am the light of the world (8.12).
I am the door of the sheep (10.7, 9).
I am the good shepherd (10.11).
I am the resurrection and the life (11.25).
I am the way, the truth and the life (14.6).
I am the real vine (15.1).

This 'I am' of deity is equally common in pagan liturgical language. 'I am,' says Isis, 'the eldest daughter of Kronos. I am she who amongst women is called god.'[6] 'I am all that has been, and is, and will be.'[7] For Jew, for Christian and for pagan alike 'I am' is the typical speech of God.

In the Greek Old Testament there occurs a use of *egō eimi*, 'I am' with no predicate at all, which is usually translated, 'I, even I am he'.

See now that I, even I, am He, and there is no god beside me (Deut. 32.39).

That you may know and understand that I am He (Isa. 43.10).

Even to old age I am He (Isa. 46.4).

This use of 'I am' with no predicate is never found in the Old Testament on the lips of anyone but God. It too occurs in the fourth gospel, in the discourses.

Before Abraham was, I am (8.58).

You will die in your sins, unless you believe that I am He (8.24; in Greek simply *egō eimi*, 'I am', with no word for 'He').

When you have lifted up the Son of man, then you will know that I am He (8.28; again simply *egō eimi*, 'I am').

It is entirely probable that this expression goes back to the name of God in Exodus 3.14: 'I am who I am', which in the Greek Old Testament is translated: 'I am he who is.'

However we look at this 'I am' it is the language of deity; it is God speaking, and in the discourses of the fourth gospel that is the way in which Jesus speaks. The inescapable conclusion is that in the discourses deity is being claimed for Jesus.

We can be fairly certain that Jesus did not make these claims for himself, at least not in the way in which the discourses make them. What we have here is not the precise words which Jesus spoke, but that which the Christian church discovered and knew him, under the guidance of the Spirit, to be. If we go back to the account in the Muratorian Canon of the way in which the fourth gospel was written, it will shed a flood of light on the matter. The Muratorian Canon[8] says:

> The fourth book of the Gospels is that of John, one of the disciples. When his fellow-disciples and bishops urged him he said: 'Fast together with me today for three days and, what shall be revealed to each, let us tell it to each other.' On the same night it was revealed to Andrew, one of the Apostles, that, with all of them reviewing it, John should describe all things in his own name.

The picture is that, when John was near the end, the church wanted him to write down his memories of the earthly days of Jesus, lest they be lost. So after they had slept on it, it was decided that John should do so, 'with all of them reviewing it'. All this happened in Ephesus nearly seventy years after Jesus had died on the cross. John and his friends must have been very old men; and for all their long lives they had lived in the presence of their risen Lord, and had remembered him and thought about him under the guidance of the Holy Spirit. So they sat down together. One of them would say: 'Do you remember how he said this or that?' And the answer would come: 'Yes, and now we know what he meant.' And down would go not only the saying, but also the meaning of it. The Spirit was indeed teaching them; the Spirit was indeed bringing all things to remembrance (John 14.26); the Spirit indeed was taking what was Jesus' truth and declaring it to them (John 16.12-15); the Spirit was indeed saying to them the things which seventy years ago they could not have taken in. Now they were able to set down not only what Jesus said, but also what Jesus meant. W.M. Macgregor has a sermon on the title 'What Jesus Christ becomes to a man who has known him long'; that might well be the title of the fourth gospel. Wordsworth's famous definition of poetry was: 'Emotion recollected in tranquillity'; that is precisely what the fourth gospel is. In a special double sense the fourth gospel is the gospel of the Holy Spirit; it gives the reader not only what Christ *said*, but also what Christ *was still saying*. The discourses are not composed of words that Jesus once said; they are composed of words which by his Spirit he was still saying. The discourses are not words of the earthly Jesus, but they are words of the risen Christ.

It will be appropriate to take in here what von Hügel said of the fourth gospel in his *Encyclopaedia Britannica* article. He said that the whole character of the fourth gospel depends on four great tendencies.

(i)   There is everywhere present a readiness 'to handle historical materials with a sovereign freedom', and yet a freedom controlled and limited by doctrinal convictions and by devotional experiences.

(ii)   There is everywhere the mystic's deep love for double and even treble meanings. In John 3.3 for instance, to be born *anothen* can equally well mean 'to be born anew' or 'to be born from above'. When Judas went out from the last supper, there come in John 13.30 the starkly dramatic words: 'And it was night' – night by the clock, night by the light of the sun, and night for the soul.

(iii)   Everywhere there is the influence of certain central ideas, partly identical with, but even more developments of, those same ideas less 'reflectively operative' in the synoptic gospels. There are six of these dominant ideas. *(a)* The idea of Jesus as the only-begotten Son; *(b)* the conception of Jesus as the Logos; *(c)* the conception of Jesus as the light of the world; *(d)* the idea of the Paraclete, the Helper, the Teacher, the Intercessor; *(e)* the idea of truth and knowing the truth, in the sense of discovering reality *(f)* and above all the idea of eternal life, the very life of God, which takes the place the kingdom has in the synoptic gospels.

(iv)   And finally, there is everywhere 'a striving to contemplate history *sub specie aeternitatis* and to englobe the successiveness of man in the simultaneity of God'. This is true of the whole gospel, but it is truest of the discourses.

5

THE AIMS AND PURPOSES OF THE FOURTH GOSPEL

Of the greatness of the fourth gospel there has never been any doubt. F.C. Burkitt in *The Gospel History* (p. 218) writes of 'the immense influence which this work has had for century after century'. 'No work,' he goes on, 'could hold so great a place before the world so long without intrinsic merit of an extraordinary sort.' We must now try to find out the aims and the purposes which prompted this extraordinary work.

One thing is certain – many of the motives which move most authors to write would not apply to John. He would not write simply to see his name in print.

> 'Tis pleasant sure to see one's name in print;
> A book's a book, although there's nothing in't.[1]

He would not write for literary fame or prestige. He would not write to propagate his own opinions. He would not write for royalties. The ordinary motives would not be there. Why then did John write?

(i) ' To put the matter at its simplest, Chrysostom said (in his *Homily* 88.2 *on John*) that love was the essential motive which made John write. Origen has the same idea. M.F. Wiles in *The Spiritual Gospel* (p. 10) says:

> Origen finds this most vividly portrayed in the picture of John reclining at supper on the bosom of Jesus. Just as it is the fact that the only-begotten Son is 'in the bosom of the Father' that constitutes him able to reveal God to men, so John's reclining on the bosom of Jesus symbolises his ability to declare the deepest truths of the Gospel.

So then at the simplest level – which is also the deepest level – it was love which wrote the fourth gospel.

(ii) Because of the love that lies behind it the fourth gospel is written, if one may put it so, in defence of Jesus. Characteristically it is neither history nor biography; it belongs, in Streeter's phrase (*The Four Gospels*, p. 365), to 'the Library of Devotion'. It begins with an experience of Jesus, which, even if it began with an historical and physical experience, has far surpassed that. Goodspeed in his *Introduction to the NT* (p. 309) says: 'The Gospel of John is a charter of Christian experience. For the evangelist, to know Christ through inner experience matters more than to have seen him face to face in

Galilee.' That experience has ended in a conviction which the author wants everyone to share. R.H. Lightfoot in his commentary (p. 33) says: 'John is seeking to produce in his readers a conviction about the person of the Lord which he is convinced is true.' Stanton in *The Gospels as Historical Documents* (III, p. 4) quotes Baur about what he calls 'the master-thought' of the Fourth Gospel:

> The manifestation of the Divine Logos in the person of Jesus, through which a separation is effected among men according as by their belief in him or their unbelief they show themselves to be children of light or darkness, while the faith even of those who believed, containing as it did an element akin to unbelief in so far as it needed the support of external signs, had to undergo a process of purification.

So Jülicher in his *Introduction to the NT* (pp. 424f.) finds the fourth gospel defending Jesus against the Jews. Beneath the surface their attack can be discerned. 'They had ransacked the whole history of Jesus to discredit him.' Had not John the Baptist baptized Jesus? And to the Jew the earlier is the greater. He had driven out evil spirits; but so did the sons of the Pharisees: Jesus himself had said so. He had chosen a band of men; he had looked on the traitor as a friend until the last minute; and to a man they forsook him and denied him. He did not dare to go to Jerusalem, the true home of the Messiah, because he could not subdue the wise of that great city, as he had the foolish mobs of Galilee, with a few high-sounding speeches. When at last he did make the venture he was quickly awakened from his giddy dream of kingship, and died in despair on a cross. This was Jewish anti-propaganda, and if the Christians denied it, the Jews would say: 'Look at your own record.' A *true* Christ was needed, 'the Christ from whose majesty the darts of Jewish calumny must glance harmlessly aside'. And so, says Jülicher, John presents the Christ of pre-existence, the Christ of foreknowledge, the Christ of self-determining free-will. Love springs to the defence of the loved one. To quote M.F. Wiles again (p. 11):

> Theodore [of Mopsuestia] states that the Christians of Asia recognized that the omission of certain miracles and certain elements of teaching, might lead in future generations to men losing sight of Christ's divinity. It was to rule out the possibility of any such misapprehensions in the future that John undertook the task of writing. Cyril gives a very similar account of the Gospel's origin and purpose. The only difference is that the danger of false teaching is not future but already present. The eternal generation of the Son and the pre-existence of the Logos are already being attacked in John's own life-time. John's purpose is therefore a full and careful statement of Christ's divinity, in correction both of present and of future heresies.

Undoubtedly one of the aims of the fourth gospel is the defence of

Jesus by a man who had experienced the uniqueness of the Son.

(iii) It has been suggested that the fourth gospel was written in order to preserve an independent line of tradition in regard to both the facts of the life of Jesus and his teaching. There have been those who believed that the fourth gospel is basically commentary on the first three. A.J.B. Higgins in *The Historicity of the Fourth Gospel* (pp. 12f.) summarizes this view (though not agreeing with it): Without the first three gospels the fourth gospel 'would have been as useless to the original readers as a biblical commentary without the scriptural text'. R.H. Lightfoot assumes a very close connection between the synoptic gospels and the fourth gospel. John, he says, did not try either to supplement or to supersede the other gospels. He aimed to interpret them and to draw out the significance of the original events. 'Without St John's gospel the earlier gospels are largely a puzzle, an unsolved problem, to which his gospel is designed to offer the key' (p. 34).

But the view that the fourth gospel is an independent production has its supporters.[2] Barnabas Lindars is at least willing to consider the view that the fourth gospel took some time to write, that it may have been begun in the early eighties of the first century and may have taken ten years or more to reach its final form. This could mean that the fourth gospel was begun *before* Luke's gospel was begun. This could mean that the fourth gospel is founded on sources identical with, or parallel to, or independent of the sources of the synoptic gospels. It is true that the fourth gospel does possess all kinds of additional information; it is there we meet Nicodemus (3.1-21) and the woman of Samaria (4.1-42); it is there we find the miracles of the paralysed man at the pool (5.1-18) and of the man born blind (ch. 9); it is there that we read the story of Lazarus (11.1-53); it is there that Andrew comes alive (1.40-42; 6.8f.; 12.22) (it is a surprising fact that in the miracle of the feeding of the five thousand, it is only John who mentions the boy who supplied the loaves and fishes); it is there that Thomas's personality emerges (11.16; 20.24-29); it is there that we have the footwashing at the last supper (13.1-11).

As we gather up these independent traditions, which are preserved only in the fourth gospel, we may notice too, with G.H.C. Macgregor (p. xxii), how rich the fourth gospel is in sheer drama. There is the moment when Jesus declares his messiahship to the Samaritan woman (4.26). There is the moment when Judas leaves the upper room to complete his terrible work. It is impossible to read the stark words, 'And it was night' (13.30) without a shudder. There is the meeting of Mary Magdalene with the risen Christ in the garden (20.11-18), which has been called the greatest recognition scene in all literature. There is not only drama; there is dramatic irony. There is Peter's boast that he will lay down his life for Jesus (13.37). There is the saying of Caiaphas that it is expedient that one man should die for the people (11.49-52).

some, but it is not necessary to see in the prologue an original hymn of the Baptist community.

(vi)   The early commentators on the fourth gospel believed that it was specially directed against two heresies. Jerome writes (*On Famous Men*, 9): 'When asked by the bishops of Asia John wrote a gospel against Cerinthus and other heretics, especially against the dogma of the Ebionites, which sprang up at that time.' And in the preface to his *Commentary on Matthew* he says that John was in Asia, when the seeds of the heretics Cerinthus and Ebion were shooting up. What then was the position of Cerinthus and of Ebion?

Let us first look at Cerinthus.[4] Irenaeus records the beliefs of Cerinthus:

> Cerinthus, again, a man who was educated in the wisdom of the Egyptians, taught that the world was not made by the primary God, but by a certain power far separated from him, and at a distance from that Authority who is supreme over the universe, and ignorant of the God who is above all. He represented Jesus as not having been born of a virgin, but as being the son of Joseph and Mary according to the ordinary course of human generation, while he was nevertheless more righteous, prudent, and wise than other men. Moreover, after his baptism, Christ descended upon him in the form of a dove from the Supreme Ruler, and then he proclaimed the unknown Father, and performed miracles. But at last Christ departed from Jesus, and that then Jesus suffered and rose again, while Christ remained impassible, inasmuch as he was a spiritual being.

Here we are face to face with thought which is basically gnostic and we cannot understand it or see its place in the fourth gospel, until we have seen the basic beliefs of Gnosticism. R.E. Brown in his commentary (p. liii) reduces Gnosticism to its barest essentials:

> All can recognize common patterns in developed Gnosticism: for example, ontological dualism; intermediary beings between God and man; the agency of these beings in producing the evil, material world; the soul as a divine spark imprisoned in matter; the necessity of knowledge gained through revelation in order to free the soul and lead it to light; the numerical limitation of those capable of receiving the revelation; the saving revealer.

The aim of Gnosticism is to explain evil. 'The Gnostic view of the world,' says Bultmann in his commentary (p. 7), 'starts out from a strict cosmic dualism.' The two opposing principles are matter and spirit. Matter and spirit are co-eternal. Matter is essentially and irremediably bad. Out of this flawed matter the world was made. This has certain consequences.

(*a*)   Matter is essentially bad; spirit is essentially good. This means that spirit cannot touch matter. There is an inevitable consequence for the process of creation. The world cannot have been created by the true God, who is pure spirit. In order to get at matter the true God, the God of pure spirit, put out a series of aeons or emanations. Each emanation was further from the true God, and more ignorant of the true God. As the chain went on a stage was reached where the aeons were not only distant from and ignorant of the true God, but also hostile to him. And so at the end of the line there is the creating God, the Demiurge, ignorant of and hostile to the real God. This is what Cerinthus said; the world was created by 'a certain power far separated' from the true God.

The fourth gospel will have none of this. It was the Word who was God's creating agent. The Word was with God; what God was the Word was; without him was not anything made that was made (1.1-5). The fourth gospel begins with a counterblast against the gnostic doctrine of creation.

  (b) Gnostic dualism has repercussions on the idea of incarnation. If matter is essentially evil, the Word cannot have become flesh. Jesus therefore could not have had a body; he was only a phantom in human form. The Gnostic *Acts of John* (89-93) tell that the appearance of Jesus was constantly changing; his eyes were never seen to close in the blink that is characteristic of the human eye; if he was touched, there was nothing to touch; when he walked he left no footprint on the ground. Either, as in the *Acts of John*, Jesus never ate at all, or, according to Valentinus: 'He ate and drank in a peculiar manner, not evacuating his food. So much power of continence was in him that in him food was not corrupted, since he himself had no corruptibility.'[5] Tertullian, writing *Against Marcion* (3.8), speaks of what was for him 'the incredibility of an incarnate God', which forced him to reject 'the bodily substance of Christ'.

This is what is known as Docetism. The Greek verb *dokein* means 'to seem', and Docetism is 'seemism', the teaching that Jesus only *seemed* to have a body, that he was no more than an insubstantial phantom in a human form.

It is the most dangerous of all heresies, for it is born of – if the phrase be allowed – a mistaken reverence. It will not take the incarnation seriously; it cannot believe that it is possible for God to assume humanity. It was specially dangerous in the ancient world, for that world had a deep suspicion of the body. *Soma sema*, said the Orphic jingle, the body is a tomb.[6] The body, said Philolaus, is the house of detention in which the soul is imprisoned to expiate its sins.[7] Plato said that the philosopher must despise the body; philosophy is nothing more than the study of dying and being dead. Pure knowledge is not possible so long as the body is with us. The soul must strive to be free from the body as from the fetters of a prison-house (*Phaedo*, 64-7). The body is a tomb and the soul is buried in this present life (*Cratylus*, 400 B,C). Man is a poor soul shackled to a corpse, said

Epictetus.[8] Seneca in his *Letters* (92.10) speaks of the detestable habitation of the body, and of the *inutilis caro*, the vain flesh, in which the soul is imprisoned, while it longs for its celestial home. Augustine said no more than the truth, when he said that he went step by step through the prologue of the fourth gospel, and found in the ancient philosophers everything there except one thing – 'The Word was made flesh, and dwelt among us, I read not there' (*Confessions*, 7.9).

John will have none of this. 'The Word became flesh' (1.14). He shows us Jesus exhausted by the well of Samaria as any man might be (4.6); tortured with thirst on the cross as any man might be (19.28); bleeding when he was pierced as any human body would bleed (19.34). F.C. Burkitt writes in *The Gospel History* (p. 233): 'In no early Christian document is the real humanity of Jesus so emphasised as in the Fourth Gospel. That Jesus was a real man is an obvious inference from the Synoptic narrative, but in the Fourth Gospel it is a dogma.'

There is one very definite reference to this in the First Letter of John. We have seen how Cerinthus thought of the divine Christ entering the man Jesus at the Baptism and leaving him again before his death on the cross. In support of this, two texts were quoted, the variant reading in Luke 3.22, 'Thou art my beloved Son; today I have begotten thee,' and Mark 15.34, 'My God, my God, why hast thou forsaken me?' in I John 4.2f. we read:

> By this you know the Spirit of God; every spirit which confesses that Jesus Christ has come in the flesh is of God; and every spirit which does not confess Jesus is not of God.

The meaning is that every spirit who confesses that Jesus is Christ come in the flesh is of God; and the spirit who does not confess this is not. But in the second half of the verse there is a variant: 'Every spirit which does not confess (variant reading Greek: *luei*; Latin: *solvit*; English, 'dissolves') Jesus is not of God.' Every spirit who *dissolves* Jesus – that is exactly what the heretics did. They drew a distinction between the human Jesus and the divine Christ; and they said that the divine Christ came into Jesus and then left Jesus; they dissolved the unity of the human and the divine which was in Jesus Christ.

So John insists on the humanity of Jesus, of Christ come in the flesh.

But these heretics had another closely connected belief. They believed that the divine Christ left the human Jesus, because they believed that the Divine One could not and must not suffer. They produced the most fantastic theories. Basilides was one of the great Gnostic thinkers. He spoke of God sending the first-begotten mind, who is called Christ, to earth. Then he goes on:

> He appeared on earth as a man, to the nations of these powers, wrought miracles. Wherefore he did not himself suffer death, but a certain Simon

of Cyrene bore the cross in his stead; Simon was transfigured by him, that he might be thought to be Jesus, and was crucified through ignorance and error, while Jesus himself received the form of Simon, and, standing by, laughed at them. For since he was an incorporeal power, and the mind of the unborn Father, he transfigured himself as he pleased, and thus ascended to him who had sent him, deriding them, inasmuch as he could not be laid hold of, and was invisible to all.[9]

Again John will have none of it; Jesus is crucified; Jesus dies.

The Gnostics produced a world created by an ignorant, distant hostile God, a botched job; they produced a Jesus, who was no more than a phantom in human form, and so destroyed the incarnation; they produced a Jesus who evaded suffering by a trick, and so destroyed the atonement. No wonder that the fourth gospel goes into battle against them.

(c) Before we come to the third consequence of Gnosticism and the mark that it has left on the fourth gospel, we must look at Gnosticism as a whole, and especially at the basic gnostic myth. To that end we shall set down two summaries of the gnostic position. The first is van Unnik's summary:

i.   The true, perfect God is unknown: he is not the Creator of this world of imperfection.
ii.   The imperfect world is produced by an imperfect God.
iii.   The true and essential being of Man belongs to and with the perfect God, but through some unaccountable mischance finds itself situated in this imperfect world and subjected to the powers of this world.
iv.   Through knowledge of himself and through awareness of his separation from God, the Absolute Perfection, Man must be set free from the tyranny of evil and return to the world of the true God.[10]

At the first two statements of this summary we have already looked; at the last two we must look a little more closely. To do so we set down Bultmann's summary of the gnostic myth:

The Gnostic myth recounts – with manifold variations – the fate of the soul. It tells of its origin in the world of light, of its tragic fall and its life as an alien on earth, its imprisonment in the body, its deliverance and final ascent and return to the world of light. The soul – or more accurately in the language of Gnosticism itself, man's true, inner self – is a part, splinter, or spark of a heavenly figure of light, the original man. Before all time this figure was conquered by the demonic powers of darkness, though how that came to pass is a point on which the various mythologies differ. These powers tore the figure of light into shreds and divided it up, and the elements of light thus produced were used by the demons as cohesive magnetic powers which were needed in order to create a world out of the chaos of darkness as a counterpart of the world of light, of which they were jealous. If these elements of light were removed, this artificial world of ours, the cosmos, would return to its primordial state of chaos. Therefore the demons jealously watch over the sparks of light which they stole. Naturally, interest is concentrated on these sparks of light, which are inclosed in man and represent his innermost self. The demons endeavour to stupefy them and make them drunk, sending them to sleep and making them forget their heavenly home. Sometimes their attempt succeeds, but in other cases the consciousness of their heavenly origin remains awake. They know they are in an alien world, and that this world is their prison, and hence their yearning for deliverance. The supreme deity takes pity on the imprisoned sparks of light, and sends down the heavenly figure of light, his Son, to redeem them. This Son arrays himself in the garment of the earthly body, lest the demons should recognize him. He invites his own to join him, awakens them from their sleep, reminds them of their heavenly home, and teaches them about the way to return. His chief task is to pass on the pass-words which are needed on the journey back. For the souls must pass the different spheres of the planets, the watch-posts of the demonic cosmic powers. The Gnostic redeemer delivers discourses in which he reveals himself as God's emissary: 'I am the shepherd', 'I am the truth', and so forth. After accomplishing his work, he ascends and returns to heaven again to prepare a way for his own to follow him. This they will do when they die and the spark is severed from the prison of the body. His work is to assemble all the sparks of light. That is the work he has inaugurated, and it will be completed when all the sparks of light have been set free and have ascended to heaven to rejoin the one body of the figure of light who in primordial times fell, was imprisoned and torn to shreds. When the process is complete, this world will come to an end, and return to its original chaos. The darkness is left to itself, and that is the judgment.[11]

There are two things to be said about this gnostic myth. The word 'gnostic' is from *gnosis*, which means knowledge; and here is the knowledge. To be saved a man must first be roused to know what he is, a spark of divinity imprisoned in a material body, which is the tomb from which he must escape. After it has been awakened, the soul must then acquire the knowledge, learn the pass-words, which will enable it to pass the various barriers in the return journey to heaven.

This demands the ability to learn. Not every man has this ability. And so the Gnostic divides men into three classes – the *hulikoi*, the material, who cannot learn at all, the *psychikoi*, those who have physical life and who can get some way on the journey, the *pneumatikoi*, the spiritual, who alone are capable of the learning which will take them the whole way. Gnosticism therefore inevitably ends in an intellectual élite; salvation, heaven, life are for the few.

Once again the fourth gospel will have none of this. It is *the world* that God loves (3.16); it is *every man* whom the light lightens (1.9); it is *all men* whom Jesus will draw to himself (12.32); it is of *the world* that Jesus is the Saviour (4.42). The exclusiveness of Gnosticism is met with the universality of Christianity.

And yet the fact remains that there is a similarity between the thought of Gnosticism and the thought of the fourth gospel. There is the same contrast between light and dark. 'He who comes from above is above all' (John 3.31). The Son of man is the one who has descended from heaven and who has ascended back to heaven (3.13) – the only one to do so. He came from glory and he returns to glory (17.15). Bultmann in his commentary (e.g. pp. 7-9) would go the length of saying that the Johannine discourses come from a gnostic sayings source. It is early oriental Gnosticism. 'The Prologue's source belongs to the sphere of a relatively early oriental Gnosticism, which has been developed under the influence of the OT faith in the Creator-God' (p. 30).

John is far from being a Gnostic in the technical and pagan and heretical sense of the term; but it is certain that a man who was a Gnostic would have known what the fourth gospel was talking about.

We saw that Jerome said that the gospel of John was written not only against Cerinthus, but also against the Ebionites. Who then were the Ebionites, and what were their beliefs?

The word *ebion* is the Hebrew word for poor; the Ebionites were the poor Christians; they were the Jewish Christians, and they traced themselves back to the experiment in Christian communism of which we read in Acts 4.34-37.

But many other interpretations were given of their name. Origen (*On First Principles*, 4.1.22) said that they were called poor, because they were poor in their understanding of the Christian faith, and that the word referred to the poverty of their intellect. He also said, in his book *Against Celsus* (2.1), that the Ebionites had adhered to their Jewish faith instead of fully embracing the gospel, and the name referred to the poverty of the law as contrasted with the wealth of the gospel. Eusebius in his *History* (3.27.1) took a similar line; he said that they were quite properly called Ebionites because 'they had poor and mean opinions concerning Christ'. In course of time the name came to be derived from an original founder called Ebion, who, of course, never existed. Tertullian speaks of those in Galatia who observed and defended circumcision and the Mosaic law. 'There runs Hebion's heresy,' he says. He speaks of Ebion, who held Jesus to be a mere man and nothing more than a descendant of David and not also the Son of God. He says that the virgin birth ensures that Jesus is not only Son of man, but also Son of God, and that he is not merely another Solomon or Jonah. He says that Ebion was the successor of Cerinthus.[12]

What then were the beliefs of the Ebionites? Irenaeus in his book *Against Heresies* (1.26.2) describes their beliefs as follows:

Those who are called Ebionites agree that the world was made by God [i.e. in contrast to Cerinthus with his belief in the inferior creating God]; but their opinions with regard to the Lord are similar to those of Cerinthus and Carpocrates [i.e. they do not accept the virgin birth and hold Jesus to be no more than a specially good man]. They use the gospel according to Matthew only, and repudiate the apostle Paul, maintaining that he was an apostate from the law. As to the prophetical writings, they endeavour to expound them in a somewhat singular manner; they practise circumcision, persevere in the observance of these customs which are enjoined by the Law, and are Judaic in their style of life, so that they even adore Jerusalem as if it were the house of God.

There are two other helpful descriptions of the Ebionites. Hippolytus writes in his *Refutation of Heresies*:[13]

The Ebionaeans however acknowledge that the world was made by him who is in reality God, but they propound legends concerning Christ similarly with Cerinthus and Carpocrates. They live conformably to the customs of the Jews, alleging that they are justified according to the law, and saying that Jesus was justified by fulfilling the law. And therefore it was that the Christ of God was named Jesus, since not one of the rest of mankind had observed the law completely. For, if any other had fulfilled the commandments contained in the law, he would have been that Christ. And they also allege that they themselves too, when in the same way they fulfil the law, are able to become Christs, for they assert that our Lord himself was a man in the same way as all other men.

Eusebius in his *History* (3.27.1-6) has a description of the Ebionites in which he distinguishes two kinds of Ebionite:

The ancients quite properly called these men Ebionites because they held poor and mean opinions concerning Christ. For they considered him a plain and common man, who was justified only because of his superior virtue, and who was the fruit of the intercourse of a man with Mary. In their opinion the observance of the ceremonial law was altogether necessary, on the ground that they could not be saved by faith in Christ alone and by a corresponding life. There were others however besides these, who were of the same name, but avoided the strange and absurd beliefs of the former and did not deny that the Lord was born of a virgin and of the Holy Spirit. But nevertheless in that they also refused to acknowledge that he pre-existed, being God, Word, and Wisdom, they turned aside into the impiety of the former, especially when they, like them, endeavoured to observe strictly the bodily worship of the Law. These men too thought that it was necessary to reject all the epistles of the apostle, whom they called an apostate from the Law. They used only the so-called Gospel according to the Hebrews and made small account of the rest. The Sabbath and the rest of the discipline of the Jews they observed like them, but at the same time, like us they observed the Lord's day as a memorial of the resurrection of the Saviour. Wherefore in consequence of such a course they received the name of Ebionites, which signified the poverty of their understanding. For this is the name by which a poor man is called in Hebrew.

We can now set down the basic beliefs of the Ebionites, and then go on to see if they have left any mark on the material in the fourth gospel.[14] W.D. Niven finds three basic principles of Ebionism: 1. An over-exaltation of the Jewish law. 2. A defective Christology; Jesus is no more than a new and greater prophet; the view of his person is inadequate. 3. Hostility to Paul and rejection of all his writings.

Niven also distinguishes three types of Ebionites. 1. There were the Ebionites who were called Nazarenes (see Jerome, *Letter* 112.13). They regarded the law as binding on themselves, but not on Gentiles. By the law they meant the Mosaic law, not the rules and regulations of the scribal or oral law. The Nazarenes did not refuse fellowship with the Gentiles and they honoured the prophets. They acknowledged the virgin birth, the divinity and the messiahship of Jesus, declaring that at his baptism 'the fount of the Holy Spirit descended on him'. They longed for the conversion of the Jews. They were not anti-Paul, and used 'the gospel according to Matthew in Hebrew' (Epiphanius, *Heresies*, 30.3). 2. There were the Ebionites proper. They strictly observed the law, and held that the observance of the law was necessary for everyone; they had no fellowship with those who did not observe the law. They were Cerinthian in Christology. They held Jesus to be the natural son of Joseph and Mary. At his baptism 'a higher Spirit' united itself with him and he became the Messiah. He became the Christ, the Messiah because he had perfectly fulfilled the law, and everyone who does perfectly fulfil the law can become Christ. They were violently anti-Paul and spread slanderous stories about him. They possessed spurious writings under apostolic names – James, Matthew, John. 3. There were the syncretistic Ebionites. These were touched by Samaritanism, in that they rejected any of the Old Testament books which came after Joshua; they had some touch of Essenism in that they abstained from flesh and wine, rejected sacrifice, and practised frequent, even daily baptism. Ebionism had run its course and vanished by the fifth century.

In two things particularly the fourth gospel may well have Ebionism in the background. First, in the fourth gospel the opposition is summed up in the generic name of 'the Jews', and the Ebionites are in fact the most intense form of Jewish Christianity. R.E. Brown (I, pp. lxx-lxxiii) notes the bitterness of the fourth gospel's polemic against the Jews.

> You are of your father the devil, and your will is to do your father's desires. He was a murderer from the beginning, and has nothing to do with the truth, because there is no truth in him. When he lies, he speaks according to his own nature, for he is a liar and the father of lies. But

The Aims and Purposes of the Fourth Gospel

because I tell you the truth, you do not believe me. Which of you convicts
me of sin? If I tell the truth, why do you not believe me? He who is of God
hears the words of God; the reason why you do not hear them is that you
are not of God (John 8.44-47).

In the fourth gospel 'the Jews' is not a racial, ethnic, geographical
term; it is the term for the sum of all that is hostile to Jesus. In the
story of the opening of the eyes of the man born blind it is said of the
man's parents (9.22): 'They feared the Jews, for the Jews had already
agreed that if anyone should confess him to be Christ, he was to be
put out of the synagogue.' Of course, they themselves were Jews, but
'the Jews' has become the expression for the opposition. In the first
mention of the detachment who arrested Jesus in Gethsemane (18.3),
they are 'some officers from the chief priests and Pharisees'; a few
verses later (v. 12) they are 'the band of soldiers, their captain and the
officers of the Jews'. In 8.18 the cross-questioners are the Pharisees; in
8.22 they are 'the Jews'. All through the fourth gospel the Jews are the
enemies. There is much less mention of particular parties and sects of
the Jews, because the fourth gospel was written after AD 70, when
Jerusalem was destroyed, and when with the exception of the
Pharisees the parties were no more. Everything is concentrated on the
Jews, who are mentioned seventy times in the fourth gospel, as against
five or six times in each of the other three gospels. Since the Ebionites
were the last and most rigid survivors of Jewish Christianity, we may
well believe that they were in the mind of John when he often spoke of
the Jews.

Second, it needs no quotations to prove that the fourth gospel is not
designed to defend Christian morality or ethics; its one aim is to
present Jesus as the Messiah, as the Son of God, as the pre-existent
Divine One; and this may well be seen as directed against the defective
and inadequate Christology of the Ebionites.

We may well believe that the mistaken notions of Cerinthus and
Ebionites were in the mind of the writer of the fourth gospel.

(vii) We have already said that apologetic is of two kinds –
negative apologetic which defends the Christian faith against errors,
mistakes and heresies, and positive apologetic which commends the
faith to those who are not yet believers, or seeks to preserve, to
strengthen and to build up the faith of those who already believe. We
have looked at the negative apologetic of the fourth gospel; we now
turn to look at its positive aims. For the basic aim we need go no
further than the gospel itself. The verses with which it originally ended
(20.30f.) before the postscript of ch. 21 was added, give us the aim:

Now Jesus did many other signs in the presence of the disciples which are
not written in this book; but these are written that you may believe that
Jesus is the Christ, the Son of God, and that believing you may have life in
his name.

So the basic aim is to produce faith in Jesus as the Messiah, the Son of God, that that faith may produce life. But even this saying may well have its problem; there is a variant reading in the Greek text. C.K. Barrett (p. 479) points out that the word 'believe' in the phrase 'that you may believe' is in some manuscripts *pisteuēte*, and in others *pisteusēte*. *Pisteuēte* is the present subjunctive, and, if John is using his tenses absolutely accurately, ought to mean 'that you may continue to believe', in which case the gospel is addressed to those who are already Christians, and is meant to establish and confirm them in their faith. *Pisteusēte* is the aorist subjunctive, and, if strictly used, ought to mean 'that you may here and now believe, and become Christians', in which case the gospel is written to non-Christians with a view to their conversion. If we are to assume that the tenses are strictly used, the two readings present us with a real problem in regard to the purpose and destination of the gospel. The United Bible Societies' Text prints *pisteusēte*, but marks it as a C reading, that is, a reading about which there is considerable doubt. On the manuscript evidence *pisteuēte* might well be preferred, for it is the reading of the original hand of Sinaiticus, of Vaticanus, of Koridethi, and of the Bodmer papyrus.

But, in the first instance, it is doubtful if we can depend on so strictly accurate a use of tenses in a Hellenistic writer. And in the second place, Bultmann would hold that the difference in tenses makes no real difference. He writes (pp. 698f.):

> So far as the Evangelist is concerned it is irrelevant whether the possible readers are already 'Christians', or are not yet such; for to him the faith of 'Christians' is not a conviction that is present once for all, but it must perpetually make sure of itself anew, and therefore must continually hear the word anew.

So we may say that the aim of the gospel is to awaken and confirm the faith of its readers in Jesus as the Messiah and Son of God, so that they may find life.

(viii)   In our search for more particular purposes of the writer of the fourth gospel we may begin with a view expressed by C.K. Barrett. He suggests that the origin of the Gospel may be obscure, and then he goes on (p. 115):

> It may not have been published during the author's lifetime; and it may be doubted whether he was very interested in its publication. It is easy, when we read the gospel, to believe that John, though doubtless aware of the necessity of strengthening Christians and converting the heathen, wrote primarily to satisfy himself. His gospel must be written: it was no concern of his whether it was also read. Again it is by no means necessary to suppose that he was aware of the historical problems imposed upon later students by his treatment of the traditional material. It cried aloud for rehandling; its true meaning had crystallized in his mind, and he simply conveyed the meaning to paper.

To use a modern phrase, John wrote it to get it out of his system, and he cared not who read it. This seems a very unlikely situation. Every author cares whether or not his book is read. He cares still more when he knows he has something new to say; and he cares most of all when he knows that what he has to say is quite literally gospel truth.

(ix) We now turn to an unusual view of the aim and purpose of the fourth gospel, the view expressed by J.A.T. Robinson in an article on 'The Destination and Purpose of St John's Gospel' in his book *Twelve New Testament Studies* (pp. 107-25).[15] It will be simplest if we begin by stating Dr Robinson's conclusion, and then examine the steps by which he reached it and the validity of his arguments. He believes that the fourth gospel was written as an appeal to the Greek-speaking Jews of the dispersion to accept Jesus as Messiah and Son of God, and thus find life, and the appeal is made in order to prevent them making the same rejection of Jesus as the Jews of Palestine made in the days of his earthly ministry. In what follows we expound Dr Robinson's position and arguments.

Long ago J.B. Lightfoot said (in his *Biblical Essays*, p. 135) that, with the exception of the Apocalypse, the fourth gospel is the most Jewish book in the New Testament. It is a remarkable fact that there is not a single reference to the Gentiles in the entire book. It is the only major work in the New Testament in which the term *ta ethnē*, the Gentiles, never occurs. In it the term 'the Jews' occurs almost 70 times, in comparison with 5 times in Matthew, 6 in Mark, and 5 in Luke. The only Gentile who appears in the fourth gospel is Pilate – and he is an outsider – 'Am I a Jew?' Pilate asks (18.35). In the synoptic gospels many Gentiles appear at least on the fringe of the narrative – the magi from the East in Matthew 2, the centurion whose faith is a great example (Matt. 8.10 = Luke 7.9), the Syro-Phoenician woman (Mark 7.28), the centurion at the cross (Mark 15.39). In Luke 2.32, right at the beginning of the story, Jesus is not only 'the glory of God's people Israel'; he is also 'a light for revelation to the Gentiles'. In the synoptic gospels Jesus does find his way to non-Jewish territory. He goes to Tyre and Sidon, and to Caesarea Philippi (Mark 7.24; 8.27). The Jewish towns are compared unfavourably with Tyre and Sidon, and even with Sodom and Gomorrah (Matt. 10.15; 11.20-24). God's preference was for the widow of Zarephath in Sidon and for Naaman the Syrian (Luke 4. 25-27). There is the warning that Nineveh and the queen of the South will fare better in the day of judgment than the Jews (Matt. 12.41f. = Luke 11.31f.). Many are to come from the east and the west to sit with Abraham, Isaac and Jacob in the kingdom of God, while the sons of the kingdom will be thrown out (Matt. 8.11f.; Luke 13.29f.). The vineyard will be taken away from its tenants and given to others (Mark 12.9). The temple is cleared so that it may really become a house of prayer 'for all nations' (Mark

11.17). The gospel is to be preached to the whole world, and the apostles are to make disciples of all nations (Matt. 28.19; Luke 24.47). The Christians will have to make their defence before the Gentiles, but this can become an opportunity to witness (Matt. 10.18; Luke 21. 12f.). The end will not come until the gospel has been preached to the whole Gentile world (Mark 13.10; Matt. 24.14). None of this appears in the fourth gospel. So Dr Robinson claims that apart from Pilate no Gentile appears in the fourth gospel.

Simply to make that statement provokes a challenge and raises a question which demands an answer. What of the Greeks who came to Philip (as reported in John 12.20-22)?

> Now among those who went up to worship at the feast were some Greeks. So these came to Philip, who was from Bethsaida in Galilee and said to him: 'Sir, we wish to see Jesus.' Philip went and told Andrew; Andrew went with Philip and they told Jesus.

Dr Robinson writes of this incident (p. 111):

> It is important to insist that these Greeks are *not* Gentiles. They are Greek-speaking Jews, of whom it is specifically stated that they had 'come up to worship at the feast' (12.20) – and there is no suggestion that they are merely 'God-fearers', or even that they had once been Gentiles. All that we can deduce with certainty is that they spoke Greek rather than Aramaic ... and that they were in Jerusalem for a specifically Jewish reason.

We shall later discuss the validity of this statement; for the moment we continue to set out Dr Robinson's argument.

For John the simple question, the basic question, is the relation of *Judaism* to the true Israel, the true vine, to Jesus as the Christ, for to John the only true Judaism is one which acknowledges Jesus as the Messiah. Becoming a true Jew and becoming a Christian are one and the same thing – and this does not mean Judaizing. It is *Jews* in whom John is primarily interested, not Gentiles. So in the gospel everything is aimed at the Jews.

Judaism is challenged and transcended. The law is overpassed. 'The law was given through Moses; grace and truth came through Jesus Christ' (1.17). Jewish ritual is set aside for the new life of Christianity; the old water of the Jewish cleansing regulations is changed into the new wine of Christianity (2.6). The very temple is for destruction (2.19). Worship localized in Jerusalem is to come to an end (4.20f.). The sabbath is subjected to a new authority (5.9-18).

In the fourth gospel Jesus is called Messiah 21 times, as against 17 times in Matthew, 7 in Mark and 13 in Luke.

The titles of Jesus are Jewish titles – the King of the Jews (19.19-22); the King of Israel (1.49); the Holy One of God (6.69); the prophet who was to come into the world (6.14; 7.40; cf. Deut. 18.15).

The images which are used are Jewish images – the manna (6.32-35); the shepherd (10.11-16); the vine (15.1-6):

The whole atmosphere is Jewish.

> The *Heimat* of the Johannine tradition, and the milieu in which it took shape, was the heart of southern Palestinian Judaism. There is nothing so far as I can see, to suggest that the great controversies of chapters 5 to 12, which comprise the hard core of the evangelist's tradition, were not the product of discussion and debate with Jewish opposition in a purely Palestinian situation. The Gentile world, except as represented by the Romans, is miles away (p. 116).

And yet the gospel is written in Greek to Greeks. To what Greeks? Dr Robinson's answer is – to the Greeks who appear in the gospel. For Paul and Luke the difference between Jew and Greek is the difference between Jew and Gentile; for John it is the distinction between the Jews of Palestine, especially of Judaea, and the Jews of the Greek dispersion. The word for 'Greeks' in John 12.20 is *Hellēnes*; the word for Greeks in Acts 6.1 and 9.29 is *Hellēnistai*. Dr Robinson holds that the *Hellēnes* of John are Greek-speaking Jews resident *outside* Palestine in the Diaspora, as distinct from the *Hellēnistai*, who are Greek-speaking Jews resident *within* Palestine. Naturally, he says, the word *Hellēnes* itself draws attention to them as non-Palestinian rather than as Jews, and indeed it is only from a Palestinian point of view that Jews could conceivably be described as Greeks. In the story of the event which led to the beginning of the end for Paul it is said that the Jews of Asia stirred up all the crowd, with the charge that Paul had introduced Greeks (Trophimus) into the temple (Acts 21.27-29). Dr Robinson suggests that John would have said; 'The Greeks (that is, the Jews of Asia) stirred up the Jews against Paul because he had introduced Gentiles (i.e. Greeks) into the temple.'

The Johannine division, Dr Robinson suggests, is not a division between Jew and Gentile, but a division within Judaism. He sees:

(a) A division between the common people and the authorities. It is the Jews who are said to question the lame man who was healed (5.10-15), and of course he was a Jew himself. For fear of the Jews (7.13) no one speaks openly of Jesus. The parents of the man born blind are afraid of the Jews turning them out of the synagogue (9.18,22). Jews are set in opposition to Jesus.

(b) A division between members of the Sanhedrin. Many of the authorities (*archontes*; members of Sanhedrin) believed in Jesus, but because of the Pharisees were afraid to say so openly (12.42). Joseph of Arimathea and.Nicodemus were members of Sanhedrin and yet believed in Jesus (19.38f.).

(c) Even within the groups there are divisions. There is a difference among the Pharisees as to whether Jesus can be from God

or not, some saying that if he was from God, he would not break the sabbath, others saying that unless he was from God, he could not do the miracles he did (9.16). There is a division among the common people. Some said that he was a good man, others said that he was leading the people astray (7.12). There was a division among the people over him (7.43).

(d) There are geographical divisions. The Jews have no dealings with the Samaritans (4.9). There is a division between Judaea and Galilee; nothing good for a Judaean could come out of Nazareth (1.46). Galilee welcomed Jesus; Jerusalem did not (7.41, 52).

The Jews were divided. And the greatest tension of all was between metropolitan Judaism and the Judaism of the dispersion. The Jews of Palestine had a contempt for the Jews of the dispersion, which can be heard in their voices when they speak of them (7.35). *And it is precisely to the Jews of the dispersion that the gospel is going as an evangelistic instrument.*

As Dr Robinson sees it, John's appeal is not to the Gentiles. His appeal is 'to Diaspora Judaism, that *it* may come to accept Jesus as its true Messiah,' even if, as Paul says, 'those who live in Jerusalem and their rulers . . . did not recognize him' (Acts 13.27). Dr Robinson finds in the fourth gospel the desire to remove this tension and to unite the two arms of Judaism into one. It is said of Caiaphas, when he argued that it was expedient that Jesus should die (11.51f.):

> He did not say this of his own accord, but being high priest for that year he prophesied that Jesus should die for the nation, and not for the nation only, but to gather into one the children of God who are scattered abroad.

'The nation' is metropolitan Judaism; those 'scattered abroad' are the Jews of the dispersion. Jesus is to bring about the final ingathering of the people of God of which the prophets dreamed.

> I lay down my life for the sheep. And I have other sheep that are not of this fold; I must bring them also, and they will heed my voice. So there will be one flock, one shepherd.

The 'other sheep' are the Jews of the dispersion; they at last are to be united in one in Jesus (cf. Ezek. 34; 37.1-28; Jer. 23.1-8; 31.1-10). Even in 17.20-26 the prayer that all may be one 'is not a prayer for broken Christendom but for scattered and disrupted Judaism, viewed as the true Israel of God'.

The one desire is to gather the whole Jewish nation into the fold of Christ. The theme, says Dr Robinson, is first introduced in 6.12f. where great importance is attached to the care with which the fragments must be gathered up after the feeding of the crowd 'that nothing may be lost'. Filling, as they do, twelve baskets, the fragments symbolize the fulness of Israel still to be gathered in after 'the Jews' have eaten their fill.

So Dr Robinson concludes his argument (pp. 124f.):

> The Gospel . . . is composed no doubt of material which took shape *within* a Christian community *in Judaea*, and under the pressure of controversy with 'the Jews' of that area. But in its present form it is, I believe, an appeal to those *outside* the Church, to win to the faith that Greek-speaking *Diaspora Judaism*, to which the author now finds himself belonging as a result (we may surmise) of the greatest dispersion of all (the result of the destruction of Jerusalem), which swept from Judaea Church and Synagogue alike. His overmastering concern is that 'the great refusal' made by his countrymen at home should not be repeated by the other sheep of God's flock, among whom he has now found refuge.

That is Dr Robinson's case for holding that the fourth gospel was not written for Greeks, but for the Greek-speaking Jews of the diaspora, in a great attempt to restrain them from also rejecting him who was the true Messiah, the Son of God, the revealer of truth, and the giver of life.

There is no doubt of the beauty of this suggestion; it is a moving thought that John should put all his effort into the endeavour to prevent the Jews of the dispersion making the same tragic mistake as the Jews of the homeland had made. Our decision must turn on the meaning of *Hellēnes* in 12.20.[16] The word *Hellēn* began by meaning a racial Greek. But very early the word *Hellēn* began to denote someone who was not necessarily racially a Greek, but who shared in Greek culture and the Greek spirit. Isocrates was born in 436 BC and in his famous speech the *Panegyricus* (50) he wrote of Athens:

> So far has our city outdistanced the rest of mankind in thought and in speech that her pupils have become the teachers of the rest of the world; and she has brought it about that the name 'Hellenes' suggests no longer a race but an intelligence, and that the title 'Hellenes' is applied rather to those who share our culture than to those who share a common blood.

As far as the Jew was concerned, the word became almost a bad word, and came very near to being a synonym for pagan. In the Septuagint, the Greek translation of the Old Testament, Isaiah 9.12 reads: 'Though God will dash down those who rise up against him on Mount Zion, Syria in the east and the Greeks [Hebrew 'Philistines', as in RSV] in the west, who are devouring Israel with open mouth.' Much later the writer of the *Clementine Homilies* can say (11.16): 'A *Hellēn* is one, whether Jew or Greek, who does not keep the Law.' With Alexander the Great, and after him, Greek culture and the Greek language spread all over the world, and those who accepted the Greek lanuage, Greek culture, Greek religion, all that the word *Hellēnismos*, Hellenization, meant, came to be known as *Hellēnes*. And the word acquired as far as the Jews were concerned an even worse meaning, when rulers like Antiochus Epiphanes made a deliberate attempt to wipe out Judaism and to substitute Greek religion and the Greek way of life. So Josephus can speak of an apostate Jew as one who has accepted the *hellenikē politeia*, the Greek way of life. There is another allied word *Hellēnistēs*, which does mean one who speaks Greek (Acts 6.1; 11.20), but a *Hellēn* is much more than merely a Greek speaker; he is one who has become a Greek.

It is therefore very unlikely that in 12.20 *Hellēnes* are Greek-speaking Jews; the *Hellēnes* are Greeks in the full sense of the term. If John had wished to refer to Greek-speaking Jews, he had the word *Hellēnistai* available and would no doubt have used it. The opinion of the commentators is consistently that the *Hellēnes* are not Jews, but Greeks. J.N. Sanders translates the passage: 'Now there were certain Gentiles among those who came up to worship at the feast.' And he then comments (pp. 290f.): 'Literally "Greeks". The emphasis is on language rather than race, but implies that these were not Jews.' J.H. Bernard (II, pp. 429f.) comments: 'These men were not *Hellēnistai*, i.e. Greek-speaking Jews, but *Hellēnes*, Greeks who had become proselytes of the gate.' And he heads the section 'The Greek enquirers'. Hoskyns and Davey (p. 423) say: 'These men were not Hellenistic Jews, named in Acts Hellenists (Acts 6.1; 9.29). They were Gentiles of Greek birth attracted to the worship of Israel.' R.E. Brown (p. 466) comments: 'Greeks, *Hellēnes*, Gentiles – not *Hellēnistai* or Greek-speaking Jews.' G.H.C Macgregor (pp. 263f.) heads the section 'The Homage of the Gentile World', and comments 'not Hellenist Jews but pure Greeks'. C.K. Barrett (p. 351) says: 'The word *Hellen* signifies not one strictly of the Greek race, but one of non-Jewish birth.' They are, he says, 'representative of the Gentile Church'. Bultmann (p. 423) describes the *Hellēnes* as 'representatives of the Greek world'; in distinction from the *Hellēnistai*, they are born Greeks. Windisch in his article in *TDNT* II (pp. 509f.) describes the *Hellēnes* as 'half proselytes of Greek language . . . Greek or Hellenised Orientals by birth who had attached themselves to the synagogue in their own lands, were described in this way rather than as Gentiles. Windisch says: 'With his two references [12.20 and 7.35] John is telling us that the idea of offering teaching to the Gentiles twice occurred in the life of Jesus, though it was never realised.'

Linguistically Dr Robinson's suggestion cannot be accepted, and the far-fetched interpretations of John 10.16; 11.50-52; and especially of 17.20-26 are very difficult, if not impossible, to accept. However attractive the theory is, it must be discarded.

(x) If Dr Robinson's theory is accepted, it would mean that the fourth gospel is a characteristically and basically Jewish book, and there are those who would agree. William Temple in his *Readings in St John's Gospel* (p. xix) wrote: 'The Gospel is through and through

Palestinian. The notion that it is in any sense Hellenistic is contrary to its whole tenour.' But truth has many streams. Clement of Alexandria said in his *Miscellanies* (1.5): 'The way of truth (i.e. the Christian religion) is one, but different streams from different quarters flow into it, as into an ever-flowing river.' The other great stream which contributed to Christian truth was the Greek stream, and, taking a view diametrically opposed to that of William Temple, B.W. Bacon in 1933 published a book on the fourth gospel entitled *The Gospel of the Hellenists*. And if we accept the tradition that the place of origin of the fourth gospel was Ephesus, then it will be natural to think of it as aimed at the Greeks.

A time for such an aim and such a gospel had to come. In a very real sense of the term the Greeks were waiting. Goodspeed writes in his *Introduction to the NT* (pp. 296-8): 'The long discipline of Greek civilization had prepared a people capable of appreciating the inward and spiritual values of the new religion.' He goes on to talk of the necessary adjustment:

Christianity was addressing [the Greek public] in Jewish terms. A Greek who felt like becoming a Christian was called upon to accept Jesus as the Christ, the Messiah. He would naturally ask what this meant, and would have to be given a short course in Jewish apocalyptic messianic thought. Was there no way in which he might be introduced directly to the values of the Christian salvation without being forever routed, one might even say detoured, through Judaism? Must Christianity always speak in a Jewish vocabulary?...The times demanded that Christianity be translated into universal terms. The Gospel of John is the response to this demand.

G.H.C. Macgregor says (p. xxix) that 'John seeks to interpret the Christian story and Christian experience to the new world of Hellenism by translating the gospel into a form intelligible to Greek modes of thought.'

It was inevitable that Christianity should begin in Jewish terms. Jesus himself was a Jew; all his early followers were Jews; the early preaching was delivered to Jews. But Christianity, to be true to its Founder's commission (Matt. 28. 18-20), had to move out to all nations and to all the world. It had to become not national but universal. B.H. Streeter in *The Four Gospels* says that Mark, Luke and John form a progressive series with

a tendency to make more and more of the idea of Christianity as the universal religion, free from the limitations of its Jewish origin, and, along with this, to lay less and less stress on the original Apocalyptic expectation of an immediate visible Return of the Master. The Fourth Gospel is thus the climax reached in the development of theology in the New Testament towards the naturalisation of Christianity in the Hellenic world.

It would be no use to talk to a Greek of Jesus as the Son of David; the Greek would never have heard of David, and when he did hear of him, David would seem to him to be no more than a petty Middle Eastern king. There was even some danger in talking of Jesus as Son of God, because the Greek mythology had many stories of how the gods had come from Olympus and seduced mortal maidens and begotten children.

We believe that it was to help the Greeks to understand that John wrote. Goodspeed writes (p. 308): 'The Gospel may be said to be intensely Greek from Prologue to Epilogue in every fibre of both thought and language.' R.H. Lightfoot in his commentary (p. 50) speaks of John in relation to the Hellenistic-Gentile world: 'It was these men, above all, as seems likely, that the fourth evangelist, although himself by origin a Hebrew, was desirous to instruct and help.'

But the help was given, and the new approach was achieved not by discarding either side, but by making a new fusion and combination of the two. R.H. Lightfoot writes (pp. 50f.):

> Jewish religion and Greek religion each had an essential contribution to make to it. Neither was capable by itself of becoming an historic universal religion, able to satisfy the needs and aspirations of humanity, but after each had received a contribution from the other, and had also been brought into relationship with the Person of the Lord Jesus, Christianity could make this claim. . . . It is probably true that in no book of the New Testament has the fusion of the two chief and very different elements, the Jewish and the Greek, been achieved with a surer touch or with greater thoroughness than in St John's Gospel.

The result of the fusion is a unique and universal gospel. Goodspeed writes (pp. 309f.) that John is not another Matthew or Mark, and is not to be treated as such.

> It is a great creative work of religious genius that has lighted the way for Greek Christianity and for universal Christianity ever since . . . Historically, it is less convincing that Mark; ethically, it is less exalted than Matthew. Yet it strikes beyond any of these to the very heart of Christianity, as above all an inner spiritual life of sonship to God and friendship with Christ.

Goodspeed concludes his study of John (pp. 314f.) by saying:

> The thoroughly Greek character of the thought and interest of the Gospel, its literary (dialogue) cast, its thoroughly Greek style, its comparatively limited use of the Jewish scriptures (roughly about one-fifth of Matthew's), its definite purpose to strip Christianity of its Jewish swaddling clothes, its intense and anti-Jewish feeling, and its great debt to the mystery religions – combine to show that its author was a Greek, not a Jew. In the Gospel of John the Greek genius returns to religion.

As R.H. Lightfoot finely puts it (p. 55), Jewish and Greek religion had each to be 'marked with the sign of the cross'.

In just what way did John move out from Judaism? Wherein lay the new thing which released and universalized Christianity?

Inevitably Christianity had begun by thinking of Jesus in messianic terms. The Jewish hope was the hope of the Messiah, and in the light of that hope Jesus was seen. But it soon became clear, as R.H. Lightfoot says (p. 49), that the office of Jewish Messiah was inadequate to account for the person and work of Jesus. This was more than Jewish history; it was world history. It was not only the preparation for a future event; 'it was itself the manifestation in history of the spiritual Power through which the worlds were made.' Earlier (p. 32) he says:

It may indeed have become increasingly clear, at any rate in certain quarters of the Church, that such a Gospel as St John's was needed, and that an interpretation of the Person of the Lord chiefly in terms of the Jewish Messiah, although already supplemented in certain respects in the other gospels, was rapidly becoming inadequate as an interpretation of Him who was now worshipped by Gentile even more than by Jewish Christians in the little churches fast taking root in the larger cities of the Roman Empire between Jerusalem and Rome.

Where then did John turn for his interpretation of Jesus?

It is in the prologue to the gospel that we see John reaching out to the Greeks, for it is in the prologue that he appropriates the Logos doctrine, the conception of Jesus as the Word. It may well be that John took over and adapted an already existing Hymn to the Logos. Different reconstructions of the underlying hymn have been offered (e.g. by R.E. Brown, p. 22, and J.H. Bernard, I, pl cxliv). C.F. Burney (*Aramaic Origin*, pp. 40f.) would omit John 1.6-10a, 12, 13, 15, 16b, 18, and would then find an original hymn in couplets as follows:

1a	1c	3a	4a	5a	10b	11a	14a	14c	14e	17a
1b	2a	3b	4b	5b	10c	11b	14b	14d	16a	17b

J. Weiss would arrange in quatrains as follows:

1a	3a	5a	11a	14ab	17ab
1b	3b	5b	11b	14cd	18a
1c	4a	10ab	12a	14e	18b
2a	4b	10c	12b	16ab	18c[17]

Whatever the origin of the prologue, whether John appropriated it or whether he composed it, it may well be said that the prologue could be called the most successful experiment in Christian communication the church has ever produced. G.H.C. Macgregor (p. xxxvii) wrote of the prologue that it is 'a philosophically conceived attempt to build a bridge between Greek and Hebrew modes of thought'. C.K. Barrett says (p. 129) that John, as no one else ever did, 'holds together Jewish, Hellenistic and primitive Christian strands of thought in a consistent unity'. The prologue, he says, can be read as 'Hellenistic philosophy, rabbinic mysticism, and history'. To do this John drew on more than one source and wove together various strands. G.T. Purves writes that John's use of the Logos idea is 'a synthesis of several elements of truth'.[18] H.A.A. Kennedy says that this drawing on differing sources was a natural step for John to take because 'syncretism is the sign-manual of the period'.[19] The fact that the Gnostics made great use of the fourth gospel is proof of both the success and the danger of the experiment. In *The Gospel of Truth* Valentinus shows that he knew and used the fourth gospel. Heracleon wrote the first known commentary on it. Ptolemaeus was the first definitely to name John as the author of the fourth gospel and Irenaeus preserves his exposition of the prologue,[20] while Clement of Alexandria quotes another exposition by Theodotus, another of the Valentinians.[21] J.H. Bernard (I, p. cxxxviii) characterizes the fourth gospel as 'a summary restatement of the Christian gospel from the philosophical side'. C.H. Dodd in *The Interpretation of the Fourth Gospel* (pp. 8f.) writes:

> The Gospel could be read intelligently by a person who started with no knowledge of Christianity beyond the minimum that a reasonably well informed member of the public interested in religion might be supposed to have by the close of the first century, and Christian ideas are instilled step by step until the whole mystery can be divulged. If he was then led to associate himself with the Church, and to participate in its fellowship, its tradition and its sacraments, he would be able to re-read the book and find in it vastly more than had been obvious at a first reading ... It seems therefore that we are to think of the work as addressed to a wide public consisting mainly of devout and thoughtful persons (for the thoughtless and religiously indifferent would never trouble to open such a book as this) in the varied and cosmopolitan society of a great Hellenistic city such as Ephesus under the Roman Empire.

What then was the key which John used to unlock the Greek mind, and to present Jesus meaningfully and intelligibly to the Hellenistic world? The key which John used was the conception of Jesus as the Word, the Logos; and the great value of this conception was that it was meaningful to people with a Greek background, to people with a Hebrew background, and to people with no religious or philosophical background at all. Let us then look at it.

(i) First, as to the word itself — in Greek the word *logos* has two meanings; it means 'word', and it means 'reason'. In point of fact there is not such a gap between these two words as might at first sight appear. Reason is that which goes on *inside* a man; when reason emerges *outside* a man, it emerges in speech. So when a man thinks things out with his inner reason, he may then in speech give a reason for the course he proposes to follow. It is the misfortune of English that it does not possess any word with the two meanings of the Greek word *logos*. For that reason Moffatt in his translation of the New Testament does not attempt to translate *logos*. He writes:

> The Logos existed in the very beginning,
> the Logos was with God,
> the Logos was divine . . .
> So the Logos became flesh and tarried among us.

In the application of the word to Jesus both meanings are combined.

(ii) The conception of Jesus as the Word has a quite general background which it requires no special background to appreciate. Two things may be said about any word. First, a word is *a means of communication*. Second, a word is *the expression of a thought*. I use words to communicate with other people, and to express my thought. So then to call Jesus the Word will mean that Jesus is God's means of communication with men, and it will mean that he is the expression of the thought of God. 'The Word became flesh' might well be translated: 'The Mind of God became a human person.'

(iii) To a Jew the conception of the Word would be completely meaningful.

> The spoken word to the Hebrew was fearfully alive. It was not merely a vocable or sound dropped heedlessly from unthinking lips. It was *a unit of energy charged with power*. It flies like a bullet to its billet. . . . There [in the East] when a curse is uttered the bystanders throw themselves flat on the ground that those words, like high explosives, may pass over their heads and do them no harm. Sir George Adam Smith tells somewhere how once as he journeyed in the desert a group of Moslems gave his party the customary greeting, 'Peace be upon you,' and failed to notice that he, a Christian, was in the group. When they learned that the Moslem greeting had thus been extended to an infidel – for the Christian is an infidel to the Moslem – they returned to ask back the greeting. A beneficent force had been released where it should not be released and they sought to recall it.

The same author quotes a saying about a certain poet who had the magic of words: 'His words became alive and walked up and down in the hearts of his hearers.'[22] G.F. Moore said that for the Hebrew a word is 'a concrete reality, a veritable cause'.

For the Hebrew then the word of God is power and effective power. The word of God is 'like a hammer that breaks the rock in pieces' (Jer. 23.29). God's word does not return to him empty. 'It shall accomplish that which I purpose, and prosper in the thing for which I sent it' (Isa. 55.11). For the Hebrew, word is action.

That action is particularly seen in two directions. First, God's word is active in *creation*. The creation story in Genesis 1 introduces each act of creation with the words: 'God said.' Creation is the act of the word of God. 'By the word of the Lord the heavens were made ... For he spoke and it came to be; he commanded and it stood forth' (Ps. 33. 6,9). 'He sent forth his word and healed them' (Ps. 107.20). 'His word runs swiftly ... He sends forth his word and melts them' (Ps. 147.15,18). Second, God's word is active in *revelation*. 'The word which Isaiah the son of Amoz saw, concerning Judah and Jerusalem' (Isa. 2.1). 'The word of the Lord came to Micah' (Micah 1.1). God's word, says C.K. Barrett (p. 127), is 'the means by which God communicates his purpose to his people'. So then to call Jesus the Word is to say that in him God's creating and revealing power has come to men.

Another part of the Hebrew background lies in the conception of Wisdom. For the Jewish thinkers Wisdom has become at least to some extent personalized. Clearly the Mind of God, the Reason of God, will have a close connection with the Wisdom of God. And many of the functions which are ascribed in John to the Word are in the Old Testament and in the inter-testamental literature ascribed to Wisdom. Wisdom was created by God before the world began; Wisdom was God's agent in the work of creation like a master-workman; and the man who finds Wisdom finds life (Prov. 8.22-36). This comes very near to the idea of the pre-existing Word, the creator of all things, the source of life (John 1.1-4). Wisdom is the fashioner of all things, the breath of the power of God (Wisd. 7.22-8.1). God has made all things by his word, and formed men by his wisdom; it is the word of God which heals all men (Wisd. 9.1f.; 16.12; cf. Sirach 24.1-12). The transition from Wisdom to the Logos, the Word, is easy.

There is another form of Hebrew expression which did not contribute to the conception of the Word, but which did familiarize people with the sound of it. The Targums are the Aramaic translations or paraphrases of the Old Testament, made for reading in the days when even the Jews had forgotten their ancient Hebrew. These Targums often found the Old Testament Hebrew rather too anthropomorphic, and substituted for the name of God himself the *memra*, the word of God. So Genesis 3.8, 'And they heard the sound of the Lord God walking in the garden', becomes: 'They heard the voice of the *memra*, the word, of the Lord God walking in the garden.' Genesis 20.3, 'God came to Abimelech in a dream', becomes: 'A word, *memra*, from before Yahweh came to Abimelech.' 'So that I come again to my father's house in peace, then the Lord shall be my God' (Gen. 28.21), becomes: '... the word of Yahweh shall be my God.' 'Moses brought the people out of the camp to meet God' (Ex.

19.7), becomes: 'Moses brought forth the people before the *memra*, the word of God.' 'My hand laid the foundation of the earth, and my right hand spread out the heavens' (Isa. 48.13), becomes: 'By my *memra*, my word, I have founded the earth, and by my strength I have hung up the heavens.' In Deuteronomy 33.7, 'The eternal God is your dwelling-place and underneath are the everlasting arms', the second half of the verse prosaically becomes: 'By his word the world was created.' 'The Lord has them in derision' (Ps. 2.4), becomes: 'The word of the Lord shall have them in derision.' Often the academic insertion of the word, the *memra*, destroys the poetry and the vividness in order to excise the anthropomorphisms. This added nothing to the meaning of 'the word', but it did mean that those who heard the Old Testament read in the synagogue were very familiar with the phrase 'the word'.

There is still one more element in the Hebrew background of thought into which the Logos fits. For the Jew the law, the Torah, is the greatest thing in the world. Torah is far more than law, far more than a code of regulations; it is instruction, and it was regarded with intense devotion. C.G. Montefiore says that the Torah is 'the "middle term" between Israel and God'.[23] In the first place, there was an increasing tendency to identify Wisdom and the Torah. We find them closely linked in Sirach:

He who holds to the law will obtain wisdom (15.1).

Whoever keeps the law controls his thoughts,
    and wisdom is the fulfilment of the fear of the Lord (21.11).

In all wisdom there is the fulfilment of the law (19.20).

The magnificent panegyric on Wisdom in Sirach 24.1-23 is immediately followed by the words:

All this is the book of the covenant
    of the Most High God,
    the law which Moses commanded us,
    as an inheritance for the congregations of Jacob.

The adoration of the Law attached to the Law all the attributes of Wisdom, and the attributes of Wisdom are the attributes of John's Logos. We shall see the resemblance if we compare what John says of the Logos and what the Hebrew sages said of the Torah.[24]

In the beginning was the Word, and the Word was with God, and the Word was God.
'Seven things existed before the creation of the world – the law, the throne of glory, the garden of Eden, penitence, the upper sanctuary, the name of the Messiah. Upon what was the Law written? With black fire upon white fire, and it lay upon God's knee while he sat on the throne of his glory.'

The law is divine; it partook of the divine nature, for the law was 'God's only-begotten daughter', married to the people of Israel.

All things were made through him.
'Through the firstborn God created the heaven and the earth, and the firstborn is no other than the Torah.'

In him was life, and the life was the light of men.
'The words of the Torah are life for the world.' The law is the light and life of the people of Israel. 'With five things is the Law compared – with water, with wine, with honey, with milk, with oil, oil which is poured out in thy name . . . As oil is light for the world, so are the words of the law light for the world. As oil is life for the world, so the words of the law are life for the world.'

Full of grace and truth.
The Torah is identified with truth.

'The Law,' says John, 'was given by Moses; grace and truth came through Jesus Christ' (1.17). It is true that the Torah was the symbol and the pledge of God's divine presence with his people. But it was given in sternness, in cloud, majesty and awe. So terrible was the sight that Moses said: 'I tremble with fear' (Heb. 12.21; Deut. 9.19). Here is the contrast. W.F. Howard in *Christianity according to St John* (pp. 52f.) points out that the old Torah was *given*; grace and truth *came*. In John 1.16-18 John dwells on the graciousness of the reality in Jesus, in the Logos; and significantly never again does he use the word *grace* in all the rest of the Gospel. The grace of the Logos is contrasted with the sternness of the law – and the rest of the gospel is an unfolding of that grace.

It is easy to see how meaningful the prologue of the fourth gospel would be to a Jew with its echoes of God in creation and God in revelation, with its memories of wisdom and of the law. Even if it is true that the Logos doctrine of the fourth gospel looks out to the Greek world, it still remains true that it also presents Jesus as the consummation of Judaism.

But we must turn now to the outreach of the fourth gospel to the Greek world. Before we turn to the special and individual contribution of the fourth gospel we must note one quite general relationship with Greek thought. One of the great contributions to the thought not only of Greece but also of the world was Plato's doctrine of forms or ideas. It was the essence of Plato's thought that there was an unseen world of forms or ideas which were the patterns from which all visible and earthly things were made. Furthermore, it was Plato's belief that it was the unseen world which was the real world, and that all we have in this physical world in which we live is but a poor shadowy copy of reality. So Plato draws his contrast between the unseen world of real things and the seen world of pale shadowy unreal copies. The fourth gospel has a way of using a certain Greek word, the word *alēthinos*. The older translations right up to the RSV translate *alēthinos* by the word 'true' – the true bread (6.32), the true light (1.9), the true vine (15.1). In Greek there are two interrelated words. There is the word *alēthēs*, which means true in contradistinction to that which is untrue or a lie. For instance, in 8.14 Jesus says to the Pharisees: 'Even if I do bear witness to myself, my testimony is true, *alēthēs*.' His testimony is accurate, no lie, the truth. The other word is the word *alēthinos*, which means true in the sense of real, genuine, as opposed to that which is unreal, that which is a substitute for reality, for the real thing. When John speaks of Jesus being the bread, the light, the vine, it is *alēthinos* that he uses, and the NEB correctly speaks of 'the real light', 'the real bread', 'the real vine'. So what John means is that with Jesus reality has entered into time. As Plato would have said, the unseen, eternal realities, which are the patterns for all things, have in Jesus Christ entered this unreal, shadowy world. In Jesus Christ man is face to face with the divine and ultimate reality. Plato held that in the unseen world there was for instance, the form, the idea of a chair, the perfect pattern of a chair of which all chairs are poor copies. He held that the supreme idea is the idea of the good, and the idea of the good, that of which all other goodness is a pale and unreal copy, is the same as God. So to call Jesus the real one is to say that with him reality, God, entered human life.

That conception of ultimate reality may underlie the fourth gospel, but there is one Greek conception, which in it becomes articulate, the conception of the Logos, the Word. G.H.C. Macgregor says (p. xxxvii):

> Through Alexandrian usage the 'Logos' had become a current philosophical term much as 'evolution' or 'élan vital' in our own day; John seized upon it as an invaluable category for the interpretation of the gospel.

E.F. Scott writing of this word Logos says:

> A middle term was discovered between Christianity and the forms of Hellenic thought, and a wide development was thus rendered possible. The new religion could now interpret itself to the Graeco-Roman world and assimilate whatever was congenial to its spirit in the intellectual life of the time.[25]

Hoskyns and Davey (p. 157) write:

> When once, however, an historical explanation of the language of the prologue was required, it seemed obvious that its author had consciously adopted the phraseology of Greek philosophy in order to interpret Christianity in terms of Greek thought and commend it to the Gentile world as a reputable philosophy.

The Logos conception has a long history in Greek thought. It begins with Heraclitus, who, like the John of the fourth gospel, lived and taught in Ephesus.[26] He flourished round about 500 BC. Only fragments of his work remain, but there is enough extant to tell us what he said, even though he was so hard to understand that men called him 'the obscure'.[27] Diogenes Laertius in his *Lives of Eminent Philosophers* (9.6) quotes Timon as calling him 'the shrill, cuckoo-like, mob-reviler, riddling Heraclitus', and Diogenes himself says that Heraclitus 'deliberately made his work the more obscure in order that none but adepts should approach it, and lest familiarity should breed contempt'.

Heraclitus said three things which are relevant to our discussion.[28]

(i)   He said that everything is in a state of flux.[29] The saying of Heraclitus most often quoted in one form or another is that you cannot step into the same river twice; step in, step out, step in again; the river has flowed on and it is a different river.[30] Everything is always in a state of motion. The Heraclitean doctrine is stated by Aristotle (*Physics*, 253b9): 'Some assert, not that some things are in motion and others not, but that *everything* is *always* moving, though this escapes our perception.' Everything *has* to keep moving. In Greece there was a well-known drink or posset called the *kykeōn*; it was made of wine with barley and grated cheese stirred into it. They do not dissolve, and therefore the drink has to be kept swirling round in constant motion until it is drunk. The universe is like that, according to Heraclitus. 'The *kykeōn* falls apart, if it is not being stirred.'

(ii)   But things are more than in motion; they are in tension; there is a harmony of opposites. 'One must know that war is common, and justice strife, and that all things come about by way of strife and necessity.'[31] 'War is the father of all and king of all; and some he reveals as gods and some as men; some he makes slaves, other free.'[32] Aristotle says:

Heraclitus rebukes the author of the line, 'Would that strife might be destroyed from among gods and men,' for there would be no musical scale unless high and low existed, nor living creature without male and female, which are opposites.[33]

'Rest and quiet?' says Heraclitus. 'Leave them to the dead, where they belong.'[34] Guthrie sums it up (p. 449):

Rest, cessation of effort, would mean the opposite of *kosmos*, for it would result in the falling apart of the opposites, whose union in 'an adjustment of opposite tensions' – locked, as it were, in an internecine strife – is what keeps in being the world as we know it.

(iii)   But, although the universe is a place in which all things are in a state of flux, a place whose very survival depends on strife, it is nevertheless not a chaos; it is a *kosmos*; it is a reliable, dependable universe. Why? Because of the Logos, even although men do not recognize it. Heraclitus says:

> Although this Logos [which I shall describe] exists for ever, men prove as unable to understand it when once they have heard it as before they heard it. For though all things come to pass in accordance with this Logos, men seem as if ignorant when they experience such words and things as I set forth, distinguishing each thing according to its nature and telling how it is. The rest of men are unaware of what they do while awake, just as they forget what they do while asleep.[35]

All things come to pass in accordance with this Logos. Don't listen to me,' says Heraclitus in effect. 'Listen to the Logos.'[36] And it is the complaint of Heraclitus: 'Although the Logos is common, most men live as though they had a private understanding of their own.'[37] Men become intelligent by breathing in the divine Logos; it works that way, Sextus explains, because when a man is asleep, breathing is 'the only point of attachment to be preserved'.[38] By this divine Logos and law men must live. 'The sun will not overstep his measures; otherwise the Erinyes, ministers of justice, will find him out.'[39] 'All human laws are nourished by one law, the divine law, which extends its sway as far as it will, and is sufficient for all and more than sufficient.'[40]

For Heraclitus the Logos is the power which puts reason into man, and the power which makes the world a cosmos and not a chaos, the power which makes man a thinking creature and the world a dependable world, the power with which a man must align himself, if he is to be one with the divine. With Heraclitus the conception of the Logos made an impressive beginning.

The thinkers who put the Logos in the very centre of their system were the Stoics. E.V. Arnold[41] says of the Stoics:

> They adopted and developed a conception which exercised an extraordinary influence over other systems, when they attributed the exercise of all the powers of deity to the divine Word, which from one point of view is the deity himself, and from another is something which emanates from him, and is in some way distinct.

Even if the ultimate source of the Stoic conception is Persian or Hebraic, he says,

> we must allow that the Stoics made use of this term with a boldness and consistency which from the time of their appearance brought it into the forefront of the religious and metaphysical controversy. Through the Stoics the doctrine of the Word passed into the systems of Judaism and Christianity, to perform in each the like service of reconciling doctrines apparently contradictory.

For the Stoics the Logos was 'the rational principle of the universe and reason in man.'[42] They used the conception of the Logos to explain how deity came into relation with the world at all. 'The Logos,' says C.K. Barrett (p. 61), 'is seen to describe God in the process of self-communication.' According to Hoskyns and Davey (p. 157), the Logos was for the Stoics 'the controlling philosophical idea by which the structure and unity of the universe was explained'.

To the Stoic the Logos was responsible for the order and for the creation of the world. 'The Logos, like Wordsworth's "Duty", kept the stars in their courses.'[43] H. Kleinknecht in his article on 'Logos' in *TDNT* IV (p. 84) says: 'In Stoicism Logos is a term for the ordered and teleologically orientated nature of the world.' Fate is defined as 'the endless chain of causation, whereby things are, or as the reason or formula (*logos*) by which the world goes on'.[44] The Logos is equated with God. 'They hold that there are two principles in the universe, the active principle and the passive. The passive principle then is a substance without quality, i.e. matter, whereas the active principle is the reason (*logos*) inherent in the substance, that is, God.' 'Fate is the Logos of God.'[45] 'God is the Logos of all things which are.'[46] Marcus Aurelius in his *Meditations* (6.1) describes the Logos as the power which controls the universal substance of which all things are made, and in 5.32 he speaks of 'the reason, the logos, that informs all substance, and governs the whole from ordered cycle to cycle, through all eternity'. The Logos is that power which makes this an ordered and reliable and dependable universe; the Logos is none other than the mind of God permeating and thus making sense of the universe.

The Word, the Logos, does not only order; it also creates. Chrysippus calls the Logos the principle which creates the world, which orders and creates it and constitutes it, the power which extends throughout matter. 'The world is a grand unfolding of the Logos,' says Kleinknecht (p. 85).

This Logos exists in different ways. We may begin from the principle that: 'Words and thoughts are the very same thing regarded under different aspects. The same idea (*logos*), which is a thought as long as it resides within the breast, is a word as soon as it comes forth.'[47] So we have the following aspects of the Logos.

(a) There is the *Logos endiathetos*, the internal logos, the logos as thought and unuttered.

(b) There is the *Logos prophorikos*, the outgoing logos, the uttered logos. So Sextus Empiricus argues: 'Man does not differ in respect of uttered reason from the irrational animals (for crows and parrots and jay utter articulate sounds), but in respect of internal reason.' But there is the counter-argument that animals are not unwise. 'For if they possess "uttered reason", they must necessarily also possess "internal reason".'[48]

(c) There is the *logos spermatikos*, the generative reason. The

spermatic logos is the active logos, the creative logos, the logos which
gives form and shape and life to all things, and out of which reason
grows. 'By the term Generative Reasons . . . must be understood the
creative and forming forces in nature which have collectively
produced the universe, and particular exercises of which produce
individual things.'[49] The spermatic logos, the Generative Reason, is
the creative formula of life.

(d)   But this phrase can also be used in the plural, *spermatikoi
logoi*. There is one overall Generative Reason, but in everything that
lives and grows there is a part of this generative reason, and it is that
particle or reason which makes the thing, the plant, the animal develop
consistently, reliably and in the way it ought.

(e)   There is *orthos logos*, Right Reason. Right Reason is that
which gives men the power of knowledge. By what standard are things
to be judged? The *orthos logos*, the Right Reason, is the 'criterion in
regard to knowledge by which what is true in our notions may be
distinguished from what is false'.[50]

It is the Logos which puts sense and order into the universe and
reason into man. 'In the Stoic *logos*,' says Kleinknecht (p. 85), 'the
rational power of order and the vital power of conception are merged
in one.' By Logos, explains W.F. Howard (*Christianity according to St
John*, p. 35), the Stoic meant 'the scheme of the world'. There remains
one thing to be said. For the Stoic the primordial reality is fire. God is
fire, ethereal, infinitely pure. But the Stoic was a pantheist, and not
only was God fire, but the stuff of the world, the substance out of
which the world was created, was that same fire, depotentiated into
matter. And that which gave life and reason to all living things was a
spark of that divine fire, a *scintilla* of the fire, dwelling in the body.
That fire was God in a man, God in a living thing, and was the same
as the Logos; and therefore in a very real sense the Logos is God, is
divine.

Here is the Stoic conception of the Logos. The Logos is creator; the
Logos puts order into the universe and reason into man; the Logos is
God in the created world and in the mind of man; the Logos gives a
man life and breath and reason and judgment; it is the Logos which
makes a man kin to God. Man came from the Logos and to the Logos
he will go. 'You will vanish into what begot you,' says Marcus
Aurelius, 'or rather you will be taken into its Seminal Reason, the *logos
spermatikos*, by a process of change' (4.14). When a soul dies it is for
a time transferred to the air; then, he says, 'it undergoes change and is
diffused and becomes fire, and is taken again into the *logos
spermatikos* of the Whole' (4.21). From the Logos we came; to the
Logos we go; and by the Logos the world exists and we live – such
was the Stoic faith.

To the Stoic, belief in the Logos was not so much a matter of philosophy as it was of devotion. The great expression of that devotion is Cleanthes's famous *Hymn to Zeus*, part of which is:

> Naught upon earth is wrought in thy despite, O God,
> Nor in the ethereal sphere aloft which ever winds
> About its pole, nor in the sea – save only what
> The wicked work, in their strange madness.
> Yet even so thou knowest how to make the crooked straight,
> Prune all excess, give order to the orderless;
> For unto thee the unloved still is lovely –
> And thus in one all things are harmonized,
> The evil with the good, that so one Word
> Should be in all things everlastingly.
> One Word – which evermore the wicked flee!
> Ill-fated, hungering to possess the good
> They have no vision of God's universal law,
> Nor will they hear . . .
> Scatter, O Father, the darkness from their souls,
> Grant them to find true understanding –
> On which relying thou justly rulest all –
> While we, thus honoured, in turn will honour thee,
> Hymning thy works forever, as is meet
> For mortals, while no greater right
> Belongs even to the gods than evermore
> Justly to praise the universal law![51]

This shows us why W.F. Howard can write (p. 34):

> The *logos spermatikos* or seminal reason was a term widely used in the centuries immediately before and after the beginning of the Christian era, and its meaning would have been understood at once in any company of educated men in Athens or Alexandria or Ephesus at the end of the first century.

The fourth gospel was presenting Jesus Christ to men in language which they could understand.

We come now to another thinker whose works are a landmark in the working out of the conception of the Logos, to Philo. Philo was a Jewish aristocrat of Alexandria, who was born about 20 BC and died about AD 50.[52] His one aim was to unite Jewish religion and Greek philosophy. He was 'the most illustrious of all those who strove to unite Jewish belief with Hellenic culture, to be the means of imparting to Jews the cultivation of the Greeks, and to Greeks the religious knowledge of the Jews. No other Jewish Hellenist was so fully saturated with the wisdom of the Greeks'.[53] W.R. Inge in *Christian Mysticism* (p. 83) writes of him: 'Philo's object is to reconcile religion with philosophy – in other words Moses and Plato. His method is to make Platonism a development of Mosaism, and Mosaism an implicit Platonism.'

W.F. Howard (*Christianity according to St John*, p. 36) tells us that in Philo's many works the Logos is mentioned about 1300 times. For Philo, says Inge (p. 84), the Logos is 'the mind of God expressing itself in act'. The Logos is the liaison between God and the world. Hoskyns and Davey (p. 158) write: 'Philo solves the problem of the relation between the supernatural, invisible, unknowable world and the material world by making use of the conception of the Logos as the active manifestation of God in the physical world.' H.A.A. Kennedy writes in *Philo's Contribution to Religion* (p. 162):

> Philo's attempts to bridge the gulf which he assumes between a God who is pure Being and the world of Becoming circle round the conception of the Logos, who is God's thought or reason, the powers of God (*dunameis*), which are manifestations of his energy working in the universe, and the angels, a considerably vaguer category.

The more men thought about God, the more they were impressed by his otherness, his transcendence, and the more necessary such intermediaries seemed to be. In the Logos Philo found his intermediary.

We begin with what H.A.A. Kennedy (p. 166) takes to be for Philo the heart of the matter, 'the most important fundamental passage' for Philo's conception of the Logos. The essential thing for Philo is that the Logos 'stands in the middle'. He quotes *Who is the Heir of Divine Things* (205f.):

> The Father, who has begotten all things, granted as his choicest privilege to his chief messenger and most august Logos, that he should stand in the middle between the Creator and the created. Now he is, on the one hand, always the suppliant for transient mortals, in presence of the Immortal, and on the other, he is the Ambassador of the Ruler to his subjects. Thus he rejoices because of the privilege and prides himself on it ... being neither uncreated like God, nor created like you, but standing between the two extremes as a pledge to both, to him who created as an assurance that created beings will never wholly rebel or revolt, choosing confusion rather than order, and in the case of the creature to give him the bright hope that the gracious God will never ignore his own work.

This may be seen also in the context of worship. In the progress of the soul towards the highest, the apprehension of the Logos is the intermediate stage which must be passed through.

> It is a boon for perishable mortals to have mediating and controlling *logoi* (the plural, i.e. rational Divine powers), because of their own awe and shrinking before the Lord of all (*On Dreams*, 1.142).

So then the supreme function of the Logos for Philo is to provide the link between God and man.

Clearly, if the Logos is the liaison between God and the world, the

Logos will have a special part in creation. The Logos is 'God's creative energy' (*On Creation*, 24; *On Flight*, 95). The Logos is the instrument (*organon*) by which God made all things, the image of God, through whom the whole universe was framed.[54]

But the Logos is not only the instrument by which God made all things; the Logos is also the pattern according to which all things are made. The Logos is at one and the same time the image of the Creator and the idea – in the Platonic sense – the pattern of creation (*On Dreams*, 2.45).

> For the constituting of the soul God seems to have used as a pattern no created thing, but only . . . his own Logos. Of this therefore . . . man was made the facsimile and copy (*On Creation*, 139).

The Logos is the ideal world as it exists in the mind of God, the image of God, 'the pattern according to which the perceptible universe has been fashioned' (*On Creation*, 24f.).

God did not make the world through his Logos and on the pattern of the Logos and then leave it; he put the Logos into the world to control and to direct it. The universe and all it contains is like a flock under the hand of God, its King and Shepherd:

> This hallowed flock he leads in accordance with right and law, setting over it his true Logos and Firstborn Son, who shall take upon himself its government like some viceroy of a great king (*On Husbandry*, 51).

In *On the Migration of Abraham* (6) Philo speaks of

> . . . the Logos who is antecedent to all that has come into existence, the Logos which the Helmsman of the universe grasps as a rudder to guide all things on their course, even as when he was fashioning the world he employed it as his instrument, that the fabric of his handiwork might be without reproach.

The presence of the Logos in man and in the universe is the seal, the sign-manual of God. 'The Logos is the divine seal by which each created thing is stamped and receives its permanent quality' (*On Flight*, 12f.). The rational soul of man is 'the genuine coinage of that divine and invisible spirit, marked and stamped by the seal of God, whose impress is the eternal Logos' (*On Noah's Work as a Planter*, 18).

The man who seeks God has the Logos as his guide.

> He who follows after God has . . . as companion on his journey these rational powers (*logoi*), who accompany God, who are commonly called angels . . . For as long as he is not perfected, he has the Divine Logos to show him the way . . . But when he has reached the summit of knowledge, after running eagerly, he will equal in swiftness him who formerly led the way, for both will become attendants of the omnipotent God (*On the Migration of Abraham*, 173-5).

The Logos of God, when he visits our earthly system of things, helps and succours those who have kinship with goodness and tend in that direction, so as to provide for them a complete refuge and salvation, but on the enemies of the good he launches ruin and incurable destruction (*On Dreams*, 1.86).

Like a king, it (the Logos) announces by decree what men ought to do; like a teacher, it instructs its disciples in what will benefit them; like a counsellor, it suggests the wisest plans, and so greatly benefits those who do not of themselves know what is best; like a friend, it tells many secrets which it is not lawful for the uninitiated to hear (*On Dreams*, 1.191).

It is hardly too much to say that the Logos is the guardian angel of the man who will have it so.

There are times when Philo writes as if the Logos were the equivalent of conscience. In a long passage in the work *On the Unchangeableness of God* (134-8) he says:

So long as the Divine Logos has not come into our souls as into its abode, the deeds of the soul are blameless; for its guardian, or father, or teacher, or whatever we ought to call that Priest by whom alone it can be warned and controlled, remains far from it; and those who sin through ignorance, without knowledge of what things they ought to do, receive pardon. For they do not even apprehend their actions as sins. Indeed they even suppose they are acting rightly in cases where they commit great errors. But when the High Priest, who genuinely tests us, enters into us like a perfectly pure ray of light, then we recognize the unrighteous designs harboured in our soul and the culpable deeds. All these the consecrated testing Power, having shown their defilement, bids us pack away and strip off, that he may behold the house of the soul clean, and, if any diseases have arisen in it, may heal them.

And then Philo goes on to liken the Logos to a prophet, the prophet Elijah in I Kings 17.18, to whom the woman whose son had died said: 'You have come to me to bring my sin to remembrance.'

For this inspired being, in the grasp of an Olympian love, and goaded by the irresistible stings of his divine frenzy, entering into the soul, created there the remembrance of her old wrong-doing and sins, not that she may again yield to them, but with loud lamentations and weeping she may come back from her former wandering, hating the issue, and may follow the promptings of the Logos-prophet, who is the interpreter of God.

The Logos, like conscience, is the guide to the right and the warning against the wrong.

The Logos, as that passage ended by saying, is God's interpreter. In a discussion of the incomprehensibility of God Philo speaks of 'the Logos-interpreter', whom he calls 'the God of the imperfect', as opposed to the Eternal, who is 'the God of the wise and perfect' (*Allegories of the Laws*, 3.207). The Logos is the interpreter of the word and the will of God to those who as yet find it hard to understand.

Philo sometimes identifies the Logos with Wisdom. In an allegorical interpretation of the river which flowed out of Eden (Gen. 2.10), he takes the river to be generic virtue and goodness. 'This issues forth out of Eden, the Wisdom of God, and that is the Logos of God' (*Allegories*, 1.65). Commenting on Psalm 65.9:

> Thou visitest the earth and waterest it,
>   thou greatly enrichest it;
> the river of God is full of water,

He says: 'As from the fountain of Wisdom the Divine Logos flows down to refresh and water the Olympian and heavenly plants of the soul that love goodness' (*On Dreams*, 2.242). It is the Logos which is the source of understanding in a man:

> Every man, so far as his understanding is concerned, is intimately related to the Divine Logos, an impress, or particle, or effulgence of the blessed nature, while, as regards his bodily status he is closely akin to the whole cosmos (*On Creation*, 146).

It is easy to see what a width and a wealth the conception of the Logos had when John annexed it. But to keep the balance two things must be pointed out. The first is that Philo never anywhere in his writings personalizes the Logos. H.A.A. Kennedy (pp. 171f.) points us to a significant passage from *On Dreams* (1.103ff.). Philo begins by observing that the Logos, obviously in the sense of *reason*, but sometimes gliding into that of *speech*, is God's choicest gift to man, his 'bulwark', his 'bodyguard', his 'protagonist', the power that 'furthers his aspirations'. The Logos is 'the saving remedy for the passions of the soul' . . . 'a counsellor and champion', whose presence gives joy and rest. But at the close of the passage all is merged in the figure of the 'Divine Logos whom the ascetic soul, renouncing itself, awaits as a visitant coming invisibly from without'. And, second, the one thing which for John is everything is absent from Philo, and impossible for Philo. For John the incarnation of the Word, the Word become flesh is everything. For Philo that could never be. Philo writes:

> There are three kinds of life – one looking Godwards, another looking to created things, and a third on the border line, a mixture of both. But the Godward looking life has never descended to us, nor has it come as far as the necessities of the body (*Who is the Heir*, 45).

J.H. Bernard in his commentary (I, p. cxliii) sums up the essential difference: 'It was left for Christian philosophy to proclaim that the only solution of those problems which metaphysic had failed to solve was *historical* – the word became flesh.'

Men already knew something of what John was talking about – but not everything.

To one other area must we go to see the kind of thinking to which the fourth gospel appealed; we must look at the Hermetic literature.[55] J.N. Sanders (p. 21) describes the Hermetic literature as 'an Egyptian syncretistic theosophy, a blend of Platonic mysticism and cosmogony, fused with elements of unorthodox Judaism'. The Hermetic literature, as it is, belongs to the second and third century AD. It was said to be the work of an ancient Egyptian sage, who was afterwards deified as the Egyptian god Thoth, who is equated with the Greek Hermes. C.H. Dodd in *The Interpretation of the Fourth Gospel* (p. 12) calls its tractates 'monuments of the cross-fertilisation of Greek and Oriental thought, which was characteristic of the Near East in the Hellenistic and Roman periods'.

Here we meet certain things relevant to the thought of the fourth gospel. Once again we meet the conception of the word, particularly in the first tractate, the Poimandres.[56] (We quote from W. Scott's translation, *Hermetica* I, pp. 114ff.) It opens with Poimandres telling the writer how the world came into being. The writer had a vision of 'a downward-tending darkness, terrible and grim-. The darkness changed 'into a watery substance, unspeakably tossed about, smoking as from fire; and I heard it making an indescribable sound of lamentation; for there was sent forth from it an inarticulate cry (*boē*)'. Then, 'Out of the Light a Holy Word assailed the wet nature, as if it were the voice of the Light.' Poimandres tells the writer that the Light is himself, for the Light is the Mind of God, who existed before the watery dark. 'And the Word which came forth from the Light is the Son of God.' The writer demands what he means by this, and Poimandres advises him to look at himself and his own nature. (C.H. Dodd in *The Bible and the Greeks*, p. 118, refers to a passage from Philo, *On the Cherubim*, 7. There Philo comments on what he supposes is the meaning of the name Abraham; he takes it to mean 'elect father of sound', and goes on: 'The uttered word sounds, and its father is the mind which has apprehended the good.' So in the Hermetic literature itself [12.14] the word is called the *eikōn*, the image of the mind. In the same way the Word which comes forth from the Eternal Mind, which is God, is the son of God.)

Poimandres continues (1.8-10): 'The watery substance ... was fashioned into an ordered world, the elements being separated out of it.' And the Word moved like a wind or a breath on the face of the water, and then, its work accomplished, it 'leapt up from the downward-tending elements of nature to the pure body ... and was united with Mind the Maker; for the Word was of one substance with that Mind.' The connection of this with the first chapter of Genesis is not difficult to see. To this Logos in creation the *Hermetic Corpus* refers again. 'The Providence in which the world is governed is "the absolute *logos* of the heavenly God." "The Creator made the whole world not with hands, but by *logos*."'[57] Scott quotes the following fragments from Cyril of Alexandria:[58]

> For God's Word, who is all-accomplishing and fecund and creative, went forth, and flinging himself upon the water, which was a thing of fecund nature, made the water pregnant.

> For it (i.e. the material world) has over it as ruler the creative Word of the Master of all. The Word is, next after him, the supreme Power, a Power ungenerated, boundless, that has stooped forth from him; the Word presides over and governs the things that have been made through him.

> The nature of his intellectual Word is generative. You may call him what you will, provided that you understand this, that he is perfect and issues from one who is perfect, and that he works perfect goods, and makes and vivifies all things. Since then he is of such a nature, he is rightly called by his name.

> The Word of the Maker, my son, is everlasting, self-moved, without increase or diminution, immutable, incorruptible...; he is ever like to himself and equal to himself, equable, stable, well-ordered; after the supreme God he stands alone.

It is clear that in the Hermetic literature the Word has a very large place in creation and in providence, in the control of the world, and in the mind of man.

The second connection of the fourth gospel with the Hermetic literature is to be found in the stress which both lay on knowledge. C.H. Dodd in *The Interpretation of the Fourth Gospel* (pp. 14-16) has collected a number of passages illustrating this.

> The only way of salvation for man is knowledge of God (10.15).

> The virtue of the soul is knowledge, for he who knows is both good and pious and already divine (10.9)

> God is the Good, and the property of the Good is to be known (10.4).

> Holy is God, who wills to be known, and is known to his own (1.31, from the hymn in the Poimandres).

> The evil of the soul ... is ignorance. The soul that knows nothing of existent things, nor of their nature, nor of the Good, is shaken blindly by bodily passions. This unhappy soul, because it is ignorant of itself, is slave to alien and oppressive bodies, carrying the body like a burden, not governing it but being governed by it. This is the evil of the soul (10.8).

The only way to know God is to be like God. Dodd puts it:

> Like is known by like; to know God is in some sense to partake of his nature ... 'Unless you make yourself like God, you cannot rationally apprehend God, for like is apprehended by like' (11.20).

The thinker who could write like that could well understand the fourth gospel. 'This is eternal life, that they may know thee the only true

God, and Jesus Christ whom thou has sent' (John 17.3). The knowledge, the saving knowledge of God, is something about which the fourth gospel and Hermeticism both know; and for both there is more than intellect in this, for the Hermetic writer can say: 'The service of God is one thing alone, to refrain from evil' (12.23).

A third thing which the thought of the Hermetic literature and of the fourth gospel have in common is their stress on light and life. Dodd (*The Interpretation of the Fourth Gospel*, p. 19) quotes the Poimandres again: 'I enter into Life and Light. Blessed art thou, O Father' (1.32). 'Save, O Life. Enlighten, O Light' (13.19). The man who could write and pray like that could well understand such sayings as 'In him was life, and the life was the light of men' (John 1.4) and 'God is light, and in him is no darkness at all' (I John 1.5). Both writers are moving in the same world.

But there is one basic difference. The Hermetic writers are sure that this knowledge and this blessedness can never be attained in this life and in this body:

> In this life we are still too weak to see that sight; we have not strength to open our mental eyes, and to behold the beauty of the Good, the incorruptible beauty which no tongue can tell. Then only will you see it, when you cannot speak of it; for the knowledge of it is deep silence, and suppression of all the senses. He who has apprehended the beauty of the Good can apprehend nothing else; he cannot hear speech about aught else; he cannot move his body at all; he forgets all bodily sensations and all bodily movements and is still. But the beauty of the Good bathes his mind in light, and takes all his soul up to itself, and draws it forth from the body, and changes the whole man into eternal substance. For it cannot be, my son, that a soul should become a god while it abides in a human body; it must be changed and then behold the beauty of the Good, and therewith become a god.[59]

> He who is not ignorant of these things can apprehend God precisely. Indeed, if I may speak so boldly, he may behold him with his own eyes, and beholding him become blessed. But it is impossible for one who is in the body to have such happiness. We must exercise the soul beforehand here, in order that, when it goes there, where it is permitted to behold God, it may not miss the way. Those men who are lovers of the body will never behold the vision of the Beautiful and the Good.[60]

The Hermetic writings can say much, but they know nothing of having life, and life more abundantly, here and now. They know nothing of a belief in Jesus Christ which here and now will bring life in his name (John 10.10; 20.31).

There is no direct contact between the fourth gospel and the Hermetic writings. They form, says R.E. Brown (p. lix), 'no significant part of the background of the Gospel'. 'No direct literary relation,' says C.K. Barrett (pp. 31f.), 'can be traced, but it seems clear that

John was working with similar presuppositions and along similar lines to those of the Hermetic writers.' C.H. Dodd, in *The Bible and the Greeks* (p. 247), says that the resemblances are 'the result of minds working under the same general influences'.

So John spoke to his day, and an examination of the facts justifies what we said at the beginning, that the fourth gospel is perhaps the most successful experiment in communication the church has ever seen.

6

THE FOURTH GOSPEL AND THE SYNOPTIC GOSPELS

No one can read the fourth gospel without seeing, even apart from any special detailed study, that it is different from the other three. And yet the fact remains that it is possible to overstate the differences and to disregard the connections too completely. F.C. Burkitt writes in *The Gospel History* (p. 220):

> The fact is that the narrative in 'Mark' and the narrative in 'John' cannot be made to agree, except on the supposition that one or the other is, as regards the objective facts, inaccurate and misleading.

That may well be much too sweeping a statement, and in any event it may well be making a comparison between the fourth gospel and the synoptic gospels on quite the wrong grounds. Before we turn to impressions and opinions and subjective judgments, we would be well to start with the factual side of the question.[1]

(i)   Obviously, the fourth gospel begins quite differently from the other. John starts with the philosophical concept of the Logos; Luke starts with an introduction such as any historian might use. R.H. Lightfoot says (p. 23): 'St Luke sets theology in an historical framework; St John sets history in a theological framework.' Luke sets his gospel firmly in history with his sixfold dating of the emergence of John the Baptist (3.1f.). John begins in the uncreated eternities before time began. The gospel writers push their beginnings always further back. Mark (1.1-4) brings Jesus on to the stage a full grown man, and his first date is the appearing of John the Baptist. Matthew (1.2) for a beginning goes back to Abraham. Luke (3.22) takes the story back to Adam. But John (1.1f.) takes the beginning back to the time before there ever was a world. John's approach to what he has to say about Jesus is quite different from the other three.

(ii)   In John the scene of the ministry of Jesus is different. In the synoptic gospels two-thirds of Jesus' work was done in Galilee and Samaria, and he does not arrive in Jerusalem until the last week of his life. In the fourth gospel Jesus' main work is done in Judaea with brief incursions into Galilee (2.1-12; 4.43-54; 6.1-7.14). It has in fact been urged (by Hoskyns and Davey, p. 63) that the topography of the fourth gospel may be said to be the topography of Jerusalem, and not even of Judaea at large. On the basis of the Fourth Gospel it may even be argued that John is declaring that Judaea is Jesus' *patris*, his native country. John writes (4.45f.):

> And after the two days he departed to Galilee. For Jesus testified that a prophet has no honour in his own country. So when he came to Galilee, the Galilaeans welcomed him, having seen all that he had done in Jerusalem at the feast, for they too had gone to the feast.

The obvious meaning of this is that Jesus was welcomed in Galilee, but had no honour in Judaea which was his native country. On the other hand the synoptic gospels have no doubt that Jesus came from Nazareth. 'He came to Nazareth, where he had been brought up, and he went into the synagogue as his custom was' (Luke 4.16; cf. Mark 6.16; Matt. 13.53-8). But here is one of these instances of what repeatedly happens in the fourth gospel. Philip's message to Nathanael (1.45) is: 'We have found him of whom Moses in the law and also the prophets wrote, Jesus of Nazareth, the son of Joseph.' And Nathanael answers: 'Can anything good come out of Nazareth?' So although the fourth gospel seems to say that Jesus' native country was Judaea, it is equally positive that he came from Nazareth.

But this much is true – if the story of the fourth gospel is to be taken as chronologically valid at all, then Jesus spent the last six months of his earthly life in Jerusalem. He goes to Jerusalem for the Feast of Tabernacles (7.2); he stays through the Feast of Dedication (10.22); and then there comes the final Passover (11.55; 12.1; 18.28). And this would cover a period of about six months. It is certainly true that in the fourth gospel Jerusalem bulks much larger in the narrative than it does in the synoptic gospels. But here we come upon the same phenomenon again. Could Jesus really on his first visit to Jerusalem have uttered the famous lament (Matt. 23.37; Luke 13.34):

> O Jerusalem, Jerusalem, killing the prophets and stoning those who are sent to you! How often would I have gathered your children together as a hen gathers her brood under her wings, and you would not!

Does not a lamentation like that carry with it the implication of a long series of previous appeals? When in the temptation story of the devil takes Jesus to the holy city, and sets him on the pinnacle of the temple (Matt. 4.5; Luke 4.9), does this not presuppose a knowledge of what the temple was like? Does not the Martha and Mary relationship with Jesus even in Luke (10.38-42) suggest a background of many visits and of intimate friendship? It is true that the fourth gospel makes Jesus move in Jerusalem much more than the synoptic gospels do on the surface of the story, but none the less the synoptic gospels also have their hints that Jesus was no stranger to Jerusalem.

(iii) In the fourth gospel the duration of Jesus' ministry is different. The synoptic gospels have only one Passover, and in them the ministry of Jesus would all go into a year. In the fourth gospel there are at least three and perhaps four Passovers. Jesus' ministry begins some time before the first Passover (2.13). Another Passover is mentioned in connection with the feeding of the five thousand (6.4). And finally there comes the last Passover (11.55). There is also the unnamed feast in 5.1.[2] To take all this in, a ministry of at least three years is necessary.

But once again the question enters in. In the synoptic gospels (Mark 2.23) we find the disciples plucking the ripe ears of grain. The harvest must have been near, and this means that it was sometime between Passover and Pentecost, that is, say, some time in May. In Mark's story of the feeding of the five thousand we find the people seated upon 'the green grass' (Mark 6.23). It could therefore be that there is something approaching a year between the two scenes. In the transfiguration incident we find Peter wishing to make three booths, one for Moses, one for Elijah and one for Jesus (Mark 9.4f.), and it is very tempting to connect that with the Feast of Tabernacles, during which the Jews lived in booths in the open air, in memory of their nomadic days in the wilderness journeyings; and its date was September-October. We then move on to the final Passover, and on this scheme there is a period of at least two years – which brings the synoptic scheme much nearer that of the fourth gospel. So again the doubt comes in.

(iv)   There is a possibility that the fourth gospel differs from the synoptic gospels in regard to the age of Jesus. In the synoptic gospels Jesus is about thirty, when he begins his ministry (Luke 3.23). But it can be argued from the fourth gospel that Jesus was about fifty when he died. Jesus declared that Abraham was glad to see his day, and the Jews reply (8.57): 'You are not yet fifty years old, and have you seen Abraham?' And there is the saying in the fourth gospel narrative about the cleansing of the temple (2.19-21). Jesus said to them: 'Destroy this temple, and in three days I will raise it up.' They replied: 'It has taken forty-six years to build this temple, and will you raise it up in three days?' And John then comments: 'But he spoke of the temple of his body.' And it is argued that the forty-six years can thus be connected with Jesus. It is of interest to note that Irenaeus knew of this tradition, and apparently accepted it, for he argued (*Against Heresies*, 2.22.6) that Jesus, because he reached fifty, sanctified all parts of life, childhood, youth, manhood and middle age. But in the passages quoted it is not by any means certain that the fourth gospel intends to say anything at all about the age of Jesus.

(v)   There are certain matters of fact in which the fourth gospel differs from the synoptic gospels. Some of them we shall take in other connections; two of them we shall take just now.

In the synoptic gospels Jesus does not begin his ministry until after the arrest of John the Baptist. 'After John was arrested, Jesus came into Galilee, preaching the gospel of God' (Mark 1.14; Matt. 4.12; Luke 3.19f.). And in the synoptic gospels Jesus does not baptize at all. In the fourth gospel the ministries of John and Jesus for a short time overlap (3.22-30), and Jesus is said to baptize more people than John (4.1f.). The reason for the overlap is not difficult to see; it is to give John the Baptist the opportunity to witness to the supremacy of Jesus, which he emphatically does.

In the synoptic gospels the cleansing of the temple comes at the end of Jesus' ministry (Matt. 21.12f.; Mark 11.15-17; Luke 19.45f.); in the fourth gospel it comes at the beginning (2.13-22). Von Hügel says that John makes the incident an appropriate frontispiece to the life of Jesus; the synoptics make it the cause of his death. It may be that John wishes to begin with an authoritative messianic act. Or it may be, quite simply, that John is right, because in the way in which the synoptic gospels are laid out Jesus' first and only adult visit to Jerusalem was in the last week of his life.

(vi) There are considerable differences in detail between the passion narrative of the synoptic gospels and of the fourth gospel. We shall see that for some of them there are possible explanations, but at the moment we shall not try to explain them, only to list them. Theodore of Mopsuestia would hold that the discrepancies occur after they had all fled and left only John, if John is the beloved disciple, there (see M.F. Wiles, *The Spiritual Gospel*, p. 18).

There is no account of the Lord's Supper, or at least of the institution of the eucharist. The date of the crucifixion is changed; in the synoptic gospels the crucifixion takes place before the Passover (Matt. 26.17-20; Mark 14.12-17; Luke 22.7-14), whereas in the fourth gospel it follows it (19.14, 31, 42). The fourth gospel has no agony in the garden. In the synoptic gospels those who have come to arrest Jesus advance towards him (Matt. 26.49f.; Mark 14.45f.; Luke 22.47); in the fourth gospel he goes forward to meet them (18.4). In the synoptics Jesus' personal claim to uniqueness is made before the Jewish investigating authorities (Mark 14.62; Matt. 26.64; Luke 22.70); in the fourth gospel (18.33-8) it is made before Pilate, and there the interview finishes with the kingdom sayings which have no parallel in the synoptic gospels. Simon of Cyrene (Matt. 27.32; Mark 15.21; Luke 23.26) is absent from John 19.17. The synoptic gospels have Christ's garments (Matt. 27.35; Mark 15.24; Luke 23.34), but the seamless robe is only in John (19.23f.). Mary, Jesus' mother, is not named among the onlookers at the cross in the synoptic gospels (Matt. 27.55f.; Mark 15.40f.; Luke 23.49), but she is there in the fourth gospel (19.25). According to the synoptic gospels (Matt. 26.56; Mark 14.50) all the disciples forsook Jesus and fled; in the fourth gospel

(19.26f.) John is there – that is, if John is to be identified with the beloved disciple. The synoptic gospels have nothing about the water and the blood coming from the wounded side of Jesus, nor of the fact that none of his bones were broken (John 19.31-7).

(vii)   The fourth gospel omits many things which the synoptic gospels contain. The fourth gospel has no parables, no exorcisms, no paralytics, no Sadducees, no scribes, no tax-gatherers. The fourth gospel omits the virgin birth, Gethsemane, the cry of dereliction on the cross, the transfiguration and the ascension. In the fourth gospel Jesus only prays, as it were, to teach and impress other people; in the synoptic gospels prayer is part of the fibre of his being (contrast Mark 1.35 and John 11.41f.). The fourth gospel has few of the great turning-point moments in the life of Jesus; it does not have his baptism, his temptations, the discovery at Caesarea Philippi, the divine approval of the transfiguration.

(viii)   The picture of Jesus in the fourth gospel is different from the picture in the synoptic gospels. It is in fact so different that there are some who think it impossibly different, and who argue that the picture in the fourth gospel and the picture in the synoptic gospels cannot both be true. In *The Fourth Gospel in Research and Debate* (p. 3) B.W. Bacon writes:

> On this question we are driven unavoidably to the alternative – either the synoptics or John. Either the former are right in their complete silence regarding pre-existence and incarnation, and in their subordination of the doctrine of Christ's person, in presenting his work and teaching as concerned with the kingdom of God, with repentance, with a filial disposition and life as the requirement made by the common Father for that inheritance; or else John is right in making Jesus' work and message supremely a manifestation of his own glory as the incarnate Logos, effecting an atonement for the world, which has otherwise no access to God. Both cannot be true.

Let us then look at the picture of Jesus in the fourth gospel, and it is here that we will see the reason for John's omission of certain things from his picture of Jesus.

(i)   There is about the Jesus of the fourth gospel a self-determining quality. He is utterly independent of other people; no one moves him to any action, or does anything for him. That is why the story of the baptism is omitted, for that story might be taken to mean that John the Baptist did something to or for Jesus. In the story of the turning of the water into wine, when Mary tells Jesus of the shortage, his response is to tell her not to interfere, but to leave things to him (2.4). When his brothers urge him to go and show himself in Jerusalem, his immediate reaction is not to go; he goes later to make it entirely clear that the decision to go to Jerusalem is his and his alone (7.3, 10).

When he receives the news that Lazarus is ill, he deliberately stays for two further days where he is, to show that he and he alone will decide when to move (11.6). In the fourth gospel account of the last supper Jesus almost orders Judas to get on with the business of betrayal (13.27). Simon of Cyrene disappears from the story; in the fourth gospel Jesus carries his own cross (19.17). 'I lay down my life,' he says (10.17f.), 'that I may take it again. No one takes it from me, but I lay it down of my own accord. I have power to lay it down, and I have power to take it again.' The fourth gospel does not say that Jesus died; none of the gospels do. Matthew (27.50) says that he yielded up his spirit; Mark (15.39) and Luke (23.46) says that he breathed his last; but John uses a word which means that Jesus, as it were of his own free will, handed over his spirit (19.30). In the fourth gospel Jesus from the beginning to the end of his life is completely self-determining.

(ii)   There is about the Jesus of the fourth gospel a certain inviolability. Until his hour comes, no one can do anything to him. In Jerusalem they sought to arrest him, 'but no man laid hands on him, because his hour had not yet come' (7.30). 'No one arrested him, because his hour had not yet come' (8.20). 'So they took up stones to throw at him; but Jesus hid himself and went out of the temple' (8.59). 'Again they tried to arrest him, but he escaped out of their hands' (10.39). In the fourth gospel Jesus does not wait for those who have come to arrest him; he goes to meet them, and 'they drew back and fell to the ground' (18.4, 6). Pilate may think that he has power to settle the fate of Jesus, but he would have no power at all unless that power had been given to him from above (19.11). All through the fourth gospel Jesus is inviolable. Sometimes it almost seems that a magic coat of invisibility concealed him. Nothing can happen to him which is outside the purpose of God.

(iii)   There is about the Jesus of the fourth gospel an omniscience which is more than human. He has already seen Nathanael under the fig-tree before he meets him (1.47f.). He knows what is in man and needs no one to tell him (2.24). He knows all about the woman of Samaria without being told (4.16). He knows beforehand what he is going to do about the feeding of the five thousand, and any question he asks is a test rather than a request for information (6.6). He knows what is going on in the minds of his disciples and he is well aware who will betray him (6.61, 64). He knows very well what Judas is going to do (13.18). He knows without being told what his disciples would wish to ask him (16.19). The Jesus of the fourth gospel does not need to ask the questions which need to be asked by ordinary people; he knows the answers already. He has a knowledge which ordinary people do not possess.

(iv)   In the synoptic gospels it is not until the incident at Caesarea Philippi that Jesus is recognized for who and what he is (Matt. 16.13-

20; Mark 8.27-30; Luke 9.18-21). And even then the disciples are charged to keep the fact of his messiahship a close secret. But in the fourth gospel Jesus is recognized from the beginning. As soon as John the Baptist sees Jesus, he says: 'Behold the Lamb of God, who takes away the sin of the world!' (1.29). Andrew goes to his brother Simon at the very beginning with the news: 'We have found the Messiah' (1.41). Philip goes to Nathanael saying: 'We have found him of whom Moses in the law and also the prophets wrote, Jesus of Nazareth, the son of Joseph.' And on being confronted with Jesus, the immediate reaction of Nathanael is: 'Rabbi, you are the Son of God! You are the King of Israel!' (1.49). The ending of the story of the miracle at Cana of Galilee is: 'This, the first of his signs, Jesus did at Cana in Galilee, and manifested his glory; and his disciples believed in him' (2.11). After the feeding of the five thousand, when many are leaving him, because he is not the kind of Messiah they expected him to be, Peter declares his loyalty: 'Lord, to whom shall we go? You have the words of eternal life; and we have believed and have come to know that you are the Holy One of God' (6.68f.). Long before the end some people are saying: 'This is the Christ' (7.41).

Not only do people recognize Jesus from the beginning in the fourth gospel; he also makes his claims quite openly. The woman of Samaria says to Jesus: 'I know that Messiah is coming ... When he comes he will show us all things.' And Jesus replies: 'I who speak to you am he' (4.26). In the story of the opening of the eyes of the man born blind, Jesus asks the man: 'Do you believe in the Son of man?' The man answers: 'And who is he, sir, that I may believe in him?' Jesus answers: 'You have seen him, and it is he who speaks to you' (9.35-8). In the fourth gospel there is no secrecy and from the beginning Jesus is recognized and openly claims to be the Son of God.

(v)   In the Jesus of the fourth gospel there is no process of development. Luke's saying (2.52) would be impossible for John: 'And Jesus increased in wisdom and in stature, and in favour with God and man.' From the beginning Jesus is, as it were, full grown, and his message is always about himself (3.16-21; 4.9-14; 5.19-46; 6.25-65; 7.14-39; 8.12-59; 10.1-18, 25-39). His claims are always astonishing. 'Before Abraham was, I am' (8.58). 'I and the Father are one' (10.30). 'No one comes to the Father but by me' (14.6). 'He who has seen me has seen the Father' (14.9). In the fourth gospel Jesus' message is about himself, and what settles any man's destiny is his reaction to these astonishing claims.

(vi)   The contrast between the essential message of the fourth gospel and that of the synoptic gospels is startling. In effect, the fourth gospel speaks of the kingdom of God only once, when Jesus tells Nicodemus that a man cannot experience the kingdom of God unless he is born again from above (3.3,5; cf. 18.36). In Matthew, however,

Jesus speaks of the kingdom 53 times, in Mark 17 times and in Luke 41 times. According to the synoptic gospels Jesus' basic message was: 'The time is fulfilled, and the kingdom of God is at hand; repent, and believe in the gospel' (Mark 1.15; cf. Matt. 4.17). And it is the simple fact that neither the noun 'repentance' nor the verb 'to repent' occurs in the fourth gospel at all. Instead of the summons to repent and the message of the kingdom, Jesus in the fourth gospel uses the words 'truth', 'true', 'truly' 55 times, the word 'life' in the special sense of the term 36 times, and the word 'light' 22 times. The message seems entirely different; in the fourth gospel Jesus seems to do nothing but talk about himself and his relationship to God, and his own divinity. Kirsopp and Sylvia Lake say in their *Introduction to the NT* (pp. 51f.) that the great difficulty in reconciling the picture of the fourth gospel with that of the synoptic gospels is not so much historical as theological.

> According to Mark Jesus never asked the people to hold any special opinion about himself. His desire was that they should repent, change their conduct, and so receive entry into the age to come. He expressly forbade his disciples to say that he was the messianic Son of man. According to John, on the other hand, Jesus freely announced that he was the Son of God, and demanded faith in himself. Those who believe in him will be given eternal life, and Jesus will raise them up at the last day.

(vii)   It is true to say that in the fourth gospel Jesus has become much less human and much more divine. In the three earlier gospels, as R.H. Lightfoot points out (pp. 42f.), Jesus' manhood is more conspicuous than his divinity; his divinity is more conspicuous than his manhood in the fourth gospel. E.J. Goodspeed in his *Introduction to the NT* (pp. 306f.) says of Jesus in the fourth gospel:

> The human qualities disappear, and he moves through the successive scenes of the gospel perfect master of every situation, until in the end he goes of his own accord to his crucifixion and his death. He does not teach in parables, and his teaching deals, not as in the earlier gospels with the kingdom of God, but with his own nature, and his inward relation to God.

E.F. Scott in *The Literature of the NT* (pp. 272-4) says:

> The humanity of Jesus falls into the background; the history is everywhere subordinated to abstract theological ideas. It is almost impossible to believe that a personal disciple could have merged the actual figure of Jesus in the conception of a divine being, answering to the requirements of Alexandrian philosophy.

Hoskyns and Davey (p. 35) say that what the fourth gospel is concerned with is to say that what Jesus *is* to the faith of the true Christian believer he *was* in the flesh. The fourth gospel gives the picture, not of the Jesus of Galilee, but of the Christ of faith.

(viii)   We look now at what Hoskyns and Davey (pp. 65-9) take to be the biggest difference of all between the synoptic gospels and the fourth gospel. The synoptic gospels consist of incidents any of which the reader or teacher may choose or use. (That is in fact the essence of form criticism). The incident can be chosen and used and interpreted as the use of it needs or desires. 'The synoptic gospels are admirably adapted to provide short public or private lections in church or at home.' But for the reader of the fourth gospel there is no such 'magnificent freedom'. The selection has been made, maybe not as we would have made it; the interpretation has been given and the interpretation is the interpretation of the risen Christ. The Spirit of Jesus has taken the things of Jesus and has shown them to us; things which could not be said in the days of his flesh are said now (John 14.26; 16.12-16). The fourth gospel is not concerned to cite crowds of witnesses. It is giving the witness of disciples who saw the glory of the Word (1.14); it is telling what they apprehended as witnesses after Christ had risen from the dead (2.22).

As Hoskyns and Davey see it, the fourth gospel is not, like the first three gospels, an arrangement of incidents; it is a literary unity. The reader has to move with the movement of the book; he has to bear carefully in mind what the author has already said, and in reading the beginning he must know the end of the whole matter. The book has to be read as a whole. Thus the end of the Lazarus story (11.43f.),

> When he had said this, he cried with a loud voice: Lazarus, come out. The dead man came out, his hands and feet bound with bandages, and his face wrapped in a cloth. Jesus said to them: Unbind him, and let him go,

must be read in the light of 5.28f.:

> Do not marvel at this, for the hour is coming when all who are in the tombs will hear his voice, and come forth, those who have done good to the resurrection of life, and those who have done evil to the resurrection of judgment;

and both are meaningless without 20.31:

> These are written that you may believe that Jesus is the Christ, the Son of God, and that believing *you may have life in his name.*

The water and the blood of 19.24 may be a matter of fact, but they become much more than a matter of fact, when they are read in the light of 6.53-6:

> Truly, truly I say to you, unless you eat the flesh of the Son of Man and drink his blood, you have no life in you; he who eats my flesh and drinks my blood has eternal life, and I will raise him up at the last day. For my flesh is food indeed, and my blood is drink indeed. He who eats my flesh and drinks my blood abides in me and I in him,

and of 7.37-9:

> If anyone thirst, let him come to me and drink. He who believes in me, as the scripture has said: Out of his heart shall flow rivers of living water.

When the book is read as a whole, no one can fail to see 'the glaring paradox' between the man who said to the woman of Samaria (4.10-14):

> If you knew the gift of God, and who it is saying to you: Give me a drink, you would have asked him and he would have given you living water ... Everyone who drinks of this water will thirst again, but whoever drinks of the water that I shall give him will never thirst; the water that I shall give him will become in him a spring of water welling up to eternal life.

and the man who in his own final agonies cried out: 'I thirst'. (19.28).

Jülicher also points out (p. 389) what he regards as the interconnectedness of the fourth gospel. 'So he came again to Cana in Galilee, where he had made the water wine' (4.46) and 'This was now the second sign that Jesus did when he had come from Judaea to Galilee (4.54) both look back to 2.1-11, the story of the wedding feast at Cana.

Again, the saying in 7.23,

> If on the sabbath day a man receives circumcision, so that the law of Moses may not be broken, are you angry with me because on the sabbath I made a man's whole body well?

is a direct reference to the healing of the paralysed man at the pool on the sabbath (5.8f.).

And there is clearly an intimate interconnection between the following three sayings:

> Little children, yet a little while and I am with you. You will seek me, and as I said to the Jews, I say to you now, Where I am going you cannot come (13.33).

> Jesus then said, I shall be with you a little longer, and then I go to him who sent me; you will seek me and you will not find me; where I am you cannot come (7.33f.).

> Again he said to them: I go away and you will seek me and die in your sin; where I am going you cannot come (8.21f.).

It is clear that 15.20, 'Remember the word that I said to you, A servant is not greater than his master,' looks back to 13.16: 'Truly, truly, I say to you, a servant is not greater than his master; nor is he who is sent greater than he who sent him.' In the same way 18.14, 'It was Caiaphas who had given counsel to the Jews that it was expedient that one man should die for the people,' clearly looks back to 11.49f.:

But one of them, Caiaphas, who was high priest that year, said to them: 'You know nothing at all; you do not understand that it is expedient for you that one man should die for the people, and that the whole nation should not perish.'

As Hoskyns and Davey say, in the fourth gospel it is not possible to isolate any one incident without interfering with the whole pattern. The whole gospel is the context of any one incident. The fourth gospel is a consistent whole in a sense that the other three are not.

The contrast between the miracle stories of the fourth gospel and those of the synoptic gospels is specially striking, and deserves a section to itself.[3]

(i)   The miracles of the fourth gospel are so important and so characteristic that Bultmann (pp. 6f.) postulates a miracle or sign source behind the gospel. In 4.54 John writes of the healing of the official's son: 'This was now the second sign that Jesus did when he had come from Judaea to Galilee.' This follows on 2.11: 'This, the first of his signs, Jesus did at Cana in Galilee.' But in between the two miracles John writes of Jesus: 'Now when he was in Jerusalem at the Passover feast, many believed in his name, when they saw the signs which he did' (2.23). It is clear that the healing of the official's son brought the total number of signs to far more than two; so Bultmann believes (p. 209) that it is called the second sign because it was so listed in a miracle source that John used. Bultmann further suggests that the sentence: 'Now Jesus did many other signs in the presence of his disciples which are not written in this book; but these are written that you may believe that Jesus is the Christ, the Son of God, and that believing you may have life in his name' (20.30f.) is a much more natural conclusion to a document containing a list of miracles than to the general narrative of a whole gospel (see W.G. Kümmel, *Introduction to the NT*, p. 151).

(ii)   Whatever we may say of the Bultmann source theory, there are certain facts to be noted. In the miracles of the fourth gospel there are no demoniacs and there are no lepers. It has been suggested that this is so because there were no demoniacs and lepers in Jerusalem while they were common in Galilee, and that the fourth gospel represents conditions in Jerusalem rather than in Galilee, while the synoptic gospels describe conditions in Galilee rather than conditions in Jerusalem.

(iii)   The fourth gospel tends to enhace the miraculous element in the stories. The lame man was lame for thirty-eight years (5.5). The blind man was blind from birth (9.1). Lazarus had been dead four days (11.39). The official's son is healed at a distance (4.46-54).

(iv)   In the fourth gospel the element of sheer compassion is not nearly so prominent. Hoskyns and Davey (pp. 62f.) say that in the synoptic gospels 'the particular poor man, the particular diseased helpless creature offered an ever-present occasion for human charity'. But in the fourth gospel the miracles are no longer to be understood as episodic, charitable, human actions; they are signs of truth, signs of the concrete action of the glory of God. Jülicher (p. 388) says: 'John does not paint the wonder-working Jesus as the one who used his power to exercise compassion, to banish trouble and misery and to dry the weeping eye . . . Even the very words for compassion are not to be found in John.' In the fourth gospel Jesus is not moved with compassion (contrast Matt. 14.14; 18.27; Mark 1.41; 6.34). In the fourth gospel a miracle is rather a demonstration of the power of God than an action of the love of God.

(v) In the synoptic gospels (e.g. Matt. 13.58; Mark 2.5; 6.6) miracles are rather the result of faith than the begetters of faith. It is a man's faith which makes the miracle possible. But in the fourth gospel the miracles produce faith and are not the product of faith (John 14.11).

(vi) In the synoptic gospels the miracles are immediate demonstrations of mercy and love; in the fourth gospel – and to this we will return – they are rather demonstrations of the timeless power of Jesus Christ. The feeding of the five thousand is not so much the feeding of a hungry crowd in mercy for their need as it is the sign that Jesus is the answer to the hunger of men's souls (contrast Mark 6.34 and John 6.25-69).

In the fourth gospel the miracles have become theological demonstrations rather than reactions of divine compassion and love.

We must now look at the general question of the connection of the fourth gospel with the synoptic gospels.[4] Every kind of view has been taken of this connection. P. Gardner-Smith believed that the fourth gospel did not know or use the synoptic gospels at all.[5] Windisch took the same view for the following reasons; i. because the evangelist says so little in actual words to show that he was consciously correcting them; ii. the agreements are too few; iii. to make divergences so wide from writings recognized by the church would be too bold.[6] On the other hand Lord Charnwood believed that the only way to make sense of the fourth gospel is to assume that it is written 'so to speak, on the top of St Mark',[7] and Kümmel can say (p. 144): 'The literary connection of John with Luke is . . . indisputable.' But the truth seems to be that, even if the writer of the fourth gospel did not know the other actual gospels, he certainly knew the gospel tradition which was embodied in them. R.H. Lightfoot makes an effective point (pp. 31f.) when he asks whether it is really credible that, if John had thought his gospel the only gospel, he would have written as he did? Would he, for instance have omitted all reference to the institution of the Lord's Supper, unless he had known that it was already there in the other gospels? Lightfoot's opinion is that, if the fourth gospel is considered by itself it is a riddle; but, if it is considered as the crown and completion of the gospel records, it falls into place.

There are many places where the fourth gospel may be said to assume the synoptic gospels. The fourth gospel knows that there were other miracles in addition to the miracles of which it tells (6.2; 21.25). It knows that Jesus used parables, although it does not include any (16.25, 29). Its references to John the Baptist presuppose the synoptic narrative (1.6, 15, 21, 30-34; 3.24). A Galilean ministry is implied (4.43-5). It is assumed that Jesus came from Nazareth (1.45f.; 18.5,7; 19.19). Capernaum is an important centre of the story (2.12). It is assumed that Jesus' leading disciples were Galileans (1.43f.). The fourth gospel knows about the unbelief of Jesus' brothers (7.3-5). Even if the fourth gospel does have different eschatological ideas (as we shall see later, pp. 219f.), the synoptic eschatological language is still there (4.21; 6.37, 40, 54; 21.22f.).

Hoskyns and Davey point out (pp. 71f.) how identical the *framework* of the passion narrative is in Mark and John, even if the detail is different:

(a)   Are you the King of the Jews? (John 18.33; Mark 15.2)
(b)   Will you have me release for you the King of the Jews? (John 18.39; Mark 15.9)
(c)   Crucify him! (John 19.6,15; Mark 15.11-14)
(d)   The scourging (John 19.1; Mark 15.15).
(e)   The mockery and the crown of thorns (John 19.2f.; Mark 15.16-20).
(f)   The inscription on the cross (John 19.19; Mark 15.26).
(g)   Golgotha; the parting of the clothes; the sponge with the vinegar (John 19.17-30: Mark 15.22-37).
(h)   The request of Joseph of Arimathaea (John 19.38-42; Mark 15.42-45).
(i)   The resurrection narrative opens with Mary Magdalene (John 20.1; Mark 16.1-4).

Hoskyns and Davey conclude that the readers of the fourth gospel already knew quite a lot, and they knew it in the form of Mark. The following passages may be compared in detail: John 5.8f. and Mark 2.11f.; John 6.7 and Mark 6.37; John 12.3,5 and Mark 14.1,5; John 14.31 and Mark 14.42; John 18.39 and Mark 15.9; the whole story of Peter's denial, John 18.15-18, 25-27 and Mark 14.66-72.

It is less than likely that the fourth gospel used Matthew. G.H.C. Macgregor (p. xi) suggests that either John did not know Matthew, or else he ignored it because of its Judaistic and apocalyptic outlook. In regard to Luke, John's account of Martha and Mary presupposes Luke's; John's story of the anointing (12.3-8) has affinities with that of Luke (7.36-8); the following detailed passages may also be compared: John 13.2,27 and Luke 22.3; John 13.38 and Luke 22.34; John 18.10 and Luke 22.50.

We may well take it that John and his readers certainly knew the story of the synoptic gospels, and almost certainly knew Mark and Luke.

7

THE FOURTH GOSPEL AND HISTORY

We cannot avoid facing the problem of the connection of the fourth gospel with history. Hoskyns and Davey write (p. 112): 'Brought up against the background of the last generation, we never escape from the problem of historicity. It always haunts us.' To this problem answers have been given which could not differ more widely. As M.F. Wiles says in *The Spiritual Gospel* (p. 22), one interpreter will regard the fourth gospel as 'the romantic creation of the mystical imagination', another as absolutely rooted and grounded in history. Hoskyns and Davey point out (p. 68) how Windisch prints at the head of his book on 'John and the Synoptics' two texts — 'All that came before me are thieves and robbers' (John 10.8), and, 'Even though we have known Christ after the flesh, yet now we know him so no longer' (II Cor. 5.16). And from that juxtaposition of texts it could be deduced either that the fourth gospel is historically the final word about Jesus, surpassing and eliminating all other accounts, or that it has nothing to do with history at all, and that 'all touch with history has been surrendered, and surrendered purposely'. C.K. Barrett asks (p. 4): 'Is the gospel to be taken as a supremely reliable' historical record of the words and deeds of Jesus, or is it a set of mystical variations on a theological theme?'

Whatever conclusion we may finally come to, we must start with the fact that to think in terms of incarnation is to think in terms of history. It is to think of the enmanning, the enfleshing of God in a particular human being at a particular time. And that John did so think there is no doubt. R.H. Lightfoot writes (p. 30): 'That St John was altogether indifferent to historical fact is out of the question; no evangelist is more insistent than he on the historical truth which he regards as essential to the gospel.' And C.K. Barrett follows up his question just quoted by saying: 'It is of fundamental importance to John that Jesus did in fact live and die and rise from the dead.' Hoskyns and Davey write (p. 107): 'There is no question that the Evangelist himself believed his Gospel to have been revealed to men and forced upon himself in history and by history.'

Inevitably we have to begin with a stage when the fact that the fourth gospel was history was not in question. M.F. Wiles (pp. 17-20) describes this early stage, and it was a stage when, since the historicity of the fourth gospel was not in doubt, the problem lay in harmonizing it and the synoptic gospels. Theodore of Mopsuestia points out that

Mark and Luke were not eyewitnesses and are therefore less reliable than Matthew and John, and says that many of the alleged discrepancies come in the passion narrative, when all except John had fled. He deals with particular points. John says that Jesus carried his own cross; the synoptic gospels say that Simon carried it. The solution is that Jesus started the walk to Golgotha carrying his cross, and that Simon was pressed into service on the way; therefore both accounts are true. Theodore, Chrysostom and Cyril all relate Philip's hesitation to bring the Greeks to Jesus to Jesus' saying in Matthew 10.5: 'Do not go into any way of the Gentiles.' That Matthew saying goes on: '... and enter into no town of the Samaritans.' This is reconciled with Jesus' conversation with the Samaritan woman, by saying that the Matthew saying forbade entry into a *town*, and that Jesus did not in fact enter the *town*; the meeting was at the well! Theodore does not find difficulty with the difference between the chronology of the fourth gospel and that of the synoptic gospels. His fundamental principle is that the synoptic gospels 'have no true chronology'. It is only John who is concerned with chronology, Theodore argued, as the precision of his dating shows. Much later William Temple was to say in his *Readings* (p. xi): 'We do not have to choose between two incompatible chronologies, for the Johannine chronology is the only one we have.' It can hardly be disputed that such arguments are ingenious rather than convincing.

Theodore extends his harmonizing endeavours from history to theology. He argues that John 20.22 is a *promise* of the Spirit, and that the word 'Receive' is to be read in the sense, 'You will receive.' In regard to Thomas' 'My Lord and my God!' in John 20.28 he makes the interesting suggestion that Thomas' exclamation is gratitude to *God* for the miracle of the resurrection rather than an affirmation of the divinity of Jesus (see M.F. Wiles, pp. 30f.).

The opposite point of view has been just as strongly held; it has been asserted that in the fourth gospel there is no history at all. In his *Introduction to the NT* (p. 419) Jülicher says bluntly: 'I know of no point, in fact, in which our knowledge of the life of Jesus receives an incontestable increase through the Fourth Gospel.' Hoskyns and Davey (p. 29) quote Harnack as laying it down that the fourth gospel cannot be treated as a historical source for the life and teaching of Jesus: 'Only little of what its author says can be accepted, and that little with caution.' Schweitzer held that the fourth gospel was far too strongly dominated by theological motives to be an historical source. 'The question is decided. The gospel of John is inferior to the synoptics as a historical source just in proportion as it is more strongly dominated than they by theological and apologetic interests.'[1] 'John,' says Kirsopp Lake, 'may contain a few fragments of true tradition, but in the main it is fiction.'[2]

So then we are poised between two points of view, the one holding that the fourth gospel is a valuable historical source, perhaps even more valuable than the synoptic gospels, and the other not hesitating to use the word 'fiction' in speaking of it.

Whatever else we may come to say about the fourth gospel and history, we shall certainly have to say that it is not only history; it is more than history. 'We must not expect,' wrote W.F. Howard, in *Christianity according to St John* (p. 21), 'to find in the Fourth Evangelist a detached spectator of events, or a disinterested chronicler of the sayings and doings of Jesus.' For John the central figure is not the Jesus of history, but the Christ of experience. E.J. Goodspeed in his *Introduction to the NT* (pp. 305f.) says that the fourth gospel is a book of a few great ideas, to which the writer returns again and again. They are all there in the Prologue – revelation, incarnation, regeneration, the impartation of life.

> It is to present them that the Gospel is written. They are of more importance in the writer's mind than mere historical facts. He is, in short, one of these men who care more for truth than for fact. The eyewitness testimony to what happened here or there is subordinated to the test of religious experience. . . . It is the inward appreciation of Jesus that supremely matters.

As G.H.C. Macgregor has it (p. xx), the object of the writer of the fourth gospel is 'not to communicate information, but to bestow upon the reader "life" through faith'.

There is nothing in this at which to be surprised. Von Soden writes: 'Interest in pure history did not exist among the writers of antiquity, certainly not among those of the East . . . History was then written as a means of conveying the author's own ideas. History is the daughter of poetry.'[3] W.F. Howard (p. 85) quotes the dictum: 'The Fourth Evangelist is not an historian; he is a seer.' The fourth gospel has been described as 'theology and not history, poetry and not prose'.[4] 'We shall never,' said F.C. Burkitt in *The Gospel History* (pp. 235f.), 'do justice to this Gospel, so long as we try to treat it as a narrative of events that were seen and heard of men. It is not a competitor with the Synoptic Gospels.' Burkitt (pp. 224f.) illustrates this from the way in which John presents the sacramental teaching of Jesus. He has no account of the foundation of the sacrament at the last supper. He transfers the sacramental teaching of Jesus to ch. 6. 'This is something more than mere historical inaccuracy. It is a deliberate sacrifice of historical truth, and, as the Evangelist is a serious person in deadly earnest, we must conclude that he cared less for historical truth than for something else.' A little later (pp. 231f.) Burkitt writes:

The true meaning of life could never have been revealed to man, if Jesus had not been sent as the Word from the Father. Who He was could only be seen after He had gone away; what He had been seen to be was nothing in comparison with the underlying reality ... It is all a different order of thought from the Synoptic Gospels or objective history.

John is writing, says C.K. Barrett (p. 39), 'so that men may recognize their relation to God in Jesus rather than to convey interesting information about him.' Gardner in *The Ephesian Gospel* (p. 75) writes:

To such a nature as his, though he is always in a sense striving to be exact, facts appear in so changed a form that their mere outward and physical side matters little... Every event for him is translated from a temporal and special setting into one which is ideal and spiritual; it has a meaning in relation to the great purpose of God.

This is very far from saying that history and facts had ceased to matter to John. In a sense they mattered even more. Hoskyns and Davey (pp. 108f.) see as the characteristic of the fourth gospel 'a truly biblical realism'. John is intensely aware of the facts of speech, the fact of paternity, the facts of light and darkness, water, bread, wine, the facts of life and death. He has a 'realistic apprehension of the theological meaning of things experienced by men in history'. He certainly sees beyond history, but not in a way 'that empties the observable world of final significance'. John brings the symbol 'out of the Hellenistic Jewish theologizing into the concrete reality of the historical Christian tradition of the person of Jesus, as living in the daily experience of the Church around him'. He is 'recounting the history of Jesus of Nazareth, not merely for the sake of its describable actuality, but also for the sake of its significance'. So then just because historical things have a significance beyond themselves, they become more, not less, important.

Because of this two writers use the same phrase in connection with the fourth gospel. G.H.C. Macgregor says (p. xxiii) that the fourth gospel is 'history written *sub specie aeternitatis*'. F.C. Burkitt says (p. 230):

The Christ of the Fourth Gospel is not the Christ of history but the Christ of Christian experience. Like St Paul the Fourth Evangelist does not care to know 'Christ after the flesh', because he saw both his Lord and his Lord's adversaries *sub specie aeternitatis*.

E.J. Goodspeed in his *Introduction to the NT* (p. 230) put it in another way:

Topography and chronology were among the least of the author's concerns. His head was among the stars. He was seeking to determine the place of Jesus in the spiritual universe and his relations to the eternal realities. These were the matters which interested and absorbed him, not itineraries and time-tables.

So then, to say that the writer of the fourth gospel is not interested in history would be wrong; but to say that he is interested only in history would be still more wrong. He is concerned to show what that which happened in time has to tell men about eternity.

This is simply to say that the fourth gospel is at least as much a theological work as it is an historical work. It might even be truer yet to say that it is altogether a theological work, and that it is not historical at all. Hoskyns and Davey (p. 24) say: 'The one way in which the Fourth Gospel cannot be interpreted is as an authentic record.' The first sentence of the introduction to their commentary is: 'The Gospel according to St John is a strictly "theological" work.' But, even when we say that, we have to remember that when someone is committed to a belief in an incarnation as the central truth of Christianity, 'his narrative', as Sanders put it (p. 64), 'cannot be theologically significant, unless it is also historically true'. What the John of the fourth gospel is writing about, say Hoskyns and Davey (p. 18), is 'the relation between time and eternity, between what is finite and what is infinite, between phenomena and reality, in fact, between man and God . . . This problem is presented to us, forced upon us, with the urgency of an ultimate demand, not by transferring us into the realm of speculative philosophy or even of spiritual experience, not by passing from a moral Jesus to a metaphysical Son of God – whatever the word "metaphysical" may mean in this context – but by confronting us with the precise and bodily history of Jesus.' The gospel is written 'by a man who had ideas, theological ideas in his head, and an experience, a religious experience, in his heart'. C.K. Barrett (p. 5) says: 'He means to write both history and theology – theological history.'

If it is true to say that the one way in which the fourth gospel cannot be interpreted is as history, it is equally true to say that one of the biggest mistakes is to think that a work cannot be historical and theological at the same time. This whole question is considered by J.N. Sanders (pp. 62-5). The two evangelists who have stated their purpose 'seem quite unaware of any incompatibility between their historical and theological interests'. Luke (1.1-4) claims to have done a considerable amount of research, and to write in order that Theophilus may have a secure basis for his faith. John (20.30f.) emphasizes that the events he describes really happened, and that he writes in order that his readers may believe that Jesus is the Christ, the Son of God. But that did not prevent them recording the life of Jesus. As Sanders says, to answer the argument that historical narrative and theological expression are incompatible, we have to consider the nature of historical narrative. There are resemblances and differences between the historian and the reporter. Neither will write what is untrue. Both can only include a tiny fraction of the actual events; to include too much would simply be to defeat their own ends. But their perspective is different. The reporter takes the short view and the historian takes the long view. The historian must be able to see the importance of things which at the moment may seem to have little or no importance. No one, for instance, could have dreamed that the death of Jesus was going to have infinitely more momentous consequences for the world than the death of the Roman Emperor Tiberius a few years later. The historian discovers what happened, and then perceives and decides what is important; and the criteria by which he decides do not emerge from the facts; he brings them to the facts. 'A historian without such criteria is not a historian but an antiquarian.' An historian cannot write without presuppositions, although he must have the humility to admit that his presuppositions are not infallible. And if we disagree with an historian, it is his presuppositions with which we disagree. The evangelists, and supremely John, are convinced by testimony and experience that Jesus is the Son of God. And their criterion is that the material they use should illustrate that truth. If we do not share that presupposition, then we will not agree that the gospels are reliable. For them the Jesus of history and the Christ of faith are the same. And this will mean that history and theology are inextricably interwoven.

This means that the fourth gospel is interpretation at least as much as it is narration. R.H. Lightfoot (p. 28) speaks of 'the large interpretative element' in the fourth gospel, and calls John 'the interpreter of the synoptists' (p. 34). John, he says, did not try to supplement or supersede the earlier gospels; he tried 'to interpret them and to draw out the significance of the original events'. John has had time to do a great deal of thinking – seventy years or thereabouts; as Streeter says in *The Four Gospels* (p. 372), 'what he gives us is not the saying as it came to him, but the saying along with an attempt to bring out all the fullness of meaning which years of meditation had found in it.' G.H.C. Macgregor says (p. xxi) that in the fourth gospel 'the reflective element is less unconsciously and more creatively and artistically present'. For John it is often the reflection which is the important thing. G.H.C. Macgregor notes (p. xlii) a characteristic of Johannine narratives. 'Just as we are looking for the climax of some dramatic scene the narrative drifts over into a doctrinal meditation.' The author introduces his characters, rivets attention upon them, only to allow them 'to evaporate from the stage'. The Nicodemus story in ch. 3 illustrates this characteristic particularly well.

John interprets Jesus partly in terms of his own experience and his own meditation, and partly in terms of the faith of the early church.

Kümmel says in his *Introduction to the NT* (p. 164) that John wishes
to put 'the absolute gospel' in place of the synoptics. He wishes to
give a representation of Jesus 'in a consummate manner', which will
make known that 'Jesus is the Christ, the Son of God' (John 20.31).
He thus 'attempts to express adequately what was already contained
in the earlier tradition'. This representation seeks 'to give perfect
expression to the Christian faith in Jesus, the Messiah and Son of God,
and thus consistently proceeds from the image of faith of the Christian
community'. John presents 'in a more systematic, more independent,
and in a more grandiose manner than the Synoptics, not what Jesus
was, but what the Christians have in Jesus'. Long ago, as M.F. Wiles
reminds us in *The Spiritual Gospel* (p. 19), Cyril had come to the
conclusion that the purpose of John is to supplement the other gospels
by providing a deeper, more doctrinal account of Jesus. To quote
G.H.C. Macgregor again (p. xxv), 'It is not merely the bodily aspect of
Jesus' story with which John presents us, but its soul.' F.C. Baur held
that the aim of the fourth gospel is not historical accuracy; it is 'the
unfolding of the dogmatic idea of the Logos', and to that purpose
everything else is subordinate.[5]

Symbolism has always been found in the fourth gospel. Loisy said:
'Tradition supplies the author with data, which he used as symbols.'[6]
Von Hügel in his *Encyclopaedia Britannica* article says of the fourth
gospel: 'The book's method and form are pervadingly allegorical; its
instinct and aim are profoundly mystical.' From Philo to Origen there
is a long line of Hellenistic, Jewish and Christian allegorism. Philo's
Life of Moses allegorized the Pentateuch so as to represent Moses

> as mediator, saviour, intercessor of his people, the one great organ of
> revelation, and the soul's guide from the false lower world into the upper
> true one. The Fourth Gospel is the noblest instance of this kind of
> literature, of which the truth depends not on the factual accuracy of the
> symbolizing appearances, but on the truth of the ideas and experiences
> thus symbolized.

In Hegelianism the universal movement is from the thesis to the
contradicting antithesis to the unifying synthesis. Strauss applied this
Hegelian formula to the movement of gospel criticism. There was first
the traditional acceptance of the gospels as historically true. That is
thesis. There was next the rationalistic criticism of the eighteenth
century. That is the antithesis. The third conception was that of myth.
J.N. Sanders (pp. 58f.) says: 'The Gospels are mythological, the
products of the faith of the early Church; on this mythological view
they cannot be accepted either as historical or as the work of the
apostles or their disciples.' This opens the door wide to interpretation
by symbolism, and it is a door which since the early days of the
church many have used. M.F. Wiles (pp. 23-5) has collected many

examples. The seamless robe of Jesus (John 19.23f.) was taken by
Origen to symbolize the wholeness of Christ's teaching, by Cyprian to
stand for the unity of the church, by Cyril to represent the virgin birth.
Only the non-allegorist, Theodore of Mopsuestia, says that a robe so
woven was woven in the ordinary way in which soldiers' uniforms
were commonly woven in the time of Jesus. Origen symbolizes John
13.30: 'He (Judas) immediately went out; and it was night.' He *went
out* not only from the room, but from Jesus himself. I John 2.19 is to
be compared: 'They went out from us, but they were not of us; for, if
they had been of us, they would have continued with us, but they went
out that it might be plain that they are not of us.' The darkness into
which he went was symbolic of the darkness of his own soul, or the
darkness which pursued but could not overtake the light (John 1.5). So
with Nicodemus. He came literally by night (John 3.2) in order to
escape the notice of the other Pharisees, but in the spiritual sense the
night was the night of his own ignorance. In John 19.34 the correct
reading is that the soldier pierced, prodded, stabbed Jesus' side, and
the word is *ēnuxen*; but there is a variant reading *ēnoixen*, reflected in
the Vulgate *aperuit*, which means 'opened'. So it is said that baptism,
the eucharist and even the church came from the opening of Jesus' side.
Augustine in his *Tractate* 120.2 *on John* says: 'He did not say "pierced"
or "wounded" or anything else; he said "opened", in order that the gate
of life might be stretched wide, whence the sacraments of the church
flow.'

M.F. Wiles (pp. 35-7) collects some of the symbolisms which Cyril
finds. The 'much grass' of John 6.10 is a symbol of spiritual
refreshment, like the green pastures of Psalm 23.2. In John 21.1-6 the
night through which the disciples fished and caught nothing is the
darkness of the dispensation before Christ. In John 13.30 the night
into which Judas departed was a cloak for his unholy thoughts, and a
picture of the hell to which he was going. In John 18.10 the loss of
Malchus' right ear is a symbol of the Jews' loss of right hearing in
refusing to accept the teaching of Christ. In John 1.39 the tenth hour
is a symbol of the lateness of Christ's coming. In John 6.9 the five
fishes are a symbol of the law expressed in the five books of Moses. In
John 20.26 the eighth day of Jesus' second appearance to the disciples
after the resurrection is a symbol of the weekly appearance of Christ
in the body to his disciples at every Christian eucharist. In John 9.1
the healing of the man born blind is a picture of Christ's mission to the
Gentiles, who, unlike Israel, have never enjoyed the gift of light. In
John 14.31 'Arise and let us go hence' is a reference to 'the spiritual
transition from the love of the world to the choosing of the will of
God, from slavery to sonship, from the earth to the heavenly city,
from sin to righteousness, from uncleanness to sanctification.

The passage on which most ingenuity has been expanded is

probably the 153 fishes of John 21.11. The simplest explanation is that of B.F. Westcott, who suggests (p. 301) that 'the record of the exact number probably marks nothing more than the care with which the disciples reckoned their wonderful draught'. R.E. Brown (p. 1076) suggests that the exactness of the number may be intended to stress the authentic eyewitness idea, which emerges in 19.35 (the witness to the water and the blood), and 21.24, the eyewitness guarantee of authenticity. These explanations do not embark upon allegory at all.

Jerome, commenting on Ezekiel 47.9-12, quotes a piece of ancient 'scientific' information that there were 153 different kinds of fishes, and one of each kind was caught to symbolize the universality of the gospel. Jerome's statement (quoted by Hoskyns and Davey, p. 554) is: 'Writers on the nature and properties of animals, who have learned the *Halieutica* in Latin as well as in Greek, among whom is the learned poet Oppianus Cilix, say that there are 153 different kinds of fishes.' But Jerome's figures have been questioned.[7] Oppian, whom Jerome quotes as an authority, lived about AD180, and what he did in fact say in the *Halieutica* was that there were 'countless' varieties of fishes, and he enumerated 157 kinds. Pliny said that there were 104 varieties of crustacea. It looks very much as if Jerome was interpreting zoology by John rather than John by zoology, and, in any event, it is not very likely that John would know any zoology. It is an attractive suggestion that the 153 represents universality, but it is a suggestion which will hardly stand up to examination.

Augustine in *Tractate* 122.7 draws a distinction between Luke 5.1-11 plus Matthew 13.47-50 as representing the beginning of Jesus' ministry, and John 21 representing the time after the resurrection. The synoptic passages represent the church as at present, containing both good and bad. In them Christ also is on the water; the draught is left in the boats; the net is let down anywhere; the nets were breaking, the boats were sinking and the catch is not numbered. In the John passage, after the resurrection, the church is perfected, there are only good. Christ is on the land; the draught is brought to land; the nets are let down in a special area, and are unbroken, and the number is exactly given. It is the difference between the imperfect and the perfected church. Later in the same *Tractate* Augustine has a numerical explanation. Ten is the number of the law, of the commandments. But the law without grace kills, so to the number of law we add seven, which is the number of the Spirit, in order to obtain the fulness of the divine revelation as a power of light. Ten and seven give us the number 17, and if the numbers from 1 to 17 are added up, $1+2+3+4 \ldots$, the answer is 153. So 153 stands for all those who are included in the saving operation of divine grace, which makes reconciliation with the law. Further, three symbolizes the Trinity; and the triple 50 evokes the idea of unity in the Spirit, for $50 = 7 \times 7 + 1$.

Westcott (pp. 306f.) has collected a number of patristic interpretations of the passage. Cyril of Alexandria and Theophylact have the same interpretation. 100 = the fulness of the Gentiles; it is 10 x 10 and is the fullest number, and is in fact the number of the Lord's flock (Matt. 18.12) and of full fertility (Matt. 13.8). 50 is 100 divided by two, which falls short of completeness, and stands for the remnant of Israel, according to election. Three signifies the Holy Trinity, to whose glory all alike are gathered.

Gregory the Great makes the point that John would not have given the exact number, unless he believed that it contained a mystery. It is in fact true that John usually says 'about so and so'; 'about the tenth hour' (1.39); 'about five thousand' (6.10); 'about a hundred yards off' (21.8). But here John does not say 'about 150'; he says precisely 153. Gregory says that in the Old Testament all action is directed by the Decalogue; in the New Testament action is ruled by the seven gifts of the Spirit. This gives us 10 + 7, which equals 17. But it is by faith in the Holy Trinity that any action becomes effective; we therefore multiply 17 by 3, and we get 51, which expresses the idea of true rest, since it consists of unity − 1 − added to the number of the year of jubilee − 50. This symbol of rest is again multiplied by 3, and we get 153, the symbol of the elect citizens of the heavenly country, the final heirs of rest.

Rupert of Deutz takes the three numbers to represent the proportion of three different classes in one faith. The 100 are the married; the 50 are the widowed or the continent; the 3 are the virgins, the fewest of all in number.

Bruno of Asti (eleventh/twelfth century) says that 3 has the same significance as 150 which is 3 x 50. There are three parts of the world, Asia, Africa and Europe. Therefore, 150 + 3 = the sum of all the faithful throughout the world.

Even quite modern times have not failed to produce their quota of ingenuity. Westcott (p. 307) quotes G. Volkmar, who in 1867 suggested that if the letters are taken as numbers − Hebrew had no separate signs for numbers − then Simeon Bar Jona Kepha adds up to 153, but, as Westcott points out, to obtain the desired result he has to leave out one letter in Kepha, and to give the Hebrew letters numerical values inconsistent with ancient usage.

This 'science' of getting figures from names is called Gematria. A further example of it is quoted by R.E. Brown (p. 1075). The Hebrew letters *qhl h'hbh* add up to 153 and mean 'church of love'; but, as Brown points out, 'church of love' is not an expression which occurs in the Johannine writings. Bultmann (p. 709 n. 2) records an ingenious suggestion put forward by R. Eisler in the present century: Simon adds up to 76; *ichthus* 'fish', the famous Christian sign, adds up to 77; the sum of both is 153!

Hoskyns and Davey (pp. 553f.) have an elaborate investigation of the meaning of the number. To begin with 153 is an interesting number. As we have seen, it equals the sum of the numbers $1 + 2 + 3 \ldots$ up to 17, so that 153 dots can be arranged in the form of an equilateral triangle, with a base line of 17 dots. That is to say 153 is a 'triangular' number. It is also a prime number of the form $2n + 1$, a numerical form of great interest to mathematicians.

But Hoskyns and Davey ask certain questions and make certain suggestions. At first sight it seems a simple record of a miraculous catch of fishes. But then the questions arise. Why do the disciples not eat the fish they have caught? Why is eucharistic language used to describe the actions of Jesus at the meal he has provided? Why is the strange number so carefully recorded? 'So long as the accuracy and supposed oddity of the number is explained as preserving the memory of the evangelist who helped to count the fish, no true interpretation of the narrative as a whole is possible.'

153 is the all inclusive number. The disciples, therefore, make the perfect catch, and by so doing fulfil concretely the prophecy of Ezekiel 47.10:

Fishermen will stand beside the sea; from En-gedi to En-eglaim it will be a place for the spreading of nets; its fish will be of very many kinds like the fish of the Great Sea.

The parable recorded in Matthew 13.47 is also fulfilled:

The kingdom of heaven is like a net which was thrown into the sea and gathered fish of every kind; when it was full men drew it to the shore, and sat down and sorted the good into vessels, but threw away the bad.

With Jesus they have made the perfect catch; but without Jesus they had toiled to no purpose. By themselves they cannot catch them, and, even if they do catch them, cannot bring them to the land. 'Apart from me you can do nothing' (15.5).

The fish symbolize the converts to the Christian religion. And for that very reason the *natural* imagery breaks down and becomes obscure at the crucial point. *The disciples cannot eat the converts.* The command, 'Bring some of the fish you have just caught' (21.20), remains incomplete. From the point of view of the story, as a story, it ought to go on, 'that we may eat some and sell others'. But to maintain the symbolism, it in fact proceeds, 'in order that they too may share in the meal I have prepared'. The narrative becomes the narrative of a miraculous eucharistic feeding. It is the counterpart of the feeding of the four thousand, in which seven, not twelve, baskets are filled (Mark 8.8; cf. Mark 6.43). It is therefore *seven* disciples who here serve as the Lord's ministers, not *twelve* (John 21.2). Once this eucharistic purpose is seen, the double meaning of other phrases becomes evident. Peter's 'I am going fishing' (21.3) echoes Jesus' words, 'I chose you and appointed you that you should go and bear fruit' (15.16). 'They went out' (21.3) – out to the Sea of Tiberias, and also out into the world, echoing 'As thou didst send me into the world, so I have sent them into the world' (17.18) and 'As the Father has sent me, even so send I you' (20.21). In the Luke fishing story (5.1-11) there are two ships and the net is rent; in the John story there is one ship and the net is unbroken; thus there is symbolized the perfection of the church and the unity of the apostles of the Lord.

There is no doubt of the beauty of the interpretation which Hoskyns and Davey give the passage. But a lingering doubt remains – would any reader see this in the passage, when he read it? Did any reader see it?

Finally we return to the passage which J.A. Emerton[8] sees as lying behind John 21.11, Ezekiel 47.10: 'Fishermen will stand beside the sea; from En-gedi to En-eglaim it will be a place for the spreading of nets; its fish will be of very many kinds, like the fish of the Great Sea.' The numerical value of the Hebrew consonants in En-*gedi* is 17, and in En-*eglaim* it is 153. So Emerton links the two passages.

The trouble is that 153 has no immediate significance as, for example, 144 has. We need never doubt that there is symbolism in the fourth gospel, but at least in this passage the symbolism has kept its secret.

We may take one other example of symbolism as seen by R.H. Lightfoot (pp. 34-6). There seems to be a discrepancy regarding Jesus' *patris*, his native country. Mark (6.1-6) seems to make it Galilee, and in particular Nazareth; the fourth gospel (4.43-5) seems to make it Judaea. The real point of the matter, as R.H. Lightfoot sees it, is that Jesus did not receive honour anywhere in the last analysis, whether Galilee or Judaea be regarded as his native country. So Lightfoot asks:

> Does not St John perhaps wish to teach that, if the Lord's *patris* is sought anywhere on earth, nowhere does he receive the honour due to him even as a prophet? For he is not of this world (8.23), and his *patris* is in heaven in the bosom of his Father (1.18); thence he came (3.13; 13.3; 16.28), and there alone he is at home (3.13), and there he does receive the honour due to him (5.22, 23, 37, 41; 8.54). And St John may be teaching in his elusive way that, whether outward recognition is accorded to the Lord (4.45) or not (Mark 6.1-4), neither Galilee nor Judaea nor any other place on earth can be regarded as his *patris*.

Lightfoot may well be right, for it will always be necessary to penetrate beyond the surface to find the meaning of the fourth gospel.

8

THE RELATIONSHIPS OF THE FOURTH GOSPEL

It is beyond question that John and Paul are the two great theological thinkers of the New Testament. It will therefore be of very great interest to enquire what relation, if any, there is between them.

There are those who think that the connection is very close. G.H.C. Macgregor (pp. xxviii f.) admits that some of Paul's greatest conceptions — faith, sin, the significance of Christ's death — are insufficiently realized by John. 'Yet, apart from special doctrines, John's whole outlook upon the Christian revelation is determined by Paul, for it was the latter, not John, who first conceived the glorified Christ of experience, rather than the human Jesus of history, as being the real object of faith.' There are 'innumerable common touches'. 'This is the work of God, that you believe in him whom he has sent' (John 6.29) might well have been written by Paul. The doctrine of Christ in creation is common to John and Paul (John 1.3; Col. 1.16f.). The Pauline conception that the new dispensation was implicit in the promise made to Abraham (Romans 4) appears in John (8.56). Macgregor finds a close and very definite relationship between Paul and John.

E.F. Scott in *The Fourth Gospel: its Purpose and Theology* (p. 46) says that in the fifty years since the death of Paul 'the mind of the Church had become impregnated with Pauline ideas'. There was much that was outdated, for example the controversy about the law. But even if 'something is always added or discarded', there is a basic debt.

There are some who believe that it is even possible to say that Paul appears in the fourth gospel. He has been identified with the beloved disciple. In particular it has been argued that the figure of Nathanael represents Paul. In the fourth gospel Nathanael is a mysterious figure. In the synoptic gospels he does not appear at all, but in the fourth gospel his call is related in detail (John 1.43-51). He cannot be identified with any of the twelve; he must therefore be either a purely ideal figure, or the symbolic counterpart of a real person. And if the second view is taken, only Paul fits the conditions. So E.F. Scott (p. 47) sums up the reasons for identifying Nathanael and Paul. (i) Paul was not one of the twelve, but he ranked with them. (ii) Both Nathanael and Paul received their call direct from Jesus himself. (iii) Paul, like Nathanael, was the last to enter the apostolic band, like 'one untimely born' (I Cor. 5.8). (iv) Both Paul and Nathanael began by being critical and hostile, and they were won over, not by the human voice of any disciple, but by the voice of Jesus himself. Nathanael was seen by Jesus when he was still under the shadow of the fig-tree (John 1.48f.), and Paul was destined for the service of Jesus, when he was still under the shadow of the law (Gal. 1.15f.). Both Paul and Nathanael could justly have been called an Israelite in whom there is no guile (John 1.47; Rom. 2.29). (v) It could be said of both Nathanael and Paul that they saw the heavens open (John 1.51; II Cor. 12.2-4). So Nathanael could symbolically represent Paul, and this could support his claim to be 'among the very chiefest of the apostles'.

So E.F. Scott says (pp. 48f.): 'John owes an incalculable debt to his great predecessor.' He even goes the length of claiming: 'For almost all his larger doctrines the evangelist is indebted, more or less immediately, to Paul . . . In some respects the Johannine theology may be considered as little more than the natural development, along one particular line, of Paulinism.' John does with Paul what he does with the synoptics – he seeks to penetrate through the outward form of his teaching to 'what appeals to him as its real and abiding import', and so he assimilates and modifies at the same time.

But both Macgregor and Scott believe that John did make a special contribution of his own. We have said that for Paul the Christ of faith and experience was more valuable than the Jesus of history. Ephesus was bound to be coloured by Pauline doctrine. 'It was John's part,' says G.H.C. Macgregor (p. xxviii), 'to prevent that doctrine being sublimated into a philosophy, by relating it to the historical facts of Jesus' life.' E.F. Scott writes (p. 51):

> The glory which Paul ascribes to the exalted Christ is thrown back by John on the actual life on earth . . . The Lord who revealed himself to Paul in the experience of faith is to the evangelist one with Jesus Christ, who had lived and taught and suffered. Even then, while he was still among us, 'we beheld his glory, glory as of the only Son from the Father'.

So, it is held, John draws largely from Paul, but with the mysticism he combines history, in the picture of the Word which became flesh. B.W. Robinson writes that Paul is the mediating link between John and the earlier gospels; but it is not, as it were, a straight series of links.

> It would be true to say that John brought Pauline religion back from its later wanderings toward a relation of the historic Jesus from which it had strayed too far . . . The Fourth Gospel is just such a Gospel as Paul would have written, had he attempted to write one . . . Paul set such store by the regenerating influence of the Spirit and felt that a knowledge of the Palestinian career of the historic Jesus was so relatively unimportant that he never thought of writing a Gospel.[1]

W. Sanday in *The Criticism of the Fourth Gospel* (pp. 212-16) listed the things which John and Paul have in common:

(i)   Both start with a conception of an incarnation (John 1.14; Rom. 8.3; Gal. 4.4; Phil. 2.7f.; Col. 1.15,19; 2.9).

(ii)   Both regard the union of the Son with the Father as not only a moral union but also a union of essential nature (John 1.1f., 14; 10.30,38; 14.10f., 20; 17.21,23; II Cor. 5.19; Col. 1.13,15,19; 2.9).

(iii)   Between the Father and the Son there is a bond of mutual love, a love that is supreme and unique. That is the significance of the term *monogenes*, only-begotten (John 1.14,18; 17.23f.,26; Rom. 8.3,32; Eph. 1.6; Col. 1.13).

(iv)   It is therefore true that the relation between Father and Son has its roots in the eternal past (John 1.1f.; 17.5,24), and was always a complete union of will (John 5.30; 6.38; 14.31; 17.16; Phil. 2.8).

(v)   Both John and Paul regard Jesus as the revelation of God (John 1.18; II Cor. 4.4-6).

C.K. Barrett (pp. 45-9) notes the things in which John and Paul agree, but also the things in which they differ. 'The reader of the New Testament cannot fail to be impressed by the considerable measure of agreement between John and Paul in their presentation of Christian theology.'

(i)   For both, 'salvation is of the Jews' (John 4.22; Rom. 9.4f.).

(ii)   For both of them God is the one Lord of the *Shema* (Deut. 6.4), a living God, transcendent in holiness, infinitely near in redeeming love. He is the creator, and his sovereign will is the beginning and the end of salvation (John 6.44; 15.16; Rom. 9. 14-18).

(iii)   Jesus of Nazareth is the divinely appointed Messiah of Israel. He lived a human life of poverty, meekness and love; he was buried and rose on the third day. Both describe Jesus as the Son of God, which is the most characteristic definition of his person in both of them. Both speak of him as the heavenly man, at once the archetype and the redeemer of earthly humanity (Rom. 5.12-21; I Cor. 15.45-49; Phil. 2.5-11; John 5.19f.; 14.9; 1.51; 6.27).

(iv)   Both John and Paul lay more stress on the Holy Spirit than the first three gospels do.

(v)   For both 'the Christian life moves about the same foci of faith and love' (John 13.34; 20.31; Rom. 13.8-10).

(vi)   In Col. 1.15-19

Paul develops a Christology which is practically a Logos Christology, though the word Logos itself is not used. It could well be argued that John's Prologue has done little more than add the technical term Logos to a Christology which he took ready made from Paul,

although it is possible that both were parallel developments of the Jewish conception of Wisdom (cf. Prov. 8), and introduced the idea of the cosmic Christ to combat the gnostic idea of creation by an ignorant and inferior God.

But Barrett sees that there are differences. He lists the things that are in Paul but not in John. John has nothing at all about justification by faith, and very little about faith and works and law. There is nothing about the circumcision controversy. In John the law is the law of the Jews (1.17,45; 7.19; 8.17; 10.34; 12.34), but there is no attempt to impose it. In John the Jews are the opposition, but 'quite unemotionally'; there is nothing in John like Paul's wishing himself accursed, if only the Jews could be saved (Rom. 9.1-3). In Paul the Jews will be saved, because God cannot and will not go back on his own word (Rom. 11.25f.). But in John the Jews are the children not of Abraham but of the devil, and their sin abides (8.44; 9.41). There is nothing in John like Paul's care of all the churches (I Cor. 11.28). John has nothing about the spiritual gifts, the *charismata*, which are so prominent in Paul (I Cor. 12.27-31; Rom. 12.6-8). But although Paul's favourite phrase 'in Christ' does not occur in the fourth gospel, John's 'abiding in Christ', with Christ's promise to abide in his disciples, is very similar.

Barrett goes on to set down the things which are in John, but not in Paul. Paul does not have a Logos Christology, although he has a Christology which closely resembles it in substance without using the term. Barrett finds this significant, because it is characteristic of Paul that he makes no attempt to use the language of the Hellenistic world. 'The double affiliation of John's language is one of the most characteristic features of his gospel, and it is unparalleled in Paul.' In other words, Paul was not making nearly so deliberate an attempt to build a bridge between Hellenism and Christianity. Paul has no parallel to John's reinterpretation of the *parousia*. John saw the coming again of Jesus in the coming of the Spirit (14.3,18,23), and this is absent from Paul. Paul does not have John's insistence that Jesus' suffering and death were actually his glorification, 'the path by which he ascended to the Father and to the glory he enjoyed before the world began'.

Barrett in the end concludes that Paul and John do not really share the same characteristics. This he finds proved by the way in which they speak differently of the same things. For Paul baptism is a dying with Christ, and a rising in union with him to new life (Rom. 6.4); in John (3.3,5) it is being born again from above. No doubt they are speaking of the same experience, but they speak of it in a different way. Paul never uses the word Paraclete, John's special word for the Holy Spirit. Paul does not use the picture of Jesus as the Lamb of God. As for faith, Paul talks about believing *in*, that is, belief in a person (Acts 16.31; Gal. 2.16); John (20.31) speaks of believing *that*, that is, the acceptance of a fact. So Barrett concludes: 'It is natural to suppose that John, the later writer, was not closely dependent on Paul.'

Jülicher in his *Introduction to the NT* (pp. 397-400) has an interesting examination of the relationship of John and Paul. He begins by saying that John's 'theological position certainly implies a knowledge of the Pauline teaching'. Two great Pauline principles, the universality of salvation, and freedom from the law, 'have entered into the writer's very marrow'. The death of Christ is not simply for the Jewish nation; it is to gather into one the children of God who are scattered abroad (11.52). Jesus speaks to, and stays with, the Samaritans (4.1-43); the Greeks are eager to enter his presence (12.20-22); there is to be one fold and one shepherd (10.16); the prayer of Jesus is that they all may be one (17.11,22). John, says Jülicher, could not have written Romans 3.1f., with its affirmation of the continuing special position of the Jews.

The law is the Jewish law (8.17; 10.34; 15.25). There is a contrast between the law of Moses and the grace of Jesus Christ (1.17). In 6.32 it is not Moses but the Father in heaven who gives the true bread from heaven. The commandments which are to be obeyed are the commandments of Jesus. 'If you love me, you will keep my commandments' (14.15). 'He who has my commandments and keeps them, he it is who loves me' (14.21). 'If you keep my commandments, you will abide in my love' (15.10). 'This is my commandment, that you love one another, as I have loved you' (15.12). 'A new commandment I give to you, that you love one another' (13.34). The important commandments are the commandments of Jesus. Questions, for instance, of circumcision and meat offered to idols belong to the past. For Paul the name of Jew is still a title of honour; but John regards the Jews as from the beginning a body alien and hostile to the Lord and his followers.

Jülicher sees theological differences between John and Paul. On the one side, he sees a process of simplification. John does not make anything of the sacrificial system, so Jülicher says, and therefore the atoning nature of Jesus' death on the cross plays little or no part in his thought. John's story of the process of salvation is simpler. It is founded on the continual struggle between the Father and the world, between darkness and light. The descent of the Son into the world, his offer of the highest good to all men, the clear demonstration of his divinity, necessarily put an end in principle to this struggle. To see Jesus is to see the Truth and to see the Father. And, therefore, if anyone denies him, he is lost beyond all help, and, if anyone recognizes him, that recognition makes him able to possess all things.

On the other side, there is a process of deepening. In John the absolute significance of the person of Christ is stressed even more than in Paul. The idea of the Jewish Messiah is no longer really in John's mind. Jesus is the pre-existent one, who came and suffered and died, and who is rewarded by the supreme exaltation. He was with God from all eternity; he is the creator of the world; he becomes the Word; for a brief period he allows his glory to be seen in the body; he then returns to his Father, not to new honour but to the honour he had before he entered the world of the body, there to prepare a new home for those who are faithful to him. So Jülicher writes: 'The deification of Jesus, for which Paul had opened the way, was inexorably carried out by John to its furthest conclusion.' So Jülicher sees John assimilating the thought of Paul, and both simplifying and intensifying what he had assimilated.

In his *Theology of the NT* (II, pp. 6-10) Bultmann has a full and penetrating examination of the relationship between Paul and John.

He has just pointed out that in John many questions which were prominent in the synoptic gospels as being characteristic of the earliest days of the church have died out – the permanent validity of the law, the coming, or the delay in the coming, of the reign of God. In John there is no longer any problem in a mission to the Gentiles. Bultmann takes Matthew 8.5-13, Luke 7.1-10 and John 4.46-54 all to refer to the same incident. In the synoptic account the story is told to highlight the faith of a Gentile; in John the story is told to illustrate the connection of faith and healing. A different situation has give the story a different point. In the fourth gospel the fulfilment of prophecy 'plays a scanty role', only occurring in 2.17; 12.14f.,38,40; 13.18; 15.25; 19.24,36f. (and perhaps 6.31,45). The one problem which is important in both the synoptic gospels and John is the place of John the Baptist (Mark 2.18 = Matt. 9.14 = Luke 5.33; Matt. 11.2-19 = Luke 7.18-35; John 1.6-8, 15, 19-36; 3.23-30; 5.33-5; 10.40-42). In John the situation of the church is acute conflict with Judaism. The theme of the gospel is faith in Jesus as Son of God. The Christian congregation in John is already excluded from all association with the synagogue (9.22; 16.1-3). So great is the estrangement that Jesus does not even seem to be a member of the Jewish people, and can speak to them of 'your law' as if he were a non-Jew (8.17; 10.34; 7.19,22). In the fourth gospel the Jews are no longer differentiated into 'pious' and 'sinners', tax-collectors and harlots, scholars in the law and fishermen. The only distinction is between the crowd and the rulers. 'The Jews' are representative of 'the world' in general, which refuses to respond to Jesus with faith.

In spite of their differences, in regard to 'the current religious atmosphere' Paul and John have certain things in common. Both come from a Hellenism that is 'saturated with the Gnostic stream'. They agree in using a dualistic terminology. Both use 'the world' (*kosmos*) in the dualistic and depreciatory sense. Both understand 'the world' as basically the world of men. John has Jesus saying that the disciples are not of the world as he is not of the world (17.14-17); Paul can urge the Romans not to be conformed to the world but to be transformed from it (Rom. 12.2). Both contrast truth and falsehood (John 8.44; I John 2.21,27; Rom. 1.25), light and darkness (John 1.5; 8.12; I John 1.5; II Cor. 4.6), earthly and heavenly (John 3.12; I Cor. 15.40).

Above all, in both John and Paul 'Christology is formed after the pattern of the Gnostic Redeemer-myth, the sending of the pre-existent

Son of God in the disguise of a man' (John 1.14; Phil. 2.6-11). For both John and Paul 'the sending of the Redeemer is the eschatological event', the turn of the ages (John 3.19; 9.39; Gal. 4.4). However the Adam-Christ parallel (Rom. 5.12-14; I Cor. 15.21f., 45f.) is not in John, while Paul does not have John's way of speaking of the 'coming' and 'going' of the Redeemer (8.14 etc.) nor his ambiguous use of 'lifted up' to refer both to the cross and the exaltation to glory (3.14 etc.). John does not use expressions which derive from Jewish apocalyptic, and which are common in Paul – 'this age' (e.g. I Cor. 1.20); 'the fulness of time' (e.g. Gal. 4.4); 'a new creation' (e.g. II Cor. 5.17).

Even so, John and Paul share to a considerable extent the use of 'a common Christian terminology'. Both speak of 'life' rather than 'the reign of God'. Both speak of 'joy' (John 17.13; Rom. 14.17) and of 'peace' (John 14.27; Rom 14.17). John everywhere speaks of 'the sending' of Jesus (e.g. 3.16), and so on occasion does Paul (Rom. 8.8; Gal. 4.4). Both speak about the exaltation of Jesus to glory (John 17.5; Phil. 2.9; 3.21). Both quote Isaiah 53.1 (John 12.38; Rom. 10.16). But Paul never uses John's favourite term 'Paraclete' about the Holy Spirit.

There is a certain amount of Pauline language which does not appear in John at all. Paul's favourite flesh-spirit contrast is rare in John (only at 3.6; 6.63). John does not have Paul's 'body, soul and spirit' anthropology. Paul's terminology relating to the history of salvation is absent from John. John has no mention of justification, and the fourth gospel never uses the noun 'faith' (it comes once in the letters, at I John 5.4), although the verb 'to believe' is common. Paul's law-grace antithesis occurs only once in John (1.17). What Bultmann calls Paul's 'salvation perspective' is not in John. John does not speak of God's convenant with Israel, nor of the new convenant. He does not speak of God's election or guidance of his people. The proof from prophecy is not widely used in the fourth gospel. *Ekklesia* as a term for the Christian congregation is not in John. There is no mention of calling, of election, of choice in John, nor are the Christians called *hagioi*, saints, in the fourth gospel. The account of the institution of the Lord's Supper is missing. Except in redactional glosses (4.1; 6.23; 11.2) *kurios*, Lord, is a title for Jesus only in chapter 20.

'Clearly,' says Bultmann, 'John is not of the Pauline school and is not influenced by Paul; he is instead a figure with his own originality, and stands in an atmosphere of theological thinking different from that of Paul.' And yet in spite of that there is a 'deep relatedness in substance'. In both, the eschatological event is seen as taking place in the present. In both, the manifestation of Jesus' glory is an actual historical occurrence (John 1.14; II Cor. 3.7-18). In both, the new life 'appears under the mask of death' (John 11.25f.; 16.33; II Cor. 4.7-12). In both, in spite of the gnostic dualism in their thought, the world continues to be understood as God's creation, and the God-concept of both retains 'the paradoxical union of judgment and grace.

Bultmann summarizes the matter (p. 6):

> The observation that in John the Pauline discussion about the Law plays no role has often led to the false deduction that John must be regarded as the culmination of the development from the theology of the earliest Church; the two lie in quite different directions. Since John is somewhat remote from the earliest Church, he is likely younger than Paul, but he does not presuppose Paul as a link between himself and the earliest Church.

This is to say that John and Paul cannot be looked on as different stages on the one road of the development of Christian theological thought; they are on different roads.

We may finally look at the view of Wernle:[2]

> John and Paul were not two theological factors, but one. Were we to accept that John formed his conception of Christianity either originally or directly from Jesus' teaching, we should have to refuse St Paul all originality, for we should leave him scarcely a single independent thought. But it is St Paul that is original; St John is not. In St Paul's letters we look, as through a window, into the factory where these great thoughts flash forth and are developed; in St John we are at the beginning of their transformation and decay.

This view would hold that John is not the culmination, but the first step in a theological process of decay – and that is not a view that many would be willing to take.

On the whole Bultmann's view is most likely, the view that Paul and John are not different stages in the same road to truth, but that each had his own road, and they were different.

We now turn to look at the relationship of John to the mystery religions. E. Hatch speaks of 'the splendid rites which were known as the Mysteries'.[3] In so far as there was anything like personal religion in Hellenistic times that religion was found in the mysteries. H.R. Willoughby in his book *Pagan Regeneration* (pp. 24-8) says: 'The mystery religions ... came nearest to satisfying the religious needs of the average man.' They were a 'real means of grace to many a convinced and sincere pagan'. They had in them a 'capacity to meet the most insistent demands of the age'.

We are in a difficulty when we turn to the mystery religions, for the initiate into them was sworn to a vow of secrecy, and that vow was rigidly kept. Once when Aeschylus was acting in one of his own tragedies the audience suspected that he was revealing certain things in connection with the Eleusinian mysteries; they would have lynched him in fury, if he had not sought refuge at the altar of Dionysus. He was later brought to trial before the Areopagus on the charge of revealing forbidden secrets, and he was acquitted because of the memory of his courage at Marathon as much as because of the defence he offered. Alcibiades, when just about to depart on the Sicilian expedition, was arrested and charged with 'impious mockery of the goddesses Demeter and Persephone' because he had 'profanely acted the sacred mysteries at a drunken meeting'.[4] Herodotus (2.171) knows what happened at the mysteries, but he will not tell. 'I could speak more exactly of these matters,' he says, 'for I know the truth . . . But I will hold my peace.' Pausanias describes Eleusis, but says (1.38.7): 'My dream forbade the description of the things within the wall of the sanctuary, and the uninitiated are of course not permitted to learn that which they are prevented from seeing.' Even Apuleius who tells more than anyone says: 'I have told you things, of which although you have heard them, you cannot know the meaning' (*Metamorphoses* 11.23). No initiate broke his vow of secrecy.

But although we do not know the details of the mystery religions, there are certain things which we do know. We know the cult stories; we know the experiences which the initiates underwent, and we know something of the methods which were used to produce these experiences. It is important to remember that, when we speak of the mystery religions, the word mystery is being used in its Greek sense. In Greek the word *mustērion* does not denote something which is complicated and difficult and obscure and hard to understand; it denotes something which may be quite simple, but which is quite meaningless to the outsider, but full of significance for the instructed initiate. Aristotle said that in the mysteries the initiate's aim was not to learn something (*mathein*), but to undergo an experience (*pathein*). The mysteries were far more emotional than intellectual.

First, then, let us look at some typical cult stories from the mysteries. Basically, the mystery religions were all centred on what we would now call passion plays, the sacred story of a god who suffered and died and rose again. The Eleusinian mysteries were the most famous mysteries in the world; they were founded on the story of Demeter. H.R. Willoughby (pp. 41f.) tells the story. Persephone the daughter of Demeter was snatched away by Pluto and carried off to the underworld to be his bride, with the knowledge and approval of Zeus. Demeter, frenzied with grief, for nine days, torch in hand, refusing to eat or drink, rushed about the world, searching for her daughter. As she rested by the well of Eleusis, she was welcomed by the daughter of Celeus, who took her to her father's house for refreshment. Here she ate and drank again, and rested for a time. But in her sorrow and anger against Zeus she brought famine on the earth, preventing the crops from growing, and thus cutting off the supply both of food for men and of offerings for the gods. Finally an arrangement was reached whereby Pluto restored Persephone to her sorrowing mother. But, since Persephone had eaten one sweet pomegranate seed in the underworld, she could never be totally free of that world, and so she was forced to spend part of each year with Pluto there. Demeter, in joy at the restoration, allowed the crops to grow once more, and gave to men the mysteries of Eleusis to give them assurance of a future life which was not the end. It is easy to see what a moving passion play this would make – the snatch, the frenzied, grief-stricken search, the sorrow that turned earth into a desert, the joy of the restoration, the agreement that Persephone spent part of her life on earth and part of her life in the underworld. It is also clear that, if we take this story far enough back, it is a nature myth of summer and winter, of the death and the resurrection of nature.

The other typical cult story we may take is that of the Isis mysteries. On earth Osiris had reigned over the Egyptians, a good king, 'making them reform their destitute and bestial mode of living, showing them the art of cultivation, giving them laws, and teaching them to worship the gods. Afterwards, he travelled over the whole earth, civilizing it.'[6] His wicked brother Set or Typhon plotted against him, and in the end murdered him, and then hid the body. Isis his wife clad herself in mourning and searched the world for the lost body. After a long search she found it. She brought it home and embalmed it. She and her sister Nephtys joined in a lament over it, which became the classical Egyptian lament over the dead. With the help of the faithful god Anubis, her son Horus and Thoth, Isis performed certain magical rites over the body, which restored it to life again. After his resurrection to life Osiris was finally translated to the underworld, where he reigned as lord of the underworld and ruler of the dead, and where he presided at the judgment at which the souls of the departed were given the reward of their virtue or the penalty of their sin. Again it is clear what a moving passion play all this would make – the good king, the loving wife, the treacherous assassins, the long search of sorrow, the finding of the body, the embalming it as dead, the raising it to life, the joy of resurrection, and the final lordship of Osiris in the underworld.

So the passion play was acted out in the presence of the initiate with only one object. The object was that the initiate should experience a total identification with the god, that he should share in the sufferings, share in the death, share in the resurrection, share in the eternal life of the god. Everything was done, says Angus in *The Mystery Religions and Christianity* (p. 61), to bring about this identification –

> tense mental anticipation, heightened by a period of abstinence, hushed silences, imposing processions and elaborated pageantry, music loud and violent or soft and enthralling, delirious dances, the drinking of spirituous liquors, physical macerations, alternations of dense darkness and dazzling light, the sight of gorgeous ceremonial vestments, the handling of holy emblems, auto-suggestion and the promptings of the hierophant

– these were the methods which were used to produce this experience of identification with the dying and rising god.

Angus writes of the mysteries (p. 117): 'In the sacrament the communicant witnessed and participated in the sorrows of his tutelar as a step towards participation in the triumphant result.' W.R. Halliday in *The Pagan Background to Early Christianity* (p. 242) says: 'The resurrection of the god was held to be a guarantee of the resurrection of the worshipper.' When the Osiris passion play had been acted out, the worshipper was able to say: 'As truly as Osiris lives, he also shall live; as truly as Osiris is not dead, he shall not die; as truly as Osiris is not annihilated, he shall not be annihilated.'[7] Here is exactly the Johannine saying of Jesus: 'Because I live, you will live also' (John 14.19). There is the closest possible connection between the thought of the mystery initiate and the thought of the fourth gospel.

The language of the fourth gospel offers many parallels with the language of the mystery religions. Proclus speaks about 'going out of ourselves to be wholly established in the divine'.[8] The initiate's prayer in the Liturgy of Mithras, 'Abide with me in my soul; leave me not', reminds us of Jesus' words to the disciples in John 15.4: 'Abide in me and I in you.' The oneness of the worshipper with his god is continually stated. Angus (pp. 110-12) has collected many examples from the magical papyri: 'Come to me, Lord Hermes, as babes to mother's wombs.' 'Enter thou into my spirit and my thoughts my whole life long, for thou art I and I am thou.' 'I know thee, Hermes, and thou knowest me; I am thou and thou art I.' 'Thou art I, and I am thou; thy name is mine, for I am thy image.' So Jesus prayed to God for his disciples 'that they may be one, as we are one' (John 17.11), 'that they may all be one; even as thou Father, art in me, and I in thee, that they also may be one in us' (17.21). Angus comments: 'The language of the Fourth Gospel, "I in you, and you in me," conveyed a familiar meaning to a world saturated in mystic thought.' There is no doubt that the fourth gospel spoke the same language as the mystery religions.

The conception of the new birth is characteristic of the fourth gospel. In John 3.3 Jesus says to Nicodemus: 'Truly, truly. I say to you, unless one is born anew, again, from above (*anōthen*), he cannot see the kingdom of God.' Angus (pp. 95f.) writes of the mystery religions:

> Every serious *mystes* approached the solemn sacrament of initiation believing that he thereby became 'twice-born', a 'new creature', and passed from death to life through a mysterious intimacy with the deity.

The watchword of the mysteries was: 'There is no salvation without regeneration.'

This is specially prominent in the Hermetic writings, attributed to Hermes Trismegistus. The thirteenth of the tractates in the *Corpus Hermeticum* is entitled: 'A secret discourse of Hermes Trismegistus to his son Tat concerning rebirth.' We quote from W. Scott's translation (I, pp. 239-45). Hermes begins by saying to Tat that, when Tat is ready to alienate himself from the world (*kosmos*), then he will speak to him. No one, he says, can be saved until he has been born again. Tat answered in exactly the same way as Nicodemus did. 'I do not know . . . from what womb a man can be born again, nor from what seed.' Hermes Trismegistus answers: 'The womb is Wisdom conceiving in silence; the seed is the true Good; the will of God is the begetter.' The ministrant is some man, who is a son of God, working in subordination to the will of God. From all this a new man emerges, and here we come to Hellenistic rather than Christian thought. The new man is not fashioned out of matter; he has an immortal and not a physical body; the bodily shape which was his before has been put away. The man who would be born again must free himself from the torments of matter – from ignorance, grief, incontinence, desire, injustice, covetousness, deceitfulness, envy, fraud, anger, rashness, vice – he must free himself from the 'prison of the body'. Then reason will be 'built up within him'. 'Such is the manner of rebirth.'

In the Liturgy of Mithras the initiate prays:

> I am a man . . . born of a mortal woman . . . and I have this day been begotten again by thee. . . . Lord, having been born again, I pass away being exalted the while. Having been exalted, I die! Coming into being by life-begetting birth and freed unto death, I go the way thou has ordered, as thou hast established the law and ordained the sacrament.[9]

The initiate is begotten by God. This is the same language as John uses (1.13), when he speaks of those who are born 'not of blood nor of the will of the flesh nor of the will of man, but of God'. Hippolytus in his *Heresies* (5.3) says that in the Eleusinian Mysteries it is said: 'August Brimo has brought forth a consecrated son, that is, a potent mother has been delivered of a potent child.'

For this reason initiation is often spoken of as a death and a resurrection. There is often a play upon the words *teleisthai*, 'to be initiated', and *teleutan*, 'to die'. Apuleius tells us that he underwent 'a voluntary death'; he 'approached the realms of death'; thereby he attained his 'spiritual birthday'; and so he entered the service of the goddess whose followers were 'as it were reborn'. Because of this the hour of midnight, the hour when the day dies and is reborn, was often regarded as the most suitable hour for initiation. Proclus tells us that in the Dionysiac-Orphic rites there was a symbolic burial. 'The priests command that the body should be buried, except the head, in the most secret of all initiations.' In the mysteries of Attis, according to

Firmicus Maternus, the candidate was known as *moriturus*, the one about to die. The mystery chapels were often underground; Halliday (p. 243) suggests that this too was a symbolizing of the grave. Sallustius tells us that in the Attis rites the newly initiated 'received nourishment of milk as if they were being reborn'.[10]

The most spectacular way to rebirth and to the initiate the most certainly effective was the *taurobolium*, the bath of bull's blood, out of which the initiate came *renatus in aeternum*, reborn for all eternity.[11] The *taurobolium* was part of the rites of Cybele, the Great Mother, and also of Mithra. It could be public or private. That is to say, it could be carried out vicariously, *pro salute imperatoris, imperii, urbis*, for the safety of the emperor, the empire or the city; or it could be carried out *de suo sumptu, sua pecunia*, at one's own expense, although it was obviously a costly undertaking for the private individual. It shows the length to which people were prepared to go in the search for rebirth. The early Christian writers often speak about it, for it seemed a dreadful and ghastly parody of the Christian conception of being washed in the blood of the Lamb.

Angus (p. 94) describes the *taurobolium* as follows:

A trench was dug, over which was erected a platform of planks with perforations and gaps. Upon the platform the sacrificial bull was slaughtered, whose blood dripped through upon the initiate in the trench. He exposed his head and all his garments to be saturated with the blood; then he turned round and held up his neck that the blood might trickle upon his lips, ears, eyes, nostrils; he moistened his tongue with the blood, which he then drank as a sacramental act. Greeted by the spectators, he came forth from this bloody baptism, believing that he was purified from his sin and 'born again for eternity'.

It is worthwhile to set down Prudentius' description of the *taurobolium*, always remembering that Prudentius was a Christian poet, and that his description is hostile.

The high priest, you know, goes down into a trench dug deep into the ground to be made holy, wearing a strange headband, his temples bound with its fillets for the solemnity, and his hair clasped with a golden crown, while his silken robe is held with the Gabine girdle.[12] Above him they lay planks to make a stage, leaving the timber-structure open, with spaces between; and then they cut and bore through the floor, perforating the wood in many places with a sharp-pointed tool, so that it has a number of little openings. Hither is led a great bull with a grim, shaggy brow, wreathed with garlands of flowers about his shoulders and encircling his horns, while the victim's brow glitters with gold, the sheen of the plates tinging his rough hair. When the beast for sacrifice has been stationed here, they cut his breast open with a consecrated hunting-spear, and the great wound disgorges a stream of hot blood, pouring on the plank bridge below a steaming river, which spreads billowing out. Then through the many ways afforded by the thousand chinks it passes in a shower, dripping a foul rain, and the priest in the pit below catches it, holding his filthy head to meet every drop and getting his robe and whole body covered with corruption. Laying his head back, he even puts his cheeks in the way, placing his ears under it, exposing lips and nostrils, bathing his very eyes in the stream, not even keeping his mouth from it, but wetting his tongue, until the whole of him drinks in the dark gore. After the blood is all spent and the officiating priests have drawn the stiff carcase away from the planking, the pontiff comes forth from his place, a grisly sight, and displays his wet head, his matted beard, his dank fillets and soaking garments. Defiled as he is with such pollution, all unclean with the foul blood of the victim just slain, they all stand apart and give him salutation and do him reverence because the paltry blood of a dead ox has washed him while he was ensconced in a loathsome hole in the ground.[13]

It is clear that regeneration, the rebirth, was an experience sought as much by the initiate in the mystery religions as by the author of the fourth gospel.

There is still another line of thought on which the language of the mystery religions will throw light. To the modern reader there is no more difficult passage in the fourth gospel than 6.53-57, which speaks of eating the flesh and drinking the blood of Jesus Christ.

Jesus said to them: 'Truly, truly, I say to you, unless you eat the flesh of the Son of man and drink his blood you have no life in you; he who eats my flesh and drinks my blood has eternal life . . . For my flesh is food indeed, and my blood is drink indeed. He who eats my flesh and drinks my blood abides in me, and I in him . . . He who eats me will live because of me.'

In the mysteries connected with Dionysus two things happened. The worship of Dionysus was the most frenzied and orgiastic worship of all. Dionysus was the god of the grape, the god of wine; and part of his worship was the drinking of wine to the extent of complete and frenzied intoxication. As H.R. Willoughby says (p. 71):

The relation of the god to the drink was not merely that of creator to the thing created . . . The god was in the wine; he was the wine even. He was not merely the god of libation. To quote Euripides' statement, he was the libation, 'the god who himself is offered in libation to the other gods'.

The god is the wine, just as the wine of the sacrament is the blood of Jesus Christ.

Dionysus was not only the god of the grape; he was identified with the goat and the bull; and part of the worship of Dionysus was 'the feast of raw flesh'. The initiate must be able to say: 'I have fulfilled his red and bleeding feasts.' The Bacchanals knew

The joy of the red quick fountain,
The blood of the hill-goat torn.

They quaff the goat's delicious blood,
A strange, a rich, a savage food.

The devotees tore asunder the slain beast and devoured the dripping flesh
in order to assimilate the life of the god resident in it. Raw flesh was living
flesh, and haste had to be made, lest the divine life within the animal
should escape. . . . The real meaning of the orgy was that it enabled the
devotee to partake of a divine substance and so to enter into direct and
realistic communion with his god. The warm blood of the slain goat was
'sacred blood' . . . The god Dionysus was believed to be resident
temporarily in the animal victim.[14]

The wine *was* the god; the bleeding flesh *was* Dionysus; and to drink
the wine and eat the flesh was to eat and drink the god himself.
However strange the words of the fourth gospel about drinking
Christ's blood and eating his flesh may be to us, they were familiar to
the age to which they were first spoken. Identification, resurrection,
regeneration, sacramental appropriation – these were all ideas
common to the mystery religions and the fourth gospel. Beyond a
doubt the fourth gospel and the mystery religions spoke the same
language.

We turn now to examine the relationship of the fourth gospel to the
Dead Sea scrolls.[15] These scrolls were accidentally discovered in caves
in the Wadi Qumran near the Dead Sea in 1947. The scrolls belonged
to a semi-monastic community, probably Essene. They comprise a
large number of biblical and apocryphal texts; an amount of
commentary material, of which that on Habakkuk is most extensive;
separate tractates, *The Manual of Discipline, The War of the Sons of
Light and the Sons of Darkness, The Hymns of Thanksgiving*. From
the same community comes *The Damascus Document*, which was
known long before the scrolls came to light. The scrolls have already
produced a vast literature, but we must confine ourselves to the
question of the connection of the Qumran literature with the fourth
gospel.[16]

There are those who have regarded the relationship between the
scrolls and the fourth gospel as very close indeed. J.M. Allegro in *The
Dead Sea Scrolls* (p. 142) writes: 'In the New Testament the richest
source of comparison (with the Scrolls) is certainly in the writings of
St John.' F.M. Cross Jr. writes in *The Ancient Library of Qumran* (p.
153): 'Linguistic and conceptual contacts between the Scrolls and the
New Testament are nowhere more in evidence than in the Gospel of
John.' On the other hand, Millar Burrows writes in *The Dead Sea
Scrolls* (p. 337): 'Direct influence of the Qumran sect on the early
Church may turn out to be less probable than parallel developments in
the same general situation.' R.E. Brown in his commentary (pp. lxiii f.)
writes:

In our judgment the parallels are not close enough to suggest a direct literary dependence of John upon the Qumran literature, but they do suggest Johannine familiarity with the type of thought exhibited in the scrolls ... What can be said is that for *some* features of Johannine thought and vocabulary the Qumran literature offers a closer parallel than any other contemporary or earlier non-Christian literature, either in Judaism or in the Hellenistic world.

Leaney in *A Guide to the Scrolls* (p. 95) concludes that examination of facts and speculations

will show all the more clearly how little solid proof there is of really formative influence on New Testament Christianity from Qumran. The sect and the early Christian Church are better regarded, from a historical point of view, as two offshoots of Judaism.

The most probable dates for the scrolls are from the last century before Christ to the middle of the first century of the Christian era. Community of background is well nigh certain: direct influence is much less likely. But let us look at the facts.

(i)   Both the scrolls and the fourth gospel have a dualistic view of life. It is not a physical dualism as in Gnosticism, in which spirit is essentially good and matter essentially bad. It is not that there are two independent forces in the world, because good and bad alike are the creation of God. It is a *moral* dualism, where good is ever under attack by evil and where the dark and the light are ever confronting each other. Cross (p. 157) speaks of light and dark as locked in 'a titanic struggle', and of 'the repeatedly contrasted themes which sound a kind of counterpoint in both Johannine and Essene literature, light and darkness, truth and error or lying, spirit and flesh, love and hate, death and life' (p. 153). So in the Qumran literature, says R.E. Brown (p. lxii), there are the two spirits, both created by God, but 'locked in combat'. On the one side the Prince of Lights, the Spirit of truth, the Holy Spirit; on the other side the angel of darkness, the spirit of perversion.

We may quote the *Manual of Discipline* col. 3 (Vermes' translation – he calls it *The Community Rule*):

He has created man to govern the world, and has appointed for him two spirits in which to walk until the time of his visitation: the spirits of truth and falsehood. Those born of truth spring from a fountain of light, but those born of falsehood spring from a source of darkness. All the children of righteousness are ruled by the Prince of Light and walk in the ways of light; but all the children of falsehood are ruled by the Angel of Darkness and walk in the ways of darkness.

So in the first letter of John we read: 'Whoever knows God listens to us, and he who is not of God does not listen to us. By this we know the spirit of truth and the spirit of error' (4.6). 'We know that we are of

God, and the whole world is in the power of the evil one' (5.19; cf. John 8.42-7).

But there is a difference. In the scrolls this battle is a permanent feature of the human situation. The *Manual* continues:

> Until now the spirits of truth and falsehood struggle in the hearts of men, and they walk in both wisdom and folly. According to his portion of truth so does a man hate falsehood, and according to his inheritance in the realm of falsehood so is he wicked and so hates the truth. For God has established the two spirits in equal measure until the determined end, and until the Renewal.

But in the Johannine literature the victory is already won. The darkness tried to conquer the light, but could not overcome it (John 1.5). The darkness is passing away and now the true light is shining (I John 5.8). The prince of this world is cast out; the victory is won (John 12.31; 16.33). In other words, the difference between the scrolls and John is Jesus Christ.

(ii)   In view of this it is very natural that both the scrolls and the fourth gospel should speak of the light of life. The *Manual of Discipline* (3) says of the man who would enter the community: 'It is through the spirit of true counsel concerning the ways of man that all his sins shall be expiated that he may contemplate the light of life.' And in the fourth gospel (8.12; 9.5; 12.46) Jesus is the light of the world. In the *Manual* the pledged initiates are sons of light. The man who does not keep his vows 'shall be cut off from the midst of all the sons of light' (2). 'It is the duty of the Master to instruct all the sons of light' (3). The followers of Jesus are urged to believe in the light that they may become sons of light (John 12.36). The concept of light is something that is equally prominent in the Old Testament. God's first creation was light (Gen. 1.5). The Psalmist says: 'The Lord is my light' (Ps. 27.1). 'Let us walk in the light of the Lord,' says Isaiah (2.5). Equally, light is a leading concept of the Hermetic literature. In the hymn of the reborn there are the prayers to light.

> O holy knowledge, by thee am I illumined, and through thee do I sing praise to the Light which mind alone can apprehend. ... O Light and Life, from you comes forth the song of praise. ... O Light, illumine thou the mind that is in us; O Life, keep my soul alive (*Corpus Hermeticum*, 13.18f.).

From the quotations which we have already made it is clear that light and life are closely connected, and in particular there is the idea of the living waters, the water of life. It is Jeremiah's complaint that the people have forsaken the fountain of living waters. It is the Psalmist's confidence that with God is the fountain of life. For the wise man 'the teaching of the wise is a fountain of life' (Prov. 13.14; cf. Ps. 36.9; Jer. 2.13). The life and water symbolism is in the scrolls also. In the *Damascus Document* (8), those who entered the new covenant and then relapsed and played false are said to turn away from 'the well of living waters'. 'The well which the princes digged' (Num. 21.18) is identified with the law. So in the fourth gospel we find Jesus speaking to the woman of Samaria of the water which he can give which will become in a man 'a spring of water welling up to life eternal,' and which, if a man drinks, he will never thirst again (John 4.14).

The idea of eternal life is one of the main ideas of the fourth gospel; it is to give eternal life that God sent his Son (3.15f.). So in the scrolls the promise to him who walks in the spirit is 'healing, great peace in a long life, and fruitfulness, together with everlasting blessing and eternal joy in life without end' (*Manual*, 4). Further, both the fourth gospel and the scrolls connect this life with *knowing*. Jesus says in the fourth gospel (17.3): 'This is eternal life, that they know thee, the only true God, and Jesus Christ whom thou has sent.' In the scrolls part of the blessing on the faithful is: 'May he (God) lighten your heart with life-giving wisdom and grant you eternal knowledge!' (*Manual*, 2).

Light, life and the water of life, the saving knowledge – the scrolls and the fourth gospel certainly speak the same language.

(iii)   The scrolls and the fourth gospel share the same doctrine of creation. In the *Manual* we read: 'From the God of knowledge comes all that is and shall be. Before ever they existed he established their whole design, and when, as ordained for them, they come into being, it is in accord with his glorious design that they fulfil their work. The laws of all things are unchanging in his hands and he provides them with all their needs' (3). 'All things come to pass by his knowledge; he establishes them by his design and without him nothing is done' (11). And the *Hymns of Thanksgiving* (no. 15, col. 10) say: 'Apart from thee nothing hath existed, and without thy will will nothing be.' 'By thy will all things exist, and without thee is nothing wrought' (Hymn 1). All these things are summed up in the Johannine affirmation of faith: 'All things were made through him, and without him was not anything made that was made' (John 1.3).

(iv)   The scrolls and the fourth gospel share a number of ways of speaking in relation to the truth.

(a)   They both speak of *doing* the truth; truth for both is not only something to be known; it is something to be practised and done. So John 3.21 has: 'He who does what is true comes to the light, that it may be clearly seen that his deeds have been wrought in God.' In the *Manual* the Master is to teach the community rule 'that they may practise truth' (1). 'They shall practise truth and humility in common' (5). The works of the twelve men who form the council will be 'truth, righteousness, justice, loving kindness and humility' (8). For both the fourth gospel and the scrolls the truth is something to be done.

(b) They both speak of *walking* in the truth. The letters of John (II 4; III 8) speak of following the truth. The *Manual* (4) speaks of walking in the ways of the spirit of truth: 'Until now the spirits of truth and falsehood struggle in the hearts of men, and they walk in both wisdom and folly.'

(c) They both speak of *witnessing* to the truth. The *Manual* (8) says of the members of the council: 'They shall be witnesses to the truth.' In the fourth gospel John 'has borne witness to the truth' (5.33). Jesus tells Pilate that the object of his coming into the world was 'to bear witness to the truth' (18.37). This also is an Old Testament conception. 'You are my witnesses, says the Lord ... I declared and saved and proclaimed, when there was no strange God among you; and you are my witnesses, says the Lord' (Isa. 43. 10-12).

(d) They both speak of *sanctification and purification* by the truth. In the *Manual* (4, Gaster's translation) we read:

Then, too, God will purge all the acts of man in the crucible of his truth, and refine for himself all the fabric of man, destroying every spirit of perversity from within his flesh and cleansing him by the holy spirit from all the effects of wickedness. Like waters of purification he will sprinkle upon him the spirit of truth, to cleanse him from all the abominations of falsehood and of all pollution through the spirit of filth.

In John 17.17-19 Jesus prays:

Sanctify them in the truth; thy word is truth. As thou didst send me into the world, so I have sent them into the world. And for their sakes I consecrate myself, that they also may be consecrated in truth.

The fourth gospel and the scrolls share the same view of the function of the truth.

(v) Both the fourth gospel and the scrolls urge the necessity of Christian unity.

Keep them in thy name, which thou hast given me, that they may be one, even as we are one ... I do not pray for these only, but also for those who believe in me through their word, that they may all be one ... The glory which thou has given me I have given to them, that they may be one even as we are one, I in them and thou in me, that they may become perfectly one (John 17.11, 21-23).

'By this all men will know that you are my disciples, if you have love for one another' (John 13.35). The *Manual* too urges love, but that love is love within the community, and hatred for those outside. The members of the community are to be taught 'to love all that he has chosen and hate all that he has rejected'. They are to 'love all the sons of light ... and hate all the sons of darkness' (1). The priests of the covenant pronounce their curse on the disobedient:

Be cursed for all your guilty wickedness! May he (God) deliver you up for

torture at the hand of the vengeful Avengers! May he visit you with
destruction by the hand of all the Wreakers of Revenge! Be cursed
without mercy because of the darkness of your deeds! Be damned in the
shadowy place of everlasting fire! May God not heed when you call on him,
nor pardon you by blotting out your sin! May he raise his angry face to you
for vengeance! (2)

The Master of the community has as a duty: 'Everlasting hatred in a
spirit of secrecy for the men of perdition. He is to leave it to them to
pursue wealth and mercenary gain, like servants at the mercy of their
masters or wretches truckling to a despot' (9). Within the community
there is the true unity: 'They shall rebuke one another in truth,
humility and charity. Let no man address his companion with anger,
or ill-temper, or obduracy, or with envy prompted by the spirit of
wickedness. Let him not hate him' (5). It is true that by the time the
Johannine literature was written Christian love was less universal and
more within the brotherhood. 'Do not love the world, nor the things in
the world. If anyone loves the world, love for the Father is not in him'
(I John 2.15).

It is true that both the scrolls and the fourth gospel urge love within
the community; it is true that both of them are acutely conscious of
the difference between themselves and the man outside; but it is also
true that the fourth gospel does not speak with the separatist bitterness
of the scrolls.

(vi) The fourth gospel and the scrolls both have the idea of a
divine Helper given by God to aid his own. The *Manual of Discipline*
(3) says: 'The God of Israel and his Angel of Truth will succour all the
sons of light.' In *The War of the Sons of Light with the Sons of
Darkness* we read: 'Thou has decreed for us a destiny of Light
according to thy Truth. And the Prince of Light thou hast appointed to
come to our support' (13). 'He will send eternal succour to the
company of his redeemed' (17). This is an idea which is kin to the idea
of the help of the Paraclete, the Helper, in the fourth gospel (14.16,
25f.; 16.7-15).

(vii) In both the scrolls and the fourth gospel there is what at least
at first sight seems to be a strong predestinarian element. In the *Hymns
of Thanksgiving* (22, col. 15) we read:

> I know that the inclination of every spirit is in thy hand;
> Thou didst establish all its ways before creating it,
>   and how can any man change thy words?
> Thou alone didst create the just,
>   and establish him from the womb
>   for the time of goodwill,
> that he might hearken to thy Covenant,
>   and walk in thy ways...
> But the wicked thou didst create

>   for the time of thy wrath,
>   and didst vow them from the womb
>   to the Day of Massacre,
>   for they walk in the way which is not good.

There is a long passage from the *Manual of Discipline* (3) parts of which we have already quoted in other connections:

> From the God of Knowledge comes all that is and shall be. Before ever they existed, he established their whole design, and when, as ordained for them, they came into being, it is in accord with his glorious design that they fulfil their work. The laws of all things are unchanging in his hands and he provides them with all their needs.

> He has created man to govern the world, and has appointed for him two spirits in which to walk until the time of his visitation – the spirits of truth and falsehood. Those born of truth spring from a fountain of light, but those born of falsehood spring from a source of darkness. All the children of righteousness are ruled by the Prince of Light, and walk in the ways of light, but all the children of falsehood are ruled by the Angel of Darkness, and walk in the ways of darkness.

> The Angel of Darkness leads all the children of righteousness astray, and, until his end, all their sin, iniquities, wickedness and all their unlawful deeds are caused by his dominion in accordance with the mysteries of God . . .

> But the God of Israel and his Angel of Truth will succour all the sons of light. For it is he who created the spirits of Light and Darkness, and founded every action upon them, and established every deed upon their ways. And he loves the one everlastingly; but the counsel of the other he loathes, and for ever hates its ways.

The matter is put most definitely of all in a passage of the *Damascus Document* (2) where it is said of the wicked:

> From the beginning God chose them not; he knew their deeds before ever they were created, and he hated their generations, and he hid his face from the Land till they were consumed. For he knew the years of their coming, and the length and exact duration of all their times for all ages to come and throughout eternity. He knew the happenings of their times throughout all the everlasting years. And in all of them he raised for himself men called by name, that a remnant might be left to the Land, and that the face of the holy earth might be filled by their seed. And he made known his Holy Spirit to them by the hand of his anointed one, and he proclaimed his truth to them. But those whom he hated he led astray.

In the fourth gospel there is an equally strong line of thought that those who believe were chosen by God to believe, and that those who accept Jesus are given him by God. 'No one can come to me,' says Jesus, 'unless the Father who sent me draws him' (6.44). 'Jesus knew from the first who would and who would not believe . . . "This is why I told you that no one can come to me unless it is granted him by the Father"' (6.64f.). 'He who is of God hears the words of God; the reason why you do not hear them is that you are not of God' (8.47). 'I know my own and my own know me . . . My sheep hear my voice and they follow me . . . My Father who has given them to me is greater than all, and no one is able to snatch them out of the Father's hand' (10.14, 27, 29). 'I am not speaking of you all; I know whom I have chosen' (13.18). 'I have manifested thy name to the men whom thou gavest me out of the world; thine they were and thou gavest them to me, and they have kept thy word' (17.6). 'This was to fulfil the word which he had spoken, "Of those whom thou gavest me, I lost not one"'(18.9). In both the scrolls and the fourth gospel there is a destiny which makes a man a believer or an unbeliever, and yet, equally clearly, both writings succeeded, while holding this, in holding personal responsibility along with it. The *Manual* can speak of a man as being stubborn, rebellious and disobedient, and turning aside from God. (2). The fourth gospel can charge the enemies of Jesus: 'If you were blind you would have no guilt; but now that you say, We see, your guilt remains' (9.41). 'If I had not come and spoken to them they would not have sin; but now they have no excuse for their sin' (15.22). For all the apparently predestinarian sayings, rejection is deliberate, and a man is himself responsible for it.

(viii)   It is just a possibility that in one matter the fourth gospel directly contradicts the scrolls. Whether or not there is direct contradiction, quite certainly in this matter the scrolls and the fourth gospel are written from diametrically opposite points of view. The Qumran community called themselves the covenanters; they entered into a covenant before God. Now the condition of the covenant was the keeping of the law (Ex. 24.3-8). And the first principle of the Qumran community was the most rigorous possible obedience to the law as interpreted by their own Teacher and priests. The very first instruction of the *Manual of Discipline* is that the Master is to instruct the covenanters 'that they seek God with a whole heart and soul, and do what is good and right before him as he commanded by the hand of Moses and all his servants the prophets . . . All those who embrace the Community Rule shall enter into Covenant before God to obey all his commandments.' Anyone who desires to enter the community 'shall undertake by a binding oath to return with all his heart and soul to every commandment of the Law of Moses in accordance with all that has been revealed of it to the sons of Zadok' (*Manual* 5). The *Damascus Document* lays it down that the only way to forgiveness with God is that 'they shall do according to that interpretation of the Law in which the first were instructed' (4). It is their obligation 'to act in accordance with the explicit injunctions of the Law' (6). This is not the outlook of the fourth gospel at all. John writes (1.17): 'The law was given through Moses; grace and truth came through Jesus Christ.' It is not impossible to feel that the fourth gospel may be directly correcting the overstressing of the law now that the gospel has come.

Such then are the facts about the relationship of the fourth gospel and the scrolls. Clearly, a case can be made out for such a relationship. Any judgment on the matter cannot escape being subjective. My own feeling is that one has only to read the fourth gospel and then to read the scrolls to see that in spirit they are poles apart. In fact it might well be true to say that the fourth gospel has a closer kinship with the Hermetic writings than with the scrolls.

Last of the relationships which we must examine is the relation of the fourth gospel to Mandaism.[17] This is a relationship which in certain quarters has been enthusiastically claimed. In 1928 Goguel could say: 'For several years a kind of Mandaean fever seems to have gripped a part of German criticism.'[18] In particular this claim had the support of Bultmann, the index of whose commentary *The Gospel of John* contains nearly eighty references to the Mandaeans. Let us then examine the facts.

Mandaism still exists as the religion of a small community in Iraq. Its sacred books are in a dialect of Aramaic and consist of the *Ginza* or *Treasure*, the *Book of John*, and various liturgical documents. The earliest manuscripts date to the sixteenth century. The earliest reference to the Mandaeans in literature is in the work of Theodore bar Khanan in AD 792; statements about the Mandaeans before then must be based on speculation. As they stand at present, the Mandaean books must be later than AD 700, because they make reference to Mohammed and the spread of his religion. Further proof of this date is that in the Mandaean literature John the Baptist is commonly referred to as Jahja, which is the Arabic form of his name used in Koran. The Mandaean literature became available through its translation into German by M. Lidzbarski between 1915 and 1920. As Kümmel points out, the first connection of the Mandaean writings with the fourth gospel was tentatively made by J.D. Michaelis in 1750. Kümmel writes:

> He even notes the anti-Gnostic polemic of the Gospel of John, and hazards the guess that he had taken 'the Word' as an expression of a divine person 'from the Gnostics', and had written 'against the disciples of John the Baptist, the Sabians' [which is another name for the Mandaeans].[19]

This view was taken further by R. Bultmann in 1923 in an article on the religio-historical background to the prologue of John's gospel, and in 1925 in an article on the importance of the Mandaean and

Manichaean sources for the understanding of the gospel of John. Since the Mandaeans do not emerge in history until the eighth century and since they are being used as an explanation of phenomena in the first century, it is clear from the beginning that we are entering on a realm of speculation. C.H. Dodd in *The Interpretation of the Fourth Gospel* (p. 115) describes the Mandaean writing as 'an extraordinary farrago of theology, myth, fairy-tale, ethical instructions, ritual ordinances, and what purports to be history'. They have, he says, no unity and no consistency, and succinct summary is impossible.

The Mandaean myth is as follows. There are two realms. There is the Realm of Light, the members of which are subject to the High King of Light or the Great Life. There is the realm of darkness, ruled by Ruha d'Kudsha, which means the Holy Spirit, and by her children, the planets and the demons of the Zodiac. The universe is a kind of compromise between these two realms. The demiurge, the creator is Ptahil. He is an offspring of the beings of light but 'there is something oblique about his birth'. According to one story his father Abathur looked into the waters of darkness, and saw his own image there, and that image was his son Ptahil.

Ptahil was both foolish and reckless. He was allowed by the beings of light, and was helped by them, to make out of the primeval chaos of darkness a world which has certain elements of light in it, but Ruha and her family constantly interfered with and harmed his work. They succeeded in creating the body of man; or, according to another version, Ptahil made the physical bodies of Adam and Eve after he was 'cut off from the light'. This is to say that the body of man belongs essentially to the realm of darkness. But the realm of light sent down the soul of man, which is thus essentially kin to the beings of light.

In view of this, the soul is a prisoner in this world, always under oppression and attack by the powers of evil. Only at the death of the body can it escape, and even then to get to the realm of light it must succeed in passsing a powerful chain of guard-houses in each of which there is a hostile demon ready to capture it. It is only the soul which has been equipped beforehand which can reach the realm of light. The soul's preparation consists of the Mandaean ritual and the impartation of a myth which describes how the powers of light have overcome the powers of darkness.

The central part of the ritual is repeated baptism in living, that is, running water, for running water has in it something of the power of the heavenly water of life which is in the realm of light. Baptism is repeated again and again, because only thus can the soul acquire the power of light, and escape from the pollution of matter. The person baptized wears a white robe which represents the white robes worn by the heavenly inhabitants of the realm of light. A crown and a staff are also part of the baptismal ritual. In the baptism the priest lays his hands on the person baptized and pronounces divine names over him. When the baptized person comes up out of the water the priest gives him his right hand, which is a symbol of his reception into the fellowship of the realm of light.

The myth, the cult story, the story which contains salvation, tells of the descent of Manda d'Hayye, knowledge of life or a son of the Great Life, or sometimes of his son Hibil, into this lower realm of earth and matter. The story tells of his terrible but victorious fight with the power of darkness, and then of his triumphant ascent and return to the realm of light and to reunion with the Great Life and all the celestial beings. And the meaning of the story is that, as Manda d'Hayye, or Hibil-Ziwa, entered the territory of the evil powers, as he faced their hostility and their attack and conquered them, as he made his triumphant way through the successive worlds between this world and the realm of light, as he overcame the demonic guardians at the guard-stations, so the human soul, your soul and mine, at present imprisoned in the world of darkness, can break through.

The story tells also how the divine champion, before he descended to earth, received the robe, the crown, the staff and the ritual handclasp, from the inhabitants of the world of light, that in the power of these he descended without fear, for 'he whom the father arms, seals, baptizes and establishes need not fear the evil one'. Mandaean baptism is the re-enactment on earth of the divine process through which the heavenly champion was empowered to win the victory. It is to be noted that the coming down and ascending of Manda d'Hayye is not an historical event; it either took place before creation, or was part of the creation process, before mankind existed as a whole.

Once man is created, the lower powers who created his body, cannot give his body life. So the Great Life sends down a soul, which is either the same as the 'hidden Adam' or as Manda d'Hayye, and the body comes to life, Adam lives.

Ruha and the planets do everything they can to get man into their power, so the Great Life sends down three helpers, Hibil, Shitil and Enosh, who give Adam a wife Hawwa, enable him to beget a family, and tell him the ritual and the story through which he and his race can at the death of the body escape and rise to the realm of light.

History is seen as in three epochs. First, there is the epoch from Adam to Nu (Noah). This epoch is ended by cosmic disasters which destroy everyone except a few individuals. The souls of the dead ascend to the realm of light, and through the few survivors the world is enabled to begin again. In the second epoch, after Noah, the powers of evil intensify their attack on mankind. One of the powers of evil, Adonai, brings the Jews out of Egypt and gives them the law through Misha bar Amra, that is, Moses. At last the seven planets lead all

Adam's children astray. One of the planets called Nbu (Hermes, the planet Mercury) is called the Christ. He revealed himself 'in another form' in which he called himself 'Jesus the Saviour'. Now there come two passages from the Mandaean writings which must be quoted in full (from C.H. Dodd, pp. 119f.).

> He [this Jesus] says: 'I am God, the Son of God, whom my Father has sent here.' He declares to you: 'I am the first Messenger, I am Hibil-Ziwa, who am come from on high.' But confess him not for he is not Hibil-Ziwa. Hibil-Ziwa is not clothed with fire. Hibil-Ziwa does not reveal himself in that age. On the contrary, Enosh-Uthra comes, and betakes himself to Jerusalem, clothed with a garment of water-clouds. He walks in bodily form, yet he is clothed with no bodily garment. There is no fiery wrath in him. He goes and comes in the years of Paltus (Pilate), the king of the world. Enosh-Uthra comes into the world with the might of the high King of Light. He heals the sick, makes the blind to see, cleanses the lepers, lifts up the crippled who crawl upon the ground, so that they can walk, makes the deaf and dumb to speak, and raises the dead. He wins believers among the Jews, and shows them: There is life and there is death, there is darkness and there is light, there is error and there is truth. He converts the Jews to the name of the high King of Light.

Then Enosh-Uthra ascends to the realm of light; Jerusalem is destroyed; the Jews are dispersed; and finally the story of the Mandaean writings ends with the coming of Ahmat son of the sorcerer Bizbat (Mohammed), and he leads the souls of men astray. In an expanded form of the story Enosh-Uthra exposes the deception of Jesus who is crucified by the Jews and whose followers are imprisoned.

So in the Mandaean myth two persons appear in Palestine not long before the fall of Jerusalem. One of them is Nbu, the malignant planet Mercury, in the form of Jesus, the other is Enosh, the last of the three divine Helpers of mankind. For the moment we will not discuss the identity of Enosh.

And now we come to the second passage in which another figure is introduced, a figure very important for our investigation:

> Further, in that age a child will be born, whose name is called Johana, the son of the gray father Zakhria, who was granted to him in his old age at the end of a hundred years. His mother Enishbai became pregnant with him, and bore him in her old age. When Johana grows up in that age of Jerusalem, faith will rest in his heart. He will take the Jordan and complete the baptism twenty-four years before Nbu takes a body and enters the world. When Johana lives, in that age of Jerusalem, and completes the baptism, Jesus Christ comes, enters with humility, receives the baptism of Johana, and becomes wise through the wisdom of Johana. But then he perverts the speech of Johana, alters the baptism in Jordan, perverts the words of the truth, and preaches blasphemy and deceit in the world.

When John came to the end of his course Hibil-Ziwa, or Manda d'Hayye, came to him in the form of a little child asking for baptism. John agreed, but when he entered the water, it receded from him. Thereupon John knew who he was, and was carried up to the realm of light; he was there baptized in the heavenly Jordan and clothed in the heavenly garments of light.

Out of all this two conclusions were claimed. First, it was claimed that 'the kernel of Mandaism' is the myth of the heavenly, primeval man, who came down from heaven to rescue the soul of man imprisoned in the world and imprisoned in matter, and who, having won his victory, reascended to heaven, the Redeemed Redeemer. This Iranian myth, it is claimed, underlies all Christian theology, and especially the fourth gospel. Jesus is the heavenly man, who descended and ascended for the rescue of the soul of man. In other words, Christian theology is based on an Iranian myth rather than on an historical incarnation. Second, it was claimed that Mandaean ritual and myth were formulated by John the Baptist, and that the later Mandaeans were the successors of the Baptist sect which appears in Acts 18.24-19.7. It is claimed that Christianity arose out of the Baptist sect. In their own scriptures the Mandaeans call themselves Nazoraeans. It is then claimed that Jesus was originally a Nazoraean in the sense that he was a member of the Baptist sect, that he broke away from the Baptist sect, taking the name Nazoraean with him, and founded a new sect. It is claimed that this is proved by the fact that the view of Jesus in the Mandaean scriptures is the same as the view of John in the Christian scriptures, that the Mandaean scriptures have a polemic against Jesus just as the Christian sect was a breakaway movement under Jesus from the Baptist sect.

So, as Bultmann sees it, the fourth gospel is a Christianized version of the myth of the descending and ascending heavenly man, the myth which was the basis of the Baptist sect, also called the Nazoraean sect and the Mandaean religion, John the Baptist is the real founder of it, and Christianity is a breakaway sect. And it is claimed that the statements made about Jesus in the fourth gospel can be extensively parallelled by the statements made about the divine figure of the heavenly man made in Mandaean literature.

C.H. Dodd (pp. 123-5) raised certain valid objections to all this. If John was the founder of the Mandaean sect, you would expect the Mandaeans to have more information about him. In fact, they have not; they do not even know how he died; for that information we have to turn to the synoptic gospels (Mark 6.14-29). The polemic against John in the fourth gospel is not against anything that the Mandaeans ever claimed John to be. 'He was not that light, but came to bear witness to the light' (John 1.8). But the Mandaeans never equate John with the Light or the High King of Light. John is not the Messiah

(John 1.20). But the Mandaeans never claimed he was; the rival of Jesus was Enosh-Uthra. Mandaean baptism was frequently repeated; the baptism of John the Baptist was a once and for all event. It is quite clear that the Mandaean scriptures date from the eighth century. All the probability is that when Mandaism came into contact with Mohamedanism, they came into contact with a religion which counted as pagans those who did not possess a 'book', as it had the Koran and the Jews the Old Testament. So then the Mandaean scriptures were concocted in self-defence. It is fairly certain that ingenious speculation elevated Mandaism to an importance it does not deserve.[20]

We left one problem unsolved – who is Enosh-Uthra? Dodd (p. 125) suggests that we reverse the question and ask, who is the Mandaean Jesus? In the Mandaean scriptures Jesus is stern and ferocious, Enosh-Uthra is gentle and kind. In one place in the *Ginza* Jesus is referred to as 'the Roman (i.e. Byzantine) Christ'. So we may say that the Jesus whom the Mandaeans condemn is the Jesus of the orthodox Church which ferociously persecuted the Mandaeans, and Enosh-Uthra is the Messiah as the Mandaeans believed the Messiah really was and ought to be.

In this case we may well hold that the Mandaean literature has no connection with the fourth gospel at all, and that it is quite unnecessary to explain Christian Christology by an Iranian myth and the Christian church as an offshoot movement from a Baptist sect.

9

THE ORIGINALITY OF THE FOURTH GOSPEL

The object of this examination of the fourth gospel was to discuss matters proper to an 'Introduction to the NT' and not to expound its theology, although it is obvious that the two cannot be kept completely separate. But it would be wrong to leave the discussion of the gospel without some mention of its most characteristic theological contribution.

In the *Timaeus* (37D) Plato discusses the relationship between time and eternity. God, says Plato, was pleased with his created universe, and decided 'to make the universe eternal, as far as might be'. But, Plato goes on, 'the nature of intelligible being is eternal, but to attach eternity to the creature was impossible'. So then God decided to have 'an image of eternity . . . and this image we call time'. So then, according to Plato, time is an image of eternity. John's central affirmation (1.14) is that the Word became flesh, which is to say that John's gospel is founded on incarnation, and this is what incarnation means. Incarnation means that events in time can be, and are, the image of eternity. In John the connection between time and eternity is unique.

The supreme theological problem which the early church had to solve was the problem of eschatology. At the time of its beginning the early church was convinced that the second coming of Jesus would happen at any moment; the first Christians looked for the immediate return of their Lord, and for the end of all things as they at present are. This did not happen, and the longer the expected events were delayed, the more acute the whole problem became. So F.C. Burkitt in *The Gospel History* (pp. 243f.) declares that one of the aims of the fourth gospel is 'the deliberate substitution of other ideals for the expected coming of the Messiah on the clouds of heaven'. Burkitt then goes on to quote a passage from a paper by W.R. Inge:

> The Synoptic Gospels, though they doubtless give us a more accurate picture of the outward circumstances of our Lord's ministry, and of the manner and style of his teaching, are pervaded by the idea of the Messianic Kingdom. To the majority of the first and second generation of Christians, the Church was regarded as merely a stop-gap till the Kingdom of God should come. Christ was to return in a few years upon the clouds of heaven to inaugurate the new theocratic kingdom. In correspondence with these ideas, a kind of legend grew up, affecting not

only the hopes of the future, but the traditions of our Lord's ministry. The demand for evidence of the Messiahship, becoming every year more urgent, was met by heightening the colours of the picture, and modifying those portions of the narrative which ascribed human limitations to Jesus. This process may be seen at work if we compare S. Matthew with S. Mark. Christianity was in some danger of being so closely identified with apocalyptic Messianic dreams that it would have perished when these hopes proved illusory ... The [fourth] evangelist wishes to lay a surer foundation, underpinning the fabric which at present rested on the crumbling foundations of thaumaturgic superstition and Chiliastic or Messianic dreams.[1]

Just what did John do? What new lines of thought did he introduce? John made an original contribution in three areas of thought.

(i)   John took a new view of the second coming. It is true that there are times when John shows us Jesus talking in the traditional way. He does show us Jesus speaking about the 'last day' (e.g. 6.39f., 44, 54). John like many an adventurous thinker could hold apparently conflicting ideas in his mind. But the really original thing about the thought of John is the idea that in the coming of the Spirit the second coming had happened, that the second coming happened at Pentecost, for then in the Spirit the presence and the power of the risen Lord came to his people in a way which never again could be taken from them. John depicts Jesus as saying: 'I will not leave you desolate; *I will come to you* ... He who has my commandments and keeps them, he it is who loves me; and he who loves me will be loved by my Father, and I will love him, *and manifest myself to him* ... If a man loves me, he will keep my word, and my Father will love him, and *we will come to him, and make our home with him*' (14.18-23). Plainly and unmistakably Jesus there speaks of his coming to his own people.

We may say that there are three kinds of eschatology. There is purely futurist, traditional eschatology, in which the second coming is expected at some future unknown date. There is realized eschatology, which holds that with Jesus the final events happened, that, in the famous phrase, D-day has taken place and V-day is certain. In Jesus eternity invaded time and the last events are here. But John's eschatology is like none of these. We might call his eschatology personalized eschatology, in that the second coming happens individually to each man personally when he turns to Jesus Christ in humble and loving obedience, and when thereupon Jesus Christ in his Spirit comes to dwell for ever within his heart.

John sees the second coming not so much in terms of a visible, shattering descent in the clouds of heaven, but in the coming of the Spirit into the world, and into the heart of a man. He sees the second coming not as a distant far-off event in an unknown future, but as something to experience here and now.

(ii)   John had something quite new to say about judgment. In the statements of the fourth gospel regarding judgment there seems at first sight to be an unresolvable paradox and contradiction.

(a)   In one set of passages Jesus says that he did not come to judge the world. 'It was not to judge the world that God sent his Son into the world, but that through him the world might be saved' (3.17 NEB). 'I judge no one' (8.15). 'I have not come to judge the world, but to save the world' (12.47).

(b)   In another set of passages Jesus seems to say precisely the opposite and to declare that his prime function is judgment. 'The Father judges no one, but has given all judgment to the Son' (5.22). 'The Father has given him authority to execute judgment' (5.27). 'For judgment I came to this world' (9.39). Here Jesus says that he came to judge just as definitely as he said in the previous passages that he had come not to judge.

(c)   There is a third saying which is the most startling of all, but which in itself contains the key to the apparent contradiction. Jesus said: 'Truly, truly, I say to you, he who hears my word amd believes him who sent me, has eternal life; he does not come into judgment, but he has passed from death to life' (5.24). Hitherto judgment has always been regarded as something which happened after death, but as John sees it judgment is a present event, happening here and now.

What is the solution of this apparent contradiction? The solution is that encounter, confrontation with Jesus is itself a judgment. When a man is confronted with Jesus, he necessarily undergoes some reaction, and in that reaction he automatically passes a judgment on himself. If, when he is confronted with Jesus, his heart goes out to Jesus, however inadequately, it is well with his soul. If his attitude is indifference, hostility, dislike, contempt, then it is ill. Confrontation involves reaction; reaction is judgment.

Let us take an analogy. Suppose I am moved and thrilled by great music. Suppose I have a friend who so far has been a stranger to music, and who has never heard great music greatly played. Suppose that I, wishing to open the door for him to a great experience, take him to a concert at which a great orchestra is playing great music under a great conductor. Suppose that within minutes he is fidgety, restless, obviously bored. He has thereby shown that he has no music in him. The experience which I intended for his delight has turned out for his boredom. The experience that I intended for his deep and lasting pleasure has shown that there are things which he is incapable of appreciating. I meant it for good, but it has turned out for judgment.

Here is the analogy. Jesus did not come to condemn or judge; he came only in love. But confronted with that love a man must have a reaction. And if in encounter with that love the man remains aloof, unmoved, hostile, then the offer of love has become a judgment, not because Jesus has judged the man, but because the man has judged himself.

If that is so, judgment is no distant and far-off event in some unknown future. Judgment is a process is always going on, every day every day and even every moment of life. And the man who answers love with love has emerged from the encounter safe from judgment.

(iii) The third of the fourth gospel's adventures in thought was in regard to eternal life. There is a difference between that which is *everlasting* and that which is *eternal*. Plato has it that the gods are eternal (*aiōnios*), but body and soul are, 'when generated, indestructible (*anolethros*), but not eternal (*aiōnios*)' (*Laws* 904A; *Timaeus* 37C). From this two things emerge. First, the word *eternal* means more than simply lasting for ever; it has more in it than simply continued existence. Second, this quality of eternity is connected with divine and not with human existence. In other words, the word *aiōnios*, eternal, can only properly be applied to God.

From this it clearly follows that eternal life is something which belongs to the future, which does not belong to this life, or this sphere of being, but to some other life and some other world, into which a man may possibly enter when this life and this kind of being come to an end. But in the fourth gospel we find the insistence that eternal life is something which through Jesus Christ a man can enjoy here and now. 'He who believes in the Son *has* eternal life' (3.36). 'He who hears my word, and believes him who sent me, *has* eternal life' (5.24). 'You refuse to come to me that you *may have* eternal life' (5.40). 'Truly, truly, I say to you, he who believes *has* eternal life' (6.47). 'I came that they might *have* life and *have* it abundantly' (10.10). Jesus *is* the bread of life (6.48,58). He *is* the resurrection and the life (11.25). This life, this eternal life, this life which is the life of God is something into which the Christian can enter here and now.

So the fourth gospel has taken three things which were formerly regarded as future events and has turned them into present realities. The second coming is the coming of the Spirit into the heart of the man who knows and loves and obeys Jesus Christ. Judgment is immediate and continuous, for judgment is what happens here and now when a man is confronted with Jesus Christ. Eternal life is a here-and-now present reality for the man who has given his heart and subjected his will to Jesus Christ. It is true that in the fourth gospel none of these ideas do away with the idea of future consummation. The triumph of Jesus Christ will be universally achieved. The here-and-now verdict of judgment will be confirmed by God. The enjoyment of life here and now is the foretaste of the perfect bliss which is to come.

When John reached these conclusions he made a real contribution to Christian thought. In an issue of *The Modern Churchman* in 1950

D.E.H. Whiteley made a most interesting and significant suggestion.[2] He suggested that there was a fundamental difference between the biblical and the modern view of history. The biblical writers see history as a series of *flash-points*, a series of events which happen in a moment of time. Modern thought sees history as a series of dynamic processes, stretching throughout ages and centuries of time. The biblical writers, for instance, see creation as a flash-point which began and finished in a week; the modern view is that creation is a dynamic process which began millions of years ago and which is not finished yet. The biblical writers see the fall of man as a flash-point event; the modern view is that the fall is a long process in which man by consistent misuse of his free will produced a sin-infected universe.

John is curiously modern. He sees the second coming not as a flash-point but as a dynamic process in the hearts of men. He sees judgment not as the flash-point of judgment day, but as the dynamic process which is continually going on in the confrontation and encounter of the soul with Jesus Christ. He sees eternal life not as something to be entered into at some distant flash-point, but as the product of a dynamic process and experience, beginning in time and ending in eternity. The truth is that John's thought is so modern that the conventional thought of the church has not assimilated it or caught up with it even yet.

The Collect for St John the Evangelist's Day

Merciful Lord, we beseech thee to cast thy bright beams of light upon thy Church, that it being enlightened by the doctrine of thy blessed Apostle and Evangelist Saint John may so walk in the light of thy truth, that it may at length attain to the light of everlasting life; through Jesus Christ our Lord. Amen.

PART TWO

THE ACTS OF THE APOSTLES

10

LUKE'S PURPOSE IN WRITING

E.J. Goodspeed declares that Acts is one of the most exciting books in the world. It is meant, he says, to be read at a sitting.

> Where will you find within eighty pages such a varied series of exciting events – trials, riots, persecutions, escapes, martyrdoms, voyages, shipwrecks, rescues – set in that amazing panorama of the ancient world – Jerusalem, Antioch, Philippi, Corinth, Athens, Rome? And with such scenery and settings – temples, courts, prisons, deserts, ships, seas, barracks, theatres? Has any opera such variety? A bewildering range of scenes and actions passes before the eye of the historian. And in them all he sees the providential hand that has made and guided this great movement for the salvation of mankind (*Introduction to the NT*, pp. 187f.).

Not only is Acts one of the most exciting books in the world; it is also one of the most essential. 'It is Acts,' says Furneaux in his commentary (p. iii), 'which bridges the gulf which separates the Church of the Upper Chamber from the churches of Europe.' It is the simple fact that, if we did not possess Acts, or if Acts should prove basically unreliable, we would know nothing of the first age of the church, except what we could guess and deduce from the letters of Paul. There is nothing to replace Acts. If we lost one of the gospels, we would still have the other three, but Acts stands alone. We may quote three more *Introductions to the NT* on this point. E.F. Scott (p. 102) says: 'It is our one account of primitive Christianity. . . . All else (other than in the Pauline Epistles) that we can discover about the primitive Church has to be set in the framework of Acts.' Wikenhauser (p. 331) says: 'Without this book, complete darkness would envelop many aspects of primitive Christianity, in spite of the evidence of the Pauline Epistles.' Kirsopp and Sylvia Lake (p. 67) say:

> The value of this book is that it affords us a unique series of glimpses into the beginnings of Christianity. It is not a complete or a perfectly connected story, but our whole knowledge of the founding of the Greek-speaking church depends on it.

But first of all we must see what it claims to offer. In the AV and RSV the title of the book is 'The Acts of the Apostles'. In the NEB it is 'Acts of the Apostles'. In the Greek manuscripts the oldest title is *Praxeis Apostolōn*, with no 'the' before either 'Acts' or 'Apostles' –

literally, 'Acts of Apostles'. The best and least misleading translation is 'Acts of Apostolic Men'. If we read of 'the acts of the apostles', we expect a comprehensive account of the exploits of the whole apostolic company. The word *praxeis*, 'acts', was a common designation of a certain kind of literature in the ancient world, a literature telling of the exploits of famous characters. Wikenhauser (p. 325) gives some examples: the *Acts of Hercules*; the *Acts of Alexander the Great*, composed by Callisthenes, the nephew of Aristotle; the *Acts of Hannibal*, composed by Sosylus. The Muratorian Canon,[1] the first list of New Testament books (*c.* AD 180), does in fact call the book 'The Acts of All the Apostles', but this is a very misleading title. There is some account of the work of Peter; we read of the deaths of Judas Iscariot (1.18f.) and of James the brother of John (12.2); John himself makes fleeting appearances (3.1-11; 4.13), but never at any time speaks; there is some information about James the brother of the Lord (15.13-19; 21.17). But after ch. 13 Acts becomes to all intents and purposes a biography of Paul. True, the apostles are listed (1.13), but only of Paul is there any extended information.

There are reasons for Luke's inclusions and omissions.

(a) There was the simple fact that any ancient writer had to be selective. He did not write in a bound book, whose size can be almost indefinitely extended; he wrote on a papyrus roll, the maximum usable length of which was about thirty feet; and Acts is just about the maximum amount of material which could be got on to any one roll. The circumstances in which he worked made it necessary for the ancient writer to be selective.

(b) There are in any event two ways of writing history. There is the way of the person who is thinking of history in terms of annals. He will try to write down everything that happened every day. He will not comment or interpret at all; he will simply list events as they happened, and he will try to be as complete as possible. The other way is to make no attempt to be complete in this sense, but rather to open a series of windows on significant events, which will illumine the decisive moments in which the direction of history is settled.

This is what Luke did. Luke was writing far more as a preacher than as a historian; he was writing for comparatively simple people. He therefore had his own technique, and his technique, as Haenchen says in his commentary (p. 103), was to write history 'in the guise of stories'. Everything he knew or could infer had to be translated 'into the language of vivid and dramatic scenes'.

As Haenchen goes on to point out, we can vividly see Luke's method in the first chapter of Acts. Simply from the point of view of conveying information, it would have been possible to write:

> Due to the treachery and the death of Judas, there was a vacancy in the apostolic company. The Christians met and appointed Matthias to fill the vacancy.

But this is not what Luke does. He dramatizes the whole scene with its meeting, its story of the death of Judas, its Old Testament quotations, its election by drawing lots. By Luke's method we not only receive the necessary information; we *see* the thing happening before our very eyes. As Haenchen puts it (p. 107): 'Tradition is not petrified but still molten lava.'

But there was more, far more, to Luke than that. Luke was far more than the dramatic painter of vivid pictures. Luke was one of theology's great pioneers. In his *Introduction to the NT* (p. 450) Jülicher says of Acts: 'The book can only be understood, from an historical point of view, as a new phenomenon in Christian literature.' Wherein then lay Luke's newness? C.K. Barrett writes in *Luke the Historian* (pp. 57f.):

> In Luke's thought, the end of the story of Jesus is the Church; and the story of Jesus is the beginning of the Church. In this proposition lie the distinctive characteristics of Luke's work. He shares with Mark and Paul the conviction that Jesus is the End, God's final word and deed; but when his work is compared with theirs, the reader finds himself asking, What does 'the End' mean? For every New Testament writer, the time that falls after the resurrection, whether long or short, is the last chapter in history. For Mark and Paul, the stress lies on the adjective *last*. For Luke, the stress lies on the fact that the last chapter is a *new* chapter. Christ is the End; but (and this is how Luke prefers to think of Him) because He is the end He is also the Beginning. He is not the close of all history, but the starting-point of a new kind of history, Church History, whose horizons are indefinitely remote. This is what Luke perceived, and this is what gives him his unique place in the New Testament. He is the Father of Church History; it had not occurred to any Christian before him that there was any such thing.

As R.H. Fuller says in his *Critical Introduction to the NT* (p. 123): 'The Church never suspected that it would have a history.' W.G. Kümmel makes the same point, when he speaks in his *Introduction to the NT* (p. 116) of Luke's 'basic theological view that Jesus' history was the beginning of the still continuing history of the church'. Dibelius had said this long before. It was an obvious necessity to collect the works and words of Jesus,

> but to write down the history of the oldest community, to give an account of its difficulties and conflicts, to describe its spread to Rome and to tell how the way was prepared for the reception of the Gentiles, and of the obdurate refusal on the part of the Jews – all this could not possibly have seemed an obviously necessary undertaking to those Christians who were waiting for the end of the world, and who had neither inclination nor ability for literary work (*Studies in Acts*, p. 103).

It is the words of Dibelius which face us with the fundamental theological revolution which Acts implies. The early church was a church waiting for the imminent end. To write its history would have seemed a sheer irrelevance. That Luke writes history at all is a new movement of thought away from imminent dissolution of life towards some kind of permanence. Evangelization had replaced the *parousia*, and the Spirit replaces the coming of the kingdom.[2]

Let us then look at this theological revolution. (In the following section I have drawn largely on Haenchen's introduction to his commentary, pp. 95-8.) For the early church the world was coming to an end. The form of this world was passing away (I Cor. 7.31). The powers of the new age were already operative (Luke 11.20). John the Baptist had been the forerunner, and Jesus had been the Messiah (Mark 9.13; 8.29). The resurrection had happened, and the second coming was soon to follow (Rom. 13.11). The brief interval must be used to awaken the belief in Jesus Christ which alone would save. For Paul, the Christian was already dead to this world, and was waiting for the body of glory which he would receive at the coming of Christ (Rom. 6.2,8; II Cor. 5.14f.; Gal. 2.19; I Cor. 15.44; Phil. 3.21).

But the trouble was that the expectation was not fulfilled. Paul was executed; James was martyred; Christians had died in agony in Nero's savage persecutions; Jerusalem was a heap of ruins, and the world was still going on. What had happened to the imminent expected end?

Two answers emerged. There was the answer that the last things were indeed happening here and now; and there was the answer that the realization of the hope would come – though not at once, but in some remote, distant and indefinite future.

The first answer was the answer of the fourth gospel. In it Jesus *is* 'the resurrection and the life' (John 11.25); and eternal life, the life of the future age, can be enjoyed here and now. When a man is confronted with the voice of the Son, which is the voice of God, he is confronted here and now with the moment of decision, and his choice will bring him life and judgment. For him the moment of judgment has come (John 5.24f.). The eschatological events are not in some distant future; they are happening in the confrontation with the Word, here and now. The second coming is not in some remote future. It is here and now; for, if a man hears Jesus and loves him and obeys him, the Father and the Son will come to him, and make their home with him now (John 14.23). Here is fulfilment here and now, whether in the Johannine eternal life, or in the Pauline 'in Christ'.

But this was not the way of Luke. Luke accepted that the second coming was no longer imminent. When it would come was God's and not man's business, and speculation was forbidden (Acts 1.7,11). But for all this Luke remains 'chronological'. The promised time will in the end come.

This is why Luke has the new thing, and the new thing is that he sees life in three periods. First, there was the time of the law and the prophets, leading up to, and ending with, John the Baptist (Luke 16.16). Then there was what Conzelmann called the middle time, the life of Jesus up to the ascension. Finally, there was the third era, and it is this third era which is the era of the church, or the era of the Spirit. This will end with the return of the Lord in judgment (Acts 1.11).

This is why it is possible to talk about the history of the church, for in this time of the church there must be a time of mission to the ends of the earth (Acts 1.8; 13.47). Since Luke had this view of things, it was perfectly possible for him to regard the life of Jesus as a chronological event; and that chronological event had a chronological sequel in the history of the church, and for Luke the history of the church was a continuation of the gospel.

But what is the connection between the two times – the middle time of Jesus and the time of the church? It is quite clear that what matters for salvation is the history of *Jesus*, not the history of the church. Wherein, then, lies the connection, and wherein lies the importance of the church? It has been suggested that the gospel is what Jesus did in the flesh, and Acts is what Jesus did through the Spirit in the apostles, that Acts is, as Harnack puts it (*Acts*, p. xviii), 'the power of the Spirit of Jesus in the Apostles manifested in history'. We shall go on to see that there is truth in that view. But what Haenchen (p. 98) calls 'the clamp which holds the two eras together' is the Word of God. In the earthly life of Jesus men are confronted with the Word of God, and in the mission of the church men are confronted with that same Word of God, and that is precisely why salvation must be preached to all, and that is also precisely why there can be such a thing as church history. So, then, Luke writes the history of the church, because he sees in the church the continuation of the gospel, in that through the mission of the church men are still confronted with the Word of God, a task which cannot cease until the return of the Lord.

This new realization of Christianity brought certain consequences.

(i) It placed Christianity firmly in the context of contemporary history. In his gospel, Luke firmly locates John the Baptist in history:

In the fifteenth year of the reign of Tiberius Caesar, Pontius Pilate being governor of Judaea, and Herod being tetrarch of Galilee, and his brother Philip tetrarch of the region of Ituraea and Trachonitis, and Lysanias tetrarch of Abilene, in the high priesthood of Annas and Caiaphas, the word of God came to John the son of Zechariah in the wilderness (Luke 3.1f.).

F.F. Bruce (p. 15) points out how this exactly parallels the method of Thucydides in his history. In the first book Thucydides assembles his introductory material; then he begins the second book:

The thirty years' truce which was concluded after the conquest of Euboea
had lasted fourteen years. In the fifteenth year, in the forty-eighth year of
the priestess-ship of Chrysis at Argos, in the ephorate of Ainesias at
Sparta, when the archonship of Pythodorus at Athens had but two
months to run, six months after the battle of Potidaea, at the beginning of
spring, a Theban force . . . made an armed entry into Plataea (II. 2).

Acts mentions Claudius twice (11.28; 18.2). Acts has begun to move
in a world of Roman emperors and their edicts. The church is in the
world.

(ii)   Acts is firmly convinced of the universal character of the
church. It represents the break-through of Christianity to
universality.[3] Luke starts his story in the temple at Jerusalem (Luke
2.2) and finishes it in Rome (Acts 28). The roll call of the countries in
the Pentecost story (Acts 2.9-11) is a way of indicating that
Christianity means a world for Christ. The Cornelius story (Acts
10.1-11.18) shows the church going out to the Gentiles, even if at this
stage it is rather the Gentiles coming into the church. Again and
again the decision to go to the Gentiles is publicly made. At Antioch
in Pisidia Paul and Barnabas say: 'It was necessary that the word of
God should be spoken first to you. Since you thrust it from you, and
judge yourselves unworthy of eternal life, behold, we turn to the
Gentiles' (13.46). In Corinth Paul says to the hostile Jews: 'Your
blood be upon your heads! I am innocent. From now on I will go to
the Gentiles' (18.6). In Rome he tells the Jews: 'Let it be know to you
then that this salvation of God has been sent to the Gentiles; they will
listen' (28.28).

Goodspeed, who takes Acts to be dated about AD 90, points out in
his *Introduction to the NT* (pp. 182f.) that the success of the Christian
movement in the Greek West made it clear that Christianity was not a
local but a universal religion. The records of its beginnings had to be
made. It begins with a picture of Jesus. Luke is the first to be
conscious of the great outside world, and fixes his narrative against
the background of imperial chronology (Luke 3.1) – this is no
eccentricity of Luke; it is exactly the way in which the papyrus
documents open and are dated. Later, he goes on (pp. 186f.): 'The
thread of the narrative is no mere biography, but the providential
fashion in which the gospel had groped its way out of Judaism into
widening circles', and so at last to the whole Mediterranean world.
With Paul, 'the gospel passes out of Asia, the continent of its origin,
into Europe, the continent of its destiny'.

For Luke Christianity had become a universal religion, and the
church a universal church.

(iii)   This universalizing of Christianity brought two immense
problems, one theological and one political. First, let us look at the
theological problem. Haenchen writes (p. 100): 'In reality Luke the

historian is wrestling, from the first page to the last, with the problem of *the mission to the Gentiles without the law.*' The essence of the problem was this – did the forsaking of the Jewish law by Christianity, and the parting of company from Judaism, break the continuity of the process and the history of salvation?

Luke's answer to that problem took various lines:

(a) The breach was not made by choice; it was made by compulsion. Men who were totally unwilling to make the separation were driven to it by the direct action of God. Acts opens in Jerusalem; it is in Jerusalem that the Christian community is assembled (1.12). the Christian leaders begin by being faithful attenders at the temple (3.1; 5.12). They have no wish whatsoever to depart from the Jewish food laws and from the distinction between things clean and unclean (10.14f.; 11.3). And then by direct message God compels Peter to open the door to Cornelius (10.1-11.18). God, as it were, meets Paul head on on the road to Damascus, when the last thing Paul is thinking of is to be a Christian missionary (9.1-19). If God pours out the Spirit on these new Gentile converts, who can argue with God (10.47; 11.17)? The breach was God's doing, God's coercion.

(b) Even then the Jews always got the first offer of salvation; it was only when they refused it that the missionaries went to the Gentiles (13.46; 18.6; 28.28).

(c) It is argued that God cannot be regarded as a partisan with special favourites. Salvation for Jews alone would obviously have been unfair. 'Truly,' said Peter, 'I perceive that God shows no partiality, but in every nation anyone who fears him and does what is right is acceptable to him' (10.34f.).

(d) In any event the Gentile Christians did not simply abandon the whole law. Paul still called himself a Pharisee (23.6). True, the scribal, oral law with its legal minutiae no longer concerned the Christian, but the Old Testament law still did. Unchastity, meat which had been offered to idols, the meat with the blood in it were still forbidden (15.21; 21.25). The God-given law was kept; it was the man-made law that was abandoned.

(e) There was a thorough search through scripture for passages which could be used to prove that the coming of Jesus, and all that had happened to him, was thoroughly in accord with the scriptures (see the sermons and speeches in chs. 2, 3, 7, 8, 10, 13, 15 and 26).

The claim in effect was that Christianity had not separated from Judaism but was in fact the real Judaism, and the breach had come under compulsion from God, and because of the stubborn refusal of the Jews to accept the offer of God.

The second problem was not a theological problem; it was much more practical than that. It was a problem of the first magnitude for the church; it was a political problem.

The problem was this. In the Roman Empire religions were classed as either *licita* or *illicita*, licit or illicit, permitted or forbidden. A licit religion was a religion which anyone might embrace and practise; an illicit religion was a religion which was proscribed, and the practice of which brought severe penalties, even death. Judaism was a permitted religion. It was so because the Jews were so inflexibly Jewish that in the end the Romans could do nothing but accept them as they were. For instance, the Jews alone of Rome's subject races were exempt from compulsory military service. What could the army do with a man who had food laws which nothing would make him abandon, and who utterly refused to work or fight on his sabbath day? In the beginning the Roman government saw no difference between Jews and Christians. Christianity began by being regarded as a kind of Judaism, and, therefore, Christianity shared the permission to exist which Judaism enjoyed. But once the separation from Judaism came that permission ceased. In fact the Jews themselves saw to it that the Roman authorities were left in no doubt that the Christians were not Jews (13.50). In the account of the martyrdom of Polycarp (13.1) it was the Jews who played a leading part in the burning. Tertullian in his *Antidote to the Scorpion's Bite* (10) calls the Jewish synagogues the 'fountains of persecution'. So, then, one of the consequences of the separation from Judaism was that Christianity became a prohibited religion and liable to persecution. And, therefore, one of the great aims of Acts to show that time and again Roman officials had been well disposed to Christianity and had treated the Christians with impartial justice and even with favour and protection. Sergius Paulus, the proconsul of Cyprus, is converted to Christianity (13.12). In Corinth, Gallio declares that there is no crime or wrong-doing with which the Christians may be charged (18.14f.). In Ephesus the Asiarchs, who were in charge of the worship of the emperor, were friendly to Paul (19.31), and the recorder of the city declares that the Christians have done no wrong, and that they are neither blasphemers nor sacrilegious (19.37). The tribune Claudius Lysias writes to Felix that, so far as he can see, Paul has done nothing to deserve death or imprisonment (23.29). Festus tells Agrippa that in his opinion Paul has done nothing to merit death (25.25). Agrippa and Bernice and Festus agree that, if he had not appealed to Caesar, Paul might well have been released (26.31f.).

It is more than once stressed that Paul was a Roman citizen, and proud of that citizenship, and on more than one occasion he used his citizenship to get justice. At Philippi it won him an unqualified apology for the way he had been treated by the local magistrates (16.35-40). The Roman tribune intervenes to rescue Paul in the riot in the temple (21.27-40). The centurion promptly abandons his intention to flog Paul when he discovers that Paul is a Roman citizen (22.25-

29). Claudius Lysias lays on the might of the Roman army to protect Paul from a Jewish plot to murder him (23.12-35). Both Felix and Festus are reluctant to condemn Paul (24.24-7; 25.6-27). On the journey to Rome the centurion in charge treats Paul with the greatest courtesy, and in the crisis of the storm to all intents and purposes accepts Paul's leadership (27.3-44).

Theophilus, to whom Luke dedicated his work, is 'most excellent Theophilus' (Luke 1.3) – as we might say in modern language, 'Your Excellency'. The Greek is *kratiste*, and Theophilus may well have been a high government official. Luke 1.4 says that Luke is sending Theophilus the truth about the things about which Theophilus has been 'informed'; but it is possible that the word used (*katēchein*) means not 'informed', but 'misinformed'; and it might well be that one of the aims of Acts was to clear the mind of Theophilus of false and slanderous information which had been maliciously given to him about Christianity. It has indeed been held by some that Acts is the brief prepared for the defence of Paul at his final trial (see Kümmel, *Introduction to the NT*, p. 114).

Quite clearly, one of the objects of Acts was to commend Christianity to the Roman government, and to remind the government that there were many magistrates and governors who had expressed their opinion that Christianity was an entirely innocent movement.

Let us turn now to another of the main aims of Acts. It is the aim of Acts to show the almost miraculous expansion of Christianity. In it we follow the story of how an obscure religion, born in the tiny country of Palestine, founded by a man crucified as a blasphemous criminal, reached Rome, the capital of the world, and became a world religion. It may well be said that the plan of Acts is to be found in the command of Jesus (1.8): 'You shall be my witnesses in Jerusalem and in all Judaea and Samaria and to the end of the earth.' Acts tells us of the expansion of Christianity in ever-widening circles. So various divisions of Acts have been suggested (see Kümmel, pp. 107f.).

(i)   1-12: Jerusalem to Antioch; the Petrine period.
      13-28: Antioch to Rome; the Pauline period.
(ii) 1.15-15.35: Expansion from Jerusalem, until the securing of the Gentile mission.
      15.36-28.31: Expansion to Rome.
(iii) 1.15-8.3: Jerusalem.
      8.4-11.18: Samaria.
      11.19-15.35: Antioch, and he Antioch mission.
      15.36-19.20: Lands around the Aegean Sea.
      19.21-28.31: From Jerusalem to Rome.
(iv) But the most interesting scheme was that worked out by C.H. Turner.[4] Turner saw Acts as divided into six 'panels', each ending with a

'progress report'. He identified the panels as follows:

(a) 1.2-6.6: The origin of the church at Jerusalem and the preaching of Peter.

Progress report, 6.7: And the word of God increased, and the number of disciples multiplied greatly in Jerusalem, and a great many of the priests were obedient to the faith.

(b) 6.8-9.30: The spread of the church through Palestine, the preaching of Stephen, the conversion of Paul.

Progress report, 9.31: So the church throughout all Judaea and Galilee and Samaria had peace and was built up; and walking in the fear of the Lord and the comfort of the Holy Spirit it was multiplied.

(c) 9.32-12.23: The extension of the church to Antioch; Peter's conversion of Cornelius; further troubles with the Jewis.

Progress report, 12.24: But the word of the Lord grew and multiplied.

(d) 12.25-16.4: The advance from Syria to Asia Minor.

Progress report, 16.5: So the churches were strengthened in the faith, and they increased in numbers daily.

(e) 16.6-19.9: Christianity comes to Europe; Paul in Macedonia and Achaea.

Progress report, 19.20: So the word of the Lord grew and prevailed mightily.

(f) 19.20-28.30: The arrival in Rome and the events which led up to it.

Progress report, 28.31: ... preaching the kingdom of God and teaching about the Lord Jesus Christ quite openly and unhindered.

If we accept this scheme, it will explain one thing – and this is a question to which we will return: it will explain why Acts finishes where it does. The modern reader wonders why he is never told what ultimately happened to Paul. Was he released or did he die? We are left for ever in suspense, never knowing the answer. But Luke was not writing the biography of Paul. He was showing how Christianity became a world religion. And when Christianity has swept across Asia and Europe and has established itself in Rome, the capital of the world, then the goal is reached, the story is told. Acts stops where it does – on this view – because for Luke it was the end of the road. C.H. Turner writes:

I believe that the Gospel and Acts form the two halves of a simple and connected scheme, and that in order to understand it we are only to attach to the two books some such labels as these: 'Volume I, How Jesus the Christ preached the Good News to the Jews, and how after his Death and Resurrection he commissioned his Apostles to preach it to the Gentiles: Volume II, How they brought the Good News from Jerusalem to Rome.'

With the two years' unhindered proclamation of the Kingdom in the capital of the world, the evolution of the Jewish-Christian sect into the Universal Church was symbolically accomplished.[5]

Streeter writes in *The Four Gospels* (p. 532): 'In a word, the title of the Acts might well have been "The Road to Rome".'

(v)   McNeile records how two writers starting from here took the matter a step further.[6] Cadoux found an earlier 'progress report' summary in Acts 2.47b: 'And the Lord added to their number day by day those who were being saved.' Starting from here, by identifying Paul's visit to Jerusalem in Acts 11 with that of Galatians 2 (see pp. 269f.), and dating his encounter with Gallio (Acts 18.12-17) by an inscription at Delphi which provides evidence that Gallio took office in AD 51 (see Haenchen, pp. 66f.), Cadoux worked out the following timetable to fit the panel 'progress reports':

(a)   2.47b: immediately after Pentecost in AD 29.
(b)   6.7: in the middle or early part of AD 34.
(c)   9.31: between AD 36 and the early months of 41.
(d)   12.24: after 1 Nisan 44, and before the beginning of 47.
(e)   16.5: a few weeks before the Passover of 49.
(f)   19.20: between January 53 and March or April 55.
(g)   28.31: in the early part of 59.

He then goes on to make the ingenious – McNeile calls it the over-ingenious – suggestion that Luke splits the history into six periods of five years each, beginning with the Pentecosts of the years 29, 34, 39, 44, 49, 54. He thus covers a total of thirty years, which is approximately the same time as is covered by the gospel.

Leaving aside the more subtle speculations, we can agree that one of the objects of Acts was to show the expansion of Christianity, to show how the faith born in Palestine, and starting from Jerusalem, reached Rome, and became a world religion.

But to this there is something to be added. Acts sets out to show that this expansion of Christianity did not happen by human means, but was the direct result of the action of the power of God. In the first chapter of Acts a command and a statement occur. The command (1.8) is the command to be the witnesses of Jesus in Jerusalem and in all Judaea and in Samaria and to the end of the earth. The statement (1.15) is that the company of the persons gathered in Jerusalem was in all about one hundred and twenty. In effect, what we are confronted with is the picture of a situation in which one hundred and twenty persons, not one of them of any education or social prestige, were told to go out and evangelize the world. There was laid on them what was literally a superhuman task. The aim of Acts is to show from the beginning that this expansion of Christianity was the act of God. We may quote three *Introductions to the NT*. First Jülicher (p. 439): Acts is 'a history of the power of God in the apostles'. . . .

The result expected from the narrative is that the divine nature of the story should be self-attested: every unprejudiced reader was to say to himself that it was solely through the power of the Spirit that the Apostles had been able to perform such marvels as he read of in these twenty-eight chapters (p. 438).

E.F. Scott (p. 95) says that the whole thing happened 'through the energy of the Spirit'. It is the story of 'how Jesus worked on after his death by the Spirit which he had imparted'. Wikenhauser (p. 326) says of Luke: 'Behind the continuous progress of the message of Christ through all lands he sees the wonderful operation of the power of the Holy Spirit, whom the risen Christ had promised and sent to his disciples.' The Acts of the Apostles might well be called The Acts of the Holy Spirit.

In Acts the risen Christ is still active. In Corinth Paul has a vision in which the Lord says to him: 'Do not be afraid, but speak and do not be silent; for I am with you and no man shall attack you to harm you, for I have many people in this city' (18.9f.) And after the episode on the Damascus road the risen Christ comes to Paul in the temple with the command: 'Depart; for I will send you far away to the Gentiles' (22.17-21). When things look black in Jerusalem, the Lord stands beside Paul during the night and says: 'Take courage, for as you have testified about me at Jerusalem, so you must bear witness also at Rome' (23.11). The risen Christ has called Paul; the risen Christ sustains him. For Paul, the risen Christ is the beginning, the middle and the end.

In the narrative the Holy Spirit is always a chief actor. In the gospel the last words of the risen Christ (24.49) are: 'Behold, I send the promise of my Father upon you; but stay in the city until you are clothed with power from on high.' And his first words in Acts (1.4f., 8) are to tell them that the promise will come true, and to say to them: 'You shall receive power when the Holy Spirit has come upon you.' So the story of Acts begins with Pentecost, when they are all 'filled with the Holy Spirit' (2.4). And from that time onwards, every leader of the church is a man of the Spirit, and no decision of the church is taken apart from the guidance of the Spirit.

The sin of Ananias and Sapphira is a tempting of the Spirit (5.3,9). The one qualification of the seven, the first office-bearers in the church, is that they shall be men of the Spirit (6.3). As Stephen, the first martyr, dies, he is full of the Holy Spirit (7.55). The sign of conversion is the gift of the Spirit, a gift so spectacular that Simon Magus is eager to buy the power to confer it (8.9-24). The Spirit is poured out on the emissaries from Cornelius, the first Gentile members of the church (10.44f.; 11.15-17).

The Holy Spirit still confers prophetic power on the Christians. It is by the Spirit that Agabus is able to foretell the famine which is to come, and the fate which awaits Paul at Jerusalem (11.28; 21.11). It is the Spirit who has given the elders of the church their office and their task (20.28).

But the most significant work of the Spirit is that it is the Spirit who directs the church on the church's outgoing task. Every new outreach is made under the influence and the command of the Spirit. It is the Spirit who bids Peter respond to the appeal of Cornelius (10.19). It is the Spirit who tells Philip to make contact with the Ethiopian (8.29). It is the Spirit who tells the church at Antioch to send out Paul and Barnabas on the first missionary journey (13.2). It is the Spirit who guides the church into the reception of the Gentiles at the Council of Jerusalem (15.28). It is the Spirit who so directs the journeyings of Paul that he is compelled to come to Europe (16.6f.).

Acts tells the story of the expansion of the church, and the way in which the story begins and continues is designed to show that that expansion is not a human achievement, but the result of the power of God, operating through the Holy Spirit.

We have now to try to deal with certain of the problems with which Acts confronts us. Foremost and most obvious of these problems is the question why Acts finishes where and how it does. Moffatt quotes the French writer Bertrand as saying that Acts finishes with an almost brutal abruptness.[7] From chapter 13 onwards, Acts has been near to being the biography of Paul. It is clear that for Luke Paul is an heroic figure. There is the build-up of the various trial appearances; there is the drama of the voyage; there is the arrival at Rome. And then we are left in suspense. How much we would like to know just what happened to Paul. Was he released, or was he condemned? Zahn writes: 'How much foolish fable-mongering even in the next century, how much laborious, minute effort and how much strife of scholars should we have been spared, had it pleased God to permit the first Greek among the writers of Christian faith to attain the completion of his irreplaceable work!'[8] Let us then look at the main explanations of why Acts ends as it does.

(i) It is suggested that the author was prevented by death from finishing it. This is something which from the knowledge that we possess no one can prove right or wrong. But it does have to be said that, if Luke is the author, the legendary and traditional material is that he lived to a good old age. The Monarchian Prologue to Luke's gospel says of him: 'Never having either a wife or children, he died in Bithynia seventt-four years old.'[9] On the whole this suggestion is less than likely.

(ii) One of the favourite suggestions is that Luke intended a third volume, in which the remainder of the story would have been told. In favour of this the first verse of Acts is cited. In the AV that verse runs:

The *former* treatise have I made, O Theophilus.

The RSV translates more accurately:

In the *first* book, O Theophilus.

In Greek the word is *prōtos*, and does properly mean 'first'. The Greek for 'former' is *proteros*. In Greek as in English it is correct to use 'former', when we speak of only two things, and 'first' when we speak of more than two things. If, therefore, language is used with meticulous accuracy if you talk of the 'first' book, there must have been more than two. But in this usage the Greeks were no more careful than we are. If we have visited a place twice, we will almost certainly say: 'The first time I was there . . .' We are not likely, unless we are very pedantic, to say: 'On the former of my two visits.' In this matter the Greeks spoke exactly as we do, and did not carefully distinguish between 'former' and 'first'. It is in fact the case that Luke never uses *proteros*, 'former', at all. We certainly cannot argue from language that Luke intended another volume. Further, if another volume was intended, it would be very odd to break off the preceding volume in the middle of a story. Someone who is writing a cliff-hanging serial story might do that, but not a responsible and conscientious historian. The hypothesis of a third volume is not very probable.

(iii)   It has been suggested that Luke stopped where he did because Paul was condemned, and the condemnation of Paul did not suit his book. His aim and purpose was to show the innocence of Christianity, and the favour which Roman magistrates had shown to it, and to end with the condemnation of the greatest exponent of Christianity would have been to ruin his case. But surely there would have been little point in suppressing from the story a fact which must have been perfectly well known. Its omission would have served no useful purpose.

(iv)   We now come to a suggestion which at the moment we can only state, and not evaluate, because, as will be clear, it is intimately bound up with the date of Acts, and the final assessment of it must wait until we deal with the date. It has been suggested that Acts stops where it does for the very simple reason that at the time Luke knew no more, that he was writing before Paul's fate had been settled, that, as Harnack puts it in his assessment of the situation (*The Date of Acts*, pp. 90-125), 'the narrative had caught up with the events'. D. Plooij writes: 'The only really easy explanation of the "abrupt" ending is that Acts has been written just on the point of time where it ends, viz., at the beginning of the trial of Paul.' Plooij held that Theophilus was the magistrate due to hear Paul's case when it came up, and that Acts was written for his information, and to gain his good-will. 'The emphasis ... with which St Luke makes his appeal to Roman justice implies ... that the book was written as information for some Roman official (or more of them) whose influence in the process of Paul was of eminent importance.'[10] This is an exceedingly attractive suggestion. It would, of course, necessitate a very early date for Acts, and we must leave the possibility of that date until we come to discuss the whole question of date.

(v) One very interesting suggestion is that the narrative in fact implies the release of Paul. This argument is stated in full by H.J. Cadbury in his essay on 'Roman Law and the Trial of Paul' (*Beginnings* V, pp. 326-32), and is sympathetically considered but rejected by Haenchen (pp. 724-6). Cadbury gives the argument of an earlier article by Kirsopp Lake. The trial of Paul was legally 'The Jews *v.* Paul'. But, Lake asks (p. 330), what happened if the prosecutors did not appear? The Roman Jews had said to Paul: 'We have received no letters from Judaea about you, and none of the brethren coming here has reported or spoken any evil about you.' Obviously, the Jews had not arrived to prosecute. Lake suggests that there must have been a time limit, and he suggests that, if the prosecutors did not appear within two years, the case was quashed. In support of this he quotes a statement by Philo from his speech *Against Flaccus* (128f.). A certain Lampo had been arrested in Alexandria for the crime of impiety against the Emperor Tiberius. The malevolent prefect of Egypt delayed the trial for a period of two years 'in order to make life more miserable for him than death by keeping the fear of an uncertain future suspended over him *pros mekiston chronon*'. This Greek phrase could mean *for a very long time*, and could just mean *for the longest possible time*. As Haenchen points out, in this case it is not a prosecutor who does not appear, it is not an appeal to Rome, and the period is drawn out by the provincial governor. And it has to be pointed out that Josephus in his *Life* (13) reports a case of men who were sent to Rome for trial in the procuratorship of Felix (AD 52-60), and who were still in custody in AD 66. There is a case in Pliny's *Letters* (10.56f.) in which provincials are given a two-year period to claim a new trial under the new governor, if they felt that they had been unjustly treated by the previous governor Julius Bassus. But this is the period, not after which a man can be released, but within which a new trial can be claimed.

Cadbury does produce one piece of evidence. There is a papyrus edict[11] credited to Nero. It lays down certain regulations for cases which are to come before Caesar. The previous emperor, Claudius, had laid it down to prevent undue delays that, if the case involved persons from overseas and outside Italy, the parties must appear within eighteen months, and if it involved persons within Italy, they must appear in nine months. It is now suggested that this may have been shortening a previous period of two years. It does not actually say that the defendant is released if no appearance is made.

It is then just possible to take it that the end of Acts means that in fact Paul was released. But, if he was, why did not Luke say so? The answer given is that this would have been a release founded on a technicality, and not on a genuine decision of innocence; and therefore Luke does not stress it, because such a verdict was not the kind of verdict in which he would find real delight. The most we can say is that a case has been made out, but not a certain case.

(vi)   The most complicated and extraordinary theory of the ending of Acts was put forward by Pfister. (It is reported by Cadbury, pp. 336-8.) One of the best loved of early Christian books (perhaps 'early Christian romances' would be a better description) was *The Acts of Paul*. The Acts of Paul carries on the life of Paul after his trial. It was a book which had a very wide vogue. Pfister believes that originally the New Testament Acts ended with a statement that Paul was condemned and executed. So now, so far as Paul is concerned, a timetable like this emerged.

(a)   Paul's last journey to Rome (Acts 27 and 28).
(b)   Paul's trial, condemnation and execution (the original ending of Acts).
(c)   Paul's departure for Spain (*The Acts of Paul*).
(d)   The last journey of Paul to Rome (*The Acts of Paul*).
(e)   Paul's trial, condemnation and martyrdom.

On this timetable Paul dies twice! So, according to Pfister, what happened was that the original ending of Acts was deleted and the present ending substituted, in order to allow for the events in *The Acts of Paul*. Cadbury says that this theory has not received the attention it deserves, but Haenchen – quite rightly – dismisses it as 'extremely improbable' (p. 726).

(vii)   So we come to the last of the suggestions as to why Acts ends where it does. This says quite simply that Acts ends where it does because the story is finished. The text on which Acts is written is 1.8: 'You shall be my witnesses in Jerusalem and in all Judaea and Samaria and to the end of the earth.' With the arrival of Christianity in Rome the promise is fulfilled (Dibelius, *Studies in Acts*, p. 134). As Haenchen puts it (p. 98): 'The path of the gospel from Jerusalem to Rome formed a complete story, a rounded whole, in itself.' Goodspeed (*Introduction to the NT*, p. 188) says that to have proceeded any farther would have been simply an anticlimax. Harnack (*Acts*, p. 42) says that with the list of nations in the Pentecost story (2.9-11) the universal character of Christianity is symbolically laid down, and with the statement of the mission to the Gentiles (28.28) the story finishes as it begins. The writer is not concerned with Peter or Paul, but with the divine plan in which the hearts of the Jews are hardened and the gospel goes out to the Gentiles. Antioch – Ephesus – Corinth – ROME. The aim is accomplished. A.C. McGiffert writes: 'The design of the book (its text is found in the eighth verse of the first chapter) was to give an account of the progress of the Church from Jerusalem to Rome, not to write the life of Paul . . . He was writing, not a life of Paul, nor of any apostle or group of apostles, but a history of the planting of the Church of Christ.'[12] The theme, says Wikenhauser (pp. 343f.), is the mission to the Gentiles; Rome is the capital of the world; therefore the entry to Rome is 'the high point of achievement'. So then it is claimed that with the entry to Rome Luke's story is finished, his purpose is completed, and there Acts ends.

11

THE DATE OF ACTS

As we noted in passing, the date of Acts is closely connected with the ending of Acts, and to the discussion of the date we must now turn. It is an extraordinary fact that the various theories have spread their suggestions as to the date of Acts over very nearly a hundred years. The various dates suggested can be grouped around five periods — some time soon after AD 60; about AD 80; some time later than AD 90; about AD 130; and as late as about AD 150. Let us look at each of these dates.

(i)   A date about AD 60 represents the orthodox Roman Catholic view. Wikenhauser (p. 321) reports the decision of the Pontifical Biblical Commission of 12 June 1923: 'Acts was written by Luke the Evangelist, towards the end of Paul's first Roman imprisonment; it is fully trustworthy.' In the earliest days of the church it was the early date of Acts which was assumed. In his *Ecclesiastical History* (3.22.6) Eusebius writes: 'In his second epistle to Timothy he [Paul] indicates [4.11,16] that Luke was with him, when he wrote, but at the first defence not even he. Whence it is probable that Luke wrote the Acts of the apostles at that time, continuing his history down to the period when he was with Paul.' In his book *On Famous Men* (7) Jerome takes the same view. Acts, he says, with Paul's two-year imprisonment reaches down to the fourth year of Nero's reign (that would be AD 58), and then he goes on to say: 'Hence we understand that the book was composed in that same city.' He apparently means that Acts was composed in Rome in the interval between Paul's arrival there and his trial. We may here take in also the account of Acts in the Muratorian Canon: 'The Acts, however, of all the Apostles are written in one book. Luke, to the most excellent Theophilus, includes events because they were done in his own presence, as he also plainly shows by leaving out the passion of Peter, and also the departure of Paul from the City on his journey to Spain.'[1] Once again the implication is that Luke's knowledge of events ends with the arrival of Paul in Rome.

The arguments of scholars who accept this early date[2] may be summarized as follows:

(a)   The ending of Acts is an impossible one. Bruce writes: 'It is almost as if the Third Gospel had come to a sudden end on the eve of our Lord's appearance before Pilate.' There is a really massive build up, with the farewell at Ephesus and the journey to Rome, and there the story ends. Was Paul freed? There is evidence that he expected it to be so. In Philippians he writes (1.25): 'I know that I shall remain and continue with you all, for your progress and joy in the faith.' He sends Epaphroditus back with the message (2.24): 'I trust in the Lord that shortly I myself shall come also.' He writes to Philemon (v. 22): 'Prepare a guest room for me, for I am hoping through your prayers to be granted to you.' And yet on the other hand in Acts (20.38) Paul leaves the elders of Ephesus 'sorrowing most of all because of the word he had spoken, that they should see his face no more'. It does seem intolerable that the story should end without an end. Further, Harnack makes a grammatical point. Acts 28.30 says: 'He lived there two whole years at his own expense.' The Greek for 'he lived' is *enemeinen*, which is an aorist tense. Now the aorist is the tense not of a continuing action, but of an event which had a beginning and an end; and if the aorist *enemeinen* can be pressed, it means that Paul's stay in Rome was an incident which finished, necessarily to be followed by something else. There was something to follow.

(b) Rackham points out that a good test of the date of a book is the date of the last event which it mentions. If Acts was written after AD 70 it is an extraordinary thing that it has nothing to say about the martyrdom of James in 62, the martyrdom of Peter and Paul, and above all of the destruction of Jerusalem and of the temple in 70. It does seem strange that Acts could be written after the terrible final war and the crowning tragedy of the destruction of Jerusalem and betray not the slightest vestige of a hint that the writer knew anything about them.

(c) The historical situation reflected in Acts seems to indicate a time early rather than late. The attitude of the Roman government to Christianity is obviously not fully decided, and is often favourable. Could such a situation possibly exist after the Neronian persecution of AD 64, for after that to be a Christian must have been automatically to be an offender? In the later days Rome is the scarlet woman, drunk with the blood of the saints and the martyrs (Rev. 17.1-6). The situation is completely changed. Harnack suggests that the generally optimistic and hopeful atmosphere of Acts would have been impossible any time after the Neronian persecution, unless the date is moved very far on.

There is further the position of the Jews. In Acts the Jews are 'the persecutors, not the persecuted'. How could the Jews act as they are shown acting after the campaign in Palestine which wiped them out as a nation? There is not the slightest indication that the Christians were criminals by definition and that the Jews were a for ever shattered people.

(d) There are certain facts about the language of Acts which make it appear early. It speaks of the *words* of the Lord Jesus (20.35), as if it was still at the stage of oral tradition, and before the time of a written gospel. The word *Christ* has not yet become a proper name, and is still a title, meaning Messiah. Paul confounds the Jews of Damascus by proving that Jesus was the Christ, that is, the Messiah (9.22). In Thessalonica his message is that: 'This Jesus whom I proclaim to you is the Christ', that is, the Messiah (17.3). In Acts 20.7 Sunday is still the first day of the week, as it is in the epistles (e.g. I Cor. 16.2), and not yet the Lord's day, as it came to be (Rev. 1.10). In Acts the Christians are still *mathētai*, disciples,[3] a word which Paul never uses. The language of Acts does seem to be the language of the early church.

(e)   Finally, there is the very surprising fact that from a reading of Acts no one would know that Paul had ever written a letter. Acts betrays not the slightest knowledge of the epistles. In fact it is hard to believe that Luke would have left us with the relationship of Acts 9 and 15 with Gal. 1 and 2 so uncertain, if Paul's letters had been available to him. It is highly probable that Paul's letters were collected, edited and issued some time about AD 90. But it seems certain that Acts knew nothing about them. Indeed it may well have been the heroic picture of Paul in Acts which in the end caused the collection of the letters.

If then there is so strong a case for dating Acts in the early sixties, why not accept it, and leave the matter there? In the first place, we have still to examine the cases for the other dates; the argument we have so far presented is totally one-sided, and at the other sides we have still to look. In the second place, it has to be remembered that Acts cannot be dated by itself. It has always to be dated in relation to Luke's gospel, for the gospel and Acts are indisputably two volumes of the one work. In Acts 1.1 the gospel is 'the first book', and therefore Acts must be later than the gospel, even if only very slightly. It is argued that the gospel must be later than the fall of Jerusalem, and Jerusalem was destroyed in AD 70. So, the argument is, the gospel must be later than AD 70, and, therefore, Acts must be later yet. On what grounds is it asserted that the gospel must date to a time after the fall of Jerusalem?

In all three gospels there is a chapter in which Jesus foretells the terror of the things to come. In that chapter the destruction of Jerusalem is foretold. In Matthew (24.15f.) part of that prophecy reads:

So when you see the desolating sacrilege spoken of by the prophet Daniel, standing in the holy place (let the reader understand) then let those who are in Judaea flee to the mountains.

Mark 13.14 says:

> But when you see the desolating sacrilege set up where it ought not to be (let the reader understand), then let those who are in Judaea flee to the mountains.

Luke 21.20f. says:

> But when you see Jerusalem surrounded by armies, then know that its desolation has come near. Then let those who are in Judaea flee to the mountains.

The argument is that in Matthew and Mark there is a prophecy, based on a saying in Daniel, but that in Luke there is no mention of a Daniel prophecy at all; there is rather a description of a historical happening which has already taken place. Matthew and Mark speak vaguely about some desolating sacrilege; Luke speaks quite definitely of surrounding armies. The deduction is that Matthew and Mark are writing, or using sources which were written, before the actual siege, while Luke is writing after it, and must therefore be after AD 70.

Is this a necessary deduction? It could be that Luke's alteration is due to the fact, not that he is writing after the siege, but that, since he was writing for Gentiles who would not know what an obscure phrase from Daniel meant, he simply substituted a much simpler phrase which his Gentile readers would more readily understand. Thus we could also argue that the surrounding by armies is no more than a simplified version of the desolating sacrilege.

But we must look at another passage, Luke 19.43f.:

> For the days shall come upon you, when your enemies will cast up a bank about you and surround you, and hem you in on every side, and dash you to the ground, you and your children within you, and they will not leave one stone upon another in you; because you did not know the time of your visitation.

When an army was attacking a fortified and walled town, they frequently built a colossal mound which overtopped the walls, and from it bombarded the town with their catapult artillery. This happened in the final siege of Jerusalem, and the argument is that only someone who knew about the mound would have put the mound into the alleged prophecy, and that Luke is wording the prophecy in terms which would only occur to someone who had actual information about the siege, and about what had happened.

Is this a necessary deduction? Far from it. During Pompey's siege of Jerusalem the better part of a hundred years before, this is exactly what Pompey's army had done, and had done it in the most famous, or the most notorious, circumstances. Josephus tells the story in his *Antiquities of the Jews* (14.61-5); also in the *Jewish War*, 1.145-7). Pompey's engineers and labourers built the mound overlooking the temple on the sabbath day, because on that day the Jews so rigorously kept the sabbath that they made no attempt to interfere with the Romans:

> If it were not our national custom to rest on the sabbath day, the earthworks would not have been finished, because the Jews would have prevented this; for the law permits us to defend ourselves against those who begin a battle and strike us, but it does not allow us to fight against an enemy that does anything else (*Antiquities* 14.63).

> Of this fact the Romans were well aware, and on those days which we call the sabbath, they did not shoot at the Jews, nor meet them in hand to hand combat, but instead they raised earthworks and towers, and brought up their siege-engines that these might be put to work the following day.

Anyone who knew anything about the history of the Jews and previous sieges of Jerusalem knew all about mounds, and would naturally deduce that in any future siege the same methods would be used again.

There is no doubt that Jesus did prophesy the fall of Jerusalem, and it is not true to say that he could not have used the language and the picture which Luke uses, and it is unnecessary to argue that the prophecy could only have been written after the event.

A more difficult point to meet is that, if we date Acts in the early sixties, then Luke's gospel must be dated in the still earlier sixties, or even the late fifties. It is an almost universally accepted hypothesis that Luke used Mark, and, if Mark is to be given time to become widely used and to have some authority, it must have been written in the early or middle forties. Is this too early a date?

Here we must leave the matter and go on to discuss the other suggested dates, but we may leave it with the decision that a date in the early sixties is by no means an impossible date for Acts.

(ii)   Let us now look at what we might call the intermediate dating of Acts, dating which, we might say, stretches from AD 70 to 100.

(a)   We begin with a view which has never been widely held. T.W. Manson suggested a date about AD 70.[4] Manson thought it possible that Acts was written in defence of Christians who in the popular view were implicated in the Jewish War (AD 66-70). This would gain them the reputation of being the enemies of Rome. Luke's object would then be to prove that, although the Christian church was the true Judaism, it was nevertheless quite distinct and separate from political Judaism. If this is the apologetic aim, it would be much less relevant after the final obliteration of the Jews in AD 70. On this view Acts would have to be dated shortly before AD 70. This may well have been part of the object of Acts, but it does not seem very likely that it was its main and primary aim.

(b)   Perhaps the most widely held view is that Acts is to be dated somewhere about AD 80-90.[5] The dating at plus or minus AD 85 comes

rather more from the relationship of Acts to the general synoptic gospel dating than from anything else. The general scheme suggested is that Luke's gospel, both from its relationship to Mark and its alleged knowledge of the fall of Jerusalem, cannot possibly be earlier than AD 70, when Jerusalem fell, and it is therefore likely to be somewhere around AD 80. Since Acts must be later than the gospel, it may be dated somewhere around AD 85. Given the generally accepted ating and inter-relationship of the synoptic gospels, this is a probable enough date.

(c) There is the dating between AD 90 and 100. E.J. Goodspeed makes a very full case for this date. In his *Introduction to the NT* (pp. 191-6) he produces fifteen reasons for dating Acts in the last decade of the first century. We may state them briefly.

1.   The literary form of the work. It is a work divided into two volumes, separate, each complete in itself, yet also closely integrated.

2.   The literary features. These include the dedication, and the preface with its account of sources, aims and method.

3.   The interest of the gospel in the infancy narratives. These are pushed back to include the birth of John. This pushing of the interest back is characteristic of the later works. For instance, the *Protevangelium*, the Book of James, pushing this interest back to the birth of Mary.

4.   The doctrine of the Holy Spirit which 'pervades both volumes'. So in the gospel the Holy Spirit is connected with Mary (1.35), Elizabeth (1.42), Zechariah (1.67), and Jesus himself (3.22; 4.1). As for Acts, the Holy Spirit 'is on almost every page of Acts, the whole narrative of which seems to float on a sea of it'.

5.   The resurrection interest. The series of appearances, the visits, eatings, penetration of locked doors, the period of forty days are all in marked contrast to Matthew, and are on the way to the long second-century accounts of conversations with the apostles.

6.   The interest in punitive miracle. This appears in the Elisha and Elijah cycles, but is 'wholly wanting in Matthew and Mark'. So in the gospel Zechariah is struck dumb (1.18-23, 57-64); in Acts dire punishment falls on Ananias and Sapphira (5.1-11); Elymas is blinded (13.6-12); Herod comes to a fearful end (12.20-23).

7.   The ending of the Jewish controversy. 'This interest, so acute in Paul's day, has become a dead issue when Luke-Acts is written.'

8.   The interest in Christian psalmody. Luke preserves hymn after hymn: the *Magnificat*, the *Benedictus*, the *Gloria in Excelsis*, the *Nunc Dimittis* (Luke 1.46-55, 68-79; 2.14, 29-32). Goodspeed says that there is no such interest in Christian poetry except in Ephesians 5.14 and in 'the arias, choruses and antiphonies of the Revelation'.

9.   Church organization. The twelve are 'a college of apostles, stationed in Jerusalem, watching over the progress of the Christian

mission', with whom the elders are associated (15.2, 6,22; 16.4). Paul is represented as appointing elders everywhere (14.23; 20.17); yet in the passage which describes Christian leadership in the earliest days (I Cor. 12.28) elders are not mentioned. Deacons are traced back to the beginning, although they are not so called, and the office is given lustre in the Stephen story in Acts 6-7. The story of Ananias and Sapphira reflects an interest in church funds (5.1-11); the Dorcas story shows an interest in charitable work for the poor (9.39). Baptism has become an essential condition of church membership, forgiveness and salvation (2.38; 8.12,36; 9.18; 10.47f.; 16.15, 33). Everywhere a fairly fully developed organization is implied.

10.   Speaking with tongues. In the Pauline letters, in I Corinthians 12 and 14, speaking with tongues is ecstatic utterance in no known language. In Acts 2, speaking with tongues has become speaking in foreign languages, a later development.

11.   By the time Acts is actually written, Paul is dead. He is still living when the curtain falls on Acts, but the clear implication of the farewell speech to the Ephesian elders is that he is dead, for they sorrow that they will see his face no more (20.25, 38). 'Such presentiments are remembered and recorded only when they have proved true.'

12.   Not only is Paul dead, but by the time of the writing of Acts he has reached 'hero stature'.

> He is not only dead; he has become a hallowed memory. He is no longer a man struggling and grappling with difficulties, as in his letters; he has become an heroic figure, and towers above priests, officers, governors and kings. This is simply the retrospect of history.

In other words, in Acts Paul has become not only a historical but a legendary figure.

13.   The emergence of the sects. Men are emerging *within* the church, teaching perverted doctrine to draw men away (20.30). It is the same kind of situation as can be seen, e.g., with the Nicolaitans in Revelation (2.6, 15).

14.   There is no acquaintance with the letters of Paul. These letters would obviously have been of great value to the writer of Acts. If he had known them, it is incredible that he should not have used them. 'It is next to impossible, if one knows Paul's letters, not to reveal the fact, when writing about his life and work', but Acts shows no hint of knowledge of them.

15.   The conception of Acts presupposes the wide success of the Greek mission.

Goodspeed's conclusion (p. 196) is: 'It is not too much to say that, wherever we sound the books of Acts, the result is the same; it reveals itself as a work of the last decade of the first century.'

There is no doubt that Goodspeed makes a powerful case for the view that Acts is to be dated about AD 90.

(iii)   The next proposed date at which we must look confronts us with one of the supreme problems of Acts. It is claimed that there are certain places in which Acts is dependent on Josephus' *Antiquities of the Jews*. The *Antiquities* cannot be dated earlier than the end of the first century at the very earliest.[6]

There are three main passages which enter into the discussion.

First, there is the speech of Gamaliel in the Sanhedrin, in which he urges that the Sanhedrin should allow time to tell whether or not the Christian movement comes from God. He quotes two cases of people who claimed divine inspiration, and whose movements came to nothing:

> For before these days Theudas arose, giving himself out to be somebody, and a number of men, about four hundred, joined him; but he was slain and all who followed him were dispersed and came to nothing. After him Judas the Galilaean arose in the days of the census and drew away some of the people after him; he also perished, and all who followed him were scattered (Acts 5.36f.)

This is an extraordinary statement for two reasons. In the first place the rebellion of Theudas took place in AD 44/45, which is about ten years *after* the date when Gamaliel was speaking. In other words, Gamaliel is reported as citing something ten years before it happened. In the second place, the rebellion of Judas of Galilee took place in AD 6; Gamaliel therefore could well have cited it, but he cites it as taking place *after* the rebellion of Theudas, when in point of fact it took place long before.[7] How, then, did Luke manage to get things so apparently mixed up? It is suggested that Luke had completely misread a passage in Josephus' *Antiquities* (20.97-102):

> When Fadus was procurator of Judea a certain magician, named Theudas, persuaded many of the people to take their possessions with them, and to follow him to the river Jordan. He told them that he was a prophet, and that he would by his word of command divide the river and thus provide them with an easy way over it. Many were deceived by his words. But Fadus did not allow him to gain any advantage from his wild attempt. He sent a troop of horsemen out against them, who fell upon them unexpectedly, slew many of them, and took many of them alive. They also took Theudas alive, and beheaded him, and took his head to Jerusalem. This happened to the Jews during Cuspius Fadus' government.
>
>   Then came Tiberius Alexander as successor to Fadus ... Under these procurators there happened in Judea the great famine during which Queen Helena bought corn in Egypt at great expense, and distributed it to those who were in want, as I have related already. Besides this, the sons of Judas of Galilee were now slan; I mean of that Judas who caused the people to rebel, when Cyrenius took a census of the estates of the Jews, as

we have shown in a foregoing book. The names of those sons were James and Simon, and Alexander ordered them to be crucified.

Josephus then quite correctly mentions Theudas and Judas in consecutive paragraphs; but he says that not Judas, but the sons of Judas were executed by Alexander. It is suggested that Luke either read Josephus very carelessly, or else from a vague recollection of what he had read put Theudas and Judas together, in spite of the fact that it was not Judas but his sons whom Josephus had been talking about, and that he not only made this confusion but misdated Theudas by ten years.

There have been many attempted explanations of Luke's apparent mistake and of the connection with Josephus. It has been suggested that the whole matter arose through sheer carelessness on the part of Luke, but this seems less than likely, because, where we can check Luke, we find him to be characteristically accurate. It has been suggested that the fault and the mistake lie with Josephus and not with Luke, because, as C.S.C. Williams says (p. 20), where we can check Josephus, we do on occasion find him to be 'wildly inaccurate' in the use of his sources. Streeter makes the interesting, and by no means impossible, suggestion that Luke had not read Josephus, but had heard him lecture, and had either taken the lecture down wrongly or had misread his notes – and any lecturer knows how easily that can happen. From about AD 70 onwards Josephus was resident in Rome and enjoyed the imperial favour. By about AD 79 he had finished his other work, the *Jewish War*. It was customary for historians to give public readings of their works, and in any event Josephus did write his history as Jewish propaganda. So Streeter says in *The Four Gospels* (p. 558):

> Josephus was extremely conceited, not at all the man to lose any opportunity for publicity, and he would do much to be in the literary and social fashion. Moreoever, his writings were largely intended for propaganda purposes; he wished to do his best to reinstate the credit of the Jewish people. He would certainly have recited parts of the *Antiquities* at intervals during the ten years before its publication. Fashionable Rome felt bound in etiquette to attend the recitations of its noble friends; but a parvenu like Josephus would have been only too glad to fill up the back seats with unimportant people like Luke.

This is speculation, but it is possible speculation, and a mistake in listening to a lecture is much easier to make, and much more forgivable, than the careless reading of a book. It has been suggested that Luke's Theudas is different from Josephus' Theudas, because the name was common – a desperate expedient. Dibelius (*Studies in Acts*, p. 187) holds that the whole discussion is pointless because, since Luke invented the speech anyway, he invented the illustration too, and it is not meant to be history.

It is by no means easy to come to any conclusion about this, but the statement that 'the argument that Luke used Josephus is not quite conclusive' (*Beginnings* II, pp. 357f.) is probably correct.

There is one other passage in which Luke makes a mistake which may have been based on a misunderstanding of Josephus. This instance is in the gospel, but since the gospel and Acts cannot be dated separately, this instance too must be considered. In Luke 3.1, one of the dating points for the emergence of John the Baptist is that it happened when Lysanias was tetrarch of Abilene. Luke was meaning to identify a date about AD 28, but Lysanias was executed in 36 BC. How did this mistake happen? Josephus in his *Antiquities* tells how Abila came into the possession of both Agrippa I in AD 37, and Agrippa II in AD 53, and in both accounts (18.237 and 20.138) he describes it as having been the tetrarchy of Lysanias. It would seem that this tetrarchy continued to be called the tetrarchy of Lysanias long after Lysanias was dead, and that because of this Luke was misled into thinking that Lysanias was still alive when John emerged. This was an entirely natural mistake to make, and has no necessary connection with Josephus at all.

One further connection with Josephus is suggested. The tribune who intervened in the riot in the temple asked Paul: 'Are you not the Egyptian, then, who recently stirred up a revolt, and led the four thousand men of the Assassins out into the wilderness?' (Acts 21.38). In Josephus there is a passage in the *War* (2.254-63) in which he speaks first of all of the Assassins, a party of terrorist nationalists, then in the next paragraph of deluded deceivers who led the people into the wilderness, and then in the next paragraph of the Egyptian who raised thirty thousand – Luke says four thousand – rebels and led them into the wilderness. This is to say that in consecutive paragraphs Josephus speaks of things which Luke's narrative speaks of in one sentence. Here the case for any connection seems very flimsy.

If we are convinced that Luke knew the writings of Josephus, then Acts must be after AD 94, although it need not be so late if it was the lectures of Josephus which Luke knew. But it must be regarded as at least doubtful that the case for the connection with Josephus has been made out.

So far we have been looking at datings of Acts which may be called conventional or orthodox. Each of them would have a good number of supporters. We now have to look at two datings which are much more individual.

(iv)   First, we look at the view of J.C. O'Neill in his book *The Theology of Acts*, the second and revised edition of which appeared in 1970. In the following section the page numbers in brackets are references to the second edition of O'Neill's book. Acts, says O'Neill, is a unique book, especially for the reason that it is the first and the only book to make the history of the early church comparable in value with the story of Jesus (p. 6). Because of this early references are rare. O'Neill, therefore, proposes to use a special method of dating it. 'The only way now left to solve the problem about the date of Acts is to decide where its theological affinities lie' (p. 1). The task which he sets himself is 'to date Acts by discovering positive theological parallels between Luke-Acts and other early Christian writers' (p. 5).

Such parallels O'Neill specially finds in the *First Apology* of Justin Martyr, with the assumption that Justin Martyr did not know the work of Luke, and that therefore the parallels are not due to quotation, allusion or reminiscence, but to the fact that both works belong to the same generation and come from the same theological climate. What then are these parallels?

(a) Apart from Luke, Justin Martyr is the first writer to assume that 'the world mission of the apostles should be told in the same breath as the history of Jesus' death, resurrection and ascension' (p. 10). 'In Matthew the world mission is commanded, not related' (p. 10). In his *Apology* (50.12) Justin writes:

> After his crucifixion even all his friends deserted, and denied him. But later, when he rose from the dead and appeared to them, he taught them to read the prophecies in which all these things that had happened were foretold. They saw him return to heaven and believed and, when they had received power which he sent from heaven to them, they went to every nation of men and taught these things, and were called 'Apostles'.[8]

This missionary activity of the apostles 'from Jerusalem' is as much part of the history of salvation as the work of Jesus (p. 11). Further, this mission is foretold in the Old Testament, for Isaiah (2.3) tells of the day when 'out of Zion shall go forth the law, and the word of the Lord from Jerusalem'.

> And there is evidence to convince you that this has come to pass; for men, twelve in number, went out from Jerusalem into the world; they were uneducated [*idiōtai*, cf. Acts 4.13] and not good speakers, but by God's power they made known to every nation of men how they had been sent by the Messiah to teach all the Word of God . . .[9]

Without theological connection between the work of Christ and the work of the apostles Luke-Acts would have been inconceivable (p. 11), and this is a viewpoint which Justin shares.

(b) The passage already quoted from Justin's *Apology*, 50.12, shows evidence of 'a detailed theology of Jesus' resurrection which in the New Testament is peculiar to Luke-Acts' (p. 11).[10] In regard to this theology of the resurrection, there are six points of agreement between Justin and Luke-Acts (pp. 11f.). First, both stress that the chief business of the risen Messiah was to persuade the apostles that his

sufferings had been foretold. Second, they both greatly elaborate the simple statement that this happened according to the scriptures, and the discovery of relevant Old Testament prophecies is a main part of the work of both. Third, they both state that during the discussions of the risen Christ with the apostles he referred back to his own predictions of his suffering. Fourth, both Luke-Acts and Justin explicitly record Jesus' ascension. Fifth, both state that after the ascension the apostles received power from above. Sixth, in both it is said that the apostles went out into all the world to teach what Jesus had persuaded them to be true, and in both this is principally the fulfilment of Old Testament prophecy in the events of Jesus' passion. None of these points is made exactly elsewhere in the New Testament and, O'Neill claims, the combination of them all in Justin and Luke-Acts is highly significant.

Further, both in Luke-Acts and in Justin the point of view is that the Jews have officially rejected the gospel, but that the Gentiles can be persuaded to receive it. Justin writes in his *Apology* (49.5):

> The Jews had the prophecies and were ever expecting the Messiah to be at hand; they not only failed to recognize him but also ill-treated him; but the Gentiles, who had never heard anything about the Messiah until the apostles came from Jerusalem and told them about him and imparted the prophecies, were filled with joy and faith and said farewell to idols and dedicated themselves to the unbegotten God through the Messiah.

Here is one of the main themes of Acts.

O'Neill further finds six detailed coincidences. First, Justin (*Apology*, 35.5f.) argues from a psalm of David to Jesus, as Peter did at Pentecost (Acts. 2.25-32). Second, both note that the apostles were uneducated (*idiōtai; Apology*, 39.3; Acts 4.13). Thirdly, both use the common idea that it is better to obey God than men, an idea going back to Socrates (Acts 4.19; 5.29; *Dialogue*, 80.3). Fourth, in both Justin (*Dialogue*, 51.2) and Acts (10.41) we find it explicitly stated that Jesus both ate and drank with his disciples after the resurrection. Fifth, both use the idea of the unknown god (*Second Apology*, 10.6; Acts 17.23). In both a Christian is accused of being mad, Paul by Festus (Acts 26.25), Justin by Trypho (*Dialogue*, 39.4).

So O'Neill argues that, first, there is a close similarity between Luke-Acts and Justin both in basic theology and in minor details, and, second, that they had not read each other's work. Therefore, they belong to the same generation (p. 17). What is that generation? O'Neill would date it – he dates Justin's *Apology* AD 138/139 – from AD 115 to 170. During that period Acts was written, and later rather than earlier because otherwise Justin would probably have known it. Can we get a latest date, now that we have fixed the earliest at AD 115? Marcion based his gospel on Luke's gospel; Marcion's date is

about AD 140, and we must allow for Luke's work having time to gain
its authority, which would put Luke's work back to AD 130.
Therefore, Acts was written, O'Neill argues, between AD 115 and 130
(pp. 17-21).

O'Neill finally has to face the problem why, if Luke-Acts is as late
as that, it shows no sign of knowing anything about the letters of Paul.
O'Neill believes that the date AD 90 which is generally accepted as the
date of the collection of the Pauline letters is too early. He argues that
the first writer to show a knowledge of all the Pauline letters is
Polycarp about AD 135. On this argument, Luke-Acts was written
before the Pauline collection of letters was made (pp. 22-25), a
conclusion which he supports by the fact that Justin Martyr never
quotes – and for that matter never even mentions – Paul.

Of the ingenuity of this argument and of the scholarship with which
it is supported there is no question; but it has failed to gain general
acceptance, if for no other reason, because an easier explanation of
the facts is that Justin knew Acts.

(v)   We come finally to the dating of F.C. Baur and the Tübingen
school.[11]   Baur   had   a   predecessor   in   M.   Schneckenburger.
Schneckenburger, unlike Baur, did not abandon the historicity of
Acts, but he argued that only the defence of Paul against his Judaistic
opponents could explain the choice of incidents in Acts, 'the
theological colouring which appears in the attribution to Peter of
distinctly Pauline characteristics, and to Paul of Judaistic tendencies',
'the assimilation of the two chief Apostles to each other' and 'the
frequency in the last chapters of Paul's speeches in his own defence'.[12]
Baur was to go very much further than this.

Baur saw everything in terms of what may be called the Hegelian
movement of life. Hegel saw the movement of things in three stages.
First, there was a *thesis*; second, in contradiction and opposition to
the thesis there emerged the *antithesis*; finally, out of this conflict
between thesis and antithesis there came the *synthesis*, in which thesis
and antithesis united to form a composite whole. Baur applied this to
the Christian church in its earliest days. The thesis was Jewish
Christianity, for it was out of Judaism that the Christian church first
came, and this Jewish Christianity centred upon Peter. The antithesis
was the Christianity which saw its duty and its destiny in the mission
to the Gentiles, and this centred upon Paul. So, as Baur saw it, the
early church was a battle-ground on which there was fought out the
struggle between a Jewish and a Gentile Christianity. But by the latter
part of the second century the synthesis had come, and the synthesis
was that catholic Christianity in which Jew and Gentile could live
together.

This, Baur claimed, was the fact of the matter. Acts, so it is
claimed, was written as a work of conciliation. Acts will not accept the

battle-ground picture of early Christianity. It was written about the middle of the second century, and its aim was to show that in the early church there was unity and not disunity. To do this, on Baur's theory, Acts is quite prepared to rewrite history, and to alter the facts. It is not trying to write history; it is trying to bring forward the synthesis between the Judaists and the Paulinists, or it is looking back, when the synthesis had been largely achieved, and it is trying to prove that there never had been anything else. How, then, does Baur claim that Acts set about the task? Add to this, that Baur held that the true picture is not the picture in Acts; it is the picture in the great undoubted Pauline letters, Romans, Corinthians, Galatians. If we want to see the facts about the early church, it is to the letters we must go, because, says Baur, Acts provides us with an unreal and idealized picture of the church.

(a) First, there is the picture of the Jews. In the Pauline letters it is *Christian* Jews, or at least Jews who claimed to be Christians, who are the trouble-makers. In Galatians the trouble-makers are not pagans from outside the church; they would claim to be Christians. It is not paganism they are preaching; it is a perverted form of the gospel (Gal. 1.6-9). On the other hand, in Acts the Jews who cause the trouble are Jews, and not Christians. The trouble comes in Acts, not from inside, but from outside the church (13.50; 14.2,19). When trouble does arise in the church, it is settled reasonably and courteously, as was the reception of the Gentiles at the Council of Jerusalem, at which the Gentiles are unanimously welcomed into the church, on condition of keeping a few laws which would make table-fellowship possible (15.1-35). The Pauline letters show war within the church between the Jewish and the Paulinist parties; in Acts there is no trouble within the church; it comes from outside.

(b) Second, it is claimed that Acts makes Peter much more Gentile than he in fact was and Paul much more Jewish than he in fact was. There is an obliterating of the differences. In Acts it is Peter who makes the initial move to accept the Gentiles in the Cornelius incident, and at the Council of Jerusalem Peter claims that he was used by God to be the first to speak to the Gentiles. In the story in Galatians the accepted arrangement is that Peter should go to the Jews and Paul to the Gentiles (Gal. 2.7-9). And yet the astonishing thing is that according to Acts it was always in the synagogue that Paul began, in Salamis (13.5), in Antioch in Pisidia (13.14), in Iconium (14.1), in Thessalonica (17.3), in Beroea (17.10), in Athens (17.17), in Corinth (18.4), in Ephesus (18.19). In Acts Paul always gives the impression of reporting back to Jerusalem. In Acts he circumcises Timothy (16.3), while in Galatians (5.2-4) he insists that Christ is of no advantage to the man who accepts circumcision, that the man who accepts circumcision is bound to keep the whole law, and has severed himself

from Christ and fallen away from grace. In Acts (23.6) Paul claims not to have been, but to be a Pharisee, while in Philippians (3.5-7) he passionately declares that his Pharisaism is one of the things that he has left behind him for ever. In Acts 21.17-26 he is perfectly willing to defray the expenses of the men who are taking the Nazirite vow, in order that he himself may show, at the request of James, that he lives in observance of the law, surely an astonishing step for a man who spoke about the law as Paul does in the letters. Jülicher says that it is not so much that Peter is Gentilized and Paul is Judaized as that both of them are Lucanized (*Introduction to the NT*, p. 438).

There is a case for holding that the portrait of Paul in Acts is different from the self-portrait of the letters.

(c)   Lastly in this matter, it is claimed that in Acts there is a deliberate equalization of Peter and Paul. Furneaux in his commentary (p. v) makes a table of it.

Peter	*Paul*
Heals a man lame from birth, 3.2.	Heals a man lame from birth, 14.8.
Denounces judgment on Ananias, 5.5.	Denounces judgment on Elymas, 13.11.
His shadow heals, 5.15.	His aprons heal, 19.12.
Is persecuted by Sadducees and supported by a Pharisee, 5.17,34.	Is persecuted by Sadducees and supported by Pharisees, 23.6,9.
Rebukes a sorcerer, 8.20.	Rebukes a sorcerer, 13.10.
Heals Aeneas, 9.34.	Heals father of Publius, 28.8.
Raises Dorcas, 9.40.	Raises Eutychus, 20.10.
His first Gentile convert a member of the noble Cornelian house, 10.1.	His first Gentile convert a member of the noble Aemilian house, 13.12.
Is led by a vision to preach to Gentiles, 10.20.	Is led by a vision to preach to Gentiles, 22.17.
Is reverenced by the centurion, 10.26.	Is reverenced by the jailer, 16.29.
The Holy Spirit falls upon his converts, 10.44.	The Holy Spirit falls upon his converts, 19.6.
Is delivered from prison by an angel, 12.7.	Is delivered from prison by an earthquake, 16.26.

The parallelism is indeed extraordinary, and, it is claimed, is artificially constructed to equate the greatness of Paul and Peter.

So then the view of Baur is that Acts was written about AD 150, by someone who wanted to obliterate the violent Peter-Paul battle of the early church, and on this view, if we want the facts, it is the letters we must read, and not Acts.

12

LUKE THE HISTORIAN

We have now reached the stage when it is necessary to examine the place of Luke as an historian. We shall do this by looking at Luke's connection with outside history, where we can check it, and looking in some detail at the relationship of Acts to the Pauline letters.

Different scholars have taken very different views of Luke as an historian. F.F. Bruce (p. 15) pays Luke the tribute of saying that he stands in the direct line of descent from Thucydides. Sir William Ramsay said that he came to the study of Acts with the belief that it was a late second-century work, but after half a lifetime spent in the study of Acts and of Asia Minor he concluded that the author was Luke and that the book is reliable history.[1] On the other hand, W.G. Kümmel in his *Introduction to the NT* (p. 113) has denied that Acts is a genuine historical work at all, or that Luke can be called the first Christian historian. Acts, he says, has none of the characteristics that real history ought to have, completeness of material, precision in historical details, complete chronology, biographical interest. F.C. Baur, as we have in part seen, will not allow that Acts even begins to be proper history. For Baur, the guiding principle is: 'The statement which has the greatest claim to historical truth is that which appears most unprejudiced and nowhere betrays a desire to subordinate its historical material to any special subjective aim.' Of Acts this, according to Baur, can never be true, for the one aim of Acts is 'a defence of the apostle Paul in his apostolic dignity and his personal and apostolic conduct, especially in the matter of the Gentiles, as against the attacks and accusations of the Judaizing party'. We have already seen the methods by which, as Baur sees it, Acts equates Paul with Peter. Baur would simply say that no one can write history in that way. 'The more closely we trace an apologetic aim in the narrative, the more questionable must it appear whether what he gives us is a purely historical narrative.' Time and time again, we shall soon see, Dibelius and Haenchen will insist that Acts is not history, and is not meant to be treated as history.

First, then, let us look at the defence of Acts. It is claimed, and rightly, that, where Luke can be checked in matters of detail, he is consistently right. A Roman province which was under the direct jurisdiction of the emperor was governed by a legate; a province which was under the control of the senate was governed by a proconsul. Broadly speaking, the distinction was that provinces with troops stationed in them were under the emperor, the provinces where there were no troops were governed by the senate. The obvious aim was that the army should be under imperial control. It frequently happened that provinces were switched from one control to the other as their circumstances changed. In such cases Luke is always right. He calls Sergius Paulus, the governor of Cyprus, a proconsul (Acts 13.7), and so he was, and Cyprus had had a number of switches. Cyprus was annexed in 57 BC; in 55 BC it was incorporated in Cilicia; in 27 BC it became an imperial province and was governed by a legate; in 22 BC the emperor exchanged it with the senate for Dalmatia, and it was governed by a proconsul. In this rather complicated succession Luke gets it right. Similarly, he calls the governor in Corinth, that is, the governor of Achaia, a proconsul (18.12), and again so he was, for Achaia was a senatorial province from 27 BC to AD 15 and from AD 44 onwards.

Acts calls the magistrates of Philippi *stratēgoi*, which means praetors (16.20). Properly, the magistrates of Roman colonial cities were called the *duumviri*, the two men; but such was the pride of these colonies, and such was their consciousness of being miniature Romes set all over the world, that their magistrates took to themselves the name of praetors, for in Rome itself the praetors came second in place only to the consuls. Cicero says of the magistrates of Capua: 'Although in other colonies they were called *duumviri*, these wished to be called praetors.'[2] Luke knew all about the pride of the colonial magistrates, who magnified their office until they had equated it with the highest in the empire.

In Thessalonica the magistrates are called *politarchs* (17.6). This is a very unusual word, the use of which was confined almost completely to Macedonia. F.F. Bruce (pp. 326f.) tells us that it does not occur in literary Greek, and in inscriptions it occurs nineteen times between the second century BC and the third century AD, and of these occurrences five refer to Thessalonica, which in the time of Augustus had five politarchs and in the time of the Antonine Emperors, six. The writer of Acts is correct in his information about Herod Agrippa I and Herod Agrippa II, and about the Roman procurators Felix and Festus. He is right about the priests of Zeus in Lystra (14.13), and about the assembly, the secretary and the Asiarchs of Ephesus (19.31f., 35).

Even in matters of local detail, where he might forgivably have been in error, the information of the writer of Acts is well nigh unfailingly correct.

But, as we have seen, there are voices on the other side. In the first place, there are those who insist that Luke is far more concerned with the development of ideas than the recording of events. E.J. Goodspeed says in his *Introduction to the NT* (p. 189): 'History is not just a record of wars and dynasties; it has to do with new ideas, currents of thought, and attitudes of mind', and of this Luke was well aware. Dibelius (*Studies,* p. 138) declares that history only becomes history when it is no longer merely 'a heap of facts', when narrative becomes interpretation, when to narrative is added judgment. History, says Dibelius (p. 102), is not the ultimate aim of Acts; the ultimate aim is preaching. Luke is concerned with 'the destination of events'. The question to ask is not the question of authenticity or historicity; the question is: 'What do these stories say?' Luke is not a mere compiler or transmitter; the question is not the question of historical reliability; the question is: What is the message? Haenchen writes (p. 110):

> For [Luke], a narration should not describe an event with the precision of a police report, but must make the listener or reader aware of the inner significance of what happened, and impress upon him, unforgettably, the truth of the power of God made manifest in it.

On this point of view, it would be almost true to say that history is the last thing for which we should look from Acts. This may well ultimately be so, but the fact remains that we cannot avoid checking, as far as we can, what Luke tells us, for his use of that which came to him will give us insight into his mind. There are three directions in which we may look at Luke's method with, and treatment of, his facts.

(i)   There is first of all the matter of *omission*. There is no doubt that there is much of the story of Paul which Acts makes no attempt to tell. Paul sets down the summary of his own life:

> Five times I have received at the hands of the Jews the forty lashes less one. Three times I have been beaten with rods; once I was stoned. Three times I have been shipwrecked; a night and a day have I been adrift at sea; on frequent journeys, in danger from rivers, danger from robbers, danger from my own people, danger from Gentiles, danger in the city, danger in the wilderness, danger at sea, danger from false brethren; in toil and hardship, through many a sleepless night, in hunger and thirst, often without food, in cold and exposure. And apart from other things, there is the daily pressure upon me of my anxiety for all the churches (II Cor. 11.24-8).

Acts is far from supplying an account of the experiences numbered in that list. Even from this it is evident that there is a very great deal of which Acts has nothing to say, and it is to be remembered that II Corinthians brings us down only to about AD 55.

Further, there is clear evidence in Paul's letters that he was in deadly peril of his life in Ephesus. He writes to the Corinthians (II Cor. 1.8-10):

> For we do not want you to be ignorant, brethren, of the affliction we experienced in Asia; for we were so utterly, unbearably crushed that we despaired of life itself. Why, we felt that we had received the sentence of

death; but that was to make us rely not on ourselves but on God who raises the dead; for he delivered us from so deadly a peril, and he will deliver us; on him we have set our hope that he will deliver us again.

And in I Corinthians 15.32, he speaks about fighting with beasts at Ephesus, whatever he means by that. Quite clearly, something very painful and very dangerous happened to Paul at Ephesus; to this day there is shown among the ruins of Ephesus a little building called Paul's prison; but of what happened Acts has no word or hint.

Time and time again the letters show Paul in serious conflict: in Galatia with the Judaizers; in Corinth with the proliferation of parties and problems, and with an opposition which in II Corinthians 10-13 produced the most broken-hearted letter Paul ever wrote; in Philippi where there are those who are out to add to his troubles. Of none of these things has Acts anything to say.

There are two things to be said about the omissions of Acts. First, a process of selection was absolutely necessary, for the maximum practical length of a papyrus roll was about thirty feet, and Acts as it stands would run to that. And second, it is sometimes said that from ch. 13 Acts becomes the biography of Paul. That is only half true. It is not the biography of Paul's personal experiences and troubles; it is the biography of Paul in so far as Paul was the key figure in the mission to the Gentiles and the expansion of the church. It is the importance of an incident in that context which is his criterion of inclusion or omission.

(ii)   There are times when Luke on the face of it does seem to be guilty of error. Perhaps the most startling difficulty which this side of the matter raises comes in connection with Cornelius (Acts 10.1-11.18). Cornelius was a centurion, and a centurion was a Roman citizen, and, R.M. Grant says, 'During the reign of Herod Agrippa (d.44) no Roman troops were stationed in his territory'.[3] In the Roman army legionaries were citizens; but the Romans made a great deal of use of auxiliary troops, and they were not citizens. It is true that the Italian cohort, which was a battalion of archers, did serve in Palestine from shortly before AD 69 until the second century. But normally, before the death of Herod Agrippa, Palestine was garrisoned by auxiliary troops who were Syrians and Samaritans. Josephus tells in his *Antiquities* (19.356-65) how Roman troops, legionaries, were brought in. On the death of Herod Agrippa the people of Caesarea broke into great rejoicing. In this rejoicing the garrison of Syria and Samaritan auxiliaries joined. They broke into the royal palace in Caesarea, stole certain statues of the late king's daughters, took the statues down to the public brothels, and treated them in the most obscene and indecent ways. Josephus (19.364f.) describes the steps the Romans took:

He (Caesar) determined in the first place to send orders to Fadus (the procurator) that he should chastise the inhabitants of Caesarea and Sebaste for the insults they had offered to the dead king, and for their insane conduct to the daughters who were still alive; and that he should remove the body of troops who were stationed at Caesarea and Sebaste, with the five regiments, into Pontus, that they might do their military service there, and that he should choose an equal number of soldiers out of the Roman legions stationed in Syria to take their places.

This is to say that Roman troops only came into Palestine following on what happened at the death of Herod Agrippa. And, if this is true, there cannot have been a serving Roman centurion in Judaea at the time to which Luke assigns the Cornelius incident.

There are three possibilities. It may be that the events connected with Cornelius should be transferred to the time after Acts 12.20-23, which tells of the death of Agrippa. It may be that Luke's mention of Cornelius can be taken as evidence that there were Roman troops in Judaea at that time, and that Luke is quite correct. It may be that Luke is not really interested at all in the precise dating of the incident, but is interested only in its place in the expansion of the church. We may have to alter the dating of the Cornelius event, but there is no necessity completely to abandon it as fiction.

(iii) Third, there are the alleged discrepancies between the account of events in Acts and the account in the Pauline letters;[4] and, it will be remembered, Baur held it as a first principle that in the case of any such discrepancy the account of the letters must always be accepted, since Paul himself wrote the letters, and presumably knew what he had done and why he had done it.

(a) The first of these discrepancies is quite unimportant, and may not be a discrepancy at all. It has to do with the movements of Paul, Timothy and Silas, after Paul had left Macedonia and journeyed to Corinth *via* Athens. Paul's own movements are clear. Due to the hostility of the Jews he left first Thessalonica and then Beroea. The Macedonian events end with the statement;

> Then the brethren immediately sent Paul off on his way to the sea, but Silas and Timothy remained there. Those who conducted Paul brought him as far as Athens; and receiving a command for Silas and Timothy to come to him as soon as possible, they departed (17.14f.).

The account then continues: 'Now while Paul was waiting for them at Athens, his spirit was provoked within him as he saw that the city was full of idols.' There is no word of an arrival of Timothy and Silas in Athens. They do appear when Paul had reached Corinth. 'After this he left Athens and went to Corinth ... When Silas and Timothy arrived from Macedonia, Paul was occupied with preaching, testifying to the Jews that the Christ was Jesus' (18.1,5). On the basis of the

Acts story, Timothy and Silas did not make up on Paul at all when he was in Athens; they did not rejoin him until he had reached Corinth.

We now turn to the letters. It is generally held that I Thessalonians was written from Corinth just at this time. In it Paul writes to tell the Thessalonians how worried about them he had been (3.1-3,6):

> Therefore when we could bear it no longer, we were willing to be left behind at Athens alone, and we sent Timothy, our brother and God's servant in the gospel of Christ, to establish you in the faith and to exhort you, that no one be moved by these afflictions ... But now Timothy has come to us from you, and has brought us the good news of your faith and love.

From I Thessalonians it would appear that Timothy had caught up with Paul at Athens, that he had been sent back to Thessalonica from there as Paul's envoy, and that he had again caught up with Paul at Corinth. In Acts there is no indication at all of Timothy's arrival in Athens. It therefore seems that Acts has missed out Timothy's journey to Athens and his return to Thessalonica as the envoy of Paul. But this is an omission of no importance. If Luke's aim was to give an account of the onward march of Christianity, the journey of Timothy had no relevance to his brief.

(b)   The second of the discrepancies occurs in connection with the story of Paul's conversion on the Damascus Road. In Acts that story is told three times. If we take the version of Acts 9.1-19 as basic, the other versions (22.8-21 and 26.9-20) make the following additions:

1.   22.6 and 26.13 add 'at midday'.
2.   26.13 adds that the light was 'brighter than the sun', and that it shone also 'on those who journeyed with me'.
3.   26.14 adds that the voice spoke 'in the Hebrew language'.
4.   26.14 adds, 'It hurts you to kick against the goads'.
5.   26.16-18 adds the long passage in which the risen Christ himself describes the work which lies ahead of Paul.
6.   26 omits the blindness and the part of Ananias in the story.
7.   9.9 alone has the information that Paul did not eat or drink for three days.

It cannot be said that any of these omissions or additions, except the omission of Ananias in ch. 26, makes any great difference to the story.

Within the story itself there are two discrepancies. Acts 9.7 speaks of Paul's companions 'hearing the voice but seeing no man', while Acts 22.9 says that 'they saw the light but did not hear the voice of the one who was speaking to me'.[5] On the face of it, that looks like a contradiction. In the second discrepancy, Acts 9.7 says that those who were travelling with Paul '*stood* speechless'; 26.14 says 'and when we had all fallen to the ground'; in 22.7 Paul says, 'and I fell to the ground'. In the one case those with Paul are said to stand; in the other case they fall to the ground.

It cannot really be said that these discrepancies make very much difference, only the difference between remaining standing and falling to the ground; and in any event it would surely be very unreasonable to demand a photographic accuracy of memory of an event like the event of the Damascus road.

What is a little more difficult is the threefold way in which the commission to Paul is given. In Acts 9.15 Ananias is the instrument by which Paul's world-wide mission is conveyed to him. In Acts 22.17-21 the mission is conveyed to Paul in a vision while he is praying in the temple in Jerusalem. In Acts 26.16-18 the commission to Paul is given on the Damascus road itself by the risen Christ. True, the difference is there; but surely the important point is not the exact moment at which the commission was given, but the commission itself.

(c) There is considerably more divergence in the narrative of events following upon the conversion of Paul as that narrative is given in Acts and in Galatians. We may set out the two accounts side by side.

Acts 9.18-30	*Galatians* 1.15-24
The part of Ananias (9.10-19)	The visit to Arabia (1.17)
The preaching in Damascus (9.19-23). Note *many days* (v. 23).	The return to Damascus (1.17)
	Three years in Damascus (1.18)
The escape from Damascus (9.23-25)	The visit to Jerusalem to Peter and James, lasting fifteen days (1.18f.)
The arrival in Jerusalem and the suspicion of the Christians (9.26)	Departure to Syria and Cilicia (1.21)
The introduction by Barnabas (9.27) 27)	Unknown by sight to the church of Judaea who had only heard of his conversion (1.22f.)
Preaching at Jerusalem (9.27-29)	
The escape to Tarsus (9.29f.)	

There are considerable divergences here. In Acts there is no mention of the Arabian visit, and the many days of 9.23 unexpectedly turn out to be the three years of Gal. 1.18. In Galatians both Ananias and Barnabas vanish from the scene, and there is no mention of the two Jewish plots against Paul's life. The stay in Jerusalem lasts for no more than fifteen days. Acts depicts Paul as preaching in Jerusalem boldly and going in and out, which scarcely ties up with the Galatians statement that he was unknown by sight to the churches in Judaea.

There are obvious differences, but it may well be that the differences at least to some extent are to be explained by the different purposes for which the two narratives are used. The one aim and object of the Acts narrative is to underline the fact that here in this incident the man who is to be the dynamic of the Gentile mission has arrived, and that his arrival is a divine act. In Galatians, Paul's one aim is to demonstrate that his call and his gospel came from no man, but were given to him direct from God. Hence the lonely visit to Arabia and the vanishing of Ananias and Barnabas from the scene. It may well be that the differences are largely due to the different purposes for which the two stories are told.

(d) The fourth of the discrepancies at which we must look concerns the Council of Jerusalem, and the connection of the material in Acts 15 with the material in Galatians 2. This is one of the most complicated and most debated subjects in the New Testament, and the literature on it is endless.[6] We may begin by noting that there are some writers who take Acts 15 to be good history, and there are others who believe that it has no historical value at all. Rackham (p. 247) writes of Acts 15: 'We now come to a narrative which bears strong testimony to the fidelity of S. Luke... The chief evidence is afforded by the speeches. These are, of course, only brief notes of what was actually said, written out afterwards by S. Luke, and yet in these few verses the characteristic attitudes of the speakers unconsciously assert themselves.' Dibelius, on the other hand, says (*Studies*, p. 100), that Luke's treatment of the event is only literary-theological and can make no claim to historical worth. And Haenchen, agreeing with Dibelius, roundly declares (p. 464): 'Luke's version of the Apostolic Council does not possess historical value.' Let us begin by investigating the connection of Acts 15 with Gal. 2. And first of all let us set down the processes of the two accounts.

To put the Acts narrative in its context we must begin far back.

1. The matter begins with Peter's defence of the reception of Cornelius the Gentile centurion into the church (11.1-18).

2. Next comes the first mention of deliberate preaching to Gentiles (11.19f.). Here is an essential difference. Cornelius asked to be admitted; in the new situation preaching goes out and invites men in.

3. The Jerusalem church, faced with this new situation, sends Barnabas to investigate and report (11.22-24).

4. Barnabas reports favourably, finds Saul (Paul) and puts him in charge (11.25f.).

5. The Antioch church determines to go further and to embark upon a deliberate mission, which covers Cyprus, Pisidian Antioch, Iconium, Lystra, Derbe, and ends with the return of Paul and Barnabas, whose report is received with joy (chs. 13 and 14).

6. Then the trouble starts. Certain persons arrive from Jerusalem and insist that circumcision is the prerequisite of salvation (15.1f.).

7. The Antioch church decides to refer the matter to Jerusalem (15.2).

8. Paul and Barnabas and certain others set out for Jerusalem, mobilizing support in Phoenicia and Samaria as they go (15.3).

9. They arrive in Jerusalem and tell the story of their mission, but certain ex-Pharisees insist that the acceptance of the law and submission to circumcision are essential (15.4f.).

10. A special meeting is convened; it consists of the apostles and the elders and the whole congregation (15.6,12).

11. Peter speaks first and claims, in virtue of the Cornelius incident, to have been the first to take the good news to the Gentiles. The saving principle for all men is faith. The yoke of the law has been an intolerable burden both for their ancestors and for themselves. It is unthinkable that this yoke should be placed on the neck of the new disciples. The way to salvation is through nothing other than the grace of the Lord Jesus (15.7-11).

12. Paul and Barnabas relate the story of what happened during their mission (15.12).

13. James speaks and comes down strongly on the side of liberty for the Gentiles, and a decision is reached that the demand from the Gentiles should be that they abstain from what has been sacrificed to idols, from blood, from what is strangled and from unchastity (15.13-21).

14. The findings of the council are embodied in a letter, and Judas Barsabbas and Silas are commissioned with Paul and Barnabas to convey the decision to the churches, which they set off to do. Paul and Barnabas remain in Antioch; the envoys, their task completed, return to Jerusalem (15.22-35).

Such is the narrative of Acts, which, taken by itself, makes a perfectly intelligible story.

Now let us turn to the narrative of Galatians 2.

1. Fourteen years after either his conversion or his first visit, Paul went up to Jerusalem with Barnabas and Titus (2.1).

2. The journey was made as a consequence of 'revelation' (2.2).

3. Paul told the leaders of the church the gospel he preached, for he did not wish his work to be in vain (2.2).

4. This was done privately (2.2).

5. Titus, though he was a Greek, was not compelled to be circumcised (this seems the more likely meaning rather than that Titus was circumcised willingly, and not by compulsion); but false brethren insinuated themselves into the discussion and did their best to take away Christian freedom and to substitute Jewish law; their efforts were strongly resisted by Paul, and were unsuccessful (2.3-5).

6. The leaders of the church had nothing to add to the gospel Paul preached; they were fully convinced that Paul's work was God's work as much as theirs was; they came to an arrangement whereby it was acknowledged that Peter was entrusted with the mission to the

circumcised, the Jews, and Paul with the mission to the uncircumcised, the Gentiles. With this agreement, Peter and James and John gave Paul and Barnabas the right hand of fellowship, and sent them on their Gentile mission, only requesting them to remember the poor (2.6-10).

7. Paul returned to Antioch. In the Galatians narrative it is not expressly said that Paul came from, and returned to, Antioch, but that is the clear implication. Peter came to Antioch, and freely mixed and ate with the Gentiles. But certain men came from James and criticized such familiarity with the Gentiles, whereat Peter withdrew from table-fellowship with the Gentiles, and carried away Barnabas with him. Paul sternly and bluntly rebuked him in public, and apparently the rebuke saved the situation (2.11-14).

Such is the Galatian chain of events, and it too makes an intelligible story.

Next, let us look at the case for identifying the events of Acts 15 and those of Galatians 2. Lightfoot long ago summed up the arguments for this identification. The *geography* is the same in both cases; the movement is from Antioch to Jerusalem and from Jerusalem to Antioch. The *persons involved* are the same, Paul and Barnabas on the one side and Peter and James on the other. The *aim* of the whole operation is the same; the opening of the door of the church to the Gentiles without circumcision and without the Jewish law is the question. The *result* is the same; the way is made clear for the Gentiles to come in. The *opponents* are the same, Jews, ex-Pharisees, who held that it was necessary to accept circumcision and the law before a man could become a Christian.

As it has been well said, the strength of Lightfoot's case lies in its affirmations; but so does its weakness. It affirms the reasons for identifying the two passages, but it does not state the reasons against identification.

What then is to be said against identification? In Galatians 2.2 Paul says that he went up to Jerusalem 'by revelation'. There is no mention of anything like this in Acts 15. In Acts 15.2 Paul and Barnabas and the rest appear to be a deputation appointed by the Antioch church. The natural reading of Galatians 2.1 is that Paul took with him only Barnabas and Titus. Acts 15.2 seems to make the deputation bigger than that. There is a real and wide divergence between the two accounts when Galatians 2.2 says that the whole matter was dealt with in private, while the narrative of Acts (15.4,6,12) makes the whole discussion very much of a full-scale public occasion. The findings of the council in Acts 15.19f. seem a good deal more elaborate that the agreement of Galatians 2.7-10, which has no conditions at all, and in Galatians there is no mention of anything having been done or of anyone being commissioned to carry the decisions to other parts of the church, as described in Acts 15.22-34.

It may be said that these are trivial differences, but there are two things which demand explanation if the events of Acts 15 are to be identified with those of Galatians 2. First, in Galatians 2.11-13 the story of the agreement is immediately followed by the visit of Peter to Antioch, during which he enters into table-fellowship with the Gentiles, until there arrive 'men from James', at which Peter withdraws from association with the Gentiles, and seduces Barnabas into a like withdrawal. Is it really credible that so soon after the events of Acts 15 Peter should refuse to associate with the Gentiles, and is it really credible that James, who so vigorously came down on the side of opening the door to the Gentiles, could have sent a deputation from Jerusalem to Antioch to stop Jewish Christians from associating with Gentile Christians? It is very hard to believe that Peter and James could have acted in any such way after what they had said, and after the decisions which had been taken at the Council of Jerusalem. They both acted as if that council had never been.

Second, the whole aim of Paul in the first two chapters of Galatians is to prove the independence of his apostleship and the independence of his gospel. His apostleship is not from men nor through man, but through Jesus Christ and God the Father (1.1). He did not receive his gospel from any human source, nor was he taught it by any man (1.12). To prove this he lists his contacts with the leaders of the church at Jerusalem, with a view to showing that he owed them nothing of the things he taught and the faith he stood for. He tells of his first visit three years after his conversion (1.18). Then he goes on to tell of what is clearly meant to be his second visit, the visit at which the matter of the mission to the Gentiles was settled (2.1). Now remember that Paul is deliberately setting down *all* the contacts he has ever had with Jerusalem, and remember also that he is doing this under a self-imposed oath: 'In what I am writing to you, before God, I do not lie' (1.20). But, if Acts is right, and if Paul is going to be strictly accurate, the visit of Galatians 2.1 was not his second visit; it was his *third visit*, for he and Barnabas had come to Jerusalem with help for the Jerusalem church at a time when the famine was severe (Acts 11.27-30; 12.25). When Paul is putting himself on oath regarding his contacts with Jerusalem, could he really have completely and altogether omitted to tell of one visit? Lightfoot thinks it possible because Acts 11.27-30 says that the famine-relief gift was given to the elders, and there is no mention of the apostles at all; he thinks that because of persecution (8.1; 11.19) the apostles were absent from Jerusalem, and that because of this Paul simply omitted all mention of this visit. But it seems most unlikely that, when Paul was carefully enumerating his visits to Jerusalem, he could have totally omitted one of them; it seems very unlikely that all the apostles fled for their lives;

and it seems very unlikely that Paul could have been in Jerusalem without seeing the apostles, even if it was to the elders that he actually delivered the gift. If the veracity of Paul is to be saved, then the events of Galatians 2 must have taken place during the visit of Acts 11.27-30, and are not to be identified with the events of Acts 15.

Before we try to reconstruct what did happen, we must note that there are a number of scholars who would hold that Acts 11.27-30 and Acts 15 are two accounts of the same visit. They hold that Acts 11.27-30 is an account of the visit from the point of view of the church of Antioch; for them it was a visit when their gift was taken to Jerusalem. And Acts 15 is an account of the same visit from the point of view of the church at Jerusalem; for them it was a visit at which the future of the Gentiles was discussed. On this basis Acts 11.27-30 = Acts 15 = Galatians 2. But the difference between Acts 11.27-30 and Acts 15 is far too wide for this to be so.

If we may venture a reconstruction, what happened may well have taken the following course. Be it noted first of all that in Galatians 2.2 Paul says that he went up to Jerusalem by revelation, and that is true of the Acts 11.27-30 visit, because it was made as the result of a revelation of the Spirit, given to Agabus the prophet. So it may be suggested that the process was this:

1.   The situation at Antioch made it absolutely necessary that the position of the Gentiles should be settled, because for the first time there was preaching to the Gentiles (Acts 11.28).

2.   When Paul and Barnabas went to Jerusalem with the famine relief contribution, they took the opportunity to discuss this matter privately with the leaders of the Jerusalem church (Gal. 2.2).

3.   It looked as if agreement had been reached, but it was only a private talk, and therefore not binding, and so further trouble about association with the Gentiles broke out, involving Peter and Barnabas and James, and, of course, Paul.

4.   Since it was proved that private talk was not sufficient, official action had to be taken, and Acts 15 describes the official action and its results.

If we were to put this down in terms of New Testament passages, the passages in chronological order would run: Acts 11.19-26; Acts 11.27-30; Galatians 2.11-14; Acts 15.1-35. This makes sense of both Acts and Galatians.

We have now to ask what the results of the Council of Jerusalem were. First of all, let us visualize the situation. The success of the Christian mission had brought its own problems. The church had begun by being 'a society of Jews with a sprinkling of Gentiles'; it was well on the way to becoming 'a society of Gentiles with a sprinkling of Jews'. Even if the problem of circumcision was settled, this did not settle the larger question. Suppose it was agreed that Gentiles might now enter the church without circumcision, this did not solve the problem of table-fellowship. What was to happen to Jewish food laws and regulations? How was it going to be possible for Jews and Gentiles to eat together? And sooner or later, this would produce an even bigger problem – how was this going to react on eucharistic fellowship? How was it going to be possible for Jews and Gentiles to sit at the Lord's table together?

There were three possible directions of action. First, the Jewish laws could have been made universal. If that had happened, as Furneaux put it (p. 230), the Judaism which had been the cradle of the church could well have become the grave of the church. Second, Jewish food laws could have been totally abrogated and Jewish susceptibilities completely disregarded. In the end the Jewish law was forgotten, but it was too soon for that. Third, there could have arisen a two-section church, one half of which observed Jewish food laws and the other half of which acted as if these laws did not exist. It is significant that no one thought of the third solution. F.H. Chase in *The Credibility of Acts* (p. 91) comments: 'The unity of the church was an axiom about which both sides were in absolute agreement.' So what happened was that the major principle of the abolition of circumcision as a prerequisite to entry to the church was agreed, but a certain basic number of regulations were accepted in order to make table-fellowship possible. What were these regulations, and what did they mean? (They are given in Acts 15.20 and repeated in 15.29; 21.25.)

It was laid down that all Christians must abstain from the pollution of idols, that is, from eating the flesh of meat offered as a heathen sacrifice, from unchastity, from what is strangled and from blood. What does this mean? In the normal sacrifice only a token part of the animal was burned, sometimes no more than a few hairs cut from its forehead. Part of the meat was the perquisite of the priests; part of it was given back to the worshipper, and often with it he gave his friends a party, which met in the temple of his god to whom the sacrifice had been made. An invitation to such a party reads:

Antonius, son of Ptolemaeus, invites you to dine with him at the table of the Lord Serapis [his god], in the house of Claudius Serapion on the 16th at 9 o'clock.[7]

It is thus laid down that a Christian cannot eat meat which has been polluted by having been used as a heathen sacrifice, still less can he eat that meat at a party in a heathen temple. (Paul treats this problem fully in I Corinthians 8 and 10.) Christians must abstain from blood. This could mean that they are to abstain from murder. Much more likely in the original context, it meant that the Jewish food law which forbade the eating of blood (Lev. 3.17; 7.26f.; 17.10-16; 19.26; Deut. 12.16, 23-5) was to be strictly obeyed. The prohibition of eating what is strangled repeats this, for the blood is not drained away from an animal which is killed by strangulation. Christians are to have nothing to do with unchastity. There are three possible meanings to this. To begin with the least likely, it could mean that they are to abstain from the worship of all false gods, because such worship is described as spiritual adultery – what the AV calls 'whoring after strange gods' (Ex. 34.15f.; Lev. 20.5f.; Deut. 31.16; Judg. 2.17; Hos.4.14). It can mean quite simply that fornication is strictly forbidden, and that it is a command to sexual purity. Perhaps most likely, it means that Christians are to abstain from marriage within the forbidden degrees (Lev. 18.6-18), which the rabbis described as fornication.

From this a very interesting fact emerges. It can be seen that all the prohibitions of the Council of Jerusalem come from Leviticus 17-18, and what distinguishes them is they that are all laws which in their Old Testament context apply not only to Jews but also to any Gentile who is a sojourner in Israel. So what the council did was simply to restate the basic minimum of the law, which was obligatory on Jew and Gentile alike. It is of interest to note that the Jews had what they called the seven commands given to the sons of Noah, which are meant not simply for Jews but for all mankind: 1. obedience to the law; 2. abstinence from blasphemy; 3. abstinence from idolatry; 4. abstinence from marriage within the prohibited degrees; 5. abstinence from blood; 6. abstinence from robbery; 7. abstinence from meat cut from a living animal. So then the regulations of the Council of Jerusalem lay down the basic minimum requirement to enable a Jew to have table-fellowship with a Gentile.

It is of interest to note that the Western text of Acts in Codex D (Codex Bezae, see pp. 299ff. below) turns the whole thing into a quartet of ethical regulations: abstention from the pollution of idols, by which it means idolatry; abstention from unchastity in general; abstention from blood, by which it means murder; and not to do to others what they would not wish done to themselves. But, interesting and relevant as this is, it is not an ethical rule that the context demands, but a ritual rule to make eating and drinking together in their homes and at the Lord's table possible.

We have looked at Acts from the point of view of history in the matter of its omissions, its errors and its discrepancies with the Pauline letters. We have proceeded so far on the basic assumption that Acts is meant to be history. It is precisely this assumption that scholars like Dibelius and Haenchen would question. They would in fact say that to try to understand Luke as a historian is the sure way to misunderstand him. Haenchen (p. 360) speaks of the 'interpenetration' of historical and theological concern in Luke, but primarily he is a theologian. He presses history into the service of the Christian message. 'He is not directly chronicling real events, but dressing up a conviction of faith . . . in the garments of history, . . . endeavouring to make the hand of God visible in the church' (p. 362). Let us see this point of view operative in two of the main stories of Acts.

(i)   Let us begin with the story of the Council of Jerusalem, which we have just been studying (see especially Haenchen, pp. 440-72). On this point of view it is impossible to regard the story of the Council of Jerusalem as history.

(a)   Acts 15.7 refers to the Cornelius story. That story itself clearly implies that the whole episode happened in a blaze of publicity. It was something that the Jerusalem church all knew all about. Now, unless the Cornelius story had been completely forgotten, the situation which is at the root of Acts 15 would never have arisen, for the reception of Cornelius settled the position of the Gentiles. The story ends (11.18) with the words: 'And they glorified God, saying, Then to the Gentiles also God has granted repentance unto life.' Either the Cornelius story is not history or the Council of Jerusalem story is not history, for they are in flat contradiction of each other. Against this it has been argued, either that the Jerusalem church knew all about the Cornelius story, but did not take it as any kind of mandate for them to extend the Christian mission to the Gentiles, or that Cornelius came *seeking* admission, and it is one thing to allow in a man who comes seeking and quite another thing to go out and invite people in broadcast.

(b)   There is Peter's reference (Acts 15.10) to the law as a yoke 'which neither our fathers nor we have been able to bear'. It is argued that Peter could not possibly have dismissed the law like that.

(c)   It is argued that the Paul of the letters would never have accepted a compromise such as was arrived at in Acts 15 and of which there is no mention in Galatians 2, that he would never have agreed to the ritual regulations with which the council ended. But F.F. Bruce (p. 289) rightly points out that, where no compromise of principle was involved, Paul was the most conciliatory of men, in support of which he cites the circumcision of Timothy (Acts 16.3), Paul's willingness to pay the expenses of the men who were taking the Nazirite vow (Acts 21.26), and also his continual willingness to make allowance for the fears and hesitations of the weaker brother (Rom. 14.1-15.6; I Cor. 8). To this the non-historicists would simply answer that the story of the circumcision of Timothy and of Paul's support of the men who were taking the Nazirite vow are simply further proof that Acts was written by some one who knew nothing about Paul. In fact the incident of the Nazirite vow is described by Windisch (*Beginnings* II, p. 320) as 'the most palpable error' perpetrated by the writer of Acts. On the historicist side we must remember that Paul himself said in his letters that, though the law had no claim on him, yet to those under the law he became as one under the law; that to the Jews he became a Jew; that he became all things to all men that he might by all means save some (I Cor. 9.19-23). It is one thing to impose regulations as necessary for salvation; it is quite another to accept them as a matter of politeness, when people have a meal together. It would have been by no means impossible for Paul to accept these basic conditions.

(d) At a first reading the impression is given of a decision which affected the whole church, and it is very doubtful if so early in the history of the church there did exist such a unity. But that is only an impression. The council's letter is addressed to Antioch, Syria and Cilicia (Acts 15.23). The decision was quite a local one, and this is clearly the explanation why Paul did not quote it when he was dealing with the question of meat offered to idols in his letter to the church at Corinth.

(e) None of these reasons would make it necessary to abandon the historicity of the council and its proceedings, but there is one matter which is very difficult indeed. James in his speech makes a quotation from Amos 9.11f. The form of the quotation in Acts (15.16-18) is as follows:

> After this I will return,
> and I will rebuild the dwelling of David, which has fallen;
> I will rebuild its ruins;
> I will set it up,
> that the rest of men may seek the Lord,
> and all the Gentiles who are called by my name,
> says the Lord, who has made these things known from of old.

Now the point is that this is a quotation from the Septuagint, the Greek version of the Old Testament. In the Septuagint the quotation runs:

> In that day I will raise up
>   the tabernacle of David that is fallen.
> I will rebuild those parts of it
>   which have fallen into decay,
>   and repair what has been demolished:
> I will indeed rebuild it as in the days of old,
>   that the rest of mankind may seek the Lord,
>   even all the nations who are called by my name,
> says the Lord who does all these things.

Of course, the point is that in the Amos prophecy it is said that the rest of men will seek the Lord, and the Gentiles who are called by his name. But in the Hebrew Old Testament this point is not there at all. Here is the Hebrew:

> In that day I will raise up
> the tabernacle of David that is fallen,

and repair the breaches,
   and raise up its ruins,
   and rebuild it as in the days of old;
that they may possess the remnant of Edom,
   and all the nations who are called by my name,
   says the Lord who does this.

In the Hebrew it is a prophecy of conquest; in the Septuagint it is a prophecy of mission. This is because the Greek translator has read the name Edom as *adām*, 'man', which has the same consonants in Hebrew.

What makes this so difficult is that of all the leaders of the church James was the most Jewish. It is quite certain that, if James were going to quote the Old Testament, he would do so in Hebrew, his native language, and not in Greek, which would be quite strange to him. And what really complicates the matter is that the point that James is making is only in the Greek and is not in the Hebrew at all. It is next door to incredible that James would have made such a quotation, and, if he did not, the conclusion must be that Luke wrote the speech himself.[8] There is no doubt that the attribution of an argument based on the Greek version of the Old Testament to James is a problem of the first magnitude.

Let us then assume Haenchen's point of view and see where it takes us. The object of Luke is to prove that the mission to the Gentiles without the law is the will of God, and that that mission was accepted and approved and set in motion by the decision of the apostles in the Jerusalem church. This for Acts is the point of the story of the Council of Jerusalem.

There is no doubt that for Acts the Council of Jerusalem is, Haenchen says (p. 461), a watershed. There are ninety-four pages in Acts, and forty-seven of them precede the Council; it is the middle point. It rounds off the past and opens up the future. Up to the council all roads lead to Jerusalem, and every area evangelized is subject to Jerusalem. It is so with Samaria (8.14-25), with Galilee (9.31), with Cornelius (10.1-11.18), with Antioch (11.19-26). Every advance has to be reported to, approved by and supervised by Jerusalem. In 16.4 the decisions of the council are conveyed to the churches. But that is the end. In Acts 15 Peter makes his last appearance; in Acts 16.4 there is the last mention of the apostles. When we come to 21.18, the apostles have vanished and the elders with James at their head, are the directors of the church. Up to Acts 15 we have apostolic rule; after that it is the rule of the elders. Further, up to Acts 15 Paul is one of many secondary figures; after Acts 15 he is supreme, but still responsible in some way to Jerusalem; but Jerusalem has legitimized the great work of Paul, the founding of the European Gentile church. Unquestionably Acts 15 is meant to mark an epoch in the history of the church.

Further, this new thing is the work and the will of God. This is what the speeches in Acts 15 are all about. The beginning was the incident of Cornelius, and that event with the vision and the command was the direct work of God (15.7-9). It has been proved by experience that the law is an intolerable burden for Jew and Gentile alike (15.19). The miracles which Paul and Barnabas have been able to work, the signs and wonders, are the direct evidence of the hand of God (15.12). The coming of the Gentiles is justified because it was foretold in scripture (15.15-17). And the things which have been laid down are, as we have already seen, the very essence of the Jewish law, that part of the law which Moses said was valid for Jew and Gentile alike (15.20,21). Come at it any way you like, the Gentile mission without the law is the will of God.

Further, the decision is sent out not with Paul and Barnabas alone; it is sent out by Judas Barsabbas and Silas, who are the direct, chosen, official envoys of the Jerusalem church. Therefore the act is not the act of any rebel or any breakaway. It is the deliberate act of the Jerusalem church.

So then if we read the Council of Jerusalem narrative as theology rather than history, we do not ask if this happened in detail. We accept the fact that this is a dramatized declaration that the mission to the Gentiles was an act of the direct will of God, and was approved and initiated by the apostles and the Jerusalem church, and thus the way is opened for the world mission of the second half of Acts.

(ii)   Now let us look at the story of Cornelius (Acts 10.1-11.18), the second of the great stories which, according to Dibelius (*Studies*, pp. 109-23) and Haenchen (pp. 343-63) must be read in the same way.

As we have already seen (pp. 262f. above), we can, if we like, begin from the fact that, as far as our information goes, there were no Roman troops in Caesarea during the reign of Herod Agrippa, and Herod did not die until AD 44. If we proceed like this, we shall argue whether or not the story is historical. We can find scholars supporting either viewpoint; for instance, F.F. Bruce (p. 214) quotes Foakes Jackson's commentary (p. 87) to the effect that this story 'bears the stamp both of probability and of truth'. On the other hand, Haenchen (p. 356) quotes Wellhausen as saying that the story is 'an unhistorical fabrication'. But then Haenchen (p. 357) approaches the question from a different aspect:

> If we wish to gain firm ground in this jostling throng of opinions, we must first set aside all questions of historical authenticity or sources and seek to understand Luke's concern in reproducing the story of Cornelius. He has told it in such a way that it can be understood only from the standpoint of its theological meaning.

At the back of it Dibelius would see a simple conversion story, the story of an occasion when Peter quite accidentally and with no principle at stake converted a Gentile centurion. The community liked stories which told of the conversion of important Gentiles. So Luke took and 'over-exploited' this story. He elevated a simply story into a principle. He sacrificed the exact reproduction of the tradition for the sake of a higher historical truth . . . the idea that the Gentile mission came neither from Paul nor from Peter, but from God.[9] What, then, are the points that are being made?

1. God shows no partiality (10.34). This cannot refer to God's choice of Israel as the chosen people. It must be a new thing which is happening in Christ.

2. We have to note who it was who was converted; it was Cornelius, a devout man, a God-fearer, a man of prayer, and a generous giver (10.2). This is continuously stressed (10,4,22,30). Conversion is not for any man, but for such a man as this.

3. We have to note who was the agent in conversion. It was Peter, no 'free-lance'. The move to the Gentiles begins with Peter.

4. Behind this is God acting irresistibly. The Christians resisted (10.14,28,47; 11.2,8,17); God insisted (10.3,11-16,22,30; 11.5-10, 13). The vision and the angel are repeated (10.22,30; 11.13). As Haenchen has it (p. 362), the reader is never allowed to forget that it is God who brought this about. A kind of passivity is lent to the characters. Haenchen complains that so strong is the guidance that the characters tend to become little more than puppets in the hands of God. The church's reluctance is overcome by the argument that, if God has given Spirit baptism, it is not for the church to refuse water baptism (11.16f.).

5. Lastly, this is no special case. The close of the story is the church's admission (11.18): 'Then to the Gentiles also God has granted repentance unto life.' As Haechen says (p. 360), this is 'the fundamental affirmative to the admission of the Gentiles'.

So once again in this story the point is not history. The point is that the Gentile mission without the law is dramatically represented as being the direct result of the action of God, and that it was begun under no less a person than Peter. When Peter set out, he did not even know he was going to baptize. All he knew was that Cornelius was 'to hear words from him' (10.22). The Gentile mission, says the Cornelius story, was not man deciding, but God guiding.

The only comment that need be made is that no one will deny that this is the very essence of the stories. The only question that need be asked is, whether it is necessary to abandon all history to reach this truth.

(iii) We may look at one more case in which this type of criticism parts with history, for in many ways it is the most surprising of all – the story of the shipwreck in ch. 27 (see Dibelius, *Studies*, pp. 134,

204-6, 213f.; Haenchen, pp. 708-11). To put it at its simplest, this
view holds that the story of the shipwreck is a story, either of the
voyage itself, or founded on other shipwreck stories – which were a
feature of ancient romances – into which references to Paul have been
deliberately and artificially inserted. 'There is more literature than
observation,' says Dibelius (p. 7), 'in the description of the shipwreck.'
Taking the story as it comes, according to this view, the first insertion
is in 27.9b-11. Paul was a prisoner on the charge of riot; he was very
probably in chains; it was extremely unlikely, if not totally impossible,
that he would have anything to do with any decision that was taken.
The story originally proceeded from v. 8 to v. 12. The next insertion is
vv. 21-26. It is ridiculous that Paul in the middle of a pounding sea
should engage in making a speech. Verse 31 is an insertion. The
incident of the sailors and the boat is quite misconceived. As
Haenchen sees it, the sailors had no intention of leaving the ship
permanently. 'To leave a safely anchored ship at night in a lifeboat on
a rough sea to get to an unknown shoreline, whose breakers could be
heard, would have been outright stupidity. Only landlubbers could
conceive such a suspicion . . . If Paul awakened suspicion against the
sailors, then he was responsible not for the rescue, but rather for the
shipwreck!' (p. 710). Verses 33-6 are again an insertion, similar to vv.
21-6. In v. 43 the words *wishing to save Paul* are an insertion, because
in any event we are not told at all about how Paul got to land. It is
quite wrong to say that Paul had acquired considerable influence
because he was an experienced traveller. He had, in fact, never made
that particular journey before. Enough has been said to show the kind
of attitude that is brought to this type of criticism.

But the point that we have to enquire about is why this was done. In
the first place, the story of the Jewish trial is followed by a highly
detailed and highly dramatized story of the voyage and shipwreck in
order to show how God kept the promise at the beginning of the book
(1.8) that the Christian witness would go out to the ends of the earth.
Neither the machinations of men nor the violence of nature can
interfere with the promise and the commission of God. Second, it is
done to present the Lucan image of Paul. Chapter 27, says Haenchen
(p. 709), 'shows Paul the prisoner as the focal point of action; he, the
prisoner, saves them all'.

> The scenes inserted correspond exactly to the Lucan image of Paul. Paul
> always stands in the limelight . . . He never despairs . . . Luke did not
> suspect – and did not let the readers suspect – that Paul could despair of
> life (II Cor. 1.8) . . . He knows only the strong, unshaken favourite of God
> who strides from triumph to triumph (p. 711).

So the argument of Dibelius and Haenchen is that Luke has taken
what was originally a purely secular narrative, and into it has inserted

idealized material about Paul to show, in the first place, how God's direct action in protecting him fulfilled God's own promise and commission. Once again the mission to the Gentiles is shown as nothing less than the action of God. Then, in the second place, the narrative is adjusted to show Paul as the undaunted hero whose personality is such that even his captors accept him as leader when they are in peril of their lives. The only comment that need be made is the obvious one – a true account would have proved both these points very much better than a fabricated one.

What we have been saying raises very acutely the problem of whether the writer of Acts really knew anything about Paul at all.[10] There are not a few New Testament scholars who feel very strongly that the differences between Acts and the letters of Paul are so wide and far-reaching that the writer of Acts cannot have known Paul at all, and that still less can he have been one of Paul's intimate friends. The case is very strongly put by Kümmel and Haenchen, and we give their arguments in outline.

1.   One of the most curious facts is that only twice (14.4,14) does Acts call Paul an apostle. Acts in fact seems on several occasions deliberately to distinguish between Paul and the apostles, particularly in reference to the events of the Council of Jerusalem (15.2,6,22f.; 16.4). On the other hand, in the letters (I Cor. 9.1f.; 15.9; II Cor. 12.11f.; Rom. 11.13) Paul is insistent on his right to this title.

2.   The attitude of Acts to the law is different from that of the letters. In the letters Paul justifies the abandoning of the law on *internal* grounds. It leads not to God but to sin; it causes a man to put his trust not in God but in his own righteousness; it has served God's purposes, but Christ is the end of the law (Rom. 10.3f.; Gal. 3.19, 21f.). It is the internal effect of the law on a man's soul and being which is its condemnation. On the other hand, Acts simply sees the end of the law in the will of God. But how can Luke prove that the end of the law *is* the will of God? He authenticates the certainty that the law has come to an end by means of the miracles, signs and wonders which accompany the mission without the law.

3.   The Paul of Acts is different from the Paul of the letters. The Paul of Acts is a top-class miracle worker. He blinds Elymas (13.6-12); he cures the cripple of Lystra (14.8-10); he exorcizes demons (16.18); his power is such that even his handkerchiefs have the ability to cure (19.12); the serpent's bite leaves him unharmed (28.3-6); he raises Eutychus from the dead (20.7-12). True, in the letters he claims the signs of an apostle (II Cor. 12.12), but there is nothing nearly so spectacular as all this.

4.   The Paul of Acts is a spell-binding orator. He has only to raise his hand and the mob is still; Jews (13.16-41; 22.1-21), Gentiles (13.9-11), governors (24.10-21; 26.2-26), philosphers (17.22-31), he has

them in the hollow of his hand. But in the letters (II Cor. 10.10) the charge against him is that his speaking powers are of no account.

5.   The theology of the Paul of the letters is different from that of the Paul of Acts. The presupposition of Paul's preaching, as he sets it out in his letters, is that all men sin (Rom. 3.23; 1.19-21; 2.14f.). They have lost the divine glory; they cannot save themselves; only Jesus Christ makes salvation possible for him who has faith (Rom. 1.22-5; 2.17-24; 3.21f., 25; 9.31f.; II Cor. 5.18-21; Gal. 4.4f.). But in the Areopagus speech (Acts 17.22-31) men are the offspring of God, not far from him, able to seek for him, and the role of the risen Christ is that of judge rather than saviour. Here is Stoicism rather than Paulinism.

6.   At the very centre of Paul's theology is the conviction that only the death of Christ on the cross brings the forgiveness of sins (Rom. 3.24-6; 5.6-11; I Cor. 1.18-25; 15.3; II Cor. 5.18-21; Gal. 3.13). But in Acts the atoning power of the cross receives only one passing mention (20.28).

The conclusion drawn by Kümmel, Haenchen and many others is that whoever wrote Acts did not know Paul, still less understand him.

There are few who would claim that Luke is a good Paulinist, but there are still at least some who do not think it totally impossible that he had known and worked with Paul. It is perfectly possible for a man to live and work with a teacher and yet to remain either untouched by, or uncomprehending of, his teaching. Goodspeed quotes an instance of this in his *Introduction to the NT* (p. 203):

> A great Old Testament scholar in his teaching constantly and characteristically used the phrase 'idealized history'. But his leading pupil and successor never used that expression; his pupils never heard it or heard of it. Some might argue that the younger man could never have known the older, much less have been his disciple. But as a matter of fact he studied under him, occupied his study with him for years as his literary secretary, became his colleague and assistant, and finally his successor. If this can happen in the twentieth century, why should it not happen in the first?

Harnack cited what is perhaps an even better example (*Acts*, p. 293):

> No one denies that Xenophon knew Socrates because his *Memorabilia* is such a defective work, and betrays so little of the spirit of the great thinker; or that Plato knew Socrates because in the Dialogues he has drawn his portrait with such freedom. We need not deny that Eusebius wrote the *Life of Constantine* because it contains about the Emperor much that is of questionable authority.

The truth is that there are critics who approach the New Testament in an extremely unimaginative way. They demand of the New Testament writers an inhuman or superhuman accuracy, and an incredible consistency. This is specially so when we remember that Paul was not writing treatises but letters. As Goodspeed well points out in connection with the passage which we have just quoted, Paul himself could be a bad Paulinist. In Galatians (3.28) he can insist that there is no difference between male and female in the church of Christ, while in I Corinthians (14.33-6) he can severely limit the share of the woman in public worship. In I Corinthians 7 he can view marriage very much as a second-best, while in Ephesians (5.21-33) he can liken the relationship of Christ and the church to the relationship of husband and wife. Anyone who has lectured and taught knows well how little may be understood and how much may be misunderstood. It might well appear to Paul very important to be called an apostle, while Luke did not believe that it really mattered at all. A Gentile would never have the same idea of the law as a Jew. Men may differ widely in their views of what man is. One man may be uplifted with the glory of the risen Christ and his eternal presence while another kneels in gratitude before the cross. Anyone who has experienced what happens in life by way of shifting emphases and half-understandings, anyone who is prepared to use his imagination, anyone who does not expect human beings to behave like computers, will still be able to believe that the writer of Acts was personally acquainted with Paul, and that he loved him even when he did not understand him.

13

THE SPEECHES IN ACTS

Nowhere is the problem of what Luke is trying to do more acute than in the speeches of Acts. Of the thousand verses of the book the speeches make up three hundred. It is the speeches which give the book its own particular flavour. It is extraordinary how much information about Paul comes to us *via* the speeches. He was born at Tarsus in Cilicia (21.39; 22.3). He was educated in Jerusalem under Gamaliel (22.3). He was a Pharisee as was his father before him (26.5f.). He was a Roman citizen (16.37), and by birth (22.25-9). All this comes out incidentally in the speeches. 'The Acts of the Apostles', wrote Jerome in a letter (53.9) to Paulinus, 'seems, it is true, to present bare history (*nudam historiam*), and to weave the story of the new born church's infancy.' Bare history is exactly what Acts would be without the speeches. Haenchen (p. 212) pays an eloquent tribute to these speeches:

> Let Acts be read in continuity, but omitting the speeches. Then the reader will notice to how great an extent these speeches give the book its intellectual and spiritual weight. Without them Acts would be like a gospel consisting only of miracle stories, without any sayings of Jesus ... In this the greatness of Luke's talent becomes clear, even if we entirely discount such a masterpiece as the sermon on the Areopagus. They are not merely accounts of Christian proclamation, but themselves offer Christian proclamation, and that even though, with the exception of Stephen's speech, they are but speeches 'in miniature', which can be read in two or three minutes. That they nevertheless have the effect of real speeches, not mere outlines, should never cease to waken our astonishment and admiration.

But the great debate is whether or not the speeches in Acts are in any way to be reckoned as reports of what was said, or whether they are to be regarded as symbolic utterances, setting out Christian truth at large rather than on any special occasion, even if they are as a literary form tied to an occasion.[1]

Opinions have differed widely. Hans Conzelmann, writing on 'The Address of Paul on the Areopagus', declares that Luke makes Paul say what is appropriate to the occasion, that 'the speech is the free creation of the author', that 'the speech is not an extract from a missionary address, but a purely literary creation'.[2] But in 1893 Curtius, the great classical scholar, said: 'Whoever disputes the historical value of the account of St. Paul at Athens tears one of the most important pages from the history of the human race.'[3]

R.H. Fuller in his *Critical Introduction to the NT* (pp. 129, 126) has no doubt that the speeches are sub-apostolic theology from the sub-apostolic age and are compositions of Luke. For Jülicher (pp. 443f., 438) the speeches are 'free inventions' of Luke; their 'authenticity is impossible'; and in them Luke has 'put his own thoughts into the mouths' of the apostles. Kümmel (p. 119) holds that 'the speeches of Acts originate with the author'. For Dibelius (*Studies*, p. 165) the speeches are the type of preaching common in Luke's own day; they are examples of how the gospel is to be preached; and the fact that the sermons of Peter and Paul are so alike is the proof that they represent a type of preaching common to all Christians. There is widespread support for the view that the real author of the speeches in Acts is Luke himself.

There have been those, like F.H. Chase, F.F. Bruce and C.S.C. Williams, who have taken a much higher view of the historicity of the speeches. It has been pointed out that the ancient memory was much more retentive than the modern memory. In the days before books were among the commonplaces of life the only way to possess a thing was to remember it. Xenophon in his *Symposium* (3.5) makes Niceratus say: 'My father, wishing me to grow up into a good man, made me learn all the lines of Homer; and now I can repeat the whole of the *Iliad* and *Odyssey* from memory.' There are forty-eight books of Homer and each book runs to about six hundred lines, and yet in that ancient world to memorize it all was no uncommon feat. Further, that ancient world knew a good deal about various kinds of shorthand writing, tachygraphy, speed-writing as it called it. Galen the doctor tells (14.11) how his students took down his lectures in shorthand. Jewish teaching was by constant oral repetition far more than by reading. The East is 'naturally meditative', and sermons would be remembered and discussed. Again, it is to be remembered that the sermons which were preached were not like conversations with single people; they were heard not by one or two people, but by scores and hundreds and even thousands. It is not the memory of one man that is in question; it is the communal memory of the church. The message, especially the part of it which dealt with proof texts, was very soon stereotyped, and would soon be printed on the church's memory. It is argued that there is nothing more easily and more quickly forgotten than a lecture or a sermon. That is only partly true. The Christian sermons were not exercises in abstract theory; they demanded action; and in the doing of what they demanded they would inevitably be remembered. And lastly, a man may forget many a sermon, but he will not readily forget the sermon by which he was converted and by which his life was changed. There were undoubtedly factors in the situation which would make for memory. F.H. Chase accepts the Lucan authorship of Acts, and he writes: 'It is hard to suppose that the Evangelist wrote down his report of Paul's words at Antioch, Lystra, Athens and Miletus without reference to the Apostle himself' (*The Credibility of Acts*, p. 120).

All this is true, but it has to be said that in the ancient world the speech had a special role in the writing of history. Instead of indirectly describing a man's thoughts or motives or the reason for his decisions, the ancient historians put a speech into the man's mouth. In this way they aimed to make their narrative dramatic and vivid. They made the characters speak for themselves, and composed a speech even when there had been no speech. The speeches were designed to show the inner thoughts and motives of the actors; H.J. Cadbury in *The Making of Luke-Acts* (p. 185) says that they were not meant to be historical tradition; they were 'editorial and dramatic comment'. Thus the works of the ancient historians were littered with speeches. Livy's history, says Cadbury, originally had two thousand speeches, of which about four hundred are still extant, and these speeches are highly praised by Quintilian, the master of Roman oratory.[4] One third of the history of Dionysius of Halicarnassus was speeches, as was one fifth of Thucydides. The only part of the *Histories* of Sallust that has survived is the speeches and the letters. The most outstanding characteristic of the ancient historians with the exception, as we shall see, of Polybius was that they scattered speeches throughout their works. The speeches were written with special care; they were the part of the work in which the connoisseurs were most interested. Demosthenes, the great orator, closely studied the speeches of Thucydides, and the speeches of Thucydides came to be regarded as his supreme achievement. Lucian in his essay *On how to Write History* (58) lays down the rule:

> If ever it is necessary to introduce anyone who will deliver an address, see to it that his words are especially appropriate to the character of the speaker, and relevant to the situation; further, that they are as clear as possible. But at such a time you are permitted to play the orator, and to exhibit your rhetorical skill.

The supreme master of the speech was Thucydides and he has left us the principle on which he worked. Thucydides was one of the most serious and one of the greatest of all the historians. In Book I, ch. 22, he tells us of his aim, and of how he aims at accuracy, unlike his predecessors with their entertainment of myths and legends:

> The absence of fable in history will perhaps make it less attractive to hearers; but it will be enough if it is found profitable by those who desire an exact knowledge of the past as a key to the future, which in all human probability will repeat or resemble the past. This work is meant to be a

possession for ever, not the rhetorical triumph of an hour.

Thucydides was not out to write a cheap best-seller. So he writes of the speeches in his *History of the Peloponnesian War*, which happened in his own lifetime:

> As to the various speeches made on the eve of the war, or in its course, I have found it difficult to retain a memory of the precise words which I had heard spoken; and so it was with those who brought me reports. But I have made the persons say what it seemed to me most opportune for them to say in view of each situation; at the same time, I have adhered as closely as possible to the general sense of what was actually said. As to the deeds done in the war, I have not thought myself at liberty to record them on hearsay from the first informant, or on arbitrary conjecture. My account rests either on personal knowledge, or on the closest possible scrutiny of each statement made by others. The process of research was laborious, because conflicting accounts were given by those who had witnessed the several events, as partiality swayed or memory served them.[5]

Clearly, Thucydides was a conscientious historian. But what was he doing? Dionysius of Halicarnassus (*On Thucydides*, 36) praises him because he wrote speeches 'suited to the persons or relevant to the situation'. There are those who think that Thucydides was inventing with a sovereign freedom; but the opinion of A.W. Gomme is far preferable. Gomme believed that, since there was no such thing as a verbatim report, Thucydides had to substitute his own words anyway. But Gomme does not believe that the speeches in Thucydides are 'free compositions', or that 'when he said he was keeping as close as possible to the general sense of the actual speeches, he was saying nothing'.[6] Thucydides unquestionably gave the speeches in his own words, but, if his claim means anything, he stuck as closely as possible to the original meaning.

However, the successors of Thucydides were not nearly so conscientious. Voltaire was to say much later: 'Set speeches are a sort of oratorical lie, which the historian used to allow himself in old times.'[7] There came a time when the speeches became pure invention, and even when, if the historian knew the original speech, he still preferred to make one up. In his *Annals* (11.24) Tacitus gives us the alleged speech of Claudius in the Roman senate on granting the franchise to the provincials of Gallia Comata. But the actual speech is extant on bronze tablets found in Lyons in the sixteenth century,[8] and the speech on the tablets is quite different from that which Tacitus gives. Plutarch (*Otho*, 15) and Tacitus (*Histories*, 2.47) agree closely in their account of the life of Otho but disagree totally in his last speech. Caesar's speech to his soldiers as reported by Dio Cassius (38.36-46) is quite different from Caesar's own account of it in the *Gallic War* (1.40). In the *Jewish War* (1.373-9) and the *Antiquities*

(15.127-46) Josephus tells the same incident from the life of Herod, but puts two quite different speeches into Herod's mouth. Josephus in his *Antiquities* rewrites the story of David and Nathan (7.147-53), and in the story of Joseph he puts long speeches into the mouths of both Joseph and Potiphar's wife (2.45-59). Cadbury (*Beginnings* V, p. 405) speaks of Josephus' misplaced moralizing, his vapid biblical paraphrases and his prosy platitudes. There is no doubt that the invention of speeches became an oratorical vice which haunted ancient history. In the *Jewish War* (5.362-74) we even have the extraordinary invented spectacle of Josephus depicting himself as standing outside the walls of Jerusalem during the siege, within earshot though out of range of weapons, and appealing to the people to surrender by delivering to them a long review of history.

So the later historians were very far from the sober research of Thucydides. They embellished their histories with a multiplicity of speeches, which were designed to do no more than to display their own rhetorical ingenuity and to entertain the reader. Even when the original speeches were available, as, for instance, in the case of Caesar and Claudius, they preferred to use their own compositions, partly, they claimed because the originals were already known, and partly not to interrupt the homogeneity of the style of the whole work. One historian and one only set his face against this whole practice — Polybius. Polybius writes (2.56):

> Surely a historian should not aim at producing speeches which might have been delivered, nor study dramatic propriety in details like the writer of a tragedy; but his function is above all to record with fidelity what was actually said and done, however commonplace it may be. For the purposes of history and drama are not the same.

He rebukes Timaeus, another historian, because in his speeches 'he has not written down the words actually used, nor the real drift of these speeches, but, imagining how they ought to have been expressed, he enumerates all the arguments used, like a schoolboy declaiming on a set theme' (12.25).

In fairness to these speech-using historians two things must be realized. First, there was no question of deception. The author knew what he was doing and the reader knew that he was doing it. The reader never for a moment thought that he was getting the actual words of the alleged speaker. He knew quite well that he was getting the historian's reconstruction or invention. Second, the author in using speeches had certain very definite aims. Dibelius (pp. 139f.) enumerates the things which the author wished to impart. 1. An insight into the total situation. 2. An insight into the historical moment. That insight might not have been known in the actual moment. The insight might well be an understanding that could not have existed at the moment, but which the author now possessed. 3. An insight into the character of the speaker. 4. An insight into the general ideas which explained the whole situation. So Dibelius says that the discussion of the speeches in Acts must not be 'prejudiced by the question of authenticity'. What matters is to find the purpose of the author, and to realize that in Acts the great aim of Luke in making the speeches is 'that the words are to reach the reader as directly as if they had been spoken contemporaneously', because they are needed contemporaneously.

So then we may say that in the speeches there are three ways of approach. 1. We may approach them as verbatim reports of what was said on each occasion. That clearly will not do, if for no other reason than that they are far too short: except for that of Stephen, not one would, as it stands, take much more than three minutes to deliver. 2. We may approach them as the composition and the invention of the author and we may concentrate entirely on finding out his purpose in inserting them. 3. We may approach them, as we have a right to approach the speeches in Thucydides, well aware that they are not verbatim reports, but none the less fairly confident that there is in them the substance of what was said.

H.J. Cadbury in his essay on the speeches (*Beginnings* V, p. 403) lists the main ones as follows:

By Peter

(i)	To the other disciples concerning a successor to Judas (1.16-22)
(ii)	To the crowd at Pentecost (2.14-36)
(iii)	To the crowd in Solomon's porch (3.12-26)
(iv)	To the Sanhedrin (4.8-12)
(v)	With the apostles to the Sanhedrin (5.29-32)
(vi)	To Cornelius and others (10.34-43)
(vii)	Report at Jerusalem (11.5-17)
(viii)	Advice at the council (15.7-11)

By James

(i)	Advice at the council (15.14-21)
(ii)	Advice to Paul with the elders (21.20-25)

By Stephen

(i)	The martyr's last defence (7.2-53)

By Paul

(i)	In the synagogue at Antioch in Pisidia (13.16-41)
(ii)	At Lystra (14.15-17)
(iii)	At Athens (17.22-31)

By non-Christians

(i) Let us begin by asking why certain scholars regard the speeches as the compositions of Luke, rather than reports of what was said.

(*a*) There is the general fact, as we have seen, that historians did, as it were, supply their own speeches.

(*b*) In general, the occasion of the speeches was not such that any record would be taken or kept. No one takes a shorthand note of events in the middle of a happening like Pentecost. No one makes a record of what is said in the middle of a riot. Who of the Christians was there to hear Gamaliel's speech in the Sanhedrin? Who of the Christians was with him when Paul made his speech at Athens? At best we have memory and recollection, not record.

(*c*) It is a fact that the style of the speeches remains always the same. No matter who is speaking, Peter, or James, or Paul, there is one style, and that style is the style of Luke. Whatever be true of the *substances* of the speeches, the *form* is the form of Luke.

(*d*) The speeches interlock and are interdependent. Psalm 16.8-11, which says that God will not allow his Holy One to see corruption, is used in Peter's speech in Acts 2, and again in Paul's speech in Acts 13. Cadbury (p. 407) points out that the use in Acts 13 cannot be understood without the use in Acts 2. It is assumed that the person who is reading Acts 13 has read Acts 2. The speeches are, so to speak, composed by some one who knows what is in all of them.

(*e*) The pattern of the speeches is the same. We shall very shortly look at what that pattern was; but at the moment we may note that no matter who is speaking, and no matter where he is speaking, the basic pattern is the same.

(*f*) The technique is the same. The same features constantly reappear. Dibelius draws attention to the technique of sudden interruption (p. 178). The crowd break in at Pentecost (2.47). Stephen is suddenly interrupted (7.54). The Jerusalem crowd will listen no more to Paul (22.22). It is as if the speaker had to be switched off once the point had been made.

(ii) Let us, then, for the moment make the assumption that the speeches are the composition of the writer of Acts, and, on that assumption, let us try to see his purpose in composing and inserting them.

(a) Let us begin with Stephen's speech, as Dibelius interprets it (pp. 167-70). In the first place, on Dibelius' view, the speech of Stephen is an insertion into a straightforward martyrdom story. The text originally proceeded straight from 6.15 to 7.55f. The content of the speech is quite irrelevant to the martyrdom. What it gives us is an insight into what happens when the world and thought of Hellenistic Judaism enter Christianity. The weapons to attack Judaism are taken from 'the arsenal of Hellenistic Judaism'. The speech is the introduction to the conflict between Christianity and Judaism, and the prelude to the Gentile mission.

(b) Dibelius (pp. 161-65) also considers the Cornelius story with its speeches. Acts very specially stresses the importance of this story. There is in turn the divine vision (10.9-16), the justification of the action after the return to Jerusalem (11.1-18), and the reference back to the episode at the Council of Jerusalem (15.7,14). The purpose of this story is to validate the Gentile mission and to attach it to no less a name than Peter, the chief of the apostles.

(c) Next there is the speech at Athens (Acts 17.22-31; Dibelius, pp. 15-24). Why Athens? Why not Philippi or Corinth? The work of Paul in Athens was not even successful. Athens itself was never important in the Gentile mission. But Athens was the beating heart of the spiritual life of Greece. It was the city which 'epitomized the spirit of Greece'. It was the centre of Hellenistic piety and Greek wisdom. And, as Dibelius sees it, the speech which Paul made was much more closely connected with Hellenistic philosophy than it was with Pauline theology. The Acts speech is inserted as a typical exposition of Christianity to the Hellenistic cultured world.

(d) Lastly, let us look at the speech of Paul on the steps of the tower of Antonia after he had been rescued by the tribune (22.1-21). Now Paul has been charged by the mob with bringing Gentiles into the inner courts of the temple (21.27-36). But the extraordinary thing about Paul's speech, as Dibelius sees it, is that there is not one single word about the charge. It has nothing whatever to do with the immediate situation. It is in fact a justification of the call to the Gentile mission and a definite statement that it came in the temple (22.17-21). The point is that the call to the Gentiles came from the God of the temple and in the temple. The God of the holy place is also the God of the Gentiles.

Here, then, is the view of Dibelius. The speeches of Acts have little or nothing to do with the immediate situation. The speech of Stephen is Hellenistic Judaism discovering Christianity; the speeches in the Cornelius event are the divine validation of the Gentile mission, through the agency of Peter. The speech at Athens is the confrontation of Christianity with the essence of Hellenism. The speech of Paul, as he faces the mob, is the claim that the God of the temple is the God of the Gentiles. The speeches are designed 'to reveal the power behind events'.

Such is the case for holding that the speeches in Acts are the composition of the author of the book rather than the words of the characters into the mouth of whom they are inserted. But there is something to be said on the other side.

(i) In the first place, this whole point of view looks at Acts as a Greek rather than a Jewish work.[9] The manufacture of speeches was characteristic of Hellenistic historians, writing for a cultured Hellenistic clientele. True, Josephus does it; but Josephus was writing in Rome for a literary public. True, it is often claimed for Luke that he is the first of the Christian writers to write for a double public, of whom Theophilus represents the cultured class. But it still remains true that Luke was not a professional, literary historian. It must be remembered that Luke was thoroughly Jewish in thought and theology, if not in race, and that indeed the Septuagint was probably the biggest influence on him, and all this makes the invention of the speeches very much less likely. Further, the Jews did preserve words. The Jews always claimed that if by any chance the whole vast oral law had been lost, or if it had been lost after it had been codified and written down in the Mishnah, then any twelve rabbis could have put it together again from memory. Against a background like that the invention of speeches becomes much less likely.

(ii) Because we possess his gospel, we know how Luke treated his sources, because we know that Luke's basis was Mark and Q. And we find that in his gospel Luke is very faithful to his sources. He can improve the language; he can rearrange the material; but he very seldom invents. It is true that there would be nothing with the authority that the works and words of Jesus had. But in view of the way in which Luke treats his sources in his gospel, we would not expect him to go in for invention in any large way. True, he did not possess sources for Acts in the same sense as he possessed sources for his gospel, but traditions and memories must have existed and we would not expect Luke radically to depart from them.

(iii) It has been claimed that the theology of the speeches in Luke is so primitive that they must come from an early date.[10] Let us briefly set out what that theology says.

1. Basic to it is the conviction that history is a preparation for the coming of Jesus Christ, whether the history be the events of the

history of Israel or the search for God among the Gentiles.

2. During this long time of preparation God was not detached from the situation. He was not far away (17.27f.); he was active in the unfolding of history (13.16-23; 17.26); he was all the time caring and providing for men in the processes of history (14.17).

3. In Jesus God acted decisively. With Jesus a new element, a new confrontation, entered into history. Life cannot be the same again. Man has been confronted with an act of God which he must accept or reject (14.16; 17.30).

4. This offer was rejected by the Jews, and the result was that Jesus was tried, crucified, put to death and buried (2.23; 3.13-15; 4.10; 5.30; 13.27-29).

5. This rejection, while being the supreme crime in history, was within the plan and the design of God (2.33; 3.18; 4.28; 13.29). Another way to put this is to say that everything that happened to Jesus, his death and his resurrection alike, is foretold in prophecy (2.16-21,25-28,34f.; 13.33-41, 47).

6. The death of Jesus is not the end. After the death there came the resurrection, which was foretold in scripture and of which the apostles are witnesses (2.24-32; 3.15; 4.10f.; 5.31; 13.31; 13.34-37).

7. The resurrection of Jesus has exalted Jesus and has given him the right of judgment. It is true that the message of Jesus is a message of salvation and of love, but the neglect of it involves judgment; Jesus is at one and the same time Saviour and Judge. Therefore the summons is to repent and to receive the Spirit; but with the summons and the promise there goes a threat (2.33; 5.31f.; 4.22f.; 13.23,32,38-41).

Here, then, is the basic theology of the speeches of Acts – and the one astonishing omission is that Acts has almost nothing about any connection of the cross and the death of Jesus with the forgiveness of sins. The theology of Acts comes from a time before Christianity was a religion of redemption through the cross. And this does seem very definitely to represent an early stage of Christian thought.

As H.J. Cadbury writes in *The Making of Luke-Acts* (pp. 278-80):

> It is plain that for this writer the resurrection of Jesus is the distinguishing article of faith for the Christian over against the Jew. . . . No New Testament writer more often refers to the resurrection as predicted in Scripture or cites more texts in its support than does Luke. . . . The resurrection is therefore the significant thing about Jesus. His death is only the prelude.

It is in point of fact the Christology of these speeches in Acts which is the best proof of their primitive character. There are three points to note about their Christology.

First, there is in Peter's Pentecost speech one indication of an adoptionist Christology: 'Jesus of Nazareth, a man attested to you by God with mighty works and wonders and signs which God did through him in your midst' (2.22). 'Jesus' – the human name; 'Nazareth' – the local place; 'a man', *aner*, a male individual creature, not simply *anthropos*, a human being; 'attested' – demonstrated, proved to be. This ties up with the variant reading in Luke 3.22, the concluding sentence of Luke's baptism narrative. The normally accepted reading is: 'Thou art my beloved Son; with thee I am well pleased.' But there is also the reading: 'Thou art my beloved Son; today I have begotten thee.' The second reading could well mean that at his baptism Jesus was *adopted* into the purposes of God. Acts 10.38, which speaks of the baptism and then speaks of Jesus being anointed by God with the Holy Spirit and with power, has a tinge of the same Christology. This is an early Christology, thought of before the problem of the relationship of Jesus to God had fully emerged.

Secondly, the Christology of the speeches is very much a Jewish Christology. The word 'Christ' has not yet become a proper name; it is 'the Christ', the Messiah; and much of the thrust of popular preaching was designed to prove this. So preaching is concerned to prove that Jesus is the Christ, or that the Christ is Jesus (9.22; 17.3; 18.5,28). Again on four occasions in Acts (3.13,26; 4.27,30) Jesus is described by the term *pais theou*, which can mean either the 'child' of the 'servant' of God. A modern parallel is the way in which the word 'boy' can mean either 'son' or a servant such as a waiter. Now in the Old Testament this word *pais* – *ebedh* in Hebrew – can be used of the great men of God – Abraham (Ps. 105.6); Moses (Joshua 1.1); David (Ps. 89.3); Job (1.1). Also, it is the word used for the servant in Isaiah (41.8; 42.1; 44.1,21; 52.13). Here, then, there are two decidedly Old Testament expressions of who Jesus was.

Thirdly, in the Christology of Acts we find in addition to the adoptionist strain and the Jewish strain, a line of thought in which the cross is not strongly connected with the forgiveness of sin, an area of thought in which Jesus as the Word and the cosmic Christ have just not appeared. This can come from one of three reasons. It can come from an astonishingly accurate reconstruction of primitive thought, a reconstruction which Cadbury in *The Making of Luke-Acts* (p. 281) calls 'a triumph of archaeology', and in *Beginnings* (p. 416) calls 'an archaeological *tour de force* which was wellnigh impossible'. It can come from the fact that Luke himself held that theology and naturally wrote it in. It can come from the fact that the speeches were written, certainly not as verbatim reports, but with good knowledge of what was said. Cadbury's final verdict (*Beginnings*, p. 427) is:

Even though devoid of historical basis in genuine tradition the speeches in Acts have nevertheless considerable historical value ... Probably these addresses give us a better idea of the early Church than if Luke had striven for realism, better than if, baffled by the want of genuine tradition, he had forgone all effort at portrayal of the apostles' preaching. They indicate at least what seemed to a well-informed Christian of the next generation the main outline of the Christian message as first presented by Jesus' followers in Palestine and in the cities of the Mediterranean world. They attest the simple theological outlook conceived to have been original by at least one Christian of the obscure period at which Acts was written.

That is the minimum that can be said, and we ourselves believe that it is possible to say more.

14

THE SOURCES OF ACTS

Before we end our study of Acts we must look at the sources from which Luke drew his material.[1] We may well begin with the quotation from Foakes Jackson's commentary (p. xv) with which F.F. Bruce begins his section on the sources of Acts: 'We should constantly remember that source-criticism in the New Testament is largely guesswork.' We shall not be long until we see how true this is.

(i) In the matter of sources Acts naturally divides into two sections, the first section being the first fifteen chapters, and the second section continuing from chapter 16 to the end of the book. We therefore begin by looking at the sources of the first fifteen chapters; and in regard to them we begin with what may be called general sources.

(a) E.J. Goodspeed in his *Introduction to the NT* (pp. 197f.) has a most interesting section on Luke's sources. A great writer, says Goodspeed, does not gather material for a particular purpose in the first instance. He simply collects material, not knowing what he is going to do with it. Then the day and the situation come when he desires to embark on some project and the material is there. 'Such minds are like magnets; they constantly draw to themselves and retain things they see the value of, long before they see how best they can use them.' That is the way the Greeks learned to write history. They wandered to Babylon, to Egypt, to the East; they saw the sights and listened to the priests tell of the ancient glories. It all lodged in their minds and they came home to tell the stories. This is how the man writes who has insight to see and a public to read. So Luke travelled with Paul to Palestine and remained there two years with him. Then he went with Paul to Rome, when Paul went to be tried.

All the time he was seeing and noting and remembering – the preaching he used, stories of Peter, Stephen, Philip, Paul. Then when the time and the call came to write, he had his written sources (Mark and Q), he had his memories, the stories gathered in Palestine thirty years before, his own knowledge of Paul and his travels. Here was his raw material. Given that the Lucan authorship of Acts is accepted, this is an attractive and convincing picture. Luke wrote as the born writer will write.

Still thinking of the generalized sources, there are two sources which would be available to any investigator. Round all the great heroic Christian characters there would gather sagas of stories. There would be the Acts of Peter, Paul, John, Philip, Stephen. Tales about each one of them would be handed down. Again, each Christian centre would have its memories, and perhaps even its records. We can see this happening in Acts. Jerusalem has its stories, and Caesarea and 'Samaria and Antioch and Damascus. For anyone prepared to travel and to question and to listen there was a vast untapped reservoir of information.

(b) Going beyond these general considerations, many scholars have attempted an increasingly detailed analysis of sources. A most convenient and lucid account of many of these theories is given by C.S.C. Williams. Torrey saw one Aramaic source document which underlay Acts 1-15. He based his argument on the conviction that there are certain difficult Greek expressions in these chapters, which can be most simply explained as mistranslations of the Aramaic. The one fact which seems to militate against that suggestion is that throughout this section the Old Testament quotations are from the Septuagint; on occasion (as in 15.16-18) the point of a quotation (in that case Amos 9.11f.) comes from the Septuagint and not from the Hebrew at all (see pp. 274f. above). If that is so, the background of this section is Greek rather than Aramaic.

F.C. Burkitt saw in Acts 1-15 a revision by Luke of an original document by Mark, which included Mark's gospel, the lost ending to that gospel, and an account of the primitive church.

Torrey and Burkitt see, therefore, one source behind Acts 1-15. But there are far more complicated methods of analysis. Harnack (*Acts*, chs. V and VI) began from the fact that this section appears to contain doublets. There are two accounts of the coming of the Spirit (ch. 2; 4.23-31). There are two accounts of the arrest of the disciples· and their appearance before the Sanhedrin (4.1-22; 7.17-42). (Jeremias[2] holds that the last two passages do not constitute a doublet, but represent a Jewish legal process. A warning had to be given, and that is what happened in the first passage. Only if the warning is disregarded will action be taken, and that is what happened in the second passage.) Harnack, beginning from the idea of doublets, distinguishes four sources. There is source A which is a good and valuable source, and which contains 3.1-5,16; 8.5-40; 9.31-11.18; 12.25-15.35. There is source B which is an unhistorical, legendary and worthless source, and which contains ch. 2 and 5.17-42. There is a Jerusalem-Antiochene source which contains 6.1-8.4, a highly valuable section which may go back to Silas; 11.19-30; 12.1-23. And there is a separate and independent source which contains 9.1-30.

Harnack's is a comparatively simple analysis, but C.S.C. Williams quotes the highly complicated analysis of Cerfaux. 1.1-14 comes from a Galilaean traditional source; 1.15-2.40 is source C[1], which is a written Caesarean source; 2.41-5.40 is source D, which consists of descriptive documents and has well-marked characteristics; 5.41-8.1a is source E^2, which is a Hellenistic dossier; source E is highly composite and supplements C; 8.1b-40 is source C^2, and, with the exception of 8.14-25, which is the work of a redactor, consists of notes collected by Luke at Caesarea; 9.1-30 is source C^3, and is Caesarean oral tradition; 9.31-11.18, except 11.1-18, which is the work of a redactor, is source C^4, and is a documentary source; 11.19-30 is source E^1, another Hellenistic dossier; 12.1-23 is source C^5, and is an oral source. This is a much more complicated analysis.

C.S.C. Williams also quotes the analysis of Sahlin. Sahlin sees three stages in Luke-Acts. Stage one is a written account of the work of Jesus and of the early church. The first part was in Hebrew, and underlies Luke 1.5-3.7a; the second part, Luke 3.7b-Acts 15, was originally in Aramaic. The author is a Jewish Christian writing perhaps in Antioch about AD 50. In the second stage a Greek Christian, very likely Luke himself, wishing to defend Paul on trial, revised and adapted the earlier work. He added Luke 1.1-4, a narrative of the work of Paul, and many intervening paragraphs. In stage three Luke-Acts, having been thus built up, is divided into two by adding an end to the third gospel and a beginning to Acts.

These, then, are specimens of the suggestions regarding the sources of Acts, and by and large the more complicated they are, the less probable they seem.

(c) Lastly, in regard to Acts 1-15 we must look at Haenchen's method (pp. 81-90) of reconstructing its sources. Haenchen's is a very great commentary, but in this matter Haenchen must be read with the greatest care, for he has a misleading habit of stating as fact that which is highly speculative and conjectural. We take his treatment of Acts 7.1-8.3, the Stephen story and the part of Paul in it. The Stephen story Luke found among his sources. But Luke's sources also depict Paul as the great persecutor, and, for Luke, to persecute the church means to persecute the Jerusalem church. So into the Stephen story Luke inserts Paul. 'And the witnesses laid down their garments at the feet of a young man called Saul' (7.58b). The insertion of Paul is entirely due to Luke. 'In this way,' says Haenchen (p. 82), 'Paul is drawn into the sombre affair; the martyrdom of Stephen did not mention Paul at all.' Paul's part is further underlined in 8.1; 'And Saul was consenting to his death.' But this is not enough. The old source knew only the one martyrdom, that of Stephen; but Luke thinks in terms of persecution, and so we read in 8.3: 'But Saul laid waste the church, and entering house after house, he dragged off men and women and committed them to prison.' 'He (Luke) suddenly turns the approving onlooker Saul into the only persecutor who is named.' Still further, Saul is made to extend his persecutions to Damascus (9.2), but Haenchen (pp. 320f.) holds that the letters which Paul received from the high priest to make his persecution official could not have existed, because the high priest possessed no such right in regard to Jews outside Jerusalem. Now in a passage of I Maccabees (15.15-21) there is a Roman rescript which quite definitely does give the Jews this right of extradition; but Haenchen, following Wellhausen, declares that I Maccabees passage to be a later interpolation. What Haenchen is really saying here is that one of Luke's main sources was in fact his own preconception of what the situation must have been, and that he rewrites history for his own purposes. To say that all this *may* be so is perfectly legitimate, even if highly arguable; to say that it *is* so is entirely misleading. Such a rewriting of history is less than likely, and would only be possible if Acts is regarded as very late.

(ii) When we turn to the second half of Acts the position is very different. In the first half it is probably true that there was no consistent source on which Luke could draw. From Acts 16 onwards we encounter a most interesting phenomenon. Sometimes the narrative proceeds in the third person – 'they did this, they did that'; and at other times the narrative proceeds in the first person – 'we did this, we did that'. The passages in which the first person is used are commonly called the 'we-sections', and they consist of 16.10-17; 20.5-15; 21.1-18; 27.1-28.16. There has inevitably been a vast amount of discussion on these passages.[3] It is possible that the we-sections begin even earlier. In Acts 11.28 the Western text reads: 'And there was much rejoicing, and when we had been in conversation together, one of them named Agabus stood up . . .' If we accept the fact that Luke is the writer of Acts, and if we accept the tradition, recorded by Eusebius in his *History* (3.4.6) and by Jerome in the preface to his *Commentary on Matthew*, that he was from Antioch, we may well regard the Western reading as very possibly correct, and date Luke's personal entry on the scene as early as the days in Antioch and the first mission.

The question is, what do these passages represent? Where do they come from, and who are 'we'? The older scholarship saw three possible answers to these questions.

(a) We start from the general principle that the passages are extracts from a travel diary, and that they represent occasions when the writer was a participant in the events which he describes. The simplest interpretation of this view is that the diary in question is the diary of the writer of Acts; we may believe that the passages are thus from the diary of Luke himself, and that they are therefore eyewitness accounts. As we shall see, however, modern scholarship would suggest considerable modification of this view.

(b) A second suggestion is that these 'we' sections are extracts made by the writer of Acts from someone else's diary, which came into his possession and was used in his own narrative.

The obvious objection to that theory is, if the author of Acts did this, why did he leave the 'we'? Why did he not integrate the contents of the diary into his own work? And if Luke is the author, then this is well-nigh incredible. Goodspeed writes in his *Introduction to the NT* (p. 201): 'The Luke who used Mark so well would never have been guilty of the absurd blunder of leaving the seventy-seven first persons' in his use of such a document. It is very difficult to think of the writer using some one else's diary as if it was his own, especially when the writer has given proof of the way in which he normally uses his sources by making them his own.

(c) The third suggestion is that the writer of Acts inserted the first-person passages as a deceptive device to make the narrative appear to be that of an eyewitness. There are two objections to that view. First, if a person wished to deceive his readers into believing that his work was an eyewitness account, why should he be so sparing with the use of first-person pronouns? Why use them in so few passages? Why not use them much more consistently? Second, Jülicher, who is no conservative critic, writes in his *Introduction to the NT* (p. 445):

> The we-document ... must come directly from the hand of a travelling-companion of Paul's ... Since its statements are never open to the slightest objection, the idea of looking on the 'we' as a deliberately deceptive fiction of the writer's is one of unusual grotesqueness.

So then we can abandon the idea that the 'we' is written to deceive the reader into thinking the account is that of an eyewitness. Had that been so there would have been far more 'we's', and in any event the material does not read like fiction.

Two things are to be noted. First, from the linguistic point of view it is to all intents and purposes certain that the author of the 'we-sections' and the author of the rest of Acts were the same person. C.S.C. Williams (pp. 5f.) says that there are twenty-one words and phrases found only in the 'we-sections' and in the rest of Acts and nowhere else in the New Testament; there are a further sixteen peculiar to the 'we-sections' and Luke; there are a further twenty-eight words and phrases which occur predominantly in Luke-Acts. On grounds of language and vocabulary the authorship of the 'we-sections' and the rest of Acts is demonstrated to be the same.

Second, there can be little doubt that the 'we-sections' are extracts from a larger work. It is incredible that they could come and go as they do. The first- and third-person sections of the book are interwoven. There is a list in *Beginnings* II, p. 158:

1.	Acts 16.1, first person.	4.	Acts 21.27, third person.
2.	Acts 16.17, third person.	5.	Acts 27.1, first person.
3.	Acts 20.4, first person.	6.	Acts 28.17, third person.

The 'we', Dibelius says (*Studies in Acts*, pp. 104f.), is only introduced to make it clear that Luke did participate in Paul's journeyings. He is modestly pointing out to Theophilus the events in which he had a share. So Dibelius holds that Luke has as his main source an itinerary of the journeys of Paul. The 'we' is simply an indication, he says (p. 136), that on that occasion the writer was present; it is not a special source. Of the itinerary Dibelius says (p. 176n.): 'I am convinced [that it] was not by any means limited to the "we passages".' Dibelius therefore (p. 197) straight away disregards the 'we' as indicating a special source. It is all part of the itinerary. This itinerary recorded the stations on the journey, and that it was merely an itinerary is proved by the way in which insignificant and unimportant stations are mentioned: Attalia (14.25); Samothrace and Neapolis (16.11); Amphipolis and Apollonia (17.1); 20.13-15 reads like a timetable. This itinerary briefly tells of the reception of the apostles, about their hosts, their activities and results, not impossibly with a view to supplying information which would be useful on future journeyings. It was customary for distinguished travellers, princes and generals of the ancient Hellenic world to have their diaries kept by some companion as an aid to memory. The stations of the route, and now and then notable events, were set down.[4] Xenophon's *Anabasis* may well have been founded on such a diary.

Trocmé suggests that the itinerary which Luke had at his disposal was a record in which Paul in his missionary journeys had got an assistant to record the day's events with a few brief notes, or even set pen to paper himself when occasion required. Eventually it was Luke who kept this journal and made use of it when he came to write Acts.[5] However that may be, Dibelius concludes (p. 104) that 'within the framework of Acts 13; 14; 15.36-21.18, we have before us a source of the first order, whether the story is told in the first or the third person.'

Into this itinerary Luke puts his own material: the speeches; the isolated stories – Elymas (13.8-12); the Philippian gaoler (16.25-34); the sons of Scaeva (19.14-16).

We may well accept the Dibelius idea of the itinerary, and, if we do, we will agree that the basic thread which holds the second half of Acts together is a first-class source.

There remains one last problem in Acts, and it is in some ways the most fascinating problem of all. Acts exists in two different texts which differ fairly widely from each other, and the same is true of Luke. There is the text which is usually printed and generally accepted, and which is now usually called the Alexandrian text, and there is the rather different Western text.[6] The main characteristic of the Western text in Acts is the number of additions it makes to the normal text.

Some of its additions are what might be called reverential additions, especially in connection with the name of Jesus. In all the following examples the italicized words are the words added by Codex Bezae.

> Of the men therefore who have companied with us all the time that the Lord Jesus *Christ* went in and out among us (1.21).

> Repent and be baptized, every one of you in the name of the *Lord* Jesus Christ (2.38).

> But he being full of the Holy Spirit looked up stedfastly into heaven, and saw the glory of God and Jesus *the Lord* standing on the right hand of God (7.55).

> God has fulfilled the same to our children in that he raised up the *Lord* Jesus *Christ* (13.34).

Sometimes the phrase *in the name of the Lord Jesus Christ* is added.

> And Stephen full of grace and power wrought great wonders and signs among the people *through the name of the Lord Jesus Christ.* (6.8).

> *And Paul* fastening his eyes upon him, and seeing that he had faith to be saved, said with a loud voice, *I say to you in the name of the Lord Jesus Christ* stand upright on your feet, *and walk* (14.10).

Sometimes references to the Holy Spirit are introduced.

> Peter rose up *in the Spirit* and said . . . (15.7).

> From which if you keep yourselves, you do well, *being sustained by the Holy Spirit* (15.29).

> Judas and Silas, being themselves also prophets, *full of the Holy Spirit* (15.32).

> When a plot was laid against Paul in Greece, '*the Spirit told him* to return through Macedonia' (20.3).

Sometimes additions or changes are made for the sake of correction.

> The next day we touched at Samos *and stayed at Trogyllium* (20.15).

> From Rhodes they sailed to Patara *and Myra* (21.1).

Gaius in the ordinary text is said to come from Derbe; in the Western text he comes from *Doberus* (20.4).

In the second and third of these examples the corrector has been just too clever. He knew that Myra was the normal port at which people trans-shipped; but he either forgot or did not know that as the crow flies it is fifty miles from Rhodes to Myra, much too long for a day's run. The normal text said that Gaius came from Derbe; but in 19.29 we read that two Macedonians, Gaius and Aristarchus, Paul's travelling companions, were hustled into the theatre. The scribe who wrote D assumed that the Gaius of 19.29 and the Gaius of 20.4 were the same person. Derbe is not in Macedonia, but in Macedonia there was a town called Doberus. So the scribe changed *Derbaios*, from Derbe, into *Douberios*, from Doberius. But it is quite clear that in 20.4 the list of delegates goes by places. Sopater, Aristarchus and Secundus are all from Macedonia; Tychicus and Trophimus are from Asia; now Timothy was from Lystra and Derbe was next door to Lystra, Lystra's natural neighbour; and so the natural assumption is that Gaius did come from Derbe, and the scribe was just too clever in attaching him by conjecture to Doberus.

Sometimes the scribe of D seemed to have another source altogether, as, for instance, in his account of the decisions of the Council of Jerusalem.

> We enjoin on them to abstain from the pollutions of idols, and from fornication and from blood, and *whatsoever they would not should be done to them you do not to others* (15.20,29).

Again and again the Western text adds vivid, dramatic and concrete details to the story.

When Simon Magus is rebuked by Peter for his attempt to buy the power to confer the Holy Spirit, we read: '*And he ceased not to shed many tears*' (8.24).

In the story of Cornelius the picture is filled out:

> And as Peter was approaching *Caesarea, one of the servants ran forward and announced that he had arrived. And* Cornelius *sprang up and* met him, and fell down at his feet and worshipped him (10.25).

In the story of Peter's escape from prison, the ordinary text says that the angel 'struck' (*pataxas*) him. D says more vividly that the angel *nudged (nuxās)* him (12.7). And a little later, when the gate had opened to them, 'they went out, *and went down the seven steps*, and passed on through one street' (12.10).

In the scene in the prison at Philippi D adds a commonsense detail:

> And he [the jailer] called for lights, and sprang in, and trembling for fear fell down before the feet of Paul and Silas, and led them out *after securing the rest* (16.30).

And there is another addition later in the story:

> But when it was day, the magistrates *assembled together into the market place and recollecting the earthquake that had happened, they were afraid* (16.35).

When Paul was in Ephesus:

> Then Paul departed from them (the Jews), and separated the disciples, discoursing daily in the school of one Tyrannus *from eleven o'clock in the morning until four in the afternoon* (9.19).

It is said of the Jews with whom Stephen argued: '*Since they were unable therefore to face the truth*, they suborned men . . .' (6.11). The word used for 'to face' is very vivid, *antophthalmein*, which means 'to look in the eyes.'

These are no more than specimens of the kind of thing which is always happening in Codex D in the Western text. More than one suggestion has been made to account for this phenomenon.

Jülicher in his *Introduction to the NT* (pp. 451f.) reports a theory put forward by Blass, that there were two editions of Acts, both from the hand of Luke. Blass suggested that the text which became the Western text represents the first draft; and that the shorter text is 'a terser, clearer and more carefully written copy'. It is further suggested that Luke arrived in Rome, found Mark's gospel, added his own material to it, or added it to his own material. The first draft was claimed by and given to the church of Rome, and then the second more careful draft was prepared for Theophilus.

Torrey (as reported by C.S.C. Williams, p. 50), saw things the other way round. He thought that the shorter text was the earlier text. This shorter text was translated into Aramaic for the use of Jewish Christians with various additions and 'improvements'. And then the Aramaic translation with its additions and improvements was retranslated back into Greek, and the retranslation is the Western text.

On the whole it is much more likely that the short text is the early text, because it is much easier to imagine someone adding new detail to an already existing short text than it is to imagine anyone extracting things from the longer text. There is no doubt sound information in the longer text, but it is the shorter text which we must accept as authoritative.

We have come to the end of our study. But it is only introductory, and it will only have served its purpose if it leads its readers back, with greater understanding, to that most readable of books, the book of Acts itself.

ABBREVIATIONS

ANCL	The Ante-Nicene Library of the Fathers, Edinburgh 1867ff.; reissued Buffalo 1887ff. (English translations of early Christian writers)
AV	Authorized or King James Version of the Bible
ET	English translation
ICC	International Critical Commentary, T. & T. Clark and Scribner
LCL	Loeb Classical Library, London and New York 1912ff. (text and translation of Greek and Latin authors, including Philo, Josephus and some Christian writers)
MNTC	Moffatt New Testament Commentary, Hodder & Stoughton and Harper
NEB	New English Bible
NT	New Testament
P	Papyrus
PG	Patrologia Graeca, ed. J.P. Migne, Paris
PL	Patrologia Latina, ed. J.P. Migne, Paris
RSV	Revised Standard Version of the Bible
SBT	Studies in Biblical Theology, SCM Press and Allenson
TNDT	*Theological Dictionary of the New Testament*, ed. G. Kittel, ET ed. G.W. Bromiley, Eerdmans 1964ff.

NOTES TO VOLUME II

1 JOHN AND HIS GOSPEL

1. See R.H. Charles, *Revelation* (ICC) I, p. 124.

2. Quoted by E.G. Rupp and B. Drewery, *Martin Luther*, Arnold and St Martin's Press 1970, p. 94.

3. R.W. Dale, *The Living Christ and the Four Gospels*, London and New York 1890, pp. 42, 46f.

4. In these passages the word for 'love' is normally *agapan*, but in 20.2 it is *philein*. But most commentators find no distinction of meaning; see pp. 68ff. and ch. 3 n. 16 below.

2 THE ATTACK ON TRADITION

1. J.A.T. Robinson, 'The New Look on the Fourth Gospel', *Twelve New Testament Studies* (SBT 34), 1962, p. 104.

2. See B.F. Westcott on John 19.25 (cf. Matt. 27.56; Mark 15.40).

3. *ton adelphon ton idion*. In classical Greek this would mean 'his own brother'; but in later Greek the word *idios* lost its meaning of 'own', and the phrase could simply mean 'his brother'.

4. Matthew is to be identified with Levi (Matt. 9.9 = Mark 2.14; Luke 5.27); and Levi and James are both called 'sons of Alphaeus' (Mark 2.14; Matt. 10.3).

5. For references see H.B. Swete, *The Apocalypse of St John*, pp. clxxiii f.; R.H. Charles, *Revelation* (ICC), I, pp. xcii f.

6. Tertullian, *On the Prescription of Heretics*, 36; Jerome, *Against Jovinianus*, 1.26; cf. H.B. Workman, *Persecution in the Early Church*, p. 45.

7. The Latin *Acts of John* are translated by M.R. James, *The Apocryphal New Testament*, pp. 257ff.

8. James, op. cit., pp. 228f., summarizes the opening chapters of the *Acts of John*, which survived only in a late Greek manuscript. The older Greek *Acts of John*, chs 18-115, are translated both by James, pp. 229ff., and by E. Hennecke, *New Testament Apocrypha* II, pp. 215ff.

9. Irenaeus, *Against Heresies*, 3.3.4; Eusebius repeats the story twice, in his chapter on Cerinthus (3.28) and in a section on Polycarp, where it is 4.14.6. Epiphanius (*Heresies*, 30.4) tells the same story of 'Ebion', but there was no such person! The Ebionites took their name not from a personal founder, but from the Hebrew word for 'poor'.

10. Irenaeus, *Against Heresies*, 3.11.8, allocates the lion to John, who begins by telling of the leadership of Christ in creation; the ox to Luke, who begins with Zechariah the priest and stresses the priestly character of Jesus; the man to Matthew, who begins with the human genealogy and the human birth of Jesus, and is the gospel of Jesus' humanity; the eagle to Mark, who

begins with the prophetic spirit coming down from on high to men, since right at the beginning there is the prophecy of Isaiah. (For other interpretations, see p. 2 above.)

11. For full discussion of this question see J.H. Bernard's commentary, I, pp. xxxviii-xlv; and his *Studia Sacra*, pp. 260-83; F.C. Burkitt, *The Gospel History and its Transmission*, pp. 251-4; R.H. Charles, *Revelation* I, pp. xlv-1; J. Drummond, *The Character and Authorship of the Fourth Gospel*, pp. 227f.; G.H.C Macgregor's commentary, p. lii; J. Moffatt, *Introduction to the Literature of the NT*, pp. 602-8; H.L. Jackson, *The Problem of the Fourth Gospel*, pp. 142-50; P.W. Schmiedel, *The Johannine Writings*, pp. 177f.; H.B. Swete, *The Apocalypse*, pp. clxxv-vii; H.B. Workman, *Persecution*, pp. 358-61; V.H. Stanton, *The Gospels as Historical Documents* I, pp. 166f.; A.E. Brooke, 'James and John the Sons of Zebedee', *Dictionary of the Apostolic Church* I, pp. 626f.

12. It is worthwhile transcribing the whole of Socrates' chapter about Philip of Sidē (*Ecclesiastical History*, 7.27), so that we may be aware of the value of this source of information on the early martyrdom of John. 'He laboured assiduously in literature, and besides making very considerable literary attainments, formed an extensive collection of books in every branch of knowledge. Affecting the Asiatic style [i.e. a florid, turgid and rhetorical style], he became the author of many treatises, attempting among others a refutation of the Emperor Julian's treatises against Christians, and he compiled a *Christian History*, which he divided into thirty-six books; each of these books occupied several volumes, so that they amounted altogether to nearly one thousand, and the mere argument [summary of contents] of each volume equalled in magnitude the volume itself. This composition he has entitled not an *Ecclesiastical* but a *Christian History*, and has grouped together in it abundance of very heterogeneous materials, wishing to show that he is not ignorant of philosophical and scientific learning: for it contains a medley of geometrical theorems, astronomical speculations, and musical principles, with geographical delineations of islands, mountains, forests, and various other matters of little moment. By forcing such irrelevant details into connection with his subject, he has rendered his work a very loose production, useless alike, in my opinion, to the ignorant and the learned; for the illiterate are incapable of appreciating the loftiness of his diction, and such as are really competent to form a just estimate condemn his wearisome tautology. But let everyone exercise his own judgment concerning these books according to his taste. All I have to add is that he has confounded the chronological order of the transactions he describes; for after having related what took place in the reign of the Emperor Theodosius, he immediately goes back to the times of the bishop Athanasius; and this sort of thing he does frequently.' The translation is by A.C. Zenos in *A Select Library of the Nicene and Post-Nicene Fathers of the Christian Church*, Series 2, vol. 2, Oxford and New York 1891.

13. Gregory of Nyssa, *Panegyric on St Basil*, Migne, PG 46, 789A; *In Praise of St Stephen*, Migne, PG 46, 725C.

14. Archigenes and Posidonius quoted by Aetius, 6.3.

15. Latin in Wordsworth and White, *Novum Testamentum Latine* I, p. 490; translation from J.H. Bernard, *St John* (ICC), p. lviii.

16. These suggestions are collected by H.L. Jackson, *The Problem of the Fourth Gospel*, p. 27 n. 2; the references are to E.I. Robson, *Journal of Theological Studies* 14, 1913, pp. 440f. (a note on Eusebius 3.39); M. Krenkel, *Der Apostel Johannes*, Berlin 1871, p. 142; W. Larfeld, *Die beiden Johannes von Ephesus*, Munich 1914, p. 184.

17. The Papias fragments are very conveniently assembled in J.B. Lightfoot's one-volume edition of *The Apostolic Fathers*, pp. 513-35.

18. *The Martyrdom of Polycarp* is given in Lightfoot, op. cit., pp. 185-211; it is also reproduced by Eusebius in the *Ecclesiastical History* (4.15.3-45); see also H.B. Workman, *Persecution in the Early Church*, pp. 306-10.

19. C.F. Burney, *The Aramaic Origin of the Fourth Gospel*, p. 141, quoted by G.H.C. Macgregor, *John* (MNTC), pp. lviii f.

20. *en tē protē hēmōn hēlikia* (Irenaeus, *Against Heresies*, 3.3.4). On this phrase and the whole question see V.H. Stanton, *The Gospels as Historical Documents* I, pp. 215-7.

3   THE BELOVED DISCIPLE

1. See the elaboration of the idea in *Acts of John*, 89. So firmly established is the description that in later Greek Christian writers John is described by the adjective *epistēthios*. *Epi* means 'on'; *stēthos* means 'breast'; *epistēthios* means a bosom friend. Cf. Eusebius of Alexandria, *Sermon* 19; John of Damascus, *On Sacred Images*, 1.19; and the eleventh-century passion play later ascribed to Gregory Nazianzen, *Christus Patiens*, 187.

2. H.V. Morton, *In the Steps of the Master*, London and New York 1934, p. 219.

3. P. Schmiedel, 'Nathanael', *Encyclopaedia Biblica* III, col. 3339.

4. J.H. Scholten, *Der Apostel Johannes in Kleinasien*, Berlin 1872, p. 110.

5. See the commentaries of J.H. Bernard, I, pp. xxxiv-vii; G.H.C Macgregor, pp. xliv-viii; also B.W. Bacon, *Research and Debate*, pp. 301-31; H.L. Jackson, *Problem*, pp. 151-70.

6. E.A. Abbott, *The Fourfold Gospel* V: *The Founding of the New Kingdom*, London and New York 1917, p. 531.

7. Judas Iscariot: L. Noack, *Die Geschichte Jesus*, 2nd ed., Strassburg 1876; see H.L. Jackson, *Problem*, pp. 164f.

8. E.g. A. Wright, *Journal of Theological Studies* 18, 1917, pp. 32f.; V. Taylor, *The Gospel according to St Mark*, pp. 534f.; H.B. Swete, *The Gospel according to St Mark*, p. 307.

9. Matthias (see Acts 1.23-5): E.L. Titus, 'The Identity of the Beloved Disciple', *Journal of Biblical Literature* 69, 1950, pp. 323ff.

10. Only Mark (10.21) says that Jesus loved the man; only Matthew (19.22) mentions his youth; only Luke (18.18) calls him a ruler.

11. By E.G. King, *The Interpreter* 5, January 1909, pp. 167ff.; see Jackson, op. cit., pp. 166f.

12. H.B. Swete, *Journal of Theological Studies*, 17, 1916, p. 374.

13. See also W. Sanday, *The Criticism of the Fourth Gospel*, pp. 99-101; V.H. Stanton, *The Gospels as Historical Documents* III, pp. 9f.; C.F. Nolloth, *The Fourth Evangelist*, pp. 92f. The originator of the theory was

Hugo Delff, *Die Geschichte des Rabbi Jesus von Nazareth*, Leipzig 1889; *Das vierte Evangelium wiederhergestellte*, Husum 1890; *Neue Beiträge sur Kritik und Erklärung des vierten Evangeliums*, Husum 1890.

14. W. Bousset, *Die Offenbarung Johannis*, Göttingen 1906, pp. 45f.

15. Lazarus: W.K. Guthrie, *The Guardian*, 19 Dec. 1906; F.V. Filson, 'Who was the Beloved Disciple?', *Journal of Biblical Literature* 68, 1949, pp. 83ff.

16. E. Hoskyns and F.N. Davey, pp. 557f. say that whatever may be true of the words outside the New Testament 'in it they are synonymous'. C.K. Barrett, p. 486, says: 'The usage of these words throughout the gospel makes it impossible to doubt that they are synonyms.' R. Bultmann, p. 711, says that the change from one word to the other 'cannot be significant'.

17. Aelian, *Varia Historia*, 9.4.

18. We list here the main discussions of John 1.14 from which we have drawn our material: the commentaries of B.F. Westcott, pp. xv and 12; J.H. Bernard, I, pp. 21f.; G.H.C. Macgregor, p. 18; C.K. Barrett, p. 138; E. Hoskyns and F.N. Davey, p. 149; R. Bultmann, pp. 67-9; and V.H. Stanton, *Historical Documents*, III, 140-3; J. Drummond, *Character and Authorship*, p. 338; H.L. Jackson, *The Problem . . .*, pp. 33f.; W. Sanday, *Criticism*, p. 77.

19. Matt. 6.1; 11.7; 22.11; 23.5; Luke 5.27; 7.24; 23.55; John 1.32,38; 4.35; 6.5; 11.45; Acts 1.11; 21.27; 22.9; Rom. 15.24; I John 1.1; 4.12,14; Mark 16.11,14.

20. On John 19.35 see the commentaries of B.F. Westcott, pp. 25-7; J.H. Bernard, II, pp. 649f.; G.H.C. Macgregor, p. 351; E. Hoskyns and F.N. Davey, p. 535; C.K. Barrett, p. 543; J.N. Sanders, pp. 412f.; R. Bultmann, pp. 678f.; also W. Sanday, *Criticism*, pp. 77f.; V.H. Stanton, *Historical Documents* III, pp. 139f.; H.L. Jackson, *Problem*, pp. 34f.; B.W. Bacon, *Research and Debate*, p. 192; J. Drummond, *Character and Authorship*, pp. 388-93; W.G. Kümmel, *Introduction to the NT*, pp. 165f.

21. C.C. Torrey, *Our Translated Gospels*, New York 1936, London 1937, pp. 50, 52f.

22. C.C. Torrey, *The Four Gospels; a New Translation*, New York and London 1934, p. 229.

23. On John 21.24 see the commentaries of B.F. Westcott, pp. xxvii f., 299; J.H. Bernard, II, pp. 687-92; G.H.C. Macgregor, pp. 369f.; E. Hoskyns and F.N. Davey, pp. 554f., 561f.; C.K. Barrett, pp. 479f., 489f.; J.N. Sanders, pp. 47f., 411; R. Bultmann, 700-06, 717f.; and J.B. Lightfoot, *Biblical Essays*, pp. 194-7; W. Sanday, *Criticism*, pp. 63f., 80-82; B.W. Bacon, *Research and Debate*, pp. 191-225; H.L. Jackson, *Problem*, pp. 35-39; V.H. Stanton, Historical Documents III, pp. 17-32; C.F. Nolloth, *The Fourth Evangelist*, pp. 31-6, 430; J. Moffatt, *Introduction to the Literature of the NT*, pp. 570-7; B.H. Streeter, *The Four Gospels*, pp. 465-81; W.G. Kümmel, *Introduction to the NT*, pp. 147-9, 166f.

24. *Gospel of Peter* 58-60, translation from M.R. James, *The Apocryphal NT*, pp. 93f. (also in E. Hennecke, *NT Apocrypha* I, p. 187).

25. A. Loisy, *Les évangiles synoptiques* I, 1907, pp. 444f., quoted by J. Moffatt, *Introduction to the Literature of the NT*, p. 573.

26. On the connection with Peter see B.W. Bacon, *Research and Debate*,

pp. 302f.; W.G. Kümmel, *Introduction to the NT*, p. 165; A. Jülicher, *Introduction to the NT*, p. 412; the commentaries of C.K. Barrett, p. 480; J.H. Bernard, II, 691f.; E. Hoskyns and F.N. Davey, p. 556; G.H.C Macgregor, p. 368; and V.H. Stanton, *Historical Documents* III, pp. 24f.

27. On John 21.20-23 see the commentaries of B.F. Westcott, pp. 299, 305; J.H. Bernard, II, p. 692; G.H.C. Macgregor, pp. 375-7; C.K. Barrett, p. 488; E. Hoskyns and F.N. Davey, p. 559; J.N. Sanders, pp. 440f., 457; R. Bultmann, pp. 715f.; and J. Drummond, *Character and Authorship*, pp. 386f.; V.H. Stanton, *Historical Documents* III, p. 20.

28. On John 21.24 see the commentaries of B.F. Westcott, p. 306; J.H. Bernard, II, pp. 712f.; G.H.C. Macgregor, p. 377; E. Hoskyns and F.N. Davey, pp. 559-61; C.K. Barrett, p. 489; J.N. Sanders, pp. 47f., 457; and V.H. Stanton, *Historical Documents* III, pp. 132-4; B.W. Bacon, *Research and Debate*, p. 305.

29. There have been many elaborate theories of additions to the gospel. This is perhaps a suitable point to give some examples of these theories. W.F. Howard summarizes a number of them in an Appendix to *The Fourth Gospel in Recent Criticism*, pp. 297-302. B.W. Bacon, for example, suggested that the following passages were all added to the original gospel: 1.6-8,15; 2.1-12,13-25; 3.31-6; 4.43-5, 46b, 54; 5.28f.; 6.39b, 40b, 44b, 54b; 7.1,14, 37-9; 10.7, 8b, 9, 22f.; 12.29f., 33, 42f., 44-50; 13.16, 20, 36-8; 18.9,14-18, 24-7; 19.34f., 37; 20.24-9; 21; 7.53-8.12; 12.8; 21.25 (*Research and Debate*, pp. 472-527). See also C.K. Barrett, p. 19.

R.M. Grant, *A Historical Introduction to the NT*, pp. 156-8, conveniently collects all Bultmann's contributions on this matter of redaction. Bultmann first of all removes 'late glosses', which are often indicated by their omission from some manuscripts – 7.53-8.11; 5.4; 6.23, 'after the Lord had given thanks'; 13.10, 'except for their feet'; 14.30, 'many things'; 16.16, 'because I go to the Father'. He then wishes to excise phrases 'which break the continuity of thought or produce confusion in a sentence' – 2.15, 'with the sheep and the oxen'; 4.1, 'the Lord knew that'; 4.11, 'you have no dipper and the well is deep' (too obvious to say!); 21.20, 'following him' and 'who had lain ... betray you'.

Then there must be removed items which were added in order to make the gospel conform to late first-century sacramental views or to synoptic eschatology or history: ch. 21; 1.6-8, 15, verses which interrupt the poetry of the prologue; synoptic sayings which have been inserted: 1.22-5; 1.32; 7.20f.; 3.24. He would also remove 4.2, which contradicts 3.22, and 18.9,32 as examples of 'mechanical fulfilment'.

Then there must be removed passages which try to relate the gospel to the church's sacramental teaching – 6.51b-58 is added to correlate the bread of life with the eucharist; 19.34b,35 is added to show that both baptism and the eucharist were established by the death of Jesus; in 3.5 the word 'water' is added; it is irrelevant since the passage is about the Spirit. John, as we have seen, had substituted a spiritual coming to replace the idea of a physical second coming, and a future judgment. Passages are put into the fourth gospel to bring it back into line with synoptic eschatology: 4.23; 5.25; 11.25f.; 3,18f.; 9.39; 5.28.; 6.27; also all the passages which speak about the last day: 6.39f., 44, 54; 12.48; 11.24.

The more one looks at these excisions the more one feels that the excisers feel free to remove whatever they do not like, and that they demand from John a consistency of mind and thought which would be characteristic of a machine rather than of a human being.

30. Lord Charnwood (G.F. Benson), *According to St John*, London and Boston 1925, p. 35, quoted by W.F. Howard, *Recent Criticism*, p. 45.

31. On the external evidence see J. Drummond, *Character and Authorship*, pp. 72-346; the commentaries of J.H. Bernard, I, pp. lxxi-viii, and of J.N. Sanders, pp. 32-44; also H.P.V. Nunn, *The Authorship of the Fourth Gospel*, Alden & Blackwell and Allenson 1952, pp. 20-38.

32. *An Unpublished Fragment of the Fourth Gospel in the John Rylands Library*, ed. C.H. Roberts, Manchester 1935; F.G. Kenyon, *Our Bible and the Ancient Manuscripts*, 4th ed., London 1939, New York 1940, p. 128; B.M. Metzger, *The Text of the New Testament*, Oxford University Press 1964, pp. 38f. (quoting Deissmann).

33. H.I. Bell and T.C. Skeat, *Fragments of an Unknown Gospel*, London and New York 1935. We quote the translation (slightly altered) from J. Jeremias, *Unknown Sayings of Jesus*, ET, SPCK and Macmillan 1957, pp. 18f. R. Dunkerley, *Beyond the Gospels*, Penguin Books 1957, pp. 137f., gives the translation of the whole papyrus.

34. J. Drummond, *Character and Authorship*, p. 255, quoting C. Taylor, *The Witness of Hermas to the Four Gospels*, London 1892, pp. 8f.

35. There is a detailed study of Justin's connection with the fourth gospel in J. Drummond, *Character and Authorship*, pp. 107-44.

36. *The Gospel of Truth*, translation and commentary by Kendrick Grobel, A. & C. Black and Abingdon 1960.

4 THE DISCOURSES OF THE FOURTH GOSPEL

1. By W. Wilkens, quoted by W.G. Kümmel, *Introduction to the NT*, p. 147.

2. Conveniently collected by R.M. Grant, *Historical Introduction to the NT*, pp. 161f.

3. H.J. Holtzmann, *Evangelium des Johannes* (Hand-Commentar zum Neuen Testament 4), Freiburg i.B., 1890, p. 269, quoted by C.F. Nolloth, *The Fourth Evangelist*, p. 169.

4. J. Armitage Robinson, *The Study of the Gospels*, London 1902, p. 148, quoted by F.C. Burkitt, *Gospel History*, p. 230.

5. On the 'I am' sayings see the commentaries of R.E. Brown, I, Appendix IV, pp. 533-8; J.H. Bernard, I, pp. cxvii-cxxi; R. Bultmann, pp. 348f.; C.K. Barrett, pp. 234, 242f., 282f.

6. An inscription quoted by A. Deissmann, *Light from the Ancient East*, ET, 4th ed., London and New York 1927, pp. 139f.

7. Plutarch, *On Isis and Osiris* 9 (Moralia 354C, LCL V).

8. Text and translation in D.J. Theron, *Evidence of Tradition*, pp. 106-9.

5   THE AIMS AND PURPOSES OF THE FOURTH GOSPEL

1. Byron, *English Bards and Scotch Reviewers*, 1.51.

2. See B. Lindars, *Behind the Fourth Gospel*, pp. 11-14; C.H. Dodd, *Historical Tradition in the Fourth Gospel*, p. 9; J. Marsh, *St John*, pp. 45f.; E. Earle Ellis, *The Gospel of Luke* (New Century Bible), Nelson 1966, pp. 55-8.

3. A tendency to give a subordinate place to John the Baptist has been noted in the commentaries of B.F. Westcott, p. xli; J.H. Bernard, I, pp. c-cii; G.H.C. Macgregor, p. xxx; E. Hoskyns and F.N. Davey, p. 144; C.K. Barrett, pp. 142f.; J.N. Sanders, pp. 74f.; R.E. Brown, pp. lxvii-lxx; also A. Jülicher, *Introduction to the NT*, pp. 423f.; J. Drummond, *Character and Authorship*, pp. 59f.; V.H. Stanton, *Historical Documents* III, 10f.; and W.G. Kümmel, *Introduction to the NT*, p. 162. W. Baldensperger, *Der Prolog des vierten Evangeliums*, Freiburg i.B., 1898, saw polemic against John as the main object of the fourth gospel.

4. Irenaeus, *Against Heresies*, 1.26, quoted from J. Stevenson, *A New Eusebius*, pp. 94f.; see also Irenaeus, 3.11.1; Hippolytus, *Heresies*, 7.33; 10.21 (ANCL 7.21; 10.17); Tertullian, *Heresies*, 10; W.D. Niven, 'Cerinthus', in *Dictionary of the Apostolic Church* I, p. 172.

5. Reported by Clement of Alexandria, *Miscellanies* 3.7 (in J. Stevenson, *A New Eusebius*, p. 91).

6. See J. Burnet, *Greek Philosophy: Thales to Plato*, London and New York 1914, p. 31.

7. Philolaus the Pythagorean, *Fragment* 14 (from Clement of Alexandria, *Miscellanies* 3.3).

8. Epictetus, *Fragment* 26 (from Marcus Aurelius, *Meditations*, 4.41).

9. Irenaeus, *Against Heresies*, 1.24.3-7, quoted from J. Stevenson, *A New Eusebius*, pp. 81f.

10. W.C. van Unnik, *Newly Discovered Gnostic Writings* (SBT 30), 1960, p. 22.

11. R. Bultmann, *Primitive Christianity in its Contemporary Setting*, Collins (Fontana) 1960, pp. 194-6.

12. Tertullian, *On the Prescription of Heretics*, 33; *On the Flesh of Christ*, 14,18; *Against All Heresies*, 3.

13. Hippolytus, *Refutation of Heresies*, 7.34 (quoted from ANCL, where it is 7.22).

14. On the Ebionites see articles by W.D. Niven, *Dictionary of the Apostolic Church*, I, pp. 318-20, and by W. Beveridge, *Encyclopaedia of Religion and Ethics* 5, pp. 139-45; G.P. Fisher, *History of Christian Doctrine*, Edinburgh and New York 1896, pp. 48-57.

15. See also W.C. van Unnik, 'The Purpose of St John's Gospel', *Studia Evangelica* I (Texte und Untersuchungen 73), Berlin 1959, pp. 382-411.

16. There is a comprehensive article on *'Hellēn'* and its related words by Hans Windisch in *TDNT* II, pp. 504-16, esp. 509-12.

17. J. Weiss, *The History of Primitive Christianity*, ET London and New York 1937, p. 790.

18. G.T. Purves, 'Logos', *Dictionary of the Bible* III, p. 135.

19. H.A.A. Kennedy, *Philo's Contribution to Religion*, p. 177.

20. Irenaeus, *Against Heresies*, 1.8.5.

21. Clement of Alexandria, *Extracts from Theodotus*, 6f.; see J.N. Sanders, pp. 37f.

22. J. Paterson, *The Book that is Alive,* Scribners 1954, pp. 3,1.

23. C.G. Montefiore in Peake's *Commentary on the Bible*, London and New York 1919, p. 620, quoted by W.F. Howard, *Christianity according to St John*, p. 50.

24. For sources see W.F. Howard, *Christianity according to St John*, pp. 50f.; E.C. Hoskyns and F.N. Davey, p. 155.

25. E.F. Scott, 'Logos', *Dictionary of Christ and the Gospels* II, p. 52.

26. On Heraclitus see Diogenes Laertius, *Lives of Eminent Philosophers*, 9.1-17; J. Adam, *Religious Teachers of Greece*, Edinburgh and New York 1908, pp. 212-40; E. Zeller, *A History of Greek Philosophy* II, 1881, pp. 1-116; W.K.C. Guthrie, *A History of Greek Philosophy* I, Cambridge University Press 1962, pp. 403-92; G.S. Kirk and J.E. Raven, *The Pre-Socratic Philosophers,* Cambridge University Press 1957, pp. 182-215.

27. Cicero, *De Finibus (Concerning Ends)*, 2.5.15.

28. The next three paragraphs are based on W.K.C. Guthrie, pp. 449-51, 446-9 and 424f.

29. *'Panta rhei.'* W.K.C. Guthrie, p. 450, says that though this statement of Heraclitus' doctrine of the 'flux' became 'almost canonical' in later ages, it occurs in only one ancient authority, Simplicius (*Phys.* 1313.11), and is unlikely to have been a saying of Heraclitus. But though the saying may not be his, the doctrine of flux is.

30. Guthrie lists seven versions of this from ancient authors, beginning with Plato, *Cratylus* 402A, and Aristotle, *Metaphysics* 1010a 13.

31. *Fragment* 80, quoted from Origen, *Against Celsus*, 6.42.

32. *Fragment* 53, quoted from Hippolytus, *Refutation of Heresies*, 9.9 (ANCL 9.4).

33. Aristotle, *Eudemian Ethics*, 1235a 25, quoting Homer's *Iliad*, 18.107.

34. Aetius, *Placita*, 1.23.7.

35. *Fragment* 1, from Sextus Empiricus, *Against the Logicians*, 1.132 (LCL II), also cited as *Against the Mathematicians*, 7.132.

36. *Fragment* 50, from Hippolytus, *Refutation of Heresies*, 9.9 (ANCL 9.4).

37. *Fragment* 2, from Sextus Empiricus, *Against the Mathematicians*, 7. 133.

38. Sextus Empiricus, 7.129.

39. *Fragment* 94, from Plutarch, *On Exile* 11, *Moralia* 604A (LCL VII).

40. *Fragment* 114, from Stobaeus, *Anthology* 3.1.179.

41. E.V. Arnold, *Roman Stoicism*, Cambridge and New York 1911, p. 19.

42. G.T. Purves, 'Logos' (see n. 18 above), p. 134.

43. W.R. Inge, 'Logos', *Encyclopaedia of Religion and Ethics* 8, p. 134.

44. Diogenes Laertius, *Lives of Eminent Philosophers*, 7. 149.

45. Chrysippus, quoted by Plutarch, *On the Contradictions of the Stoics* 47 (*Moralia* 1056C).

46. Quoted from Origen, *Against Celsus*, 5.14.

47. E. Zeller, *Stoics, Epicureans and Sceptics*, rev. ed., London 1892, p. 73.

48. Sextus Empiricus, *Against the Logicians*, 2.275, 287 (LCL II).

49. E. Zeller, *Stoics* ... p. 172; see also W.F. Howard, *Christianity according to St John*, pp. 34f.

50. Zeller, op. cit., p. 75.

51. Cleanthes, *Hymn to Zeus* (from Stobaeus, *Eclogae*, 1.1.12); translation from F.C. Grant, *Hellenistic Religion*, Liberal Arts Press, New York, 1953, pp. 152-4; for another translation see E.V. Arnold, *Roman Stoicism*, pp. 85-7.

52. On Philo see the commentaries of R.E. Brown, pp. lvii f.; G.H.C. Macgregor, pp. xxxvi f.; J.H. Bernard, I, pp. xciii f.; E.C. Hoskyns and F.N. Davey, p. 158; also W.F. Howard, *Christianity according to St John*, pp. 36-8; H.A.A. Kennedy, *Philo's Contribution to Religion*, pp. 157-77; C.H. Dodd, *The Interpretation of the Fourth Gospel*, pp. 54-73; E. Schürer, *The Jewish People in the Time of Jesus Christ*, ET, Div. II vol. III, Edinburgh 1900, pp. 374-6; H.A. Wolfson, *Philo* I, Harvard University Press, 1947, pp. 200-95, 325-60; E.R. Goodenough, *An Introduction to Philo Judaeus*, 2nd ed., Blackwell 1962, Barnes and Noble 1963, pp. 100-111; J. Drummond, *Philo Judaeus* II, London 1888, pp. 156-273.

53. E. Schürer, op. cit., p. 322.

54. *Allegories of the Laws*, 1.21; 3.96; *On the Unchangeableness of God*, 57; *On the Cherubim*, 127; *Special Laws*, 1.81.

55. The text and translation of the Hermetic Literature is in W. Scott, *Hermetica* I, ('The Poimandres' is on pp. 114-33). See also the commentaries of C.K. Barrett, pp. 31f.; R.E. Brown, pp. lviii f.; J.N. Sanders, pp. 20f.; and C.H. Dodd, *The Bible and the Greeks*, pp. 99-248, esp. 115-21; C.H. Dodd, *The Interpretation of the Fourth Gospel*, pp. 10-53; W.F. Howard, *Christianity according to St John*, pp. 39-41, 200f.

56. C.H. Dodd, *The Bible and the Greeks*, p. 99 (also *Interpretation of the Fourth Gospel*, p. 30), tentatively accepts the derivation of the name Poimandres from the Coptic *p-eime-n-rē*, which means 'knowledge of the Sun God'.

57. C.H. Dodd, *Interpretation of the Fourth Gospel*, p. 29, quoting Scott's Excerpt 12.1 (from Stobaeus), and the *Hermetic Corpus*, 4.1.

58. Scott, fragments 27-30, I pp. 544-7, quoted from Cyril of Alexandria, *Against Julian* (PG 76. 552f.).

59. *Hermetic Corpus*, 10.5f., Scott's translation, *Hermetica* I, p. 191.

60. Scott, Excerpt 6.18 (from Stobaeus); Dodd's translation (*Interpretation of the Fourth Gospel*, p. 17).

6   THE FOURTH GOSPEL AND THE SYNOPTIC GOSPELS

1. F. von Hügel's article 'John, Gospel of' in the *Encyclopaedia Britannica* (11th ed., 1911) remains one of the best summaries of the evidence.

2. B.F. Westcott in his commentary (pp. 92f.) has a long and careful note on the feast of 5.1. The manuscripts vary between *a* feast and *the* feast, but there is little doubt that *a* feast is the better reading. The evidence for what the feast was is 'obscure and slight'. Different authors have identified it with Passover, Pentecost, Tabernacles, the Day of Atonement, the Feast of

Dedication and Purim. *The* feast, Westcott says, would be Tabernacles, for Tabernacles and not Passover is 'emphatically *the* feast of the Jews'. The two fixed points are the two Passovers of 2.23 and 6.4; the feast of 5.1 comes between them. There are a number of subsidiary indications of date:

1. We learn from 3.22 that Jesus stayed in Judaea and baptized, long enough to present a problem to John's disciples (3.26) and to attract the notice of the Pharisees (4.1).
2. But the stay could not have been very long, for the events were still fresh in the minds of the Galileans (4.45).
3. We learn from 5.35 that the ministry of John the Baptist is over, although he had still been at liberty after the previous Passover.
4. Jesus' disregard of the sabbath was already known: 'He was in the habit of breaking (*elue*) the sabbath' (5.18).
5. Obviously 4.35 would be specially relevant if the harvest was ripening.
6. 7.2-4 seems to indicate that Jesus had not visited Jerusalem since the unnamed feast, and now it is Tabernacles. The unnamed feast must therefore fall between Passover and Tabernacles.

It is not likely to be one of the feasts John names: Passover (2.13; 6.4; 11.55), Tabernacles (7.1) or Dedication (10.22). It could thus be Purim, Pentecost, the Day of Atonement or the Feast of Trumpets. Purim, March, suits for date, but since it celebrates the events of the book of Esther, it provides no connection whatever for the discourse. Pentecost suits for subject matter, but the seven weeks between Passover and Pentecost do not seem to allow enough room for the events of chs. 3 and 4. It is not likely that the Day of Atonement, the greatest of all Jewish days, would be called *a* feast. Westcott decides for the Feast of Trumpets. It came at the September new moon, at the 'beginning of the year'; it was 'a memorial'. It had a *national* significance, in that it commemorated the giving of the law with the 'sound of a trumpet' (Ex. 19.16), but it also had a *universal* significance, calling to that spiritual warfare in which God gives peace. There was an old tradition (*Mishnah*, Rosh Hashanah 1.2) that on that day God held a judgment of men, as on that day he had created the world. So the main thoughts of the discourse − creation, judgment, law − have a very close connection with the thoughts of the festival. If the unnamed feast is not a Passover, then in the fourth gospel the length of Jesus' ministry must be about three years.

3. On the miracles see the commentaries of J.H. Bernard, I, pp. clxxvi-xxxvi; J. Marsh, pp. 61f.; G.H.C. Macgregor, pp. xvi f.; C.K. Barrett, pp. 62-5; E.C. Hoskyns and F.N. Davey, p. 62.

4. On the connection with the synoptic gospels in general see J.H. Bernard, I, pp. xciv-cii; E.C. Hoskyns and F.N. Davey, pp. 58-85; G.H.C. Macgregor, pp. x-xix; C.K. Barrett, pp. 14-16, 34f.; R.H. Lightfoot, pp. 26-41; J.N. Sanders, pp. 6-16; R.E. Brown, pp. xlii-iv; J. Marsh, pp. 44-7, 59-64, 75f.; also C.F. Nolloth, *The Fourth Evangelist*, pp. 111-71; W.F. Howard, *Recent Criticism*, pp. 128-43; W.G. Kümmel, *Introduction to the NT*, pp. 142-54.

5. P. Gardner-Smith, *St John and the Synoptic Gospels*, Cambridge 1938.

6. H. Windisch, *Zeitschrift für die neutestamentliche Wissenschaft* 12, 1911, pp. 174f., quoted by A.H. McNeile, *An Introduction to the Study of*

the New Testament, rev. ed., p. 269.

7. Lord Charnwood, *According to St John* (see ch. 3 n. 30), p. 89.

7 THE FOURTH GOSPEL AND HISTORY

1. A. Schweitzer, *The Quest of the Historical Jesus*, 3rd ed., A. & C. Black 1954, p. 87.

2. K. Lake in *The Albert Schweitzer Jubilee Book*, p. 431.

3. H. von Soden, *The History of Early Christian Literature*, ET London and New York 1906, p. 417.

4. By Maurice Jones, summarizing the views of many writers, *The New Testament in the Twentieth Century*, 3rd ed., London and New York 1934, p. 395.

5. F.C. Baur, quoted by J. Drummond, *Character and Authorship*, p. 68.

6. A. Loisy, quoted by W.F. Howard, *Recent Criticism*, p. 86.

7. By R.M. Grant, *Harvard Theological Review* 42, 1949, pp. 273-5, quoted by R.E. Brown, p. 1074. Pliny's statement is in his *Natural History*, 9.4.3.

8. J.A. Emerton, *Journal of Theological Studies*, new series 9, 1958, pp. 86-9.

8 THE RELATIONSHIPS OF THE FOURTH GOSPEL

1. B.W. Robinson, *The Gospel of John: a Handbook for Christian Leaders*, New York 1925, p. 34.

2. P. Wernle, *The Beginnings of Christianity*, ET London and New York 1903-4, II, p. 275, quoted by E.C. Hoskyns and F.N. Davey, p. 37.

3. E. Hatch, *The Influence of Greek Ideas and Usages upon the Christian Church*, London and New York 1890, p. 283.

4. Plutarch, *Alciabiades* 19, quoted by H.R. Willoughby, *Pagan Regeneration*, pp. 46f.

5. Synesius of Cyrene, *Dion* 7.

6. Plutarch, *Isis and Osiris* 13 (Moralia 356AB, LCL V). The story is told in chs. 12-20; see also H.R. Willoughby, *Pagan Regeneration*, pp. 170-4; S. Dill, *Roman Society from Nero to Marcus Aurelius*, pp. 578f.

7. Quoted by H.R. Willoughby, *Pagan Regeneration*, p. 175; S. Angus, *The Mystery Religions and Christianity*, p. 46.

8. Proclus, *On the Republic* (of Plato), (Teubner, II, p. 108).

9. Quoted by H.R. Willoughby, p. 164; cf. S. Angus, p. 110.

10. Apuleius, *Metamorphoses* 11. 21,24; Proclus, *On the Theology of Plato*, 4.9; Firmicus Maternus, *On the Error of Pagan Religions*, 18; Sallustius, *On the Gods and the World*, 4; (all quoted by S. Angus, *Mystery Religions*, pp. 96-8).

11. The phrase is found in inscriptions, see e.g. *Corpus Inscriptionum Latinarum* 6, Berlin 1894, nos. 510-12, 736.

12. The Gabine girdle was a way of wearing the toga on the occasion of sacrifice and other solemn rites. The part of the toga which was usually worn

thrown over the shoulder was worn wound round the waist. It is not known why the name Gabine was given to this way of wearing the toga.

13. Prudentius, *Crowns of Martydom*, 10.1011-50 (LCL II); see also Tertullian, *On the Prescription of Heretics*, 40; Firmicus Maternus, *On the Error of Pagan Religions*, 27; H.R. Willoughby, *Pagan Regeneration*, pp. 130-2; S. Dill, *Roman Society*, pp. 555f.

14. H.R. Willoughby, pp. 75-8, quoting a fragment of Euripides from Porphyry, *On Abstinence*, 4.19, and Euripides' *Bacchae*, 140 (in two versions).

15. The story of the discovery of the scrolls is told by J.M. Allegro in his Pelican book, *The Dead Sea Scrolls: A Reappraisal*, pp. 17-21. Most of the quotations below are from G. Vermes, *The Dead Sea Scrolls in English* (also a Pelican). Another translation is that of T.H. Gaster, *The Scriptures of the Dead Sea Sect*.

16. On the connection between the fourth gospel and the scrolls see especially R.E. Brown, 'The Qumran Scrolls and the Johannine Gospel and Epistles' in *The Scrolls and the New Testament*, ed. K. Stendhal, Harper 1957, SCM Press 1958, pp. 183-207; also Brown's commentary, I, pp. lxii-iv; G.R. Driver, *The Judaean Scrolls: the Problem and a Solution*, Blackwell 1965, Schocken Books 1966, pp. 544-60; M. Black, *The Scrolls and Christian Origins*, Nelson and Scribner 1961, pp. 170f.; J.M. Allegro, *The Dead Sea Scrolls*, pp. 142-5; Millar Burrows, *The Dead Sea Scrolls*, Secker and Warburg and Viking Press 1956, pp. 338-41; A.R.C. Leaney in *A Guide to the Scrolls* (with R.P.C. Hanson and J. Posen), SCM Press 1958, pp. 95-103.

17. The material on Mandaism can most conveniently be studied in the chapter on it in C.H. Dodd, *The Interpretation of the Fourth Gospel*, pp. 115-30; and in W.G. Kümmel, *The New Testament: A History of the Investigation of its Problems*, Abingdon Press 1972, SCM Press 1973, pp. 350-62.

18. M. Goguel, *Au seuil de l'évangile, Jean Baptiste*, Paris 1928, p. 113, quoted by Kümmel, op. cit., p. 358.

19. J.D. Michaelis, *Einleitung in die göttlichen Schriften des Neuen Bundes* (Introduction to the Divine Scriptures of the New Covenant) Göttingen 1750, II, pp. 1137, 1140, quoted by Kümmel, op. cit., p. 69.

20. See also H. Lietzmann, *Ein Beitrag zur Mandäerfrage*, 1930, reprinted in his *Kleine Schriften* I (Texte und Untersuchungen 67), Berlin 1958, pp. 124, 131, 139f.

9 THE ORIGINALITY OF THE FOURTH GOSPEL

1. W.R. Inge, in the *Proceedings of the Oxford Society of Historical Theology* for 1903-4, pp. 58f., 65 (quoted by F.C. Burkitt, *The Gospel History and its Transmission*, pp. 243f.).

2. D.E.H. Whiteley, 'The Religion of the New Testament Writers', *Modern Churchman* 40, 1950, pp. 235f.

10   LUKE'S PURPOSE IN WRITING

1. Text and translation of the Muratorian Canon in D.J. Theron, *Evidence of Tradition*, pp. 108f.

2. See W.G. Kümmel, *Introduction to the NT*, p. 120.

3. See W.G. Kümmel, op. cit., p. 115.

4. C.H. Turner, 'The Chronology of the New Testament', *Dictionary of the Bible* I, p. 421, quoted by A.H. McNeile, *Introduction to the Study of the NT*, rev. ed., 1953, pp. 97f.

5. C.H. Turner, *The Study of the New Testament, 1883 and 1920* (Inaugural lecture), Oxford 1920, p. 30.

6. C.J. Cadoux, *Journal of Theological Studies* 19, 1918, pp. 333-41; B.W. Bacon, *Harvard Theological Review* 14, 1921, pp. 137-66 (quoted by A.H. McNeile, op. cit., pp. 98f.)

7. E. Bertrand, *Essai critique sur l'authenticité des épitres pastorales*, Paris 1888, p. 50, quoted by J. Moffatt, *Introduction to the Literature of the NT*, p. 285.

8. T. Zahn, *Die Apostelgeschichte* (Kommentar zum NT 5), Leipzig-Erlangen 1919-1921, p. 862, quoted by H.J. Cadbury, *The Making of Luke-Acts*, p. 323.

9. D.J. Theron, *Evidence of Tradition*, pp. 60f.

10. D.J. Plooij, *Expositor*, 8.8, 1914, pp. 514, 516, quoted by C.S.C. Williams, pp. 16, 18.

11. *Berl. Griechisch. Urkunden* 628 recto, see Cadbury, *Beginnings* V, p. 333.

12. A.C. McGiffert, *The Church History of Eusebius* (Nicene and Post-Nicene Fathers, New Series, vol. I), Oxford and New York 1890, p. 124n. 14.

11   THE DATE OF ACTS

1. This translation is from J. Stevenson, *A New Eusebius*, p. 145; cf. Haenchen, p. 12, and B.F. Westcott, *History of the Canon of the New Testament*, London 1855, p. 479. It is based on an emended text. The original text by Theron, *Evidence of Tradition*, pp. 108f., reads: *Acta autem omnia apostolorum sub uno libro scripta sunt. Lucas optimo Theophilo comprehendit, quae sub praesentia singula gerebantur, sicut et remote passionem Petri evidenter declarat, sed et profectionem Pauli ab urbe ad Spaniam proficiscentis.* Theron's translation of the latter part reads: '. . . as he also evidently relates indirectly the death of Peter (?) and also Paul's departure from the city as he was proceeding to Spain'. The emended text reads: *semota passione . . . et profectione* for *remote passionem . . . et profectionem.*

2. E.g. A. Harnack, *The Acts of the Apostles*, pp. 291-7; the commentaries of Rackham, pp. l-lv; and F.F. Bruce, pp. 10-14.

3. The word *mathētēs* occurs 30 times in Acts, e.g. 1.15; 6.1; 9.1; 11.26; 14.28; 15.10; 18.27; 19.30; 20.1; 21.16.

4. T.W. Manson, *Bulletin of the John Rylands Library* 28, 1944, p. 403, quoted by C.S.C. Williams, pp. 13f.

5. See B.H. Streeter, *The Four Gospels*, p. 540; E.F. Scott, *Introduction to the Literature of the NT*, pp. 92-4; F.B. Clogg, *An Introduction to the NT*, 3rd ed., London University Press 1948, pp. 235-9; H.A. Guy, *The Acts of the Apostles*, Macmillan 1953, p.13.

6. The earliest appearance of the view that Acts is dependent on Josephus is to be found in J.B. Ott, *Spicilegium sive excerpta ex Flavio Josepho ad Novi Testamenti illustrationem*, 1741, and J.T. Krebs, *Observationes in Novum Testamentum e Flavio Josepho*, Leipzig 1755. The question is discussed in most modern commentaries and Introductions; see e.g. Foakes Jackson and Kirsopp Lake, *Beginnings* II, pp. 355-9; the commentaries of Williams, pp. 19-21; Haenchen, p. 252 (very briefly); F.F. Bruce, p. 147; also M. Dibelius, *Studies*, pp. 186f.; B.H. Streeter, *The Four Gospels*, pp. 557f.; J. Moffatt, *Introduction to the Literature of the NT*, pp. 29f.; P.W. Schmiedel, articles on Lysanias and Theudas in *Encyclopaedia Biblica* III and IV.

7. 'After him' (Acts 5.37) is in Greek *meta touton*. C.S.C. Williams, p. 20, records that T.W. Manson made the suggestion that *meta touton* could possibly mean, 'My next example is', which is very improbable.

8. Cf. also Justin, *Dialogue with Trypho*, 53.5.

9. Justin, *First Apology*, 39.2f.; cf. 42.4; 45.5; 49.5; 50.12; 53.3; 61.9; 67.3; *Dialogue* 109.1; 110.2.

10. Cf. *Dialogue*, 53.5; 106.1; Luke 24.25-7, 44-6.

11. F.C. Baur, 'Die Christuspartei der korinthischen Gemeinde', *Tübinger Zeitschrift für Theologie*, 1831, pp. 61ff.; *Paulus, der Apostel Jesu Christi, sein Leben und Wirken*, Stuttgart 1845, 2nd ed. Leipzig 1866; ET, *Paul the Apostle*, London 1873-5. See B.H. Streeter, *The Four Gospels*, pp. 541-6; H. Windisch, *Beginnings*, II, pp. 298-300; F.F. Bruce, pp. 33ff.; E. Haenchen, pp. 17-24; A. Jülicher, *Introduction to the NT*, pp. 17-25.

12. M. Schneckenburger, *Uber die Zweck der Apostelgeschichte*, Berne 1841. See Windisch's account in *Beginnings* II, p. 298.

12 LUKE THE HISTORIAN

1. Sir William Ramsay, *Pauline and Other Studies*, London and New York 1906, p. 199.

2. Cicero, *De Lege Agraria*, 2.34.93.

3. R.M. Grant, *Historical Introduction to the NT*, p. 145; see T.R.S. Broughton, 'The Roman Army', *Beginnings* V, pp. 427-45; Haenchen, p. 346.

4. On the alleged discrepancies between Acts and the Pauline letters see A. Jülicher, *Introduction to the NT*, pp. 441-3; H. Windisch in *Beginnings* II, p. 298; A.H. McNeile, *Introduction to the Study of the NT*, pp. 111-123; A. Wikenhauser, *NT Introduction*, pp. 332-8; C.S.C Williams, pp. 22-30; F.F. Bruce, pp. 34-40.

5. Two explanations have been offered. (i) It is suggested that the voice in 9.7 is Paul's, the meaning being that they heard Paul speaking and saw no one to whom he was speaking. (ii) It is noted that the Greek for 'hearing the voice' is in 9.7 *akouein phōnēs*, genitive, which could mean 'hear the sound', while in 22.9 it is *akouein phōnēn*, accusative, which could mean 'distinguish the words'. So 9.7 could mean that they heard the sound but saw no one, and

22.9 could mean that they heard the voice but could not make out what it was saying.

6. On the Council of Jerusalem see, among much else, the following: J.B. Lightfoot, *A Commentary on the Epistle to the Galatians*, 3rd ed., London 1869, pp. 124-7; A.H. McNeile, *Introduction . . .*, pp. 117-23; the commentaries of C.S.C Williams, pp. 24-30; F.F. Bruce, pp. 287-9; R.B. Rackham, pp. 247-56; E. Haenchen, pp. 455-72; K. Lake, 'The Apostolic Council of Jerusalem', *Beginnings* V, pp. 195-212; M. Dibelius, *Studies in Acts*, pp. 93-101.

7. P. Oxyrhynchus 523; see G. Milligan, *Selections from the Greek Papyri*, Cambridge and New York 1910, p. 97.

8. Haenchen, p. 448, cites what he calls desperate attempts to save the quotation for James. Zahn, *Apostelgeschichte* (see ch. 10 n. 8), p. 521 n. 83, suggests that the Greek text may be older and better than the current Hebrew, and may have existed in Aramaic in Galilee in the time of James; or maybe James throughout the years had grown familiar with the Septuagint, and cited it in courtesy to Paul and the Antiochenes, who knew Greek better than Hebrew. Haenchen grimly comments: 'It is a sorry business when a viewpoint has to be defended with such arguments.'

9. This is Haenchen's summary (p. 357) of Dibelius' essay, 'The Conversion of Cornelius', *Studies in Acts*, pp. 109-22.

10. On the question whether Luke knew Paul see H. Windisch, 'The Case against Tradition', *Beginnings* II, pp. 298-348; the commentaries of F.F. Bruce, pp. 34-40; C.S.C. Williams, pp. 22-30; E. Haenchen, pp. 112-16; and W.G. Kümmel, *Introduction to the NT*, pp. 129f.

13   THE SPEECHES IN ACTS

1. On the speeches in Acts see the essays of H.J. Cadbury, *Beginnings* V, pp. 402-27; of M. Dibelius, *Studies in Acts*, pp. 138-85; and of E. Schweizer, in *Studies in Luke-Acts*, ed. L.E. Keck and J.L. Martyn, pp. 208-16; the commentaries of F.F. Bruce, pp. 19-21; C.S.C. Williams, pp. 36-48; also Foakes Jackson and K. Lake, *Beginnings* II, pp. 13f.; H.J. Cadbury, *The Making of Luke-Acts*, pp. 184-90; F.H. Chase, *The Credibility of Acts*, pp. 105-22; F.F. Bruce, *The Speeches in Acts* (Tyndale Lecture for 1942), London 1943; and the *Introductions to the NT* of A. Jülicher, pp. 443-5, and W.G. Kümmel, pp. 117-20; and cf. R.C. Jebb, 'The Speeches of Thucydides' in *Hellenica: Essays on Greek Poetry, Philosophy, History and Religion*, ed. E. Abbott, 2nd ed., London 1898, pp. 244-95.

2. H. Conzelmann, in *Studies in Luke-Acts*, ed. L.E. Keck and J.L. Martyn, p. 218.

3. E. Curtius, in an article translated in *The Expositor*, 7.4, 1907, p. 455, and quoted by Cadbury, *Beginnings* V, p. 406.

4. Quintilian, *Institutes of Oratory*, 10.1.101.

5. Thucydides, I.22; translation from R.C. Jebb, 'The Speeches of Thucydides' (see n. 1 above), p. 251.

6. A.W. Gomme, *Essays in Greek History and Literature*, Oxford 1937, p. 166; *A Historical Commentary on Thucydides* I, Oxford University Press 1945, pp. 140-8.

7. Quoted by R.C. Jebb, op. cit., p. 253.

8. *Corpus Inscriptionum Latinarum* 13, Berlin 1907, No. 1668.

9. C.S.C. Williams, pp. 38-40, also citing B. Gärtner, *The Areopagus Speech and Natural Revelation*, Uppsala 1955.

10. Cf. C.H. Dodd, *The Apostolic Preaching and its Developments*, 2nd ed., London 1944; A.M. Hunter, *The Unity of the New Testament*, London 1943 (= *The Message of the New Testament*, Philadelphia 1944).

14   THE SOURCES OF ACTS

1. On the sources of chs. 1-15 see the commentaries of F.F. Bruce, pp. 21-26; E. Haenchen, pp. 81-90; R.B. Rackham, pp. xli-iv; C.S.C. Williams, pp. 7-13; the *NT Introductions* of J. Moffatt, pp. 286-96; R.H. Fuller, pp. 123-6; W.G. Kümmel, pp. 123-32; also F.H. Chase, *The Credibility of Acts*, pp. 14-24.

2. J. Jeremias, *Zeitschrift für die neutestamentliche Wissenschaft* 36, 1937, pp. 205-21.

3. On the 'we-passages' see Foakes Jackson and K. Lake, *Beginnings* II, pp. 158-67; H. Windisch, ibid., pp. 328-31 and 343-5; the commentaries of C.S.C. Williams, pp. 5-7, and Haenchen, pp. 489-91; the *Introductions* of J. Moffatt, pp. 294-6; A. Jülicher, pp. 445-8; A.H. McNeile, pp. 105-9; A. Wikenhauser, pp. 328f.; W.G. Kümmel, pp. 125-7; also A. Harnack, *Luke the Physician*, ET London and New York 1907, ch. II.

4. See J. Moffatt, *Introduction to the NT*, p. 294; M. Dibelius, *Studies in the Acts*, p. 199.

5. E. Trocmé, *Le livre des Actes et l'histoire*, Paris 1957, quoted by Haenchen, pp. 84f.

6. The most massive treatment of the 'Western' text is in *Beginnings* III: *The Text*, ed. J.H. Ropes, 1926. Other special treatments are J.M. Wilson, *The Acts of the Apostles. Translated from the Codex Bezae*, London and New York 1923; A.C. Clark, *The Acts of the Apostles*, Oxford and New York 1933; F.G. Kenyon, *The Text of the Greek Bible*, London 1937; A.F.J. Klijn, *A Survey of the Researches into the Western Text of the Gospels and Acts*, Part 1, Utrecht 1949; Part 2, Leiden 1969. See also the commentaries of F.F. Bruce, pp. 40-47; E. Haenchen, pp. 51-60; C.S.C. Williams, pp. 48-53; M. Dibelius, *Studies in Acts*, pp. 84-92; and the *Introductions* of J. Moffatt, pp. 309-11; and A. Jülicher, pp. 451-6.

The main authorities for the so-called Western text are Codex Bezae (D); the African Latin (especially Codex Floriacensis); quotations in Tertullian, Cyprian, the Latin version of Irenaeus, and Augustine; the Old Syriac; the Harclean Syriac (text and margin); quotations in the commentary of Ephraem the Syrian; P^{29} (3rd-4th century: Acts 26.7f., 20); P^{38} (3rd-4th century: Acts 18.27-19.6; 19.12-16); P^{48} (3rd century: Acts 23.11-16, 24-29). It can be seen that it is far more than a 'Western' text.

BIBLIOGRAPHY

(of books frequently cited; more specialist works may be found in the notes)

I   General

Allegro, J., *The Dead Sea Scrolls: A Reappraisal*, Penguin Books 1956

Angus, S., *The Mystery Religions and Christianity*, London and New York 1925

Barrett, C.K., *Luke the Historian in Recent Study*, Epworth Press and Allenson 1961; reissued Fortress Press 1970

Baur, F.C. *Paul the Apostle*, ET London 1873-5

Bultmann, R., *Theology of the New Testament*, ET, 2 vols., SCM Press and Scribner 1952-55

Burkitt, F.C., *The Gospel History and its Transmission*, Edinburgh 1906

Bernard, J.H., *Studia Sacra*, London 1917

Cross, F.M., *The Ancient Library of Qumran and Modern Biblical Studies*, Doubleday and Duckworth 1958

Charles, R.H., *Revelation* (ICC), 2 vols., 1920

Dibelius, M., *A Fresh Approach to the New Testament and Early Christian Literature*, London and New York 1936

Dictionary of the Apostolic Church, ed. J. Hastings, 2 vols., Edinburgh and New York 1915-18

Dictionary of the Bible, ed. J. Hastings, 4 vols., Edinburgh and New York 1898-1904

Dictionary of Christ and the Gospels, ed. J. Hastings, 2 vols., Edinburgh and New York 1906-08

Dodd, C.H., *The Bible and the Greeks*, London and Toronto 1935

Encyclopaedia Biblica, ed. T.K. Cheyne and J.S. Black, 4 vols., Edinburgh and New York 1908-26

Encyclopaedia of Religion and Ethics, ed. J. Hastings, 13 vols., Edinburgh and New York 1908-26

Fuller, R.H., *A Critical Introduction to the New Testament*, Duckworth 1966

Goodspeed, E.J., *An Introduction to the New Testament*, Chicago and Cambridge 1937

Grant, R.M., *A Historical Introduction to the New Testament* (1963), Collins (Fontana) 1971

Halliday, W., *The Pagan Background to Early Christianity*, Liverpool 1925

Hennecke, E., and Schneemelcher, W., *New Testament Apocrypha*, ET, ed. R. McL Wilson, 2 vols., Lutterworth Press and Westminster Press 1963-65, reissued SCM Press 1973-4

Inge, W.R., *Christian Mysticism* (1899), 7th ed., London and New York 1933

James, M.R., ed., *The Apocryphal New Testament* (1924), corrected ed., Clarendon Press 1953

Jülicher, A., *An Introduction to the New Testament*, ET London and New York 1904

Kümmel, W.G., *Introduction to the New Testament*, ET Westminster Press and SCM Press 1966

Lake, K. and S., *An Introduction to the New Testament*, New York 1937, London 1938

Lightfoot, J.B., *The Apostolic Fathers*, 5 vols., 2nd ed., London and New York 1889-90; one-vol. ed., London and New York 1891

— *Biblical Essays*, London and New York 1893

—'Papias of Hierapolis', *Essays on the Work entitled Supernatural Religion*, London and New York 1880, pp. 142-216

McNeile, A.H., *An Introduction to the Study of the New Testament*, 2nd ed., revised by C.S.C. Williams, Oxford University Press 1953

Moffatt, J., *An Introduction to the Literature of the New Testament*, Edinburgh and New York 1911

Robinson, J.A.T., *Twelve New Testament Studies* (SBT 34), 1962

Scott, E.F., *The Literature of the New Testament*, New York and London 1932

Scott, W., *Hermetica*, 4 vols., Oxford and New York 1924-36

Stanton, V.H., *The Gospels as Historical Documents*, 3 vols., Cambridge 1903-30

Stevenson, J., *A New Eusebius*, SPCK and Macmillan 1957

Streeter, B.H. *The Four Gospels* (1924), 5th imp. revised, London and New York 1936

Swete, H.B., *The Apocalypse of St John*, London 1906

— *The Gospel according to St Mark*, London 1898, New York 1908

Taylor, V., *The Gospel according to St Mark*, Macmillan 1952

Theron, D.J., *Evidence of Tradition*, Bowes & Bowes and British Book Service, Toronto, 1957

Vermes, G., *The Dead Sea Scrolls in English*, Penguin Books 1962

Wikenhauser, A., *The New Testament Introduction*, ET Nelson and Herder & Herder 1958

Willoughby, H.R., *Pagan Regeneration*, Chicago and Cambridge 1929

Wordsworth, J., and White, H.J., *Novum Testamentum Latine* I: *Quattuor Evangelia*, Oxford 1889-98

Workman, H.B., *Persecution in the Early Church*, London 1906

Zahn, T., *Introduction to the New Testament*, ET, 3 vols., Edinburgh and New York 1909

II   The Fourth Gospel

Commentaries

Barrett, C.K., SPCK 1955

Bernard, J.H., (ICC), 2 vols., 1928

Brown, R.E. (Anchor Bible), 2 vols., Doubleday 1970, Geoffrey Chapman 1971

Bultmann, R., (1941) ET of 1964 printing, Blackwell and Westminster Press 1971

Hoskyns, E.C., and Davey, F.N., rev. ed., Faber & Faber 1947

Lightfoot, R.H., edited by C.F. Evans, Oxford University Press 1956

Macgregor, G.H.C., (MNTC), 1928

Marsh, J., Pelican New Testament Commentaries, 1968

Plummer, A., Cambridge Greek Testament, 1882

Sanders, J.N., edited and completed by B.A. Mastin, A. & C. Black and Harper 1968

Westcott, B.F. (Speaker's Commentary, vol. 2, 1880), reissued separately 1896

Books on the Fourth Gospel

Bacon, B.W., *The Fourth Gospel in Research and Debate*, 2nd ed., Newhaven and London 1918 (often cited as *Research and Debate*)

Burney, C.F., *The Aramaic Origin of the Fourth Gospel*, Oxford and New York 1922 (often cited as *Aramaic Origin*)

Dodd, C.H., *Historical Tradition in the Fourth Gospel*, Cambridge University Press 1963

The Interpretation of the Fourth Gospel, Cambridge University Press 1953

Drummond, J., *An Inquiry into the Character and Authorship of the Fourth Gospel*, London and New York 1903 (*Character and Authorship*)

Gardner, P., *The Ephesian Gospel*, London and New York 1915

Higgins, A.J.B., *The Historicity of the Fourth Gospel*, Lutterworth Press 1960

Howard, W.F., *Christianity according to St John*, London 1943, Philadelphia 1946

—*The Fourth Gospel in Recent Criticism*, 4th ed., revised by C.K. Barrett, Epworth Press 1955 (*Recent Criticism*)

Hügel, F. von, 'John, Gospel of', *Encyclopaedia Britannica*, 15, 11th ed., Cambridge 1911, pp. 452-8

Jackson, H.L., *The Problem of the Fourth Gospel*, Cambridge 1918 (*Problem*)

Lindars, B., *Behind the Fourth Gospel*, SPCK 1971

Nolloth, C.F., *The Fourth Evangelist*, London 1925

Robinson, J. Armitage, *The Historical Character of St John's Gospel*, London 1908

Sanday, W., *The Criticism of the Fourth Gospel*, London and New York 1905 (*Criticism*)

Sanders, J.N., 'Who was the Disciple whom Jesus Loved?', in *Studies in the Fourth Gospel*, ed. F.L. Cross, Mowbray 1957, pp. 72-82

P.W. Schmiedel, *The Johannine Writings*, London and New York 1908

E.F. Scott, *The Fourth Gospel; its Purpose and Theology*, Edinburgh 1908

Temple, W., *Readings in St John's Gospel* (1939-40), one-volume edition, Macmillan 1945

Wiles, M.F., *The Spiritual Gospel*, Cambridge University Press 1960

III   The Acts of the Apostles

Commentaries

Bruce, F.F. Tyndale Press 1951

Furneaux, W., London 1912

Haenchen, E., ET Blackwell 1971, Westminster Press 1972

Jackson, F.J. Foakes, (MNTC), 1931

Rackham, R.B. (Westminster Commentaries) (1901), 4th ed., London 1909

Williams, C.S.C., A. & C. Black and Harper 1957

Other books

Cadbury, H.J., *The Making of Luke-Acts*, 1927, reissued SPCK and Allenson 1958

Chase, F.H., *The Credibility of the Acts of the Apostles*, London and New York 1902

Dibelius, M., *Studies in the Acts of the Apostles*, SCM Press and Scribner 1956

Harnack, A., *The Acts of the Apostles*, ET London and New York 1909

Jackson, F.J. Foakes, and Lake, Kirsopp, *The Beginnings of Christianity* I: *The Acts of the Apostles*, 5 vols., New York and London 1920-33, reissued Eerdmans 1966 (cited as *Beginnings*)

Keck, L.E., and Martyn, J.L., eds., *Studies in Luke-Acts*, Allenson 1966, SPCK 1968

INDEX OF NAMES

INDEX OF BIBLICAL REFERENCES